The Movies

Miss Sebastian

THE MOVIES

Texts, Receptions, Exposures

edited by Laurence Goldstein and Ira Konigsberg

ANN ARBOR

THE UNIVERSITY OF MICHIGAN PRESS

Copyright © by the University of Michigan 1996
All rights reserved
Published in the United States of America by
The University of Michigan Press
Manufactured in the United States of America
♾ Printed on acid-free paper

1999   1998 1997 1996   4   3   2   1

A CIP catalog record for this book is available from the British Library.

Library of Congress Cataloging-in-Publication Data

The movies   :   texts, receptions, exposures / Laurence Goldstein and
    Ira Konigsberg, editors.
        p.   cm.
      ISBN 0-472-09640-0 (cloth). — ISBN 0-472-06640-4 (paper)
      1. Motion pictures.   I. Goldstein, Laurence, 1943–   .
    II. Konigsberg, Ira.
    PN1994.M78   1996   96-31169
    791.43—dc20   CIP

Title page illustration: Buster Keaton on the set of *Free and Easy.*
© Metro Goldwyn Mayer.

CONTENTS

"All American history, past, present, and to come, is a gigantic movie," wrote the poet Vachel Lindsay in the mid-1920s. The souvenir program for D. W. Griffith's epic film, *America* (1924), seems to be making the same point.

LAURENCE GOLDSTEIN
IRA KONIGSBERG

INTRODUCTION

The centennial of motion pictures in 1995 brought a spate of retrospective commentary, including two special issues of the *Michigan Quarterly Review*, from which much of the contents in this book is derived. The novelty of celebrating the birthday of a major art form became infectious, even giddy, and yet more than a few tributes adopted an elegiac tone in looking back over the history of this triumphant visual medium. Just as the fin-de-siècle atmosphere of the 1890s favored the infant film industry as a symbol of the electrifying new century to come, the animated spirit of a reinvigorated public imagination, so the decadent spirit of our own fin de siècle sees film art as at a crossroads, fat with profits yet declining in vitality as it slouches toward some horizon where it may virtually disappear into the technology of video or the computer. Susan Sontag claims that what has disappeared at the end of the hundred year run of motion pictures is cinephilia itself, not just the love of films but a certain taste common to audiences of the first, say, seventy years of movie history. "If cinephilia is dead, then movies are dead, too," she writes, in the most extreme of the public epitaphs inscribed in this decade.

This book has been assembled in order to assert the opposite point of view. Though some of the authors see signs of decline, the contents as a whole locate in the hundred-year history of cinema dynamic forces certain to impel filmmakers and audiences alike toward a continuous series of satisfying encounters in the dark. Though there is no monolithic ideological program observable in the writings that follow, they do testify to the ways a great tradition of film texts becomes embedded in the cultural imagination. Thanks to the prolonged experience of spectatorship, our fundamental human passions have been rendered into the compelling and gratifying shape of enduring art. Moviegoing has become a social habit in part because a heritage of masterpieces has entertained and astonished spectators over such a long period of time. Barring some radical change in public consciousness on a scale almost unthinkable, movies will certainly maintain their appeal to all levels of society, according to the structures and practices described in the following pages.

In order to defend this premise, the editors felt that it was necessary to begin this volume with a set of "readings" of particular films. The six essays in the first section provide formal interpretations of important films and do so in each case by reference to their interaction with the audience. That is, each critic defines the rhetoric of the film to account for its artistic significance. The most successful films, these authors imply, are those that make the most sophisticated use of psychology and sociology to frame their narratives. The characters in the films change from reel to reel, and the spectators who identify with the characters' lives also change; indeed it is for the experience of vicariously occupying the lives of others that people attend movies, leaving the theater with an enlarged understanding of themselves and their social environment. Such has been the trajectory of audience response since the silent era, according to Ira Konigsberg, when films like G. W. Pabst's *Secrets of a Soul*, drawing directly upon Freud's theories of psychoanalysis, revealed the effect of unconscious desires and personal trauma upon the Everyman on the screen and in the theater. By transposing the activities of the unconscious into dramatic form, this expressionist film revealed opportunities for the new artform that filmmakers have exploited ever since.

Secrets of a Soul is the paradigm for the revelatory film, disclosing to the viewer the interior constraints of the psyche. Bonnie Friedman takes *The Wizard of Oz* as a model for Everygirl's education in the biological and cultural limits to her freedom. Dorothy's dreamlike impulse toward independence and power, rendered monstrous by its association with the Wicked Witch, collapses under the unremitting pressures exerted by the memory and example of Aunt Em, the matronly destiny toward which Dorothy herself is compelled to return, repentant and defeated. It is one of the signal achievements of Adrienne Donald's essay on *Silence of the Lambs* that she finds the same nexus of attitudes in that horror film as Friedman did in the M-G-M comedy. Clarice Starling ventures into the patriarchal world just as Dorothy did, in a quest for knowledge, freedom, and self-control. She too transgresses into the forbidden world of monsters where the wizard Hannibal Lecter waits to reveal to her, and to a susceptible audience, a terror-inspiring lesson about what happens to those who subvert cultural authority. For all the differences in these films, both conjure the perils of role-playing and gender-changes, as well as the possibilities for love and productive work in an America that may be scarier than we like to acknowledge.

Likewise William Ian Miller probes "the deep-seated ironies of the social and the psychological" in Martin Scorcese's great film, *The King of Comedy*. This film, scripted by movie critic Paul Zimmerman, is a self-reflexive study of how the celebrity culture involves every spectator in its own voyeuristic hysteria. We are embarrassed for Rupert Pupkin, the delusional fan who aspires to displace his favorite late-night tv talk-show host, because of the likely oedipal jealousy we too have for the famous figures who dominate our subliminal experience. Just as *Silence of the Lambs* mortifies our desire for absolute power, the power of the cannibal that consumes his enemies, so *The King of Comedy* mortifies our desire for fame by chronicling the humiliations we would undergo, if we were crazy enough to try, in usurping the magic of a media wizard. Another moral lesson is the life of that famous victim, the last emperor of China. In Robert Zaller's analysis of Bernardo Bertolucci's masterpiece, *The Last Emperor*, Freudian and Marxist methodologies are once again deployed to explain how the film explodes Pu Yi's fantasy of omnipotence. "Bertolucci has found a perfect political analogue for the Freudian human comedy of which the social order is ultimately a projection," Zaller remarks. Pu Yi is constrained by his oedipal past but also by historical forces—the Japanese occupation, the Communist regime—that render his expectations of supreme leadership ridiculous. The movies' moral structure, in all these cases, lies in their recognition of the constraints, more ironic than tragic, upon actors and audiences who dream of inflating their lives in some extraordinary fashion.

The social constraints depicted in *Menace II Society* could hardly be more obvious. The characters live in the southcentral Los Angeles ghetto, in which economic and physical violence of the most cannibalistic sort is an everyday fact of life. Grant Farred shows how images of captivity abound, if not the actual prisons of *The Last Emperor* and *Silence of the Lambs*, then the soul-numbing limits of opportunity and emotion endured by men and women alike in this milieu. Here too the film makes itself useful to its audience by revealing secrets of a world unknown to most Americans—the codes, language, and activities of young people whose desire for independence is closed down daily by their gang rivals and the police alike. As with Bertolucci's film, this work by the Hughes brothers focuses on bad faith and betrayal, the collapse of history into fantasy. The documentary realism of these films lends them precisely the kind of authenticity that citizens of this country require in a postmodern period when so many of the sources of belief have vanished, not least because of the influence of the movies themselves.

Part Two of this book moves behind the screen to collect some expert testimony on how films are produced. Here too the notion of constraint is a common theme as writers, directors, and producers describe how they cooperate, or not, toward the goal of a hit film. Arthur Miller reports on the technicians of an earlier age of motion pictures: "They thought of movies as a sort of primitive drum that beat out the simplest, basic emotions—greed, lust, fear, bravado, sobriety, drunkenness, and so on. . . . It was an unalienated art designed for the masses. And that I believe is what it is." Miller asserts that movies have always offered "not reality but hope" as part of their quotidian glamour. William Harrison finds out in his odyssey through the deal-making world of contemporary Hollywood that most financiers, and some filmmakers, still want to make nothing but formula films, like cars rolling off the assembly line. He shifts in cinematic style from contact to cynical contact, showing in each case how obstacles rise up in the path of an artist and kill the spirit. Occasionally, almost by accident, some masterpiece gets made; after all, "Michelangelo was hired by the Pope." The oeuvre of Billy Wilder is a perfect example of how the Hollywood system produced great art by offering vast resources to proven talent, and in his interview with Burt Prelutsky Wilder chats amiably about some of his brilliant inspirations, and some of his bad judgments, during a long career.

The M-G-M producer Samuel Marx sees the matter from a different angle in his memoir. When he committed himself and his studio to making the first film about the atomic bomb, he gained access to the movers and shakers who altered history radically by their actions. What is the truth about the bomb? and how should its creation be represented? Marx's conversations with President Truman, Leslie Groves, and J. Robert Oppenheimer among others make for fascinating reading, and his admission that the final product, *The Beginning or the End*, was an artistic disappointment reminds us again of how even the most massive resources and privileged networking can lead to an inferior result. An interesting counter-example is the filming of *Tabu* in Tahiti, a shoestring operation that resulted in a compelling, if flawed, motion picture in the silent mode. Jim Shepard's fictional recreation of director F. W. Murnau's sojourn in Tahiti shows us a visionary artist weaving together the romanticism of his exotic scenario and the erotic romance he enjoys with a young native.

Not all directors can make a seamless unity of art and life. The career of Orson Welles provides the perfect example of the way Hollywood can sunder the visionary from the mercenary. In Michael Anderegg's analysis of Welles's "bracketed performances"—those in which he is deliberately recognizable as Orson Welles, commodifying himself in order to raise a bit of cash—the true nature of postmodern film reveals itself. The crowd-pleasing cameo ironizes and compromises not only reputations but narrative itself, a concession to the impurity of film form and its cannibalistic tendency to swallow the life of its agents in the act of representation.

Once again we are compelled to see how difficult it is to speak of filmmaking without reference to the audience. And so Part Three of this book follows the products of Hollywood out to the community of spectators, critics included, who consume and make judgment upon the tradition they have grown up with. The essays from the 1920s by Vachel Lindsay and H.D., on film censorship and Greta Garbo respectively, remind us of the binary attitudes the studios have had to address whenever they fashioned a film. Lindsay, who wrote the first book of film criticism in America, claims that movies "should have the apocalyptic gleam that will be the glory of the future" but deplores the way Edison's magical creation has released "floods of unutterable stupidity." To halt the vapidity and vice-ridden products of the mid-1920s Lindsay calls for censorship to stop the moguls from further corrupting their audiences. H.D., a modernist poet of major interest to us today, celebrates the beauty of Garbo as a heaven-sent boon to the glamour-starved audiences of her time. A case study of such revelation is Venezuelan author Laura Antillano's vignette of a woman enchanted by Vivien Leigh's "imposing figure" in *Gone With the Wind*. Likewise Janset Berkok Shami explores in a powerful short story the fatal effect of Hollywood musicals on a Turkish family. Like all products of machine technology, movies have an impact on spectators unknowable except through testimony like this rising from the impacted themselves.

How much thought do people give to the visual monitor that makes it all possible? William Paul has researched the history and technology of the screen in order to set straight some of our assumptions about the viewing process itself. What are the properties and effects of small and large screens, especially? Using case studies and the record of disputes among experts since the 1920s, Paul establishes some important points about the size and shape of the canvas on which our film experience depends. A different kind of canvas is the subject of Diane Kirkpatrick's survey of responses by artists to the movies. She shows that film imagery was eminently adaptable to the immobile canvas. Artists could put quotation marks around a star, a director, a moment in the movie palace, and thereby disturb the moviegoer's transfixed gaze for the sake of some conceptual discovery. These secondary frames, whether of painting, drawing, or photograph, inflect the judgment of spectators no less than the fleeting images on the screen.

Leo Braudy's historical essay returns us more than halfway to the practice of the film critics in Part One. He examines some key films of the 1950s—*On the Waterfront, Viva Zapata!, Rebel Without a Cause*— but not before describing a zeitgeist that foregrounded images of the male body in everyday discourse. These ambiguous and idiosyncratic films belong to the social environment of method acting, rock 'n' roll, the Beat Generation, and the Cold War in ways that require careful elucidation. "Reading" a decade's dominant themes as a cultural historian, Braudy explains why such films achieve a centrality in the culture, and thus why *any* films, given the right set of historical circumstances, impress themselves on the public imagination in ways that create a need, and a market, for films of equivalent power in succeeding decades.

Film scholars are the acknowledged historians of our movie heritage, but surely poets remain the unacknowledged keepers of our public dreams. One of the most important topics in contemporary poetry has been the status of the movies and their effect upon audiences that include poets. Part Four of the book, then, is a forum for a range of poets to reframe the film experience in a rival medium. Some focus on a star (Margaret Atwood on Ava Gardner, Pier Paolo Pasolini on Marilyn Monroe), some on a director (David Wojahn on Orson Welles, Laurence Goldstein on Alfred Hitchcock), some on a special film (Charles H. Webb on *Color of Night*, Janet Sylvester on *Andy Hardy's Double Life*), and others like Mordechai Geldmann, David Lehman, and Diann Blakely Shoaf, on the general condition of moviegoing, its joys and sorrows, its iconography of erotic illusion and nostalgia, the hope it sponsors for a happy ending. "Maybe there's an afterlife already composed of / our favorite scenes," Ira Sadoff speculates. A place of hope over the rainbow, in the next century, thanks to the magic of all the movies that came after the first.

In John Updike's novel of this year, *In the Beauty of the Lilies*, movies are described as an expression of this nation's religious imagination, full of pieties and virtue, and promissory of eternal life. "The movie theater and the church often existed side by side in small towns," Updike noted in an interview. The cinephilia of American citizens became a perennial condition, he implies, because movies nourished the profound need of people in an era of radical change for structures of feeling that did not

change, that preserved the capacity for unselfish compassion and wonder. The editors of this collection hope that readers will return to the
cinema refreshed with new understanding and enhanced appetite for
the best work that the next generations' filmmakers can create. The
movies may or may not be the old-time religion that Updike supposes,
but the more we know about them the more stringent demands we can
make upon the independent minds that will craft the great movies of the
future. It is in that spirit, a cinephilia informed by social responsibility,
that we present this collection of writings to the public.

Ann Arbor
April, 1996

I. Analyzing Films

[Top] In *Secrets of a Soul*, the husband (Werner Krauss) feels a strong compulsion to stab his wife. [Bottom] Doctor Orth (Pavel Pavlov) helps him to resolve his emotional illness through psychoanalysis.

IRA KONIGSBERG

CINEMA, PSYCHOANALYSIS, AND HERMENEUTICS: G. W. PABST'S *SECRETS OF A SOUL*

In the 1948 film *The Snake Pit*, a psychiatrist (played by Leo Genn) has a long therapeutic session with a patient (played by Olivia de Havilland) in which he slowly opens up to her two earlier traumas that have resulted in her nervous breakdown and incarceration in a mental institution. A photograph of Sigmund Freud prominently appears on the wall behind them throughout much of the scene. *The Snake Pit* was Hollywood's fifth highest box-office success for the year and earned an impressive list of Academy Award nominations. Freud and psychoanalysis have on occasion been good box office and have also been treated with a certain amount of reverence in commercial cinema. We should remember that many Hollywood filmmakers were under the influence of psychoanalysts at the time, an influence evident in the many films of the 1950s and 1960s that employ psychotherapists, and here I mean both analysts and non-analysts, as an important and positive element in their plots. One looks back with nostalgia to a time when psychotherapists were not fools like Richard Dreyfuss in *What About Bob* (1991), lovesick fools like Dudley Moore in *Lovesick* (1983), corrupt lovesick fools like Richard Gere in *Final Analysis* (1991), or cannibals like Anthony Hopkins in *The Silence of the Lambs* (1991).

Psychotherapists were certainly portrayed as comic or horrific figures in earlier films, but they were also treated with a good deal more respect than in recent years. The number of relatively high-profile films during the past decade with depraved, demented, dysfunctional, or simply incompetent therapists, however, seems to be making a statement — a statement, perhaps, about the way psychotherapy is currently perceived in the public mind. Psychotherapists are receiving their share of abuse in film along with other professional types like lawyers or doctors—there has always been a democratic undercurrent of disdain for authority figures in our popular culture (more so, I might add, than for our wealthy class) and the times are ripe for disdaining authority. But we are talking about the movies, a popular art form that establishes a historical context and a set of conventions in which professional types are caught: for example, Richard Gere's role as the duped psychotherapist is certainly a spinoff from William Hurt's performance as the incompetent lawyer in *Body Heat* (1981). Hannibal Lecter in *The Silence of the Lambs* is the modern equivalent of the deranged scientist or doctor in the earlier horror film—only in this case we have moved from the attempts of the earlier figure to control the human body to an attempt to control the mind, from Dr. Frankenstein putting together the parts of dead bodies to Hannibal disassembling the layers of the human psyche. His cannibalism is a metaphor for his wish to devour the mind of the heroine—he is our culture's ultimate depiction of the "shrink."

These contemporary portrayals of the "shrink" in cinema may also be a defensive reaction of our culture against the truth that our time is in considerable need of psychotherapy, that the psychotherapist potentially carries significant power. An important essay by Claude Lévi-Strauss, "The Sorcerer and his Magic," demonstrates apparent differences and interesting correspondences between the shamans of primitive cultures and the psychoanalyst in ours, especially in their role of causing a "conversion" in an individual and thus integrating his or her "contradictory elements" into more acceptable "systems of reference" (178). I would like to take this parallel in another direction and add to the shaman and psychoanalyst such figures from a variety of cultures as the psychotherapist in general, the witch doctor, the alchemist, the priest, the artist, and the scientist, and claim that they all perform a similar role in the popular minds of their respective cultures, acting as both an intermediary and a transitional object between this world and another, between everyday reality and some other type of reality, between the known and the unknown. *The Exorcist* (1973) combines the priest and psychiatrist in the figure of Father Karas. In such films as *The Cabinet of Dr. Caligari* (1919), *I Was a Teenage Werewolf* (1957), *Dressed to Kill* (1980), *The Howling* (1981), *Manhunter* (1986), and *The Silence of the Lambs*, the psychiatrist becomes a focal point for the fears and terrors we associate with unknown worlds, but, interestingly, none of these figures are analysts.

The 1926 silent film *Secrets of a Soul*[1] is the first of a different group of films in which the psychoanalyst specifically becomes our savior from such fears and terrors. I am referring to a group of salvational films in which Freud hovers in the background — in one version of *Secrets of a Soul* a portrait of Freud appears on the screen after the opening titles that praise his contributions[2] — in which psychiatry and psychotherapy are considerably influenced by psychoanalysis, in which the unconscious and the methodology of psychoanalysis that discloses that unconscious are treated with reverence and fascination.[3] I shall mention as examples four films in this category after the Pabst film: Alfred Hitchcock's *Spellbound* in 1945, a film that in spite of all its outrages finds most of its suspense and twists of plot in the unconscious mind of its hero and that brings the surrealistic images of Salvador Dali to its dream sequence; *Mine Own Executioner*, a British film about a lay analyst that appeared in 1947 and that has been totally forgotten;[4] *The Snake Pit* in 1948; John Huston's well-intentioned if misguided *Freud* in 1962 that focuses on the great man's early life and theories. We might do better to concentrate on these films than the counter-transference films in which we have met the enemy, who also happens to be a psychotherapist, and he is us. Aggression and violence have generally been film's particular forte, satisfying the public's id as a type of socially acceptable pornography; and films about psychotherapy have been quick to tap into film's romance with violence, to exploit and explore the death instinct more than other aspects of the psyche in order to satisfy the audience's vicarious taste for thrills. Though some of the salvational films fall into this vast category, all of them present the analyst not as the perpetrator of violence but as our savior from self-destructive impulses.

The opening titles to *Secrets of A Soul* immediately identify the film as salvational in nature while also placing it in a historical context.

> In everyone's life, there are desires and passions that remain unknown to our conscious minds. In dark hours of emotional conflict, such unconscious drives try to assert themselves. Such struggles engender mysterious illnesses, the explanation and healing of which are the professional province of psychoanalysis. The teach-

held in Berlin to celebrate Freud's seventieth birthday in 1926 and was well received after its opening in Europe and the United States.

Freud's prejudice against cinema is curious, especially since his theories and the film medium were born at virtually the same time and both offered entries into the human mind. At the end of *The Interpretation of Dreams*, Freud compares the psyche "to a compound microscope or photographic apparatus, or something of the kind [in which] . . . psychical locality will correspond to a point inside that apparatus at which one of the preliminary stages of an image comes into being" (V. 5, 536); yet in his "A Note Upon the Mystic Writing Pad" (1925),[9] some twenty-five years later and published only a year before the appearance of *Secrets of a Soul*, when he again seems to be in earnest search for some kind of apparatus that will act as a metaphor for the operations of the mind, he rejects devices such as the "photographic camera" because they cannot receive new impressions while holding onto memory traces of earlier perceptions. The writing pad with its thin plastic layer on top of a wax base seems a much better representative of the mental process he wishes to suggest. It is interesting to speculate why Freud was so resistant to the film medium and its potential for dealing with the human mind, especially since this is the direction that some of the earliest theorizing on film was to take. Perhaps his distrust was due to the newness of the medium in general and its appeal to a wide public — there has always been a certain vulgarity associated with film because of its popularity, its tendency to simplify human nature, and its exploitative appeal to the audience's less civilized emotions. But, ironically, was not this dark, emotional world the very landscape of the human psyche that Freud himself explored, and was not this the reason for Goldwyn's offer to him? Freud might also have been resistant to film because he was still unaware of its imagistic potential, its capacity to use superimpositions, split screens, dissolves, models, matting shots and other special effects to create a mental time and space, as it was to do in *Secrets of a Soul*.

Ten years before the appearance of *Secrets of a Soul*, Hugo Münsterberg, a German psychologist teaching at Harvard, published *The Photoplay: A Psychological Study*, a significant attempt to show the correspondence of film to the human mind, at least in its conscious aspects:[10] "We recognize that in every case the objective world of outer events had been shaped and molded until it became adjusted to the subjective movements of the mind. The mind develops memory ideas and imaginative ideas; in the moving picture they become reality" (58). As early as 1916, someone is noticing how the motion picture, with its use of close-ups, flashbacks and flashforwards, and movement in space "obeys the laws of the mind rather than those of the outer world" (41). At the same time as the production of *Secrets of a Soul* in Germany, a group of avant-garde filmmakers in France was beginning to use film as an expression of the unconscious. Although we can find various theoreticians in later years discussing film as a psychological art form, the most significant advance in this direction took place in the 1960s, especially with the writing of Jean-Louis Baudry and Christian Metz in France. Baudry and Metz were influential in laying upon film theory the burden of Jacques Lacan and his concept of the mirror phase, but they are especially interesting in their use of Freud to explicate the viewer's response to the film medium. The relation between film and dream has often been suggested in film theory, but Baudry and Metz are the first writers to make the correspondence seem convincing. I have no time to go into the analogy but let me say that sitting in a darkened area, passive in an immobile state, with images appearing before their consciousness, viewers loosen their hold on reality and undergo a type of regressive experience that puts them in a state akin to that of dreaming and day-dreaming. The fact that the images themselves are signifiers without any reality, are a two-dimensional imprint of a world that does not exist in reality, reminds us of the images of our dreams that also have no actuality. The crucial mechanism here is the way, in a state of reverie, we project our fantasies into the images on the screen, the way in which our fantasies interact with those on the screen so that what we see seems to emanate from ourselves, just the way the dream images are a creation of our own psyches.

If viewing a film is akin to the dream experience, if the special power of film is to give presence to a fantasy world, a film such as *Secrets of A Soul*, which offers a dream as a central portion of its narrative, is creating for us the experience of viewing a dream within a dream. Just as the play within the play discloses some hidden truth about what takes place in the outer world of the literary text, so does the dream within the film, itself experienced as a dream, disclose a similar hidden truth about the world that surrounds it. Freud comments that "What is dreamt in a dream after waking from the 'dream within the dream' is what the dream-wish seeks to put in the place of an obliterated reality. It is safe to suppose, therefore, that what has been 'dreamt' in the dream is a representation of the reality, the true recollection, while the continuation of the dream, on the contrary, merely represents what the dreamer wishes" (338). Freud's point is that the inner dream discloses some reality, some truth that the outer dream hides. *Secrets of a Soul*, therefore, indicates that films about psychoanalysis, and psychoanalysis itself in its reading and use of dreams, function according to already-established practices and rules of narrative art and are influenced by the same basic strategies of interpretation.

Psychoanalysis in general functions according to methodologies similar to those we use when analyzing both a literary and film text, when we first understand the manifest content while searching for a latent meaning, but when we also put all of our information, manifest and latent, into some type of structure or developmental order.[11] The Russian formalists have given us a set of terms that help us better understand the second part of this interpretive strategy, the "sujet" and the "fabula" — the first term referring to the text in the order that we find it, and the second referring to the text that we both discover and rearrange in our own mind so that we finally have a logically ordered sequence of events that tell the larger story.[12] Interpreting texts according to their "sujet" and "fabula" is close to the analytical method where the material as it is given and then deciphered is put into some type of logical ordering, some kind of cause and effect relationship, some kind of sequence and development that also tells the larger story. I am discussing what in psychoanalytic terms is referred to as "construction" or, more accurately, "reconstruction," concepts that I shall turn to in more detail later in this essay, after we look at Pabst's film and are ready to make some larger cultural generalizations. The most obvious type of narrative text that fits the "sujet/fabula" and "reconstruction" paradigms is the mystery, where the reader or viewer is impelled to discover some hidden events that will explain the present situation, some hidden cause and effect relationship between events, some logical and chronological order that transcends the material as presented. This may explain why psychotherapy is often presented in film in the context of a mystery. In such works there seem to be two mysteries — the mystery involving the external events and the mystery of one of the character's psyches, often some trauma or traumatic event that explains the outer mystery or contributes to its explanation.[13] Indeed, what also takes place in a number of these films is the conflation of both aggressor and victim so that the mysteries we seek to answer are explained by such characters' self-victimizations — so that these characters are, indeed, their own executioners.[14]

Let me specify how most of the psychoanalytic salvational films fit into this general category. In the psychoanalytic films, where the focus is usually on a character's self-victimization, we seem to resolve a mystery about the character that only covers up another mystery; we seem to discover something that answers to the course of present events only to discover that there is another mystery to be answered, another level of psychic events that is a truer explanation of what has taken place — it is as if these films are never satisfied with what they at first explain, as if they are suggesting that the mystery of the mind goes deeper and deeper. In *Mine Own Executioner*, a man nearly strangles his wife and, with the help of his analyst, is able to remember a traumatic experience in which he killed a guard while escaping from a camp for prisoners of war. But while the patient feels grateful that he now understands the buried past that has led to his irrational behavior, the analyst feels that the patient is still dangerous because some earlier traumatic experience remains buried and unrecognized. This other trauma is only hinted at and never fully exposed before the tragic ending of the film. In *The Snake Pit*, the therapist, through the use of truth serum, encourages the patient to remember the car accident that caused the death of her male friend, but immediately we discover some interior, earlier experience, an event when as a young girl she wished for the death of her father just before he actually died.[15] This backward direction of the *sujet* in order to propose the forward direction of a larger *fabula* is most obvious in *Freud*, a work that dramatizes Sigmund Freud's self-analysis and his parallel analysis of the composite character Cecily, showing him pushing further and further into the psyche, back in time, until his discovery of childhood sexuality which is the first step in the development of the oedipal complex that explains his, Cecily's, and our present mental states.

In a curious way, *Secrets of A Soul* satisfies the type of structure I am describing — the mystery behind the mystery, the explanation behind the explanation, the psychic trauma behind the psychic trauma. On the surface, the film's story is quite simple. A husband and wife live together congenially, but are unable to have children.

A murder next door and the announced visit of the wife's cousin, a childhood friend of the couple, precipitate in the husband an emotional reaction and strange dream, at the end of which he repeatedly stabs his wife. The actual visit of the cousin and a childhood photograph exacerbate his condition to the point where he is unable to hold a knife because of his fear of stabbing his wife. He undergoes psychoanalysis, while living apart from his wife with his mother, and is finally cured when he and the analyst, with the help of the dream and photograph, trace his present emotional state back to an event in his childhood that caused him to become jealous of his wife's relationship with her cousin. The cousin goes off and the couple go on to parenthood and a happy life. But the explanation that the film puts forth for the husband's knife phobia, for his present irrational actions, cannot possibly be the full reason — the events from the past recounted in the film suggest earlier events that are a truer explanation for the patient's present behavior, though these earlier events are not articulated in the film itself.

The structure of the film indicates the kind of inward movement that I am referring to as a series of frames — of frames within frames. The titles that begin the film, the statement concerning Dr. Sigmund Freud and his teaching as well as Freud's photograph (everything that appears on the screen is part of the film's *sujet* and also part of its fiction) create for us a level of "reality" in which the film's narrative action is to be embedded. The portrait of Freud appears in the Rohauer print of the film, where it is immediately followed by a brief scene showing Dr. Orth writing, "Facts of the case of Martin Fellman, a chemist . . .," a scene paralleled in the final shots of this version when we see him writing,

> Case History #326
> Martin Fellman
> Illness: Knife Phobia[16]

The framing device of Dr. Orth writing his case history not only encloses the narrative actions in another frame, but also attempts to place them in a larger context of which they are only a part — case #326 means that there have been 325 other cases for this particular psychoanalyst. In this version of the film, then, the narration of the husband, his wife, and her cousin actually begins within two frames, the first, that of Freud and psychoanalysis; the second, that of Dr. Orth and his case histories. But the narrative itself is obviously the frame for the larger and more significant action and imagery of the husband's dream, which itself becomes a frame for the story of the childhood event that led to the dream — and, I wish to argue, this childhood event is only a frame for a deeper configuration and dynamics that we must figure out for ourselves.

The pamphlet that Hanns Sachs wrote as a guide to the film is of help to us now. In this pamphlet Sachs attempts to write a primer concerning psychoanalysis and an explication of the film in psychoanalytic terms. An opening explanation of parapraxis[17] (a misaction like a slip of the tongue or misplacing an object that results from unconscious motives) leads to a discussion of the hero's breaking of the test tube in the film and then an extensive explication of the film, with citations of other examples of parapraxis. Sachs also provides explanations of phobia and compulsion to explain the behavior of the film's protagonist. The central portion of the explication is an analysis of the husband's dream. For the most part Sachs' explication of the film is no more satisfying than the analyst's explication within the film, but Sachs lets us in on the secret of Secrets of a Soul toward the end of his pamphlet when he tells us that "Erotic problems, which have been especially important for psychoanalysis, are touched upon at various points but could be clarified only to a certain degree" (29).

A good deal in the film is not clarified. I suppose we can say that even though the film is dealing with a talking cure, the images must speak for themselves, tell us more than the film's titles — logically this must be the case since this is a motion picture and a silent one at that, but more is suggested and hidden in the narrative than in even the most ambiguous and subtle of silent narrative films. The explanation that the husband's desire to kill his wife and the resulting knife phobia are the products of a jealousy that can be traced back to the childhood event in which his wife gave a doll to her cousin might cure the husband in the film, but it hardly satisfies the viewer. I will suggest briefly what I believe the film wants us to interpret for ourselves. When the husband shaves the back of his wife's neck, at the start of the narrative, and then cuts her as the result of a shout of "Murder" from a neighboring house, his act is clearly connected to the actual murder announced by the shout, which, we later learn, was committed with a razor and "prompted by jealousy." His accidental injury of his wife is thus made to suggest his own jealousy and the possibility of his committing some greater violence on her; but it

[Top] The husband's emotional illness seems to be connected to his relationship with his wife and her cousin. [Bottom] He turns to his mother (Ilke
Grinning) for help.

also suggests an act of violence that we cannot yet perceive, one that seems to disturb and threaten the characters in the film. The razor and the gash on the wife's neck suggest from the start that on some still unrecognizable level we are dealing with violent sexuality.

We soon find out that the couple is childless, that their childlessness is the product of their dysfunctional sexual life which we are led to attribute to the husband. There is a telling moment when a little girl, to whom the husband has just given a piece of candy in his laboratory, is told by her mother, "Come, Daddy is waiting for us," as if to indicate to us that the husband is not the little girl's Daddy or a Daddy in general, that Daddy is elsewhere, and that, by not being a Daddy, the husband is still a child. We should note at this point that Daddy is also missing from the interior story of the film, that though the husband's mother is alive, apparently his father is not, and that in his memories of the past, only his mother appears.

The absence of the husband's father allows for the ready identification of the wife's cousin with this figure. The cousin had sent them a statue of Kwanon, the Japanese mother-goddess, with a child in her lap, and a Japanese dagger. The dagger is both phallic and destructive, yet it is important that the statue with which it is associated is a statue of maternity and not fertility. The statue stands for the wife who is potentially a mother and the dagger for the husband's phallic desires but also for the fact that his impotence has murdered life. But we must, of course, relate the dagger to the razor with which he lacerated his wife's neck and see it as a symbol for the rage and destructive impulses that he seems to hold for the woman (and, perhaps, for women in general). The husband slowly pulls the dagger out of its scabbard and then throws it down with repulsion. His later inability to hold either razor or knife, after his dream and the scene the following night when he feels a compulsion to plunge the dagger into his wife's neck, indicates that the razor and knife have become instruments of potential destruction for him personally, in part as instruments of aggression to overcome his own phallic weakness, but also, we begin to surmise, because of his jealousy of his wife and her cousin. But the film is starting to force us to surmise something else, that, on some level, the husband associates his wife and her cousin with his mother and father, and that the razor and dagger represent his own feared punishment of castration by his father for his oedipal wishes for his mother.

Earlier in the film, when the analyst asks the husband why he and his wife cannot have babies, the husband describes to him "wild fantasies" in which he sees himself looking unhappily through some kind of trellis while his erotically clad wife makes love with her cousin. What is constantly hinted at, then, through the film's very apparent suggestion of violence in the interactions of the men and women, in the phallic symbols of the razor and knife, in the female symbol of the slash, in the closed bedrooms and separating doors, is the primal scene and the child's association of violence both with the sexual act performed between the parents, but also the punishment with which he is threatened by the father for sexually desiring his mother. No wonder the husband is unable to consummate his relationship with his wife. In his adult life, he has taken the place of the father by becoming a husband; but in his inhibition to take the place of his father he has taken upon himself a symbolic castration in his inability to have sex with his wife. Thus as castrated husband he also assumes the role of the punished son.

All of this is carefully suggested by the events in the dream, replete with sexual imagery. The large tower, shaped like a penis, for example, that suddenly arises in the middle of the Italian village indicates the sexual nature of the husband's own inadequacy but also the threatening penis of both the cousin and the father whom he represents. The husband's sexual inadequacy and his fear of castration are indicated both by the anxious way in which he rushes up the tower (three times we see the same middle-long shot of him running up the steps on the side of the tall structure), frantically leans out and gestures, and then drops his hat; and by the faces of three women — his servant, wife, and assistant — superimposed over the tolling bells, laughing at him derisively for his impotence.

The husband's guilt, not only for cutting his wife's neck and for his murderous impulses toward her, but also guilt from early childhood for his feelings toward his mother, lead to a court trial with his father-surrogate, the cousin as prosecutor. The wife bares her neck and points to the slash from her husband's razor. The storm outside melts into the world of his dreams and produces the drum rolls that announce his guilt and his execution but also announce the key sequence of the film.

The husband's laboratory has become his cell; he rushes to the window, lifts himself to the bars, and down below sees a boat with his wife and her cousin. Close-up shots of the husband frantically screaming are interspersed throughout the scene viewed in a high-angle, point-of-view shot from the husband's perspective. His wife catches a doll that is meant to represent a baby and that seems to leap into her arms from the water. She cuddles the baby and then gives it to her cousin, waving to her husband as the boat moves off. The dream ends violently, with the husband, over and over, thrusting the dagger into an image of his wife, thrusting it as if performing a savage act of intercourse. Later, during his therapy, when the analyst tells him that the baby coming from the water signifies "impending" or "desired" birth, the husband has the clue that weakens his defenses and allows him to find the episode in his past that can explain his present phobia and compulsion. The solution he works out falls short of the solution that we are supposed to read into the film, partly because the husband has not realized whose birth he has been witnessing in his dream — that his wife and her cousin as stand-ins for his parents have actually given birth to him,[18] that he has witnessed the primal scene responsible for his own existence, that his screaming throughout the scene has been his screaming as a baby first entering the world, that the savage thrusts of his dagger into his wife were his angry reaction to his parents' copulation and an act of desire for his own mother.

Another psychodynamic element that ought to be noted is the strong attraction that the husband feels for his wife's cousin.[19] I have suggested that in his unconscious, the husband sees in this man the usurping and threatening figure of the father who has taken his mother from him and who threatens him with castration. But though the husband may feel anger toward this man, he is strongly drawn to him. Their embraces are worth noting, but so is that moment when the two meet after so many years and the cousin pats the husband on the stomach, an action that suggests a fond husband patting the swollen belly of his pregnant wife. The screenplay for the film strongly implies that such feelings exist especially for the husband when it describes his nervous tension while he continuously and demonstratively strokes the cousin's face during their greetings. The film, then, very much suggests that part of the husband's problem may also be the strong attraction he feels for his wife's cousin, an attraction that may draw its source from his unconscious identification of this figure with his father — or perhaps I should say unconscious substitution of this figure for his father since the latter never appears in the film nor in the husband's memories. It is conceivable that the husband is also angry with his wife for taking her cousin's affections from him. The child never shakes loose of the attraction it feels for the father, a buried attraction that in the male child leaves a residue of homosexual feelings that can in later years fix on a male replacement for the father.

I shall explain this relationship further in a moment, but first I must turn to the final scene to complete our survey of the work and introduce one more interpretive level. The final scene in *Secrets of A Soul* always reminds me of the penultimate scene of Ingmar Bergman's *Wild Strawberries* (1957). The scene in the later film is dreamed by Isak Borg, but the conclusion of *Secrets* is also dreamlike and unreal. In Bergman's film Isak redreams and revises the primal scene, nay sets it right by fantasizing the pastoral scene in which his parents sit by the lake, his father fishing with a long pole, and wave to him to join them. The film ends with the seventy-six year-old man smiling as he falls into a deep sleep, smiling because he has substituted for his original fantasy of the primal scene this ideal vision which now includes him. The final scene in *Secrets* celebrates the husband's successful psychotherapy by demonstrating that he has overcome his impotence and become a father. He fishes with a long pole in a rich pastoral setting and then rushes to his wife who holds their baby. But the husband's passionate rush to his wife, the fact that he throws his basket of fish into the water, the wavering hand-held shot of him as he rushes up the hill suggest another level, another story for us to discover — the husband still acts like a child at the conclusion of the film, acts like he is rushing to his mother.

Although Abraham had written on the oral stage and made an important contribution with his work on oral sadism, I think that the advisors to the film intended us to interpret it largely on an oedipal level; but in dealing so fully with this level of the psyche, they inevitably, though unwittingly, opened up the husband's soul to other levels of interpretation. Immediately before viewing the photographs of himself, his wife, and her cousin, the husband views one of himself and his mother, suggesting, I believe, another subtext in the film and another level to his psychic conflicts. The husband feels both a bonding with and rage for his mother that seem to derive from an earlier time of his childhood than that which we have been discussing. Hanns Sachs, in his pamphlet, describes a scene that appears in the screenplay but in none of the versions of the film now available. Overwhelmed by his compulsion and the feeling that he will never be able to control it, the husband rushes to his laboratory to take poison. About to end his life, his eyes focus on a picture of his mother, and he realizes "that yet another woman plays a role in his life, one with a love that reaches farther back and is deeper than the one which joins him to his wife" (10). Bringing the picture of his mother to his lips for a parting kiss, he knocks over the bottle of poison and is saved. Sachs means the incident to indicate the saving power of his love for his mother, but this love may also be regressive and paralyzing. In the Rohauer print of the film we read the title, "In mental distress, Martin's mind turned to his mother." Unable to live at home with his wife because of his compulsion to mutilate her with a sharp instrument, the husband goes to live with his mother while he is in therapy. There is an especially impressive scene in which his mother cuts his food before hiding the knife upon his arrival. The husband then sits at the table, eating his meat with a spoon with obvious childish pleasure. A considerable reversal and regression has taken place in his life — in this instance it is his mother who wields the phallic knife and it is the husband who regresses to helpless childhood. The husband's relationship with his mother might also further explain his homosexual feelings for the cousin in a psychoanalytic context. Freud discusses the process whereby young boys with such maternal attachments, after puberty, internalize the mother and identify with her to the point of taking on her love objects. Although he at first suggests that such a process satisfies the boy's narcissism since the love-object becomes a substitute for his childish self, he later argues that the object can also be identified with the mother's other love, the father.[20] I would argue that at the same time that the child feels this excessive love for the mother, he also feels a rage at this dependency and attachment.

Indeed, the husband seems to feel rage at all the women in the film, as we can see in the dream — the derisive laughter of the three women with their heads superimposed upon the tolling bells is an indication of the shame and inadequacy he feels from his relationship with women in general. His behavior in his dream when he slashes wildly with the knife at the image of his wife, a slashing repeated at the end of his therapy as a type of abreaction that is supposed to indicate his cure,[21] reminds me of Melanie Klein's terrible infant, venting its rage on the body of its mother in its fantasies (128–30). Part of the husband's rage may derive from the fact that he will never be able to father a baby with his mother; but the rage seems to date from a more primitive time, when he saw the woman as giving but also depriving—as a totally controlling figure. The husband's regression to childhood when he dines with his mother suggests that he has not yet been able to separate from her in a healthy way—she remains an internalized object that controls his dreams, his memories, and his marriage. The statue of Kwanon that the cousin has sent to the husband and his wife is more than a symbol of maternity; she also represents the powerful mother who still holds control over the husband's emotional life. The dagger that the cousin has sent them, then, and all the razors and knives in the film, take on another level of meaning. The husband stabbing wildly with a knife at the image of his wife, who, in his unconscious has come to represent his mother, is the husband attempting symbolically to cut the umbilical cord that still has him connected to this powerful figure. The husband's dream, his phobia and compulsion in the film, are all symptoms of his struggle for separation and individuation.

Secrets of a Soul, then, is a far more subtle and complex work than film history has allowed.[22] The dream-sequence, an innovative and bold attempt to use the spatial and temporal flexibilities of the film medium to portray the labyrinthine and many-leveled workings of the mind, is worth the price of admission and certainly seems no less effective than dream sequences in later psychoanalytic films that were to have far more technical advantages from special-effects cinematography. But what is most compelling for the modern viewer is the film's openness to multiple interpretations, none of them contradictory. To read the film is an experience akin to reading the psyche of an individual—levels of meaning overlay one another and fuse together at the same time.[23] Although we discern some kind of developmental order when viewing the film, some type of *fabula*, this type of ordering imposed upon the film is largely theoretical and tentative, and exists beyond the text and the immediate presence of the main character who remains a complex amalgam. The multivalenced quality to the film that I am describing achieves a significant connection with hermeneutics and interpretation in general as they have developed in the twentieth century. It is not *Secrets of a Soul* that has changed but the ways in which we read it. Even though the makers of the film had already undermined any clear and unequivocal meaning by compromising on what would be manifest through explicit explanation in the film and what would remain latent in the film's visual imagery, they still were certain about the work's ultimate meaning.

We might, at this point in our discussion, be more sympathetic to Freud's ultimate rejection of the motion-picture camera in his search for some kind of mechanical metaphor for the operations of the mind. Certainly film can project images on a screen in such a fashion that they resemble thought, fantasy, and dream; but Freud wished to find a sufficiently complex metaphor to describe the way the brain operates. We must admit that he was right about the limitation of film emulsion as a metaphor for the storing power of the brain, about its inability to repress and store an endless series of images of reality. The filmic process is a good metaphor for the way in which the brain registers and then recalls to consciousness at a later time some series of events — but the emulsion is limited, normally, to only one such registration. The mystic writing pad at least has the virtue of countless registrations, even though the images cannot again be reconfigured. It has the virtue of suggesting the layers of "memory-traces" that can be received, absorbed, and fused together by the mind. Freud's writing pad is an apt metaphor for the multivalenced and complex network of representations and significations of the "mnemic systems" stored in the mind (1925, 230).

An ambivalence about the validity and authenticity of any single psychoanalytic interpretation in analysis in general may be suggested by the way in which Freud seems to minimize the difference between the the terms "construction" and "reconstruction" (between putting together something for the first time and putting together something that has already existed in the past) in his essay "Construction in Analysis." He claims that "interpretation" is something "one does to a single element of the material while "construction" is "when one lays before the subject of the analysis a piece of his early history that he has forgotten." But he also writes, "We do not pretend that an individual construction is anything more than a conjecture which awaits examination, confirmation or rejection" (259–65). Construction, then, is dependent upon both individual interpretations of isolated elements in the analysis but also upon a broader conjecture or interpretation of the material that awaits confirmation on the part of the analysand. Freud seems fairly certain, however, that the past, for the analyst, is recoupable: "His work of construction or, if it is preferred, of reconstruction, resembles to a great extent the archaeologist's excavation of some dwelling-place that has been destroyed and buried of some ancient edifice." Both the analyst and archeologist must "reconstruct by means of supplementing and combining the surviving remains" and both are "subject to many of the same difficulties and sources of error"; but the analyst works under better conditions since he is dealing with material, none of which is permanently destroyed and all of which is finally accessible. In spite of the partial story that *Secrets of a Soul* explicitly unfolds, its screenplay, like the film itself, demonstrates the same confidence we find in Freud's essay for reassembling the past when it tells us that at one point, during the analytic sessions, the Doctor's eyes light up—"the reconstruction has worked for him" (107). From then on the analytic sessions in the screenplay are divided between the husband's memories of events and sections marked "Picture of the Doctor's Reconstruction."

Such confidence in interpretation and the recuperation of the past has been undermined in recent years in the psychoanalytic literature. Donald P. Spence, for example, has argued that the creation of the patient's life into a logical narrative is "evidence more of a general preference for closure and good fit than for the effectiveness of the technique or the usefulness of the theory" (123).[24] Harold P. Blum's balanced work on the subject, *Reconstruction in Psychoanalysis: Childhood Revisited and Recreated*, states that reconstruction is a dynamic, contextual, and developing process that "is never 'what really happened,' as might be proposed by external observers or historians" (37).

This shift in analytical thinking resembles a similar change that has taken place in literary interpretation, a movement from the interpretive strategy that E.D. Hirsch, Jr. argues for in *Validity in Interpretation*, first published in 1967, when he says that "even though we can never be certain that our interpretive guesses are correct, we know that they *can* be correct and that the goal of interpretation as a discipline is constantly to increase the probability that they are correct" (207), to the type of thinking by such deconstructionists as Paul de Man and J. Hillis Miller in the 1970s and 1980s and represented by Jonathan Culler's statement in *On Deconstruction: Theory and Criticism after Structuralism*: "In reading particular works and rereadings of these works, deconstruction attempts to understand these phenomena of textuality—the relations of language and metalanguage, for example, or effects of externality and internality, or the possible interaction of conflicting logics" (225). The group of salvational films I am discussing are structured to produce the type of reading suggested by Culler. They are mystery films *par excellence* and their multiple mysteries concern the human psyche and our ability and inability to understand that psyche. These films are ultimately about processes, the process of the psychotherapist and his patient to solve the mysteries of the soul but also the process of the viewer to understand the mysteries — the various textualities and logics — of the film. If one thinks of these films as finished artifacts, as finitely definable and describable, then they must fail — *Secrets of A Soul* in this context would be a most unsatisfactory film.

The non-existence of any single work of art called *Secrets of a Soul*, the fact that there are differing versions at this time and no authorative, original version, emphasizes the impossibility of placing any closure on our attempt to get at the work's meaning. Nor do I think that we shall ever "reconstruct" such an original and definitive print. When I began researching this film, I was advised by a distinguished scholar of German film that I could not possibly write on *Secrets of a Soul* without using the restored print available at the Film Museum in Munich. When I finally was able to view this print, I was struck by a number of important shots and titles missing from it and available in the Rohauer print — and also impressed by a number of shots in the Munich print not present in either the Rohauer or West-Glen versions. My letter to the present director of the Film Museum in Munich, questioning why shots clearly filmed during production were not used in the original release, resulted in a reply admitting that the "restored" print must not be fully restored and asking for information on the location of the missing material. We may ultimately have a print that puts together all of the available shots, but I doubt we shall ever know the version exactly the way Pabst released it — especially since there are also some major discrepancies between the subtitles and intertitles of the available prints. Any hermeneutics concerning *Secrets of a Soul* must satisfy the poststructuralist and deconstructive scriptures about interpretation and meaning in general — lacking both the author's presence and any single originary visual or verbal text, the film offers instead a play of texts and meanings.

Secrets of a Soul also raises questions about the privileged status given to language in the theory of interpretation. It does so by asking us to consider whether the film's titles tell us the whole story — or even a piece of one. And it also asks us why its language, the titles we see on the screen, is to be given privileged status, is to be seen as an outside intervention and transcendent truth, and is not to be seen instead as part of the film, as another of the images that we see on the screen, as another element in the secrets and mysteries of the soul, as another text. The uncertain state of the verbal text to the film reinforces this point about the circumscribed nature of language. In the West-Glen version available in this country and in the "restored" version in Munich, which seems to be a fuller version of the former, the all-powerful analyst has disappeared from the opening and closing—we no longer see him framing the film with his act of writing. We must relate to this omission the fact that the West-Glen print has fewer titles than both the "restored" version and the one available in this country from the Rohauer Collection, and that both the West-Glen and Munich prints are missing a long series of titles that convey Dr. Orth's explanation to the husband of the nature of his illness at the end of the therapy.[25] *Secrets of a Soul* seems to demonstrate a struggle with language through the differences between its available versions—a struggle exacerbated, nay motivated by the simple fact that the film is silent, silent of spoken language. If psychoanalysis is dependent on language, if language is the passage to the unconscious, what we have in this film is a futile struggle to get to that unconscious. But I must also connect the missing shots of the analyst writing in both the West-Glen and "restored" versions to the the missing father in the film as well as to the missing language. I borrow, at this point, a bit of Lacan that reinforces my matriarchal interpretation of this film. What we find in the form and substance of *Secrets of a Soul* is the struggle to move from the imaginary to the symbolic, the imaginary that fosters a feeling of oneness to the mother, the symbolic that is the realm of the prohibiting language that belongs to the father. If film is truly an oral experience, a taking in of the images and sounds emanating from the screen, and if the screen is itself a residual memory of the dream screen, then it follows that the very nature of film is matriarchal, and the struggle of film to move into the realm of language must be doomed.

The missing language and missing father inevitably lead us back to the role of Dr. Orth in the film. Significantly missing from his interaction with the husband are the issues of transference and, concomitantly, counter-transference—issues not absent from such later salvational films as *Mine Own Executioner* and *Freud*. The missing transference and counter-transference become especially obvious in the film's problematic handling of the husband's neurosis and cure, forcing us to impose them on the film ourselves. While we are making, for ourselves, a host of interpretations from the husband's life and dream, the analyst is creating a very limited and circumscribed story, one that emphasizes his own control over the material and over the husband. The powerful analyst has himself become an author in the act of reading, and the patient for him is a "readerly text" on which to inscribe his own meaning, a process we see in the behavior of a large number of the therapists we meet in non-comic films about psychotherapy — a process that savagely erupts in the portrayal of Hannibal Lecter in *The Silence of the Lambs*.

At one point in *Secrets of a Soul*, the husband looks at some photos that his wife has been showing to her cousin. The husband looks fondly at the picture of himself as a young boy and his mother, then one of himself, his wife, and her cousin as children, but appears disturbed when he next views a photograph of the three of them from the same period evidently taken at a Christmas celebration.[26] During his psychotherapy the husband remembers the time during the Christmas party when the disturbing photograph was taken — there are two interesting aspects to his memory. The first is the doll held by the little girl since in the actual photograph we have viewed earlier in the film she is empty-handed.[27] We must ponder, then, whether events took place exactly as the husband remembers them — or what we are seeing, and what he and the analyst are taking for reality, have instead been changed by projections from the husband's unconscious, altered by his own fantasies. The second interesting element in this memory is the photographer taking the picture, who seems to be aiming his camera right at us, the audience, with a mirror behind him showing his own reflection.[28] The presence of the photographer almost seems to authenticate the scene of the three children the way we now see it, but this photographer appears in the husband's memory and is, therefore, only as reliable a recorder of reality as that memory itself — the photographer's reflection in the mirror specifically suggests the separation of memory from reality, the fact that memory shows us a version and reflection of actual events. The shot of the photographer, however, is also a self-reflexive image that makes us ponder more than the mind as a

recorder of reality — makes us ponder the issue of art and representation, especially cinema as photography, as moving pictures with the
ability and inability to represent reality, both external and internal.

But the photographer is also aiming his camera at us, involving us
in his picture-making process and in the world of the film as well,
involving us in the impossible search for some original source and
original meaning to all these images. Both the uncertainty about the
visual representations and the failure of language in the film put the
burden of meaning on our interpretive faculties. *Secrets of a Soul* is
ultimately a self-reflexive film about hermeneutics, about interpretation in general, about the process of looking for meaning. The film
becomes a "readerly text" for us, an analysand, and we become the
empowered analyst. We are invited to play this role, to get into this
process, so long as we remember the openness of the film to multiple
readings but also to our own counter-transference, the infusion of
our own fantasies and defenses. Or perhaps I might say that the film
on the screen becomes a unique transitional object for each of us. In
analyzing the film I watch it over and over — in fact, it is the nature
of film to be seen over and over, pretending to be fixed with the
same images, the same titles, the same sequence. But the very act of
viewing, the fact that I watch the film each time in a different
frame of mind and with a different day's residue, the fact that each
print will be seen in a different theater, with a different quality of
image and sound, by a different audience, and by different individuals in the audience means that it can never be fixed or determinate
in meaning.

And here is the final lesson we learn from viewing *Secrets of a
Soul*: searching the film for any single neurotic pattern or pathology
that explains the husband's behavior, like searching for any original
or authoritative print of the film, can only be a partial success at
best — meaning does not ultimately reside in the work itself but in
the person making the interpretation. The three versions of the film
(four if we include the one referred to in Sachs' publication) and the
multiple interpretations inherent in the text open up the work to
contemporary deconstructive readings, reader-response theory, and
psychoanalytic concepts of counter-transference and reconstruction.
Perhaps now we can understand the natural and increasing appeal
of film for psychoanalysts:[29] its presentation of images that create an
experience not far from dreaming or daydreaming, that provoke us
to interpret them not only in terms of what the film presents to us as

its meaning but also in terms of something hidden and subversive; our attempt to put image into language and to fix the meaning of image through language; the fact that we are always interpreting in spite of the fact that we are always misremembering; and the fact that our discovery of the latent in the manifest and our construction of the *fabula* from the *sujet* are together a creative act that is part of the entire work's development. Films may pretend to have their own meanings, but there can be no meanings without someone doing the interpreting and, I must add, taking part in the fantasy — the viewing experience is the experience of analysis, but the true film critic realizes that he or she is both analyst and analysand. The frequent appearance of psychotherapists in film, the frequent stories that involve psychotherapy, are a tautology because film viewing, to begin with, is an analytic process — but because all tautologies are self-reflexive, such films draw attention to what the film medium is all about.

NOTES

[1]The German title is *Geheimnisse einer Seele*. Translated as "Soul" in the English title, "Seele" maintains its original meaning rather than being deprived of its spiritual significance as when Strachey translates Freud's use of the word as "psyche" or "mind" in the *Standard Edition of the Complete Psychological Works of Sigmund Freud*. See Bettelheim for a discussion of the English translations of Freud's works.

[2]The portrait appears in an English-language version of the film available in this country as part of the Rohauer Collection. The Filmmuseum of the Münchner Stadtmuseum claims that its version of the film is "restored," even though the print is missing the photograph of Freud as well as a number of other shots available in the Rohauer print. Also missing the portrait, and somewhat close to the "restored" print in Munich but without all the titles, is an English version of the film available in this country through West-Glen. I shall have something more to say on these various prints of the film below.

[3]I am excluding from this category several films in which psychotherapists perform similar ameliorative roles, but which do not quite fit the category I am defining. I exclude, most notably, *The Three Faces of Eve* (1957) because the focus is more on the sensational issue of multiple personalities than the therapeutic alliance, *David and Lisa* (1963) because the film is most concerned with the pathologies and relationship of the two main characters, and *I Never Promised You a Rose Garden* (1973) because the film, though certainly about the therapeutic alliance, does not follow the particular narrative structure of mystery and discovery that I will be describing in the following pages.

[4]No mention of the film appears in a recent history of the psychiatrist in cinema by Gabbard and Gabbard.

[5]I shall directly translate the German titles from the Munich print since they are likely to be the original titles and since the English translation in the Rohauer print

seems to me more discursive and melodramatic. *Spellbound* begins with similar titles extolling the merits of psychoanalysis in "open[ing] the locked doors of [the] mind."

[6]The story of the genesis of the film from the perspective of Freud and his circle is told in detail in Chodorkoff and Baxter. Friedberg also gives an account of the film's genesis.

[7]I am grateful to Jan-Christopher Horak, Director of the Filmmuseum in the Münchner Stadtmuseum, for making a copy of the screenplay available, and to my colleague Peter Bauland for his help in translating the German.

[8]I am grateful to the Deutsches Institut For Filmkunde in Wiesbaden-Biebrich, Germany, for a photocopy of this work.

[9]Browne and McPherson cite this quotation from *The Interpretation of Dreams* and then refer to Derrida's "Freud and the Scene of Writing" in which the French philosopher discusses Freud's discovery of an adequate model for the operations of the mind in "Note on the Mystic Writing Pad" (36).

[10]In *Psychotherapy*, published in 1909, Münsterberg clearly argued against the unconscious as developed by Freud and argued instead for one filled with memories and learning, one directly connected to but unnoticed by the conscious mind (15–26).

[11]Interpretation as the single most important activity in literary criticism received much emphasis from the New Criticism that was so pervasive in the years following the second world war, an emphasis that was not diminished by the deconstructive movement. Indeed, deconstruction itself became an interpretive strategy, e.g., the work's meaning was the difficulty or impossibility of meaning (see Culler for a discussion of interpretation in the context of the New Criticism and deconstruction, 3–17). The New Criticism can be seen as part of the development of hermeneutics in Western thought from the writing of the German philosopher Wilhelm Dilthey in the late nineteenth century. Paul Ricoeur's *Freud and Philosophy: An Essay on Interpretation* is essential reading for understanding the relationship of Freud's thinking to hermeneutics.

[12]See especially Tomashevsky's "Thématique," 267–69.

[13]An obvious example of this process takes place in Alfred Hitchcock's *Psycho* (1960) when the psychiatrist at the end of the film explains the mystery and the pathology of Norman Bates that has been responsible for that mystery; but in such films as Robert Siodmak's *The Dark Mirror* (1946) and Robert Benton's *Still of the Night* (1982) the psychotherapy plays a more pervasive and crucial role in solving an external mystery.

[14]Variations on this theme appear in Stanley Kramer's *Home of the Brave* (1949) and Barbara Streisand's *Prince of Tides* (1991).

[15]There is an interesting variation on this type of double exposure in *Spellbound* when the hero discovers his earliest trauma, his reaction as a young boy to his accidental killing of his brother, and, as a result, then remembers the more recent trauma that has caused his present amnesia, his reaction to the murder of the doctor. In this film the solving of the two internal mysteries frees the character from suspicion and allows for the solution to an external mystery.

[16]The "restored" version in the Munich Museum and the West-Glen print begin with the opening titles concerning psychoanalysis followed by the narrative itself, which begins with a shot of the husband sharpening his razor and then a mirror shot of him shaving himself — this entire shaving sequence is missing from the narrative proper in the Rohauer print, which begins with the husband entering his wife's bedroom. While the husband is identified as Martin Fellman in Dr. Orth's notebook

as well as on two occasions during the film and his wife's cousin is identified as Erich at the end of his letter to the couple in the Rohauer print, their names are totally missing from both the Munich and West-Glen prints.

[17]Sachs uses the word "Fehlhandlung" or faulty action instead of Freud's "Fehlleistung" or faulty function. The editor of the *Standard Edition* of Freud's works tells us that no equivalent term to "Fehlleistung" existed in English and the word "parapraxis" had to be invented (1901, viii).

[18]A point also made by Browne and McPherson in their discussion of the film's oedipal theme.

[19]A relationship first touched upon by Chodorkoff and Baxter.

[20]Freud at first identified the loved object with the self because his theory of homosexuality was partly based on the life of Leonardo da Vinci, who was raised for the first three years of his life without a father (1910, 98–100). Since the husband's father is totally absent in *Secrets of A Soul* such an interpretation has some credence, but the oedipal elements in the film clearly show the husband's identification of the cousin with his father. It is certainly possible that the strong mother and the absence of the father in early childhood can later produce a homosexual configuration where the love object represents both the self and the missing father, a fusion that further compensates for the parental absence. Later, in "Some Neurotic Mechanisms in Jealousy, Paranoia, and Homosexuality," Freud argued that homosexuality may be induced by the high regard for the male organ and also by either regard for the father or fear of him (in the later case his danger is removed by making him the loved object). Both "the clinging to a condition of the penis in the object, as well as the retiring in favor of the father — may be ascribed to the castration complex" (231).

[21]The analyst points out that the husband is cured because he is now holding a knife. Abreaction is a type of catharsis, normally achieved through language, that frees the patient from an affect that is the product of some early trauma. The concept is associated with Freud's early work on hysteria and was frequently achieved through hypnosis, though some form of abreaction continued to be sought in psychoanalytic treatment under certain conditions. Many films featuring psychotherapy, including most of the salvational psychoanalytic films, use abreaction as the denouement of their plots because of its dramatic nature.

[22]The work has generally been judged as visually interesting but intellectually superficial (see, for example, Kracauer's assessment, 170–72).

[23]There are obviously more interpretive possibilities than the series I have outlined here, each dependent on one's psychoanalytic leanings. In addition to 1) Dr. Orth's logical, though incomplete narrative; 2) the oedipal interpretation as suggested by the film's visual imagery; 3) the implications of homosexual feelings between the two male figures from their interactions; and 4) my pre-oedipal reading, the film can easily support 5) an object-relations approach in terms of the husband's relationships with his mother and father as projected onto his involvement with his wife and her cousin; 6) a self-psychology interpretation through a focus on the husband's narcissistic injuries and the structure of his self.

[24]He also states that "The preferred explanation for a series of symptoms tends to be cast in terms of single events — the primal scene is the outstanding example" (144).

[25]The titles in this portion of the Rohauer version appear as subtitles, except for the last part of this explanation that appears as intertitles. The West-Glen and "restored" versions use only subtitles for the analyst's explanation.

[26]In the screenplay, the oedipal significance of this photograph is underscored when the wife and her cousin are described as playing husband and wife with a

cradle and doll while the husband watches sadly from a distance. Later that night, the husband again looks at the photograph which seems to undergo a strange transformation before his eyes: both his wife and cousin grow older continuing to play mother and father, while he remains the young child looking sadly on.

[27]The husband remembers that at this Christmas celebration his mother gave him her new baby to hold. In his mind, he must have felt that he was no longer the play father, but his own father, and his little sibling was his and his mother's child. When his wife, as the little girl, felt deserted by him as a result of his mother's action and gave the doll to her cousin, the husband conflated the two women in his mind and felt rejected by his mother. Because the husband associated the little girl with his mother, he, in fact, also became the doll that she gave to the cousin, and the girl and her cousin his parents. The doll in his memory is related to the doll that his wife holds while in the boat with her cousin at the end of the husband's dream, when he dreams his own birth.

[28]August Ruhs suggests that the man with the camera is the husband's father reminding us of the filmmaker with his constant cinematic references to the primal scene beneath the sublimated events of the film itself (31). Browne and McPherson also relate the primal scene to this photograph and the husband's memory of the photograph being shot (44).

[29]I refer not only to the large number of classes on film now part of psychoanalytic training and the multitude of lectures on films given by psychoanalysts, but also to such groups as The Forum for the Psychoanalytic Study of Film in Washington D.C., which promote these activities as well as further communication between analysts and film scholars on the subject of film.

REFERENCES

Abraham, Karl. 1924. "A Short Study of the Development of the Libido, Viewed in the Light of Mental Disorders." *Selected Papers*. London: Hogarth Press, 1927. 418-501.

Baudry, Jean Louis. 1970. "Ideological Effects of the Basic Cinematographic Apparatus." Trans. Alan Williams. *Film Quarterly* 28 (1974–75). 39–47.

Bettelheim, Bruno. *Freud and Man's Soul*. New York: Alfred Knopf, 1983.

Blum, Harold P. *Reconstruction in Psychoanalysis: Childhood Revisited and Recreated*. Madison, Conn.: International Universities Press, 1994.

Browne, Nick and Bruce McPherson. "Dream and Photography in a Psychoanalytic Film: *Secrets of A Soul*." *Dreamworks* 1 (Spring 1980): 35–45.

Chodorkoff, Bernard and Seymour Baxter. "*Secrets of a Soul*: An Early Psychoanalytic Film Venture." *American Imago* 31 (Winter 1974): 319–34.

Culler, Jonathan. *The Pursuit of Signs: Semiotics, Literature, Deconstruction*. Ithaca: Cornell University Press, 1981.

Eberwein, Robert T. *Film and the Dream Screen: A Sleep and a Forgetting*. Princeton: Princeton University Press, 1984.

Freud, Sigmund and Karl Abraham. *A Psycho-Analytic Dialogue: The Letters of Sigmund Freud and Karl Abraham*. Ed. Hilda C. Abraham and Ernst L. Freud. Trans. Bernard Marsh and Hilda C. Abraham. London: The Hogarth Press, 1965.

Freud, Sigmund. 1900. *The Interpretation of Dreams. The Standard Edition of the Complete Psychological Works of Sigmund Freud.* Ed. James Strachey. London: Hogarth Press, 1953–74. Vols. 4 and 5.

———. 1901. *The Psychopathology of Everyday Life. Standard Edition.* Vol. 6.

———. 1910. "Leonardo da Vinci and a Memory of his Childhood." *Standard Edition.* 11:59–137.

———. 1922. "Some Neurotic Mechanisms in Jealousy, Paranoia, and Homosexuality." *Standard Edition.* 18: 221–32.

———. 1925. "A Note Upon a Mystic Writing Pad." *Standard Edition.* 19: 226–232.

———. 1937. "Construction in Analysis." *Standard Edition.* 23: 256–269.

Friedberg, Anne. "An *Unheimlich* Maneuver between Psychoanalysis and the Cinema: *Secrets of a Soul (1926)." The Films of G. W. Pabst: An Extraterritorial Cinema.* 1990. Ed. Eric Rentschler. New Brunswick: Rutgers University Press, 1990. 41–51.

Gabbard, Krin and Glen O. Gabbard. *Psychiatry and the Cinema.* Chicago: The University of Chicago Press, 1987.

Hirsch, E. D., Jr. *Validity in Interpretation.* New Haven: Yale University Press, 1967.

Jones, Ernest. *The Life and Work of Sigmund Freud.* Vol. 3: *The Last Phase, 1919–39.* New York: Basic Books, 1957.

Klein, Melanie. 1932. *The Psycho-Analysis of Children.* Trans. Alix Strachey. Revised H. A. Thorner. New York: Delacorte, 1975.

Kracauer, Siegfried. *From Caligari to Hitler: A Psychological History of the German Film.* Princeton: Princeton University Press, 1947.

Lévi-Strauss, Claude. "The Sorcerer and his Magic." *Structural Anthropology.* Trans. Clair Jacobson and Brooke Grudfest Schoepf. Anchor Books. New York: Doubleday, 1967. 161–80.

Metz, Christian. *The Imaginary Signifier: Psychoanalysis and the Cinema.* Trans. Celia Britton, Annwyl Williams, Ben Brewster and Alfred Guzzetti. Bloomington: Indiana University Press, 1982.

Münsterberg, Hugo. *Psychotherapy.* New York: Moffat, Yard and Co., 1912.

———. *The Photoplay: A Psychological Study.* New York: D. Appleton, 1916.

Ricoeur, Paul. *Freud and Philosophy: An Essay on Interpretation.* Trans. Denis Savage. New Haven: Yale University Press, 1970.

Ross, Colin and Hans Neumann. Manuscript. *Die Geheimnisse der Seele, Psychoanalytisches Filmwerk. Zweiter Teil: Das Geheimnis einer Seele, Ein Psychoalytisches Kammerspiel.* Berlin: Kulturabteilung der UFA, n.d.

Ruhs, August. "Geheimnisse Einer Seele: Ein Freud-Loses Projekt." *G. W. Pabst.* Ed. Gottfried Schlemmer, Bernard Riff, and Georg Haberl. Münster: Maks Publikationen, 1990. 20–32.

Sachs, Hanns. *Psychoanalyse: Rätsel des Unbewussten.* Berlin: Lichtbild-Bühne, 1926.

Spence, Donald P. *Narrative Truth and Historical Truth: Meaning and Interpretation in Psychoanalysis.* New York: W.W. Norton & Company, 1982.

Tomashevsky, Boris. "Thématique." *Théorie de la littérature.* Ed. Tzvetan Todorov. Paris: Éditions du Seuil, 1965. 263–307.

"A nightmare vision of feminine power, a grotesque of female appetite": The Witch of the West threatens Dorothy with the curse of independence.

BONNIE FRIEDMAN

RELINQUISHING OZ:
EVERY GIRL'S ANTI-ADVENTURE STORY

I was always stricken, as a child, at the moment when the Wicked Witch in *The Wizard of Oz* cried, "I'm mellllting!" The shocked anguish on her face, the way she crumpled to the floor—guilt overcame me. As much as I'd hated her before (and I had: she was cruel and she was voracious. She wanted everything for herself), suddenly, to my surprise, remorse washed over me, and painful sympathy: She was my own mother, dissolving!

Quick, she mustn't be let die! Prop her up! A terrible mistake must have been made! And the moment I had expected to feel thrilled triumph (as we would have if this were a boy's story: we're glad the knight slays the dragon) turned out to be in fact spiked with a baffling sense of betrayal.

But wasn't the girl supposed to win? Wasn't the wicked witch evil? And how had my mother snuck into it all?

The boy's coming-of-age story is about leaving home to save the world. The girl's coming-of-age story is about relinquishing the world beyond home. It is about finding a way to sacrifice one's yearning for the big world, the world of experience, and to be happy about it. At its center is the image of the hungry woman, the desirous, commanding, grasping woman who shows herself with a blow to our heart—her ultimate weapon—to be the woman we love most.

Or is she?

As a child, I wasn't sure. Watching the witch suddenly dissolve, I knew I'd glimpsed something. I was snagged. Distracted. The story stopped for me right there. I was no longer immersed. Because maybe one wasn't meant to vanquish the dragon. Maybe one shouldn't have hated that witch so much. Maybe, maybe . . . and a sort of unraveling happened— one had misunderstood, one had got one's signals crossed, one was too impulsive, eager, girlish. Precisely because it never got looked at—in girls' stories, in my own life, the plot rushed on—this unease remained:

41

a suspicion of one's flaring impulses. A tendency to go vague. The sort of dubiousness that makes a student shoot her hand up in class, but then, quite slowly, lower it, and afterward trail home unsettled, head bent.

At a certain point in my own life, everything partook of this same confusion. I had gotten something I craved—a writing contract, a broomstick of my own—only to find to my dismay it wasn't what I wanted at all. I was blocked, locked, grounded. How had I learned to be paralyzed? In the absence of my own particular memory, I found myself obsessed with the great cultural memory of Dorothy in Oz. Besides the moment the witch's face alters, I kept thinking about the scene in which Dorothy is locked in the witch's keep. "Auntie Em!" she cries, in Judy Garland's signature throbbing voice, while Em, in the crystal ball, calls "Dorothy! . . . Where are you? We're trying to find you!" turning and peering and vanishing into Kansas.

"Oh, don't go away," cries Dorothy. But it's too late. Em, never even suspecting the possibility of Oz, is gone. How far the daughter has traveled from her mother! Into realms unimaginable. Like a girl who leaves home for erotic love and can't come back. Or a daughter whose ambitions transport her far from her mother's values. "Oh, don't go away!" rang in my mind, and my eyes dripped. Locked in my own prison, blocked in my work, I identified without knowing why. Gradually, though, I began to see how Dorothy's story is the story of many women and men who find ourselves stuck.

The Wizard of Oz is so familiar it resembles a childhood ritual more than a concocted work of entertainment. Even though I hadn't seen the movie in twenty years, when I watched it again the other night I found myself murmuring key lines with the characters. The rhythms were in my body like the rhythms of Mother Goose, like the pulse of a song that's on the radio so low you don't notice it, yet your feet tap to its beat, and you are nodding your head.

Dorothy is racing up the road, all in a frazzle. "Auntie Em!" she cries. "Uncle Henry!" Her little charge, Toto, has gotten into some natural, even hormonal mischief chasing Miss Gulch's cat. Yet the punishment will be dreadfully severe. It just doesn't seem fair! But Dorothy, like a quintessential adolescent, comes off as all elbows and histrionic gasps. She's only in the way. "Dorothy, please! We're trying to count!" her aunt chastises. "Don't bother us now," says Uncle Henry. They're gathering up eggs, and Dorothy will make them lose track. Financial troubles threaten the farm; there's no time for Dorothy's breathless complaints.

The situation is the same with the rest of the people in this dusty, grim world; the farmhands are all busy, or give silly heedless advice. "You going to let that old Gulch heifer buffalo you? Next time she squawks, walk right up to her and spit in her eye. That's what *I'd* do," counsels Zeke.

"Aw, you just won't listen, that's all!" says Dorothy. Her sense of what's crucial is so different from the adults', and no one really regards what she says as important at all, although it's obvious they love her. Her aunt seems impatient for Dorothy to grow up and realize what really matters (counting eggs; perhaps she'd like Dorothy to start noticing the eggs inside her), to give up childish concerns and take responsibility for the womanliness her body suggests she already has. Dorothy wears a pinafore that crams her breasts against her and spills into a frothy white yoke of blouse; every other woman in the movie wears a dress. Dorothy seems to have outgrown her childish frock without noticing, or perhaps she's installed in a sort of transitional training dress, like the training wheels on a bicycle before a child knows how to maintain her balance, or like a "training bra," those concoctions of padding and lace meant to train—not one's breasts, certainly. Well, then, one's mind into an acceptance of one's breasts. Or the boys in one's class into an acceptance of one's acceptability.

How tired out Aunt Em looks! One of the characters describes her face as "careworn," as if she'll soon be erased, rubbed away. Perhaps Em would like Dorothy to fill in for her, but Dorothy won't take the bit. She frolics, she indulges in what others see as self-absorbed emotion. In her exuberance, she tries idly walking the balance beam of the fencetop between the animal pens, tomboyish, but tumbles right into the hogs' slovenly pen. The big loud beasts start to trample her. She shrieks. Finally, a man rescues her and the other farmhands rush up. Their circle of warm laughter is descended upon by the irate Aunt Em.

Dorothy's first fall is due to her carelessness, her carefreeness, her animal high spirits (she is like Toto, wandering after "trouble." If she were a witch, as the munchkins instantly recognize her to be, we'd call Toto her familiar). Dorothy can't keep her balance. It's as if, with those recent breasts of hers, she no longer knows how to hold herself; she is not used to the weight of being a woman yet. And, in this good middle-American tale, her burgeoning, fence-flouting femaleness lands her flat in the mire of—what? Degradation, being overrun by beasts, and, if unrescued by a good man, even death. Perhaps Dorothy falls *so that* a man will rescue her. The farmhands all come running. She gets them to show concern when Aunt Em won't. Unrescued, though, she would become a "Miss Gulch."

Who exactly is this Gulch? The word gulch comes from the Middle English word meaning to gulp, and refers to "a deep or precipitous cleft or ravine, especially one occupied by a torrent" and "containing a deposit of gold." The word gulch also meant "to swallow or devour greedily," the way a glutton or drunkard might, and the act of "taking a heavy fall."

A woman who is a gulch is a devouring, appetitive, carnal woman, a torrential woman who will swallow you up into her vacuumous cleft; she is a fallen woman who gulches others and makes them fall too, and she inhabits the sunken places (I think of Shakespeare's witches on the "blasted heath," that obscure, gashed watery wasteland. Those hags also draw their power from arousing taboo cravings.) The gulch is aligned with the Devil, with his clefts and his knack for snaring men by using their earthly wants against them. And, in the case of Kansas' particular Elvira Gulch, she is an aging spinster, which, in the era of the movie meant she occupied a certain realm of death—undesired, undesiring of men, her sexuality considered a waste, her reproductivity a redundancy, sterile and thwarted. And yet, unlike Aunt Em, she pays a *lot* of attention to Dorothy.

We know from the start that Miss Gulch is a wanting woman—it is *her* demands that set the world of the movie in motion, that set Dorothy rushing up that road of dust in Kansas. The very first words of the picture are "She isn't coming yet, Toto. Did she hurt you, Toto? She tried to, didn't she?" with Judy Garland's frightened face staring straight into the camera toward the impending, wrathful She. In fact, the real, scarcely noticed precipitating event is Dorothy's choosing to go past Miss Gulch's house on the way home. She might have predicted Toto would again invade Miss Gulch's garden. When a farmhand suggests she choose a different way home, Dorothy exclaims, "You just don't understand."

When we see this acquisitive woman, she is anything but fat, as we might expect a ravenous "gulch" might be. She flies into the movie on her bicycle (historically the symbol of a liberated woman: the first bikes were made in retooled corset shops and gave middle-class women freedom of movement; bike makers, in turn, built the first airplanes. Stays to spokes to wings). Miss Gulch is a gnarled skinny vixen stoked with a purposeful fury. She almost trembles with energy. She *will* be satisfied.

Many of the scenes I focus on come from the black-and-white section, by the way. These scenes are like a person's own early history, crucial to understanding the color parts in the same way childhood explains an adult's demeanor, or Rosebud explains Citizen Kane.

"Ga-yle!" trumpets Miss Gulch, saluting Uncle Henry with his last

With Toto at stake, Dorothy and Miss Gulch make their appeals to Aunt Em.
Uncle Henry stands outside the circle of decision.

name in a sort of perfunctory military way. "I want to see you and your
wife right away. It's about Dorothy."

Uncle Henry stages a few jokes at Miss Gulch's expense. She says
she's here because of Dorothy, but she keeps talking about her dog. She's
conflated the two. "Dorothy bit you?" he asks. "She bit her *dog*?"

He blinks, holding a whitewashing brush. Apparently he's whitewashing the fence (walls and gates and doors of all sorts figure enormously
here). Miss Gulch claims she's almost lame from where Toto bit her on
the leg, but she's obviously lying—she immediately glances down and
her face takes on an almost guilty look. Besides, she's nowhere near
lame; she's one of the most vigorous women imaginable. She announces
that Toto is "a menace to the community," when, from the looks of him,
he could hardly hurt a fly—he's a tiny, yappy, bright-eyed terrier who extends a paw when Dorothy feels blue, and who remains patiently beside
her while her mind roams in daydreams. In fact, he is the only one who

pays much loving attention to Dorothy at all—he *is* her all, her "toto," her soul. He is also her mutual-gazer, her adoring lover, her loyal friend.

"He's really gentle. With gentle people, that is," Aunt Em points out.

Bizarrely, Miss Gulch does seem to have an impulsive shrinking terror of the dog—at one point she drops way back in her chair when he is near. It is as if she fears he might recognize her when no one else does, that he might expose her the way he later exposes Oz (it is Toto who drags the curtain away from the man operating the smoke and thunder machine: he has an instinct for truth).

Dorothy would give up everything she has to save him (she proves this when she runs away). Yet Miss Gulch wants to "take him to the sheriff and see that he's destroyed." Why? Out of mere vindictiveness? A warped desire to make Dorothy as lonely as she?

"Their magic must be very powerful or she wouldn't want them so badly," the good witch later says about the Wicked Witch's desire for the red shoes. Aunt Em also identifies the issue as power. "Just because you own half the county doesn't mean you have power over the rest of us!" she exclaims.

But Miss Gulch does. She comes equipped with magic: a slip of paper from the sheriff. If they don't give her the dog, she rants, "I'll bring a suit that will take your whole farm. There's a law protecting people from dogs who bite." How fast the dog has turned into the farm! No one questions this logic.

She claps open her basket (it seems like a torture device), and Aunt Em nods to Uncle Henry to pry the dog from Dorothy, who stares from Henry to Aunt Em, then runs weeping from the room. Aunt Em seems about to lose her composure to the gloating Gulch as she bursts, "Elvira Gulch, for 23 years I've been dying to tell you what I think of you—" yet, in classic fashion she concludes, "but now, being a Christian woman, I can't say it!"

Being a "Christian woman," being a woman gagged by the strictures of decorum, Aunt Em is left with the sole response of acquiescing to tyranny and holding her tongue. This is what a "Christian woman" does, her example teaches: she sequesters herself away in her house with her good name (although of course her remark is a marvelous example of passive aggression), while the Miss Gulches of the world cycle off in bitter triumph, what they want secure, for the moment at least, in their woven box.

"Boxes, cases, cupboards and ovens represent the uterus," Freud noted. Miss Gulch has Dorothy's genie, her wild pleasure, caged up for herself. But her lock can't keep Toto; her basket is not secure. Toto pushes free and gallops back to his rightful owner.

This is a story about who owns what, as any archetypal story about women must be. It is about kidnapping and re-kidnapping and ultimate possession. Merged with our mothers, unsure of our boundaries, women's drama often enacts the story of the self in jeopardy, the self that has been absconded with—raped, ravished, invaded, and annexed—and the struggle to get that self back. Demeter and Persephone, Hera and Io, Cinderella, Snow White, Sleeping Beauty, all are about self-possession and the struggle with a rapacious, devouring outside force.

Toto leaps in Dorothy's window (the window is one image for the mind here) and she embraces him. Quick, she realizes, "they" will be back: her own home is in league with "them" (Aunt Em doesn't even consider challenging the sheriff's order or explaining her viewpoint to this invisible, commanding man. As with Oz's diplomas, what's on paper holds supreme magic). Dorothy heaves her suitcase on her bed. She will run away.

Frog or dragon figures often begin archetypal stories, according to Joseph Campbell, who writes: "The disgusting and rejected frog or dragon of the fairy tale . . . is the representative of that unconscious deep . . . wherein are hoarded all the rejected, unadmitted, unrecognized, unknown, or undeveloped factors, laws, and elements of existence . . . Those are the nuggets in the gold hoard of the dragon."

What is Miss Gulch's gold? The powers locked inside Dorothy that are yet unknown. Miss Gulch reveals her home's fragility, its inability to keep Dorothy content; it is so much cardboard and whitewash before Miss Gulch's roar, "Then I'll huff, and I'll puff. . . ." Miss Gulch sets Dorothy on her way.

At the end of a long dry road, when she is merely a lonely figure, vulnerable and fatigued, Dorothy comes upon a caravan. It announces the presence of the celebrated Professor Marvel. The man is camped under a bridge, like the proverbial gnome. Clad in a threadbare cutaway and frilled shirt, and roasting wieners like a hobo, this fancy gentleman is obviously a fraud. Yet before Dorothy utters hardly a word, he gazes at her and proclaims that she is running away because "They don't understand you at home. They don't appreciate you. You want to see other lands. Big cities, big mountains, big oceans."

"Why, it's like you could read what's inside me," she exclaims.

Ah, so her motive isn't just to save Toto! Or, perhaps her two aims are one: to save her animal spirit, she must go out into the world. She is like the midwestern farm boy who wants to come east to college or west to make his fortune; she wants to leave behind the consuming farm. Home is the gulch, really.

Discussing why women through history hardly ever wrote, and why, when they did, they rarely achieved the free flight of genius, Virginia Woolf invokes women's confined experience. Women were kept home. They were kept knowing little. "Anybody may blame me who likes," she quotes Charlotte Bronte. And then Woolf asks, Why does Charlotte Bronte's character feel she deserves to be blamed? Because this character—Jane Eyre—climbs up on the roof while the housekeeper makes jellies, and looks over the fields at the distant view.

Jane Eyre longs for "a power of vision which might overpass that limit; which might reach the busy world, town, regions full of life I had heard of but never seen . . . practical experience . . . it is narrow-minded in their more privileged fellow-creatures to say [women] ought to confine themselves to making puddings and embroidering bags." Suddenly, though, Jane Eyre recalls Grace Poole's laugh. It is like being interrupted, as Dorothy so often is at the height of her happiness, by the mocking glee of Elvira Gulch: the cackle of a woman who flew off over the horizon and paid the price. (Air, pool, gale, gulch: women are nature, ephemeral or eerie. How interesting that Jane Eyre mounts a house much the way Dorothy does to fly over the rainbow.)

"Ah," remarks the professor when Dorothy is amazed by his grasp of her innermost wishes. "Professor Marvel doesn't guess. He *knows*."

Perhaps he recognizes something of himself in her. But he also knows the world is no place for a young girl, and, like a good gate-guardian, he contrives to send her home.

He will read his crystal ball, he announces. He dons a turban with a central jewel on it reminiscent of the circular mirror doctors used to wear over their eyes when they wanted to see inside you. He swipes from inside Dorothy's basket a photo and looks at it in secret. It shows her and her aunt side-by-side at their front gate, both wearing fancy ironed dresses. It is a formal, posed picture in which the two show a quite public face. It is a startling photo, and it takes a moment to realize why. In all the informal scenes until now, not once have we seen Mrs. Gale smiling.

The professor gazes into the cloudy ball. Again it's as if he were seeing into Dorothy's head. He does what his sign urged her to let him do. He reads her "Past, Present, and Future in His Crystal."

He sees an older woman in a polka dot dress, he says. She has a careworn face. She's crying, he says. "Someone has hurt her. Someone has just about broken her heart."

"Me?" Dorothy asks.

"Well, it's someone she loves very much. Someone she's been very kind to, taken care of in sickness."

"I had the measles once. She stayed right by me every minute."

"She's putting her hand on her heart. What's this?! She's dropping down on the bed. Oh, the crystal's gone down."

Dorothy leaps up. She must get home! Her independence, it seems, will kill the woman who sacrificed herself for Dorothy, who allowed her own face to be worn away—who effaced herself—so Dorothy could have her girlhood and perhaps her beauty, the woman who literally *runs* about the farm from chore to chore. Why, she *chose* to be Dorothy's mother when she didn't have to (she's Aunt Em—Aunt Mother. The use of mother-surrogates in fairy tales, of course, allows the more frightening emotions to surface). Dorothy's going out into the world is such an abandonment of the mother it may kill her.

How weak Aunt Em suddenly seems! It's as if, in leaving, Dorothy stole *her* Toto, her soul. The daughter belongs to the mother at least as much as she belongs to her own self. If she will have the world for herself, she must steal herself from her mother: it feels like seizing the cornerstone of a house—the other person topples.

Maybe the mother really believes she will die without the daughter, and she might, heartbroken: the daughter is the well in which the mother glimpses her own face. The daughter may be the part of herself that her mother loves best. Dorothy has kidnapped herself. The leaping dog and the scarlet shoes are symbols for Dorothy's own soul. Yet when the daughter leaves the mother, she too loses part of herself. She feels alone in an alien place: Dorothy when Em vanishes from the witch's crystal ball.

When Rapunzel flees her mother's tower she becomes an exile. Her lover is her means of escape (she is also literally his way out; she braids her body into a ladder for him, and knots her sheets for her own freedom, using bed as an escape). For seven years she and her lover live in a Sahara. Devoid of mother, the world is punitive, desolate, as Hades must be for Persephone, who also chose between sex and daughterhood (casting the daughter's rapture as abduction spares the mother from having to be angry at her own offspring). Ice is the punishment for sex: for each pomegranate seed the daughter savored, the mother inflicts a frozen month.

Luke Skywalker, in comparison, is evicted. His family home is destroyed *so that* he'll be forced to assume his manhood duties. He must relinquish home to save the world, like Hamlet or Superman, all of whom experience the destruction of their childhood homes. They are thrust out to make the world right. Men leave home to restore it. If they don't leave, sickness and decay result. Oedipus' ignorant enjoyment of his parents' bed, Hamlet's prolonged aggressive fascination with his mother's sexuality, the Egyptian prince Moses' delayed departure—all plague the land. Even *Sunset Boulevard*, which depicts the story of a young man who lives in what is symbolically the narcissistic mother's mansion, selling his soul for a gold cigarette case, is about social and inner corruption. Men must leave home or they themselves will destroy it.

The professor reads the fears Dorothy cannot admit to herself, and he knows just when to stop—at the brink of the unthinkable. The crystal's gone down; the mind obscures itself. Guilt drives Dorothy back home.

"I thought you were coming with me!" the wandering man says, in mock surprise.

"I have to get to her right away," Dorothy cries as she flees.

And now a curious thing happens. A tornado gusts up, just when Dorothy is coming back. Nobody seems to have predicted this. Again the farm is in jeopardy. It's not from Miss Gulch this time or because Dorothy is running away, but because Dorothy is returning.

The storm expresses Dorothy's own tempestuousness, the cyclone within her that she cannot allow herself to admit. She must be furious at having to give up the world for Aunt Em! Yet how guilty she would feel if she allowed herself to know this! Now it's Dorothy's own projected fury that threatens to wipe out the farm. Doesn't she wish it were wiped out? Then she would be released. Em's spell would be broken. But no— she mustn't, can't, shall not think that.

Quite a squall is brewing. A twister is coming in which everything—all objects, all meanings—will get twisted. It whirls across the horizon, a dark ascending coil like the probing mouth of a vacuum cleaner. The horizon itself is inhaled. Aunt Em, Uncle Henry, and the farmhands vanish into the storm cellar. Dorothy finds a deserted house. She stamps on the door of the cellar; they do not open up. It is as if she has projected her own abandoning behavior on them or as if they are punishing her for her anger by withholding their presence. They have walked down into the underworld, marched into a grave in the earth. In fact, this may be exactly what Dorothy unconsciously wishes: if they abandoned her, she would not have to feel guilty about abandoning them.

On the surface, though, her sudden solitude is terrifying. Trees are ripped up. The front screen door blows off in Dorothy's hand. "Aunt Em!" she cries. In a twist, her own life is now in peril. The house looks just like what Elvira Gulch revealed it to be: balsa and paint, weightless and frail, like the court in which Queens and Kings judged Alice in Wonderland only to watch Alice surge bigger and bigger until she declares, "Why, you're just a pack of cards!" while they whirl away.

But Dorothy's return home might literally cost her her life: the house attacks her. The frame of her window (her own crystal) knocks her on the head as it goes down. She swoons onto her bed, and a peaceful expression comes over her. Her face divides. Her face looks superimposed on itself. The twin faces permeate each other, rock through each other, brows, noses, smiles nodding up and down as if agreeing to something marvelous.

In Dorothy's delicious dream her house flies into the air. It spins high, looking like a doll's house, a toy house, but when it comes down to earth its landing is real enough: it kills someone. Dorothy's first act is to crush a faceless woman. "She's gone where the gardens grow. Below, below, below," just like Aunt Em. Of course, it's an accident. But, as the Wicked Witch of the West cries, understanding precisely the nature of "accidents": "I can cause accidents too, you know." (This, ironically, is just what does her in: she incites an accident that dissolves her. Dorothy is capable of violence only under the guise of an accident.) The murder implement of this first act? Why, it's death by house, as if domesticity itself could bear down like the medieval torture of pressing, or as if the incarnated burden of housework could be hurled like a thunderbolt. Riding her house like a broomstick, Dorothy had lethal power.

Yet, ring the bell! This is cause for celebration. The wicked old witch at last is dead! Who is the wicked witch? Well, we can't quite see yet; nothing is visible but her feet on which gleam the scarlet power shoes.

Shoes figure in other tales about young women: in Cinderella they unlock the secret of the heroine's identity and liberate her from servitude; at the end of Snow White the evil queen is forced to dance in fiery-hot metal shoes, a punishment for her burning passions. Cuplike as a brassiere, snug as a vagina, shoes are both confining and emblematic of freedom. They are a potent fetish. How significant that the totalitarian Mrs. Marcos should have assembled an empire of shoes, a vast treasure trove of them, and that Marla Maples, Donald Trump's faux-royal bride, would return to the tabloids over the theft of shoes.

When the ruby slippers are removed, the dead woman's feet curl like party favors. What look like eensy bound feet beneath peppermint-striped stockinged legs retract under the house—she is gone; the house subsumed her. Hidden within those shoes was a stunted root of a woman. But her sister remains, summoned, it seems, by the other's death, or summoned—could it be?—by Dorothy's joy!

Like the dour Em who descends on Dorothy and the farmhands the moment they are all laughing, an incarnation of guilt, the Wicked Witch always appears at the height of Dorothy's festivities. And what are the festivities? In this case it's that Dorothy is being celebrated as the national heroine of a land peopled by adults the size of children, adults who sing songs (in Kansas, Dorothy was the only one who sang), adults who hang on Dorothy's every word and then repeat them to one another as she recounts the story of the ride that made her a sort of Abraham Lincoln to this race of people who will henceforth regard the day she fell (How liberating it is to fall!) as "A day of independence for all the munchkins and their descendants."

In this dream all her wishes have been fulfilled. Here they understand her. Here they appreciate her (And how!). Here are her other lands, her big cities. In the background rise giant mountains. And in the foreground—oh, the colors! The fabulous pinks, the paintbox oranges, the plant-leaves gleaming like lollipops, and a river the Dippity-Do blue of a millionaire's pool. Here is a place drenched in rainbow colors, where a woman in a billowing white gown like an ambulatory cloud and with a voice like a trilling flute floats down in a bubble with words of welcome.

Glinda, the only witch with a name, is the very opposite of the skinny wicked witch. She is a vision of celestial femininity, clean and blonde as can be, and swathed all in gossamer layers of veil as if she were incorporeal, almost rarefied out of existence. She contains a voice that could make your teeth ache it's so thin and high and cloying, a soprano on helium, a woman whose throat is so constricted she seems to be strangling, exquisitely. When I was a child, Glinda seemed more of a fraud to me than any of the other characters. She frightened me. Could I ever be like her? Impossible as being Tinker Bell or Jo or Julie Andrews as a nun in *The Sound of Music*. These women were perfectly clean. "P.U.," I thought when Glinda spoke, my childhood response when threatened by ultra-femininity.

It is Glinda who sets Dorothy on her yearning, winding way to Oz even though she knows from the outset that Dorothy has the power to go home now, if she'll only click her heels. But wait. I'm wrong. For the shoes to work, Glinda claims, Dorothy must believe they will. She must acquire a certain transformative faith. In other words, there's no point in running home until she's learned her lesson.

From the outset, from the *outset*, she wants to go home. As a child this baffled me. What was the matter with that girl? Why was she so pathetically homesick? Couldn't she have any fun? Even now it seems sad. Oz is a place for *her*. It is sensually delicious; it is full of magic, play and song. Dorothy never names the witch as a reason she wants home. As Dorothy weeps outside the shut gates to the Wizard (and these are the words that make the locked doors swing wide, this is her liberating "Open Sesame!"): "Auntie Em was so good to me and I never appreciated it. . . . She may be dying, and it's all my fault. I'll never forgive myself—never, never, never, never."

How you goin' to keep 'em down on the farm? The answer is near at hand. Just look in the nursery. See under: Oz. The word "Oz," in fact, stands for the second half of the alphabet. Frank Baum was wondering what to call the magical land when he saw his filing cabinet, divided A-N and O-Z. Dorothy gives up half of everything in giving up Oz.

The quest is about reversal. Dorothy must reverse herself. Instead of satisfying her own need for appreciation, she needs to appreciate Em. Em didn't really fall on the bed, clutching her heart. Dorothy fell; her frame of mind attacked her. Health will return when Dorothy relinquishes her fury at Em. She must get angry at own selfish self. Aunt Em has run away: she vanished into the earth, flinging Dorothy into the sky. How to restore the balance? Through empathy with Em.

"I had an Aunt Em too, you know," says the weeping gate-guardian, swinging open the door to Oz.

Her heart's desire has become Em, not the big world. She can't have both. Perhaps this is the answer to why Dorothy wants home so fast. Oz is exile, without a mother's love. Guilt spoils beauty. Kansas blights Over-the-rainbow already. The solution is to choose A-N, the land of definite articles: an egg, an acre, an aunt, the land of factuality, not Ozymandias.

But not until Dorothy believes she deserves Em can she have her back. Em is the Toto now. She's what's locked away. To earn her, Dorothy must turn every ounce of anger to guilt. She must convert desire for the world to desire for home.

"The pure products of America go crazy," wrote William Carlos Williams.

"I'm afraid you've made rather an enemy out of the wicked witch," Glinda remarks, although it was Glinda herself who managed this. She put the glitter shoes on Dorothy's feet. Why does she ensure that Dorothy can't live peacefully with the witch of the west?

A person becomes taboo "for the simple reason that he is in a condition which has the property of inciting the forbidden desires of others and awakening the ambivalent conflict in them," says Freud. There is something compelling about the woman who flies on her own stick, who is mistress of her own castle, who keeps in her thrall men whom she uses for her own devices and beasts like boys that flock at her command. All this female power might *attract* Dorothy, so better make that woman verboten—better yet, her nemesis—from the start.

"You must prove yourselves worthy," Oz roars to Dorothy and her friends.

How?

"Bring me the broomstick of the Wicked Witch of the West"—again *making* the Witch an enemy.

"We'll have to kill her first!" cries the smart scarecrow.

Oz sets a test like the type set for a knight. The reward, traditionally, is the hand of the king's daughter. Here the romantic object is Em. Oz is lodged at the end of a long glistening red hallway, a passage of ribbed arches like a gallery of wishbones: scarlet, internal, echoey. Oz is aim and obstacle. Egglike, legless, with an ample cranium that presages Marvel's balloon, he hovers, a floating head, thronged with salvers of green smoke and flames like an incarnation of Kubla Khan's "ancestral voices prophesying war." Dorothy has ascended into the fomenting, highly defended throne of the Mind-king. He gives her reason to accomplish what she may have secretly wished to do all along (she rehearsed this death from the instant she arrived; in fact arriving was synonymous with killing). She will be worthy of home when she destroys the Wicked Witch.

The Witch of the West is a woman who wants. She provides all the obstacles to Dorothy's quest—the malicious trees, the soporific fields. In fact, the whole place sometimes seems to exist in her control: as Dorothy and her new friends sing and stroll blithely along the Witch watches them in her ball. They inhabit a small globe owned by her; the world is her paperweight. What do we actually know about her? She is thin and green, as if painted with the brush of mortality, the taint of envy. Something in her is already rotting. She is friendless, all who serve her enslaved by a spell broken only at her death.

"It's so kind of you to visit me in my loneliness," she croons when Dorothy arrives, kidnapped, into the rocky, remote fortress—and despite the sarcasm, there's a poignance to the words. Surrounded by robotic men, attempting to warm herself with a million flickering fires (she is a nightmare image of who Aunt Em might become if Dorothy left), wouldn't she actually like a daughter for herself? "My pretty," she calls

Dorothy, a term of droll cherishing. Wouldn't a daughter be a balm for those gaunt arms, that scraped raw voice? The woman's starved! With her face thin as a chisel, her raggedy black dress binding her bony waist, she looks broken apart, fragmented, all the parts of her jutting in the fractured angles of a stovepipe rather than flowing in ample round maternal shapes. She is a sort of vicious pauper lusting for the impossible.

This depiction of an autonomous woman is of course a nightmare vision of feminine power, a grotesque of female appetite—as if to say that to be a woman who wants is to be a woman who can only want, whose wants are by definition out of control, oceanic, threatening to swamp the world like nature gone awry, or liable to suck back spitefully into herself on a salty tide all that she has engendered, a birthing in reverse. The suppressed has surfaced, and, volcanic, might blot out the world. "What is it that woman wants?" How strongly Freud resisted knowing, although all day long women told him their secrets. The fear of what women would want if they could want runs through literature like an underground river.

But can one imagine the bejeweled slippers on the witch's frame, with her ascetic mourner's garb? Ludicrous! It would be like a crone in a tutu or a child in a negligee. No, the scarlet heels are not meant for the witch no matter how she stretches out her elongated green fingers, gesturing first toward her mouth then toward the shoes, then toward her mouth again as if thoughtfully beckoning. They are an emblem of youth and sexuality. They are all this female pariah lacks. The shoes are glamorous, they cast a delightful glamour over others, a web of enchantment.

If the witch had the shoes, Dorothy is warned, the witch's power would be absolute. Would men then fall in love with her? After all, Dorothy's power is her ability to inspire love. If the Wicked Witch could make others love her while she retained her own controlling will, wouldn't her power be complete?

Across the very sky, writ in giant charred letters, the witch spells "Surrender Dorothy." Not surrender the shoes but surrender yourself.

The drama of the daughter's journey is: who will control her. Will she capitulate to the Wicked Witch or will she make it home? Will she celebrate her own stubborn, lonely will, or will she become a selfless woman, freed from isolation? Locked in the witch's keep, she calls out to Aunt Em like Jonah crying from the whale where, as he put it, "the earth with her bars closed upon me."

"I'm frightened, Aunt Em! I'm frightened!" She sounds as if she is making atonement or admitting something at long last.

In response, Em emerges in the crystal, calling "Dorothy! It's me! It's Aunt Em. Where are you? We're trying to find you!"

"I'm here in Oz, Aunt Em," cries Dorothy. "I'm trying to get home to you. Oh, *don't* go away!" for already Em is clouding and darkening and twisting until she reveals herself to be—what a shock!—the gloating Wicked Witch.

"I'll give you Auntie Em, my pretty!" she sneers.

And doesn't she? In the crystal of the mind, the two are merged. The deathly witch is the other face of the nurturant Em; M is W from another angle.

How does it clarify matters to see Em as the witch of the West? When I thought about Em, I always remembered a kind, loving woman. Yet viewing the movie as an adult, I noticed how grim Em is, and how forcefully nasty she can be.

"What's all this jabberwocking about when there's work to be done?" Em demands, descending on Dorothy and the farmhands, implying that the sort of daydreaming Alice was partial to through the looking-glass will not be countenanced here. 'Twas brillig and the slithy toves, indeed! And when there's work to be done!

"I know three shiftless farmhands who'll be out of a job before they know it," she continues.

One of the men explains, "Well, Dorothy was walking along—"

"I saw you tinkering with that contraption, Hickory," she practically spits. "Now get back to that wagon."

Contraptions and tinkering! Why, it's almost as bad as jabberwocking.

"All right, Mrs. G," he replies. He lifts a finger in the air. "But one day they're going to erect a statue for me in this town—"

"Well, don't start posing for it now!" she cuts.

Even when she offers the farmhands a tray of phallic crullers she holds at waist-height it's because "you can't work on an empty stomach."

"You got my finger!" Hank exclaims when the flat-bed of a cart is lowered on his helping hand.

Rakes, fingers, and crullers; incubators and wagons—the farm is a suggestive place, and what it suggests to Em is work and more work.

In contrast, the principle of the Emerald City is idleness. "We get up at 12 and start to work by 1. Take an hour for lunch and then by two we're done. Jolly good fun!" sing the urbanites. Dorothy, who loves freedom, liberates as she goes. She unhooks the scarecrow from his nail, oils the tinman where he's rusted (Hickory wanted to have a statue. Well, fine. The witch has made him a statue), cajoles along the lion who was so tormented by fears.

The men of Oz are all missing one key organ (the lion wants "the nerve!"). One suspects that, in Dorothy's mind, the men on Aunt Em's farm all lack an organ, too. The farmhands are embodied in the galley-slaves whose long-proboscised faces mirror that of the Wicked Witch (these people almost have an *extra* organ). They are cruel to Dorothy only because they are under a spell. In Dorothy's dream, the farmhands appear in both their defiant and their servile incarnations.

From being a doting Mom, Mrs. Gale comes across as an iron-gray matron who knows quite well, thank you, how to lay down the law. She is a sort of strict schoolmistress who won't stand for a moment of spring fever, not when there's multiplication tables to recite. Which is why it comes as a shock when she appears so terribly fragile as soon as Dorothy attempts to leave.

From the start of the movie, Aunt Em is angry. She is *furious*. Is she envious of Dorothy's ability to daydream and sing while she herself is shackled to the farm? Is she jealous of the girl's latent fecundity (why doesn't Em have children)? Is she afraid of becoming old and lonely? Perhaps she is angry that she has so much to protect Dorothy from.

Dorothy's unbridled growth ruptures the old unity with Em. "Who killed my sister?" Em demands in her witch incarnation. The dead sister is the childhood Dorothy, the female who disappeared and who the new Dorothy has the most vital part of. In Dorothy's nightmare vision, Em stretches long fingers toward her. She is an ugly starveling who wants to make Dorothy like her. She can pursue Dorothy anywhere. Why, she even appeared when Dorothy ran clear across the county and into the carnie man's tent.

Em imprisons Dorothy. The terrifying hourglass the witch overturns resembles a voluptuous scarlet woman draining red dust. If only Em could remove Dorothy's womanliness, the old joy would be restored! If only Dorothy could give Em back some years and return her femininity, she wouldn't need to feel so guilty! (The ashen menopausal farm can't sustain its eggs. "This old incubator's gone bad," Uncle Henry reports. Em's badness is threatening). "Give them back to me!" cries the Wicked Witch when she sees the ruby shoes on Dorothy's feet. They were hers once, apparently. "Give them *back*!" she insists.

But they are time, sexiness, red-mouthed beauty (Dorothy's lush lips are the first thing one notices in color). "Keep tight inside them," Glinda cautions. "Never let them off your feet."

And yet of course one's body does loosen and slip. Time is the movie's villain, in fact. The film begins mythically, with a scroll of words which name Time as the enemy: "For nearly 40 years this story has given faithful service to the Young in Heart; and Time has been powerless to put its kindly philosophy out of fashion."

By faithfully serving her mother, a girl can resist the pull of time, a force so like mitosis, when a cell's twin nuclei fling in polar directions. In seeing her mother, in fact, a girl sees herself plus time. Can't the daughter restore to the mother what she herself has apparently devoured? Mother and daughter drain into each other like two halves of an "ourglass," two crystals merged, two minds fused. How can they separate?

"Why didn't you tell Dorothy earlier that she just needed to tap her heels?" the scarecrow demands at the end.

"She wouldn't have believed me," says Glinda, neatly. "She had to learn something for herself first."

What has she learned?

"It's that . . . it wasn't enough just to want to see Uncle Henry and Aunt Em. It's that—if I ever go looking for my heart's desire again, I won't go any further than my own backyard. Because if it isn't there, I never lost it in the first place."

To return to her family, Dorothy must redefine her heart's desire. She must stay home and not feel anything has been lost. The daughter must not come home resentfully. That might destroy home, much as the caged woman in Rochester's attic and the chained woman in Roderick Usher's basement finally burn down their mansions. She must choose home happily.

The story is a mother-romance. The girl had thought it was her own self that was missing. But the cost of finding that self was mother.

"Think to yourself, 'There's no place like home,'" Glinda instructs.

Dorothy shakes her head from side to side as if to say no to Oz, no to Oz, and murmurs the words hypnotically, casting a spell over herself: "There's no place like home." Her whole family appears.

No place like home. For men, the situation is different. Home and world aren't either/or. Odysseus leaves to fight and find adventure knowing home waits. Men go and are loved. They are in fact loved more for going: that's brave. Penelope weaves and unweaves. Her calendar is filled and unfilled. But her marriage bed is rooted in the earth. It won't blow away.

Odysseus is valued for his rich experience. Experience in a girl means just one thing, and it's no good. Leave home and you lose it, girls learn. Leave home, and home leaves you. The photo in your basket will transform: the woman who had smiled will die. The world is an alien, forsaken place; go into it and you will be alien and forsaken. Leave home, and you murder it. Only if you stay, can it, and you, be safe.

"We thought for a moment she was going to leave us," Uncle Henry says.

"But I did leave—"

"Lie quiet now," Em interrupts. "You just had a bad dream."

"But it wasn't a dream. It was a place. . . ."

"Sometimes we dream lots of silly things when—"

"No Aunt Em, it really existed . . . Doesn't anyone believe me?"

"Of course we believe you, Dorothy."

Em does seem to believe for a moment, although it's not clear exactly what. That the experience was real for Dorothy? Em interrupts talk of departures; that's "a bad dream." Perhaps she's willing to concede an internal departure happened, and the fever is quenched at last. Or perhaps really, mysteriously, Em actually *does* believe in Oz. For one enchanted moment this seems true.

Dorothy, thrilled to be back and believed, smiles at Em's smiling face. Maybe Em wanted to trust all along in Dorothy's "jabberwocking," maybe she secretly values what she feels impelled to mock. Maybe dreaming will heal her too.

But Dorothy's not dreaming any more, she vows. "I'm not going away ever, ever again. Oh, Auntie Em," she cries in her final declaration of love to the woman she quested for so well and long: "There's no place like home."

ADRIENNE DONALD

WORKING FOR ONESELF:
LABOR AND LOVE IN
THE SILENCE OF THE LAMBS

The Silence of the Lambs' sweep at the Academy Awards—best picture, best director, best leading actress and leading actor—was remarkable not only because rarely does one film win all of the major categories but also because it was the first "horror" film to win best picture. And while it is bemusing that some of the other films nominated—such as *Bugsy, JFK,* and *Beauty and the Beast*—don't also count as horror movies, *The Silence of the Lambs* was clearly a controversial choice. It seemed unlikely that the Academy of Motion Pictures Arts and Sciences, an institution more often dedicated to the art of compromise than of the cinema, would embrace a film featuring serial murder, homicidal transvestism, and cannibalistic psychoanalysts—or would court the outrage of gay activists who have attacked the film's homophobia and misogyny. The picketing at the Oscars wasn't the first demonstration against the film. Before its official premiere, Richard Jennings of the Los Angeles chapter of Gay and Lesbian Alliance Against Defamation called the film "an atrocity against women and one more instance of an industry that can't seem to create a positive gay character." Michelangelo Signorile of the now-defunct New York queer magazine, *Outweek,* vilified one of the film's stars, Jodie Foster, for being involved in such a homophobic project.[1] Indeed, it's possible to see the Academy's decision to honor *The Silence of the Lambs* as the industry's professional refusal to bend to outside political pressure.

While the criticism of the film has been justly sobering, the emphasis on gender and sexuality nonetheless limits an account of other forms of violence in it. What is truly frightening is that viewers may take for granted or overlook the silent humiliations endured by women workers and the brutalizing stigmas of class. *The Silence of the Lambs*'s homophobia and misogyny are inextricable from economic violence. Economic violence shapes everyone in the film, the police as well as their prisoners, the gainfully employed as well as the wantonly destructive, the powerful as well as the powerless. Every character — not just the victimized women and the murderous gay transsexual — struggles with what might figuratively or literally cannibalize us all: work.

In the film, as in life, work powerfully informs human identity. Theorists from Locke to Marx have valued work as the potential means by which people may shape the material world around them to reflect and embody a sense of self. In the film, as in life, however, different kinds of work narrowly determine different kinds of identity — or rather, different kinds of alienation. There are two kinds of workers in *The Silence of the Lambs*: wage laborers — the police, the transsexual serial killer called Buffalo Bill, and most of the women whom he murders — and professionals — the FBI, psychologists, and psychotherapists. The wage laborers in the film do not gain a sense of self from what they do for a living or what they're paid. On the other hand, since their work expresses nothing about them as unique individuals, what they do in their free time doesn't contribute to the ways in which their work subordinates them in the administered world. In contrast, the professionals in the film are paid for the intelligence, training, and personality which is indistinguishable from their sense of identity.[2] Nonetheless, their work is no more self-expressive than wage laborers'. By locating their skills within their personalities, professionals undermine the distinction between what they do and who they are. They have more control than wage laborers over how they work but in exchange they internalize administered labor as a sense of self. They don't produce commodities — they are commodities.

The Silence of the Lambs opens with a scene depicting the process which creates the internally disciplined professional. We see a young woman by herself, working her way through an obstacle course. When an FBI instructor briefly steps into the frame, we realize that she is not alone because she is watched; her solitude is that of the student displaying her resourcefulness and self-control for an audience which invisibly observes and judges her. For her, the purpose of the exercise is to show that she has internalized the discipline of her audience of teachers. As we watch the FBI instructor's thoughtful gaze after the dutiful young woman, we, too, are metaphorically part of her administered world, if we observe, even take deep interest in her without intervening in or aiding her progress.

Her name is Clarice Starling and her prime teacher and exemplary disciplinarian at the FBI Academy is Dr. Jack Crawford, a psychologist who is hunting down Buffalo Bill, the serial murderer who flays his female victims. She finds Crawford in a small, cinderblock room, the walls of which are covered with newspaper clippings and photographs of unsolved crimes, as well as a few professional plaques and citations. His office is not much different from another room which we see later in the film, the cell occupied by Dr. Hannibal "The Cannibal" Lecter, psychoanalyst and serial murderer; the resemblance indicates not only the impersonality of Crawford's professionalism, but also that the places of institutional power and correction oddly resemble each other. Crawford's colorless austerity is perfect for training Starling in the professional rigors of transference and counter-transference. He assigns her an apparently simple exercise: since he's busy with Buffalo Bill, Starling is to give Lecter a questionnaire with which the FBI is creating a profile of serial killers. Above all, Crawford warns her, she should not tell Lecter anything about herself: "Believe me, you don't want Hannibal Lecter inside your head."

Only later does she learn from Lecter that Crawford is really using her to get information on Buffalo Bill. When she confronts Crawford on his reasons for sending her to Lecter, he argues that, had she known about her visit's purpose, Lecter would have wheedled it out of her without giving her any information in exchange. She shouldn't feel personally betrayed since, Crawford assures her, he had only professional reasons for manipulating her ignorance. Such disinterestedness distinguishes his behavior from Lecter's — and from her sense of personal betrayal. Crawford's managerial foresight blandly masks and contains his sadism; since he takes no personal pleasure in it, he can justify manipulating Starling professionally.

If impersonality is Crawford's mode of aggression, it is supposed to be Starling's defense against Lecter's perversely brilliant insights. For her psychic security and professional authority, Starling needs to analyze Lecter before he analyzes her. Her model for interpretive strategies is Crawford in his use of her against Lecter; and, obviously and eventually, *vice versa*. Crawford and Lecter thus become frightening mirror images of each other in the account of Starling's professional education. Lecter bizarrely extends and parodies transference and counter-transference; his cruel, reductive, yet canny "reading" of Starling's personality and past is part of an interpretive will to power, of which his cannibalism is the most radical and literal form of internalization. Crawford, conversely, wants Starling to emulate him and his Freudian strategies of effacing the interpretive self, withdrawing from the patient's constructions and projections; Crawford's model of professionalism is a form of self-cannibalism. His impersonality makes him an easy character for Starling to internalize and yet distance herself from. He is a cool mentor, who comes to congratulate Starling at her graduation from the Academy but who hesitates to shake hands, as if the gesture might be a little too intimate for him. At that moment she's more perfectly professional than he is; she is so bumptiously sure of her newly-authorized self that she doesn't even recognize the possibility for an unseemingly private gesture.

The scene concludes the film's account of Starling's professionalization. Her transformation begins in earnest when, on Crawford's assignment, she meets Frederick Chiltern, the psychiatrist who runs the hospital where Lecter is imprisoned. Like other shrinks in the film, Chiltern is a little unstable himself — he gleefully flirts with her by showing off his "specimens" of insanity. (Later, we learn that he systematically abuses Lecter.) While Starling artfully frustrates his advances,[3] Chiltern gets his revenge as he leads her toward Lecter's cell. While warning her about the security protocol for Lecter — which includes staying away from the glass, passing him only soft objects, and so on — he pulls a picture out of his wallet as evidence of what Lecter did to a nurse administering an EKG to him years before. Chiltern tells her that doctors reset her jaw and saved one of her eyes; when Lecter swallowed her tongue, his heartbeat never got above eighty beats per minute. The horror isn't simply what we and Starling infer that Lecter did — it is that Lecter didn't physiologically register the horror of his act; his violation of the nurse's body simply didn't arouse him at all.

But it does move Starling, and it does move us, as we avidly take in her struggle for composure. With the camera angled up toward Starling's face, we never see the photo. Instead, we watch her, bathed in red light, looking down at the picture — and obliquely at us — while Chiltern vengefully describes the results of Lecter's attack. Jodie Foster's performance is finely controlled at this moment: we see her eyebrows knit slightly with intensity as she looks at the photo but we don't see simple disgust, horror, or morbid fascination. We watch her contain and conceal strong feeling; we see the depth and strength of her character. As we hear what Lecter did to the nurse's face and our own pulses beat with calm self-control or speed up — with surprise, horror, pleasure — we see Starling's guarded reaction which we consume and internalize. And, most powerfully, we see her obliquely watch our fascination with her reaction to horrifying violence. The audience's aesthetic appetite for violent sensationalism becomes complicit with Chiltern's assault on her.

When the film locates the audience's reactions alongside those of its characters, its central dilemma emerges: is the ability to experience horror without getting excited a sign of calm professionalism or madness? When Chiltern leaves her to face Lecter on her own, Starling has just discovered that her quest for knowledge is going to be much harder than she expected. What she had thought would protect her — that is, the impersonality of her aspiring professionalism — reveals its own dangers in the world which she has entered. The blurring of the distinction between psychosis and the impersonality of professional self-commodification takes on further importance for the moviegoer who watches Starling's struggles with and for impassivity. That is, what kind of aesthetic pleasure can be gained from the representation of pain? On the one hand, the audience needs to distinguish its aesthetic and moral or political reactions to the film; for example, there is a difference between the character Jodie Foster plays and how she performs the role. Yet on the other hand, the audience's aesthetic competence which enables such distinctions results from a commodification of personal responses analogous to that in professionalism. Aesthetic competence shares professionalism's containment and splitting off of intimate, helpless, useless feeling. Slipping the restraints of empathy that makes us mutely feel pain for others' pain, aesthetic competence and professionalism frees the sadistic pleasure of witnessing and causing what we can't feel in others, and fear in ourselves: vulnerability. Starling's poised tact reverses the pedagogic relation between her and the audience; walking down the subterranean corridor to Lecter's cell, assaulted by the shrieks and whispers of the criminally insane, balancing professional competence against psychotic disinterestedness, she shows the audience how to weigh its fear for, and pleasure in, her vulnerability.

Washed in the analytic glare of white light, fastidious even in his prison uniform, alert, formal, and arch, Lecter fuses extraordinary

Top: Hannibal Lecter at his work table, with his drawings of aesthetic objects. Bottom: Clarice Starling receives her certification of identity from the F.B.I.

intellectual self-control and irruptive emotional abandon. Almost immediately, he parodically treats Starling as a training analyst, evaluating her interviewing technique to show off his own expertise. And going further, he nastily reads her cool professionalism as a vain flight from her white trash origins. What distinguishes Starling from other figures in the film — such as Chiltern and even the mother of one of Buffalo Bill's victims, whom Lecter taunts — is that she doesn't angrily deny and thus confirm his insight; like a good analyst, she calmly turns it back against him: "You see a lot, Dr. Lecter," she says, "but are you strong enough to point that high-powered perception at yourself?" That he has hurt her is confirmed by her tears as she leaves the hospital, and by her flashback to the poor, rural childhood which Lecter accurately guessed at; but when she is with him, she coolly exploits her own feelings to get him to talk to her.

What develops between Starling and Lecter is a bizarre form of analytic exchange. Rather than giving memory for insight about herself, insight for money, Starling trades her childhood memories for Lecter's riddling clues about Buffalo Bill. The challenge for Starling, then, is that she must produce for Lecter her private memories of a past from which, he has already pointed out, she wants to escape by becoming a professional; in order to gain the professional and class advancement which Lecter says she loves most, she must reveal the personal identity which she wishes to repress.

Unfortunately, the portrait of Starling which emerges from her sessions with Dr. Lecter and from her two flashbacks is a little disappointing because Lecter's first hunch about her is absolutely right. It is in part a sign of our interpretive voracity that Starling's lack of narrative resistance is comparatively uninteresting; a larger problem with Lecter's reading of her is that it is both couched in and about psychological clichés. As a child growing up in rural West Virginia, she was orphaned when her father, a town marshal, was shot to death in a burglary. She was sent to a nameless, "decent" uncle and aunt who supported their family by raising livestock for slaughter; her identification with innocent, helpless, bleating lambs is the narrative key to her professional vocation, the emblem of her own moral worth, and the explanation for the film's enigmatic title. As a story, it is too formulaic in its grief, in its resolution of guilt and rage. Her professionalism is too clearly a mode of self-protection which distances her from memories of loss and impoverishment and a means of idealizing her grief by projecting it onto the innocent victims with and for whom she works.

Such obsessions have an ostensible moral dignity which attempts to redeem Starling's submersion of her identity in work. Yet by the end of the film, she has become a cliché, not a character. In the climactic scene, she stalks Buffalo Bill around his own darkened basement maze of torture. Our viewpoint at that moment is identical with Buffalo Bill's, who's wearing infra-red goggles, so we see her terrified expression, her blind clumsiness, her gun shaking violently in her hand. The scene is startling since Foster's performance, like almost all of the film, is otherwise tastefully understated. Indeed, it is bizarrely comic, not only because Foster overacts with a prop but because she is being stalked so closely by the person whom she's stalking. From the beginning of the film, we've seen her rehearse for this moment. But rather than being heroically revealed, her personal courage and strength collapse into merely professional behavior. As a character, Starling never recovers from this moment of conflation. Hereafter, she's the successful student at her graduation who has earned not freedom from her past but professional advancement. She acts like a cartoon because she has been reduced to one.

While the scene's crudeness seems at odds with *The Silence of the Lamb*'s refusal of slasher and suspense clichés it suggests deeper consistencies. The film's tasteful symmetries are too pat, too fungible to offer the exhilarating and frightening revelation of the private, the individual, the vulnerable. For the audience, the commodification of Starling's personality as a professional identity is manifested through the sentimental clichés of her narrative. It's hard to imagine that Hannibal Lecter would be at all interested in her nightmares about screaming lambs. Yet his alertness to her class narrative indicates the political and aesthetic flaw in the film's sense of its own good taste: it assumes that Starling's desire to escape her class and regional identity is completely creditable and empathetic. According to the ethos of *The Silence of the Lambs*, there's not much difference between being a psychotic serial murderer (or his victim) and being poor white trash. The narratives of sexual deviance and gender oppression which the film explores with such morbid relish and tactful sensitivity, respectively, are thus disturbingly underpinned by a common economic narrative of class resentment and aspiration. For example, closeups of Jodie Foster, especially during her flashbacks to her childhood, visually sustain the account of her upward escape from her shameful class origins. These shots, unusual both for their angularity and Foster's lack of adornment, suggest a geometry of bone structure, muscle, and gaze that charges her luminous face with the intelligence to contemplate the gawky, sorrowful, underprivileged child she once was in order to transcend that past.

Starling is not the only character in *The Silence of the Lambs* who wants to escape a past identity; the other is Buffalo Bill, or Jame Gumb who presents a still more parodic and grotesque version of class identity than does Starling. But while Starling's sexuality and class are equally ambiguous and universal, Gumb's class is explicitly and viciously mediated through his sexuality. According to Lecter, Gumb thinks he's a transsexual but he's not really—he's simply unhappy being what he is. So just as Starling uses work to escape her past, he uses his; but while she cultivates a pure, classless professional identity, he is a tailor who must literally stitch together a suit of clothes for a new identity as a woman. The film cynically manipulates the audience's voyeuristic fascination and disgust by sexualizing Buffalo Bill's pathology and by identifying the hatred and envy of women with gay men. Yet such homophobia becomes apparent within the film's overarching treatment of class. Buffalo Bill is dirty, inarticulate, artisanal (as opposed to artistic), vulgar, faggy, misogynistic, violent, perverted, tattooed, and mutilated; he listens to heavy metal, he drives a van, he lives in the suburbs, he owns a toy poodle named Precious, he is a Vietnam veteran. In short, he is an unformed, shadowy, vaguely working-class, gay composite non-character, a study in suburban Gothic, an appalling stereotype of class and erotic loathsomeness.

One may hope in vain that audiences would perceive Jame Gumb/Buffalo Bill to be the homophobic caricature that he is. While his erotic and class identity is anathematized, however, Hannibal Lecter's intelligence, class, sophistication, and power make him an evil ideal. For example, when Starling first visits him, another prisoner hisses that he can smell her cunt. After forcing her to repeat the comment, Lecter says that while he cannot smell *that*, he can describe her shampoo, perfume, and cosmetics in virtuosic detail; he smells her culture, not her biology—and in drawing that distinction, he reveals his mastery of the former and disdain for the latter. In every sense, Dr. Lecter is a perfect gentleman.

Lecter's austerely rational, even neoclassical aestheticism is the essence of his violent insanity. He doesn't rape people; he eats their livers with fava beans and Chianti or swallows their tongues with perfect calm. To cultivate such Promethean tastes is beyond the dreams of *Bon Appetit* (a copy of which is unconvincingly placed in Lecter's cell for a rather flat joke). He is an amateur artist who compensates for the aesthetic boredom of incarceration by drawing the Palazzo Vecchio, the Duomo of Florence, parodies of Renaissance masterpieces.[4] He sneers at Starling's badges of class — her good bag and her cheap shoes — with epigrammatic panache. He murders two men while listening to a tape of the *Goldberg Variations.*

Lecter's brutal dandyism has distinct erotic undertones. His cannibalism is a literalizing return to the atavistic origins of sexual desire: the craving for the flesh that gives the feeling of satiety. His ability to comprehend and manipulate other people's eroticism is astonishingly polymorphous; for example, he verbally compels the prisoner who hisses at Starling to swallow his own tongue. In the film, Lecter's reading includes J. D. McClatchy; in the book, the Italian edition of *Vogue.* The evidence may be as strong as a scent and just as disembodied: Hannibal Lecter is a gay dandy.

The dandy's deliberate cultivation of a sense of self invested not in fictions of commodified power but in style, gesture, irony, and parody both marginalizes him within a world governed by exchange relations and privileges him as a unique and therefore — within the terms of that world — authentic personality. With the medicalization of sexuality, the dandy and the deviant homosexual were by the end of the nineteenth century all but identified with each other as frightening, antithetical versions of the stable, autonomous bourgeois subject, who enters exchange relations as a professional. The gay dandy subverts his own commodification and classification with his dangerous uselessness, his exquisite sense perception, his social and erotic production of nothing more than style. In the opening section of *Minima Moralia* (appropriately entitled, "For Marcel Proust," a consummate gay dandy), Theodor Adorno describes the double-edged threat of the unprofessional personality:

> The occupation with things of the mind has by now itself become 'practical', a business with strict division of labour, departments and restricted entry. The man of independent means who chooses it out of repugnance for the ignominy of earning money will not be disposed to acknowledge the fact. For this he is punished. He is not a 'professional', is ranked in the competitive hierarchy as a dilettante no matter how well he knows his subject, and must, if

he wants to make a career, show himself even more resolutely blinkered than the most inveterate specialist. The urge to suspend the division of labour which, within certain limits, his economic situation enables him to satisfy, is thought particularly disreputable: it betrays a disinclination to sanction the operations imposed by society, and domineering competence permits no such idiosyncrasies. The departmentalization of mind is a means of abolishing mind where it is not exercised *ex officio*, under contract. It performs this task all the more reliably since anyone who repudiates the division of labour — if only by taking pleasure in his work — makes himself vulnerable by its standards in ways inseparable from elements of his superiority.[5]

Is Lecter, a figure of aristocratic privilege, aesthetic hauteur, and raving self-indulgence, more compelling aesthetically and morally for his pure defiance of every authority figure (Dr. Chiltern, Jack Crawford, the police) or more abhorrent for the exquisitely disinterested manner in which he clubs a man to death? While Lecter may be a more interesting, complex, and sympathetic character than Buffalo Bill, does he play upon anything other than the same class and erotic ideologies in the audience?

Privileging the homosexual dandy as a figure who defiantly resists the administered world problematically assumes that a marginalized sexuality is in some sense authentically oppositional. In Volume One of *The History of Sexuality*, Michel Foucault conversely argues that marginalized sexualities are created by power which anathematizes them.[6] Thus a Foucaultian reading of *The Silence of the Lambs* would emphasize all of the ways in which Lecter recuperates the power and privilege which are too explicitly exercised and recognizable in characters such as Crawford and Chiltern; it would portray his relations to Starling and Gumb as means of exploring those characters' ambivalently differentiated relation to power. However, such a reading subsumes the aesthetic thrill of Lecter's resistance within a political analysis of its potential homophobia and classism. If the audience is utterly repelled by Buffalo Bill, it is both fascinated with and horrified by Lecter, who thus embodies however ambivalently the hope and desire for the reconfiguration of class and sexuality.

It is through his own aestheticized attentions that Lecter holds open to Starling the possibility of transformation and resistance. While Chiltern and more minor characters are interested in her sexually, and Crawford is interested in her professionally, Lecter's feelings for her are fundamentally disinterested, a point which he sardonically makes when, as she visits him one last time, he says, "People will say we're in love." While she begs him for Buffalo Bill's true identity, he makes her retell the story of her own, by reconstructing with her an account of her victimization. In effect, he devotes their last minutes together to redeeming her slightly boring, slightly unconvincing account of her professionalism by translating it into an explanation of why she feels compelled to rescue Buffalo Bill's latest victim. As before, the narrative is a cliché: soon after arriving at her uncle's and aunt's ranch, she tried to save a screaming spring lamb from slaughter. At Lecter's insistence, she recognizes in her desire to be an FBI agent her empathy with innocent suffering, which will always exist and will always haunt her. Lecter shows her that she wants to be like Jack Crawford and have his power because she cannot help but identify with Buffalo Bill's powerless victims.

Starling wants clues about a killer; she also gets from Lecter an empathetic attention which sees personal dignity in her ambition. Lecter's counter-transference — which is, of course, highly unprofessional — results in his disinterested love for Starling. When he finishes the story of the lambs for her, describing the nightmares that awaken her still, her eyes fill with tears even while she demands Buffalo Bill's real name. Lecter thanks her, and when he looks up and then down to say hello to the approaching Dr. Chiltern, his own eyes have tears in them. Before she is escorted from the room, he calls her back, saying she's forgotten her case file and in passing it through the bars to her, while the police with Chiltern drag her away (one of her few moments of defiance), his index finger momentarily caresses hers.

After that scene, while Starling dwindles into a white-collar stereotype, Lecter is crucially transformed by his disinterested love for her. He thanks her, with a quiet nod of his head, for the closure of memory. His tears well up both in empathy with hers and in anticipation of losing her, when Chiltern arrives. Like the gesture of a secret lover whose touch momentarily overcomes obstacles and surveillance, his tiny caress of farewell reveals the pleasure of mutual recognition, rather than of possession and domination. At the moment when he must let her go, Lecter abandons, if for just a moment, his psychological and literal cannibalization of others by loving the one person in the film who cannot sustain (however much she tries) an identification with the power of the administered world. While Starling may identify with Buffalo Bill's victims, Lecter recognizes rather than identifies with her. To paraphrase Jessica Benjamin's description of mutual recognition, he accepts Starling's otherness but nonetheless feels for and with her; he is compensated for his loss of absolute power by the pleasure of communion with her.[7] And the recognition is mutual. After Lecter escapes, Starling is unconcerned for her safety because, as she tells her roommate, Lecter would not be so rude to attack her. He himself tells her in their last conversation, "The world's more interesting with you in it." All he wants is for her to be.

The concept of recognition, rather than of identification, enables a reading not only of Lecter's love for Starling and of the film's movement away from its homophobic representation of Buffalo Bill but also of the film's sexual politics in general. The dangerous, rather than liberating, power relations in *The Silence of the Lambs* — Starling's relation to Crawford, Buffalo Bill's relation to women — are founded on false identifications whereas Starling and Lecter's moment of mutual recognition eroticizes and subverts the barriers of prison cells, professionalism, even sexual orientation which divide — and perhaps align — them. For just as the disinterestedness of his love is grounded in his sexual indifference to her as a woman, so Starling's disinterestedness is grounded in her indifference to or toleration of the horrors of his psychosis. Starling and Lecter's recognition reveals and affirms their difference from each other, as well as from other people. By empathetically recounting Starling's recurrent nightmare, Lecter shows that he can be moved by a vulnerability which he himself does not possess. Similarly, Starling's ability to "read" his riddles, anagrams, manners, and desire suggests her interpretive familiarity with the language of shared secrets and silent acknowledgement. After all, a closeted person is implicitly recognized by some, but not all; is someone who is known speculatively by action and relations rather than by identity. It could thus be asserted about Starling and Lecter, with as much certainty as it could be asserted about any other such couple, that she is a closeted lesbian and he is a gay dandy. It could also be argued that criticism of Jodie Foster's appearance in a film ostensibly without positive images of gays and lesbians is perfectly wrong: unlike identification, which enforces similarity, recognition respects and preserves differences both between individuals as well as between them and their impersonal masks, whether they be of professionalism or aestheticism. Those who assert that Foster herself is closeted in the film thus unwittingly register the power of recognition.

The film's final moment of recognition occurs not so much between

its characters but between itself and the audience. Just after her graduation from the Academy, Starling receives a call from Lecter, who is
on a tropical island. As a final joke, he tells her that he's having an old
friend for dinner; and we see, as Starling cannot, Dr. Chiltern — the
sadist who tortured him, who made passes at Starling, whose vanity is
matched by his stupidity and aggression — whom Lecter is evidently
about to kill and eat. The line makes audiences cheer; it makes Lecter
a hero. At that point, his cannibalism is no longer a threat to Starling
and to us but is a form of subversive energy turned against a figure of
administered life. His appetite is for, rather than simply of, evil; the
murderous gay dandy for at least a moment represents for the audience the possibility of a cultural subversiveness which aligns rather
than divides him from Starling at her most resolute — the West Virginia woman struggling against sexism, poverty, and death. Of
course, the greatest change isn't in Lecter — it's in the audience which
at the beginning of the film is aligned with the administrative apparatus supervising Starling and which at the end of the film cheers
Lecter on to a dinner in which he'll be eating yet another man. What
had been a source of fear and revulsion at the beginning of the film
becomes a liberating ideal. The audience's desire for terror can be
seen at that moment not only as a potentially horrifying, masochistic
worship of power which overwhelms the viewer but as the subversive,
thrilling pleasure of imagining the forbidden.

Hannibal Lecter is an odd figure to encounter on the way to liberation; why tout a final scene of rebellious evil eating away at evil
authority? I suspect, too, that those who found Buffalo Bill a vicious
stereotype will not be happier thinking of Hannibal the Cannibal as a
gay dandy. Delighting in a fiendish gay killer is ultimately not that
much different from hating him, if it means identifying his ambivalent power with his marginalized sexuality. Nor is Starling's dispirit-
ing fate of becoming a *successful* FBI agent more encouraging. At
best, Lecter and Starling mark only provisional moments of liberating
recognition.

But what more could one ask of a film? We turn to the passing
distractions of art not for a substitute for the world but for a shock
that will make us recognize our desire for another world. For Adorno,
the fantasy element of art which rejects reality offers the hope of a
melancholy utopianism: "Truth is inseparable from the illusory belief
that from the figures of the unreal one day, in spite of all, real deliver-
ance will come" (121–122). The viewers who cheer Hannibal Lecter's
final scene in *The Silence of the Lambs* both register the burden of

living in the administered world of work, governed by all of our Dr. Chilterns, and recognize, as much in Lecter's love for Starling as in his appetite for his warder, the hope of being without work.

NOTES

For their reactions which immeasurably improved this essay at various stages of its composition, I thank Eduardo Cadva, Lawrence Danson, Maria DiBattista, Claire Fowler, Jonathan Freedman, Walter Hughes, David Kaufmann, and Sherri Wolf.

[1]Larry Kramer and Stephen Harvey, "Writers on the *Lamb*," *The Village Voice*, 5 March 1991: pp 49, 56; David J. Fox, "Gays Decry Benefit Screening of 'Lambs'," *Los Angeles Times*, 4 Feb 1991: p. F9; "Gossip Watch," *Outweek*, 27 February 1991: pp. 44–45, 60, and 6 March 1991: pp 58–59.

[2]According to Magali Larson, the modern professional emerged during the nineteenth century with economic qualifications invested in a definition of personality ostensibly free of specific class definitions yet nonetheless anchored within monopolistic cultural institutions. See *The Rise of Professionalism: A Sociological Analysis* (Berkeley: University of California Press, 1977) pp 14–15.

[3]Although Starling's sexuality is not made explicit, she keeps all interested men at arm's length. On the other hand, toward the end of the movie she repeats with the black woman who is her roommate at the Academy, Lecter's advice (taken from Marcus Aurelius) on the first principles in finding Buffalo Bill: "What need does he serve by killing? He covets. How do we begin to covet? We begin by coveting what we see every day." With each sentence, the camera cuts back and forth in reverse angle shots of the women's faces, looking at each other with growing revelatory excitement. The scene would seem to suggest that they, too, covet what they see every day. While the reasons for reading Starling as a closeted lesbian will become clearer later in the essay, for the moment it is enough to say that heterosexual eroticism is only an obstacle and a danger for her throughout the film.

[4]Later in the film, he draws Starling, swathed in drapery, holding a lamb. It would be generous to describe the picture as "cheesy" and it represents a failure of taste which I would rather ascribe to the film's set designer than to Lecter himself. I will admit, however, that Lecter's aesthetic tends toward Walter Pater's more lurid excesses.

[5]Theodor Adorno, *Minima Moralia: Reflections from Damaged Life*, trans. E. F. N. Jephcott (London: Verso, 1974) p. 21.

[6]See for example Michel Foucault, *The History of Sexuality, Volume I: An Introduction*, trans. Robert Hurley (New York: Vintage, 1980) p. 48.

[7]One of the more helpful discussions of identity, domination, and recognition can be found in Jessica Benjamin's *The Bonds of Love: Psychoanalysis, Feminism, and the Problem of Domination* (New York: Pantheon, 1988).

Rupert Pupkin's triumphal moment as he delivers the opening monologue on a late-night TV show in Martin Scorsese's film, *The King of
Comedy*. Robert De Niro plays The King.

WILLIAM IAN MILLER

"I CAN TAKE A HINT":
SOCIAL INEPTITUDE, EMBARRASSMENT,
AND *THE KING OF COMEDY*

The phrase "I can take a hint," when said seriously, contains its own denial. It reveals that the speaker has not been very adept at recognizing the hints already given, nor very graceful about not making a scene once he has recognized them. Its very utterance has the effect of punishing the hint-giver by making her hint fail as a hint. The truly successful hint works by gaining its end with no extra awkwardness added to the social encounter. The good hint should be barely perceived by the person toward whom it is directed. We could even say that it should not really become a part of his active consciousness. It should simply trigger a sense that it's time to go or that the line he is pursuing needs to be terminated. The good hint achieves the invisibility of the natural.[1]

People vary in their sensitivity to hints. The vast majority of us, in most settings, seem to pick up on them with reasonable facility. But we shouldn't be picking up on too many of them. That would be a sign of paranoia or self-loathing, if we are being hypersensitive, or a sign of how little we are in fact esteemed, if we are only middlingly sensitive. Yet we should worry if we are picking up on no hints. Few of us are so delightful all the time that we could never be the object of a distancing hint. It might be that our competence in reading signals is so habitual, so much a matter of second nature, that we are not conscious of the hints we discern and act upon properly. But it might also mean that we are being somewhat dense.

We are hint-givers as well as hint-receivers. And this fact should help us hone our skills as hint-receivers. But not necessarily. Hints can be given with focused intention, or hints can just be read (rightly) into rather unfocused unconscious distancing signals. There is no reason that the unconscious hint-giver need have any special aptitude for discerning when she is the object of someone else's hint. The person skilled in giving intended hints, however, should also be proficient in discerning when she is the object of someone else's hint. That skill is often what we think of as the very substance of good manners and tact, of refined social sensitivity. I am assuming, of course, that these hints are successful ones, that is, those that do their work anonymously.

The situation needs to be complicated a little more by noting that hints whose failure has the capacity to produce scenes come in two varieties: those that are distancing, that reveal the hinter as wishing to be free of the other, and those that seek greater closeness, as in hints of sexual attraction, of continued social relations, of desires to give or receive gifts. Each type involves somewhat different social and psychological risks. The risk of making distancing hints is of giving offense and the attendant awkwardnesses that accompany giving offense: embarrassment, regret, maybe even guilt and remorse. The risks of making hints of desired contact are the risks of rejection and its attendant pains: as before, embarrassment, but more seriously and centrally, humiliation, shame, chagrin, indignation and resentment. Both hints of distance and closeness tend to establish a moral and social hierarchy in which the distancer or the desired one has a higher status. There is a certain moral economy here. The two types of hint often appear in tandem: the hint of closeness, not unusually, provokes hints to keep away, while the distancing hint often prompts desperate and pathetic hints of closeness and reassurance from the rejected party. It is clear that a certain right inheres in the distancing position, a right to be free of relations not consented to.[2] The person seeking closeness is always cast in the role of a seeker of favors, or more accurately, of the other's consent to have her social spaces intruded upon.

The structure of this moral economy means that, somewhat perversely, we are inclined to find the seeker of closeness to be more off-putting than we are to find the distancer off-putting. Social obtuseness in the former produces in others contempt, disgust, annoyance, emotions that motivate removal and distancing; social ineptness in the distancer produces hatred, indignation, resentment, emotions that, though hostile, impel us to get closer even if only to wreak havoc or take vengeance. The seeker of closeness is thus a nudnick, a nerd, a creep, a dork, a schnorrer (Yiddish seems to make a myriad of refined distinctions in this social type), and more recently, a harasser or a stalker; the distancer is rude, boorish, a cold fish, or more charitably, shy or reserved. Ineptness in the distancer is not, however, simply a matter of giving offense. There is another kind of ineptness: failing to keep others off, being too accessible. Thus the patsy, pushover, chump, on the one hand, or the gracious, sweet, long-suffering soul on the other. Gender figures in this also. We usually envisage men as more likely to violate the norms of distance than women: it is men who are usually treated to epithets like nerd and creep. A woman who doesn't pick up on distancing signals might be pushy, or aggressive, whiny or dependent, but not a dork or a nudnick. Men, on the other hand, are cut more slack for being rude as distancers than woman are, even though women are caught in the double bind of being condemned both for not being circumspect enough about men approaching them and for not being generally more welcoming when approached.

"I can take a hint," as I indicated above, is already a sign that a hint has not succeeded in doing its work without social disruption, that is, without giving offense and without that offense becoming the basis for "making a scene," for "I can take a hint" makes a scene. It is the indignant response of someone who feels that he hasn't been treated to the respect he feels himself entitled to. But if indignation is the emotion of the nudnick who finally gets the message, embarrassment and mortification, or a more generalized sensation of awkwardness, are likely to characterize the emotional position of the hinter and observers of the scene. Embarrassment figures more insistently in the world of hints than just as a response to making a scene. The inept reader of distancing signals embarrasses us even before he must be disciplined by being forced to "get the hint" or "get the message." It is his denseness that makes the situation awkward for others long before it degenerates into a "scene."

This is a long prologue to a tale which I must make a bit longer still, for the failure of hints and the embarrassment generated by inept hint takers are the central motifs of *The King of Comedy*, which is my subject in this essay. Let me sketch briefly some salient features of embarrassment. It has been observed that embarrassment and certain closely related sensations of awkwardness and social discomfort can be experienced vicariously. We can feel embarrassed on someone's behalf even though that person does not feel embarrassed but, as our own sensations judge, should feel so. This allows us to experience a doubling of the embarrassment. Not only do we feel the embarrassment we would feel if we were in Rupert Pupkin's predicament, but we also sympathize with the embarrassment that Rupert's ineptitude has caused the other party. In fact, it is this latter embarrassment that triggers the former. Because Rupert embarrasses others, we imagine to our own embarrassment what it would be like to be so embarrassing and so dim as not to have perceived we were.

Embarrassment is also contagious; that is, we can catch it from another who does feel it. In these instances it is not the case that we are feeling embarrassed by what the other is feeling embarrassed by — that would simply be another example of vicarious embarrassment. The contagion of embarrassment is a function of the fact that the display of embarrassment can itself be embarrassing. Embarrassment can thus feed on itself, producing more embarrassment in the embarrassed person who now can add the embarrassment of a loss of poise to whatever failings gave rise to the initial embarrassment. The manifest embarrassment of another also embarrasses others who witness it. Blushes produce blushes because embarrassment makes demands on our tact which we are not always up to. Do we pretend not to notice? Do we notice and say something to defuse the situation? Or does our embarrassment at their embarrassment do just the right thing by making us a community of equals again? Embarrassment, it has been observed, is not only disruptive of a smooth social order; it is called upon in many situations to do the remedial work of restoring smoothness to a disturbed social setting.[3] Embarrassment works, as we all well know, to effect apology, to make amends for our gaffes and awkwardnesses. In fact, if we are not embarrassed or embarrassable we are unlikely also to be very adept at picking up on the distancing signals that others give us.

There lurks here an issue which may be of special interest to film theorists: the process by which the viewer develops identifications with characters, themes, or the camera's eye might vary with the particular emotion at stake. Certain depicted emotions, like embarrassment, because contagious and vicariously experienceable, prompt the reproduction of themselves in the viewer; other emotions cannot reproduce themselves. Compare, for instance, jealousy: one does not feel jealous on someone else's behalf. We can sympathize with their jealousy or understand it, but we do not feel it. In this regard, it is unlike embarrassment. Any theory of the identificatory process in film will remain forever oversimplified without a more detailed consideration of how spectator sympathy works in conjunction with different kinds of emotions.

Embarrassment is an emotion that has a strangely insistent connection with laughter and comedy. We might think of embarrassment as occupying the middle ground between humiliation on its dark side and amusement on its light side. Embarrassing incidents are the same things that provide mirth to observers and even to the poor embarrassed soul within hours or days of the event. Embarrassing events are thus distinguishable from humiliating ones. We will regale others to our own and their delight with our embarrassments, but we will guard our humiliations and reveal them to no one unless we are engaged in certain ritualized degradations like confession or psychoanalysis.[4] Yet humiliation too partakes of the comic world, for our humiliations often occur to the delight of others, producing in them Hobbes's "sudden glory"[5] and the gray mirth of Schadenfreude.

The emotion we name amusement,[6] and by this I mean the feeling that we have in response to things deemed humorous rather than the sense of amusement as when we say we amuse ourselves by playing basketball, seems to find in the embarrassing much of the occasion for its elicitation. Not only is it that the same events that are embarrassing can with a slight shift of perspective also appear amusing, but also that embarrassment itself provides amusement, if not to the embarrassed person then surely to others. But this is tricky, for we think of embarrassment as an unpleasant emotion; indeed it is sufficiently painful to provide much of the discipline and threat that keeps us functioning as mannerly and sociably presentable people. Embarrassing situations are embarrassing for all concerned, the one who embarrasses, the one who is embarrassed by the one who embarrasses, and those that witness the spectacle. At some level watching others make fools of themselves is painful. We do not want our humanity so utterly vulnerable, our bases for self-respect so fragile. Yet it is precisely the fragile basis of our respectability that produces the comic: what is a clown, what are the grotesque, slapstick, black humor, burlesque, if not the spectacle of our ineffable foolishness? We are dealing here, rather obviously, with some pretty deep-seated ironies of the social and psychological.[7]

Here I note as an aside that it has been a commonplace of literary theory since Aristotle that certain emotional experiences in the observer may be as constitutive of a particular artistic genre as its other formal generic structures. Aristotle was clearly onto something when he made the elicitation of certain emotions the signature of tragedy. We have even come to the point where we categorize films by the emotions we expect them to elicit: horror film is named after a type of fear, revenge films engage the passion of vengefulness and its close associates: indignation, resentment, and the satisfaction of justice done. Tear jerkers often elicit a range of emotions from wistfulness to pity. Action films exhilarate and partake of aspects of apprehension, revenge and horror. We would need to distinguish more precisely the differences between the emotion we experience as an observer of a fictional representation from the one we give the same name when the representation is not fictional or to the one we say we feel when we are one of the principal actors. We would also want to recognize that our precise emotional responses depend to some extent on what we figure the emotional situation of the observed party to be. Thus the apprehension we experience in horror films may well have a different structure depending, say, on whether the character in the film is also experiencing fear and terror or whether she is blithely oblivious to the danger that lurks behind the closet door.

Embarrassment and amusement also share some of the same somatic features. Laughter, central to the bodily presentation of amusement, is no stranger to embarrassment either, although distinctly less central than blushing. Laughter, as we all know, can mark a variety of psychic, social, and somatic states: embarrassment, malice, contempt, joy, anxiety, awkwardness, getting tickled, being amused, or simply supplying the necessary signs of engagement in amiable conversation. It may be that these states share nothing more than the fact that they all can trigger laughter. Is there anything really similar between the awkward laughter of embarrassment, and the laughter of genuine amusement? It is never too difficult to tell one from the other. Yet they are both laughters; they are not different genera, but species within a genus and they share a certain common relation with the ridiculous, the ludicrous, the humiliating, and the embarrassing, and the comic universe in which they thrive.

Like laughter, comedy cuts across a number of emotional domains. Comic laughter is not only the laughter of amiability. Most any laugh provoked by the comic (we may thus except the laugh of being tickled) is over-determined: part nervous, part "sudden glory," part just joining with others who are laughing, part amusement and mirth and part relief in the style of "oh please be funny enough, so that I don't have to feel embarrassed by your not being funny." This last item is surely some of what motivates laughter at the performances of that most vulnerable of souls, the stand-up comedian, the modern clown. Is it possible to separate our fear of his embarrassing us by his being embarrassing from the total experience of the comedy? Consider the emotions elicited by observing an unfunny comedian, something we will take up again shortly when we meet Rupert Pupkin. If humiliation lies in pretending to bigger shoes than you can fill, then the unfunny comedian humiliates himself and one of the sure indications that you are watching someone humiliate himself is that you will be embarrassed by the display.

*   *   *

Embarrassment, comedy, stand-up comedians, and the norms of respectable and competent social behavior, especially as these have to do with the practices surrounding leave taking, conversation and interaction closure all come together in Martin Scorsese's under-appreciated classic, *The King of Comedy*.[8] The movie, according to press critics and Scorsese in interviews, is about the American obsession with celebrity. The film presents the story of Rupert Pupkin's obsessive drive to get his break on network television as a stand-up comedian. Rupert (Robert De Niro) is a pathetic 34 year-old messenger boy who enjoys an active fantasy life imagining himself the host of his own talk show which he stages in a room of the house he shares with his mother amidst life-size cardboard cutouts of Liza Minelli and Jerry Lewis.[9] Jerry Lewis plays Jerry Langford, the popular host of a late night talk show and the object of Rupert's emulation and fixation. One night Rupert insinuates himself into Jerry's car after having helped him brave a throng of autograph hounds and groupies like himself; he confesses his ambitions to Jerry, asks Jerry if he would listen to his act, and extracts from him an unfelt concession to contact his office. The film then treats us to the painful experience of Rupert's numerous attempts to see Jerry as he remains oblivious to the rebuffs and brush-offs from Jerry's staff people. Interspersed with scenes of Rupert cooling his heels in the reception area of Jerry's office are Rupert's fantasies: Jerry begging Rupert to take over his show, Jerry declaring Rupert a comic genius, Rupert getting married on the Langford show to Rita, a bartender who was once the object of Rupert's fantasies from afar when they were in high school. Pursuant to Jerry's invitation in one of these fantasies to visit Jerry's summer home, Rupert actually shows up with Rita and is rudely sent packing. In the next scene, Rupert, with the assistance of another psychotic Langford fan, Masha (Sandra Bernhard), kidnaps Jerry and the end of it all is that Rupert uses Jerry as a hostage to secure his own appearance on Jerry's show after which he blithely goes off to jail, but not before he, we, and Rita view his monologue on network TV in Rita's bar. The movie closes with various voice-overs in the style of the evening news in which we find that Rupert Pupkin's name has become a household word, that his performance was viewed by 87 million households, that he was sentenced to six years in the white collar minimum security facility in Allenwood, PA, that Rupert's memoirs have been purchased by a New York publishing house for more than a million dollars, that Rupert was released after serving two years and nine months of his sentence, that his best-selling autobiography will be appearing as a major motion picture. And in the final scene the resonant voice of an announcer introduces the one and only King of Comedy Rupert Pupkin who now has his own network show. "Rupert Pupkin, ladies and gentlemen, let's hear it for Rupert Pupkin. Wonderful. Rupert Pupkin, ladies and gentlemen. Rupert Pupkin, ladies and gentlemen. Let's hear it for Rupert Pupkin. Wonderful. Rupert Pupkin, ladies and gentlemen."

Let me touch on a few small items before taking up the issues of misreading social cues and the emotional responses such misreadings provoke that are so central to the movie's feel. Rupert loves his name; thus his first words to Jerry in the car: ". . . my name is Rupert Pupkin and I know the name doesn't mean very much to you but it means an awful lot to me. Believe me." At some level he seems to know it may be his best joke. He leads with it when he gives his comedy routine, even after it has been given by the announcer. Names, some think, dictate our destiny. Rupert's surely dictates his. It takes a very special person to overcome a name. Nerdy names go a long way to making their bearers nerds. In any event, the movie industry operates on such an assumption, for if names can't quite make a star, they surely can prevent one from being born. We thus have Clark Gable and Rock Hudson, names which have a style every bit as parodiable as the names we give residential subdivisions. Could Rupert possibly be a skilled social actor with such a name? He does not disappoint our expectations.

The movie ends by obsessing on Rupert's name and getting it right, something no one but Rupert in the movie does. To others he is Mr. Pumpkin, Mr. Puffer, Mr. Pipkin, Mr. Pubnik, Mr. Krupkin, Mr. Potkin, etc. Together with the improbable number of households (the entire US) viewing Rupert's night on the Langford show, this repetition of his correct name by someone other than himself, presented somewhat slower than it would be in reality, is a very insistent indication that the extravagant news items and voice-overs at the end of the film are just another one of Rupert's fantasies. Critics have taken it straight, some going so far as to chastise Scorsese's irresponsibility in depicting the rewards obtainable by criminal devotion to celebrity.[10] In the beginning of the film Rupert's fantasies are clearly marked as such. When Jerry finally extricates himself from Rupert after their first encounter, Rupert falls into reverie and the scene breaks to Jerry and Rupert having lunch. Here it is Jerry who is importuning a reluctant Rupert to take over his show for six weeks which a self-satisfied Rupert deigns to do. Scorsese makes sure we do not mistake the reverie for reality by breaking to Rupert in his room acting the part of Rupert in the fantasy. Rupert must even suffer the indignity of his mother's off-screen interruptions ("What are you doing down there so late?"). It is striking that the Rupert of the fantasy speaks with more reserve (but still it is a reserve with many indicia of "showbiz" vulgar) and less volume than he is actually uttering the lines in his room. We thus see explicitly the metamorphosis Rupert's self-conception effects on the raw reality of Rupert's self that others see. Rupert does not hear himself as others hear him, nor does he see himself as others see him. Maybe. There is more than an occasional indication that Rupert is not without some strange access to insightful self-knowledge, of which more anon.

If the reality of the final scene is less obviously the stuff of fantasy, that is only because Rupert and the movie have insistently moved to make his fantasy and his reality converge into a kind of "fan-reality" in which fans become the performers. Earlier fantasies were clearly signaled as such, but now we, like Rupert, are not sure anymore where fantasy ends and reality begins. This is a film that delights in all kinds of ambiguities that arise when the boundaries between

It's fantasy time as Rupert daydreams doing lunch with talk-show host Jerry
    Langford (Jerry Lewis).

reality and fantasy, play-acting and playing at acting, television and
life, good jokes and bad jokes, are not clearly demarcated. Was
Rupert's monologue supposed to be funny or supposed to be bad?
The critics split on this question, as have people I have polled; even
Scorsese and De Niro split, the former thinking it weak, the latter
thinking it great.[11] Ambiguities and ambivalences figure in the casting. We thus have dramatic actors such as De Niro trying to do
comedy just as Rupert Pupkin is trying to do comedy and as De Niro
as Jake LaMotta did comedy at the conclusion of *Raging Bull*, Scorsese's film before *The King of Comedy*. Sandra Bernhard, a stand-
up comic, gets her acting debut as a dramatic actress. Tony Randall,
Victor Borge, Joyce Brothers play themselves, but they are not just
being themselves, but playing themselves, self-enacting. And if De
Niro is remarkable because he seems to come less determined by his
prior roles than most big stars, less encumbered with the sludge of
his public person, the opposite is the case with Jerry Lewis, about
whom no one does not have an opinion, and, unless French, usually
a negative one. Lewis is a comedian playing a dramatic role, but

playing a comic in that role. Lewis figures greatly in what I take to be one of the central implicit issues raised by the film: the unfunny comedian, the generally inept social actor, and the embarrassed discomfort he creates in his auditors. For every occasion someone might have actually laughed at Lewis one has cringed in embarrassment at least three times. The real Lewis, in other words, has caused us almost as much discomfort as Rupert will cause us.

Rupert's fantasies are wonderful stuff. They are pure wish-fulfillment, but they are not ends in themselves; rather they motivate Rupert to actualize them. The strength of his fantasies seems to overwhelm the embattled reality of others. When Jerry, in a desperate attempt to bring closure to Rupert's verbal barrage in the car, tells Rupert to call his office and ask for his secretary, Rupert replies: "You know how many times I had this conversation in my head? This is beautiful." Jerry responds with cool patronizing contempt: "And did it always turn out this way?" Rupert: "Yeah, it did." Later, he goes to Jerry's summer home with Rita because Jerry, in a fantasy, invited him. In these fantasies Rupert, more successfully than he can in real life, adopts Jerry's cool competence, while Jerry is reduced to acting like Rupert (or the real Jerry Lewis) as he fawns, importunes, and tells lame jokes. Yet Rupert's visions are indelibly Rupert's, still manifesting tastelessness and bad social judgment. In one he imagines his high school principal as a special guest on the Langford show, called there to pay homage to Rupert and marry him to Rita on national television. The taste mimics the tackiness of Tiny Tim but reproduces it as something to aspire to rather than to parody (as even Tim was able to do). And the irredeemability of his smallness of character manifests itself in the apology his vision extracts from the principal on behalf of all those who made Rupert's high school life miserable. Rupert thus constructs humiliation rituals (pathetic ones in the form of fantasized apology and deference) for others as a source of his pleasure. At dinner with Rita, Rupert links himself with one well-attested Christian tradition which makes the joys of heaven the delight of watching the pains of the damned in hell. He paints Rita a future of bliss in which they will be able to "look down on everybody and yell, 'Hey, tough luck, suckers. Better luck next time.'"

Triumph is the contempt of losers for losers, Nietzschean *ressentiment* writ small. Rupert thus consistently manifests contempt not only for Masha but for the other autograph seekers outside Jerry's studio. But there is something about Rupert's sheer obliviousness that makes him an object of a kind of reluctant awe. Don't we root for him because his triumph will come at Langford/Lewis's expense? Our willingness to discover appealing characteristics in this psychotic nebbish is not quite separable from the fact that he annoys Jerry Langford, someone for whom we have as little love as we do for the actor who plays him. Thus do we participate in Rupert's Schadenfreude.

Rupert is so inept that his ineptitude produces perverse consequences, that is, ones that cannot readily be distinguished from aptitude. De Niro's Rupert is a wonderfully subtle portrait of someone who lacks subtlety, who gets all the little things wrong and misreads everyone else's hints and cues. His hair, his dress, his body posture, his facial posture, his verbal and tonal tics all capture precisely someone who just doesn't quite get it. The remarkable thing about human sociability is how subtle we are in discerning the slightest deviation in these matters. But Rupert lacks key components of this competence: he is largely clueless. We need, however, to distinguish between at least two kinds of clueless person: the one who is simply oblivious and the one who at some level of consciousness uses his ineptitude strategically.[12] We all know cases of each. The difficult matter is what kind of consciousness to attribute to the latter. They are not sufficiently clued in to have the ability to become properly socialized, yet they are not without some awareness that the offenses they give others get results. Others back off, others don't want to make scenes, others are too well socialized to be so rude as to call them on their rudeness, their intrusiveness, their boringness, boorishness, etc. These are the people who prey off the general sociability of the majority. Yet it would be hard to attribute to them the classic mentality of the predator: that preternatural hyperawareness of each move of its would-be victim. The Ruperts of the world are not subtle hunters, nor are they generally cruel in a focused way. Such persons don't pretend, convincingly that is, not to want what they want; in this they are unlike the predator who studies how not to tip off danger alarms in his prey.[13] Yet at some level of consciousness they are not displeased with the consequences of their behavior. In straight economic terms the cost of their nerdiness, the cost of their violating all these myriad of social norms, does not outweigh the benefits they obtain by violating them.

Rupert is at different times both kinds of clueless. He really does think the excruciatingly awful jokes he tells are funny. He thinks the picture of his Pride and Joy, a card picturing the household products of the same names, is witty. Yet at the same time he is not without awareness that the way to get where he wants to go is to make it very uncomfortable for others not to let him get there. But only some of the time, for his fantasies do not make him the best of cold rational actors. He does, after all, overplay his hand by showing up at Jerry's summer home for the weekend with Rita in tow. That blunder finally provokes Jerry into making a scene of his own, the one in which Rupert finally acknowledges that he can take a hint. And when the violation of little norms won't get Rupert where he wants to go, he shows little reluctance at violating big ones, such as kidnapping laws. It is not without interest that the movie cuts from Rupert's finally admitting he can take a hint at Jerry's place to him and Masha in the car with the toy gun waiting to abduct Jerry.

There is in this another clue as to what constitutes so much of the offensiveness of the socially clueless person, whether instrumentally so or not: clueless people are not forgiving of other people's similar lack of competence. Masha embarrasses Rupert as he does her; Rita embarrasses Rupert when she makes herself a little too at ease at Jerry's before Jerry arrives, putting on the record player ("You really shouldn't put that on, you know; it's not polite.") or when she takes herself on a sightseeing expedition upstairs ("No, Rita, I . . . No, Rita, I wouldn't go up there. Rita. Rita, Rita. I don't think it's a good idea. . . . Rita, I don't think you have the right to go upstairs. Rita, please, don't go up. . . Rita."). Rupert's incompetence is not a general incapacity to feel embarrassment, or even a lack of knowledge of broad ranges of appropriate behavior. It is just that he can only feel embarrassed by another and only recognizes inappropriate behavior when it is someone else's. Thus it is that Rupert will brazenly maintain to Masha that he didn't get thrown out of the building in which Jerry's office is located even though she saw him get unceremoniously chucked out by two security guards. To Rupert's mind the grossest violations of the norms of appropriate social interaction are Jerry's, not his.[14] Jerry's tact fails him and thus is Rupert forced to have to take a hint:

> Jerry: You understand English? Take your things and go.
> Rupert: All right, all right. I can take a hint, Jerry. I just want

to ask you if you'll listen to my stuff for fifteen minutes, that's all. Is that asking too much?

Jerry: Yes, it is. I have a life, okay?

Rupert: Well, I have a life too.

Jerry: That's not my responsibility.

Rupert: Well, it is when you tell me to call you and then you don't. . . .

Jerry: I told you to call to get rid of you.

Rupert: To get rid of me?

Jerry: That's right.

Rupert: Okay. All right, I can take a hint.

Jerry: If I didn't tell you that, we'd still be standing on the steps of my apartment.

Rupert will not suffer such rude treatment and he now feels justified in taking revenge.

An actor of less genius would have made this movie into the satire on celebrity that at one level it is and nothing more.[15] But with De Niro doing Pupkin we have a serious piece of social psychology, the kind of insightful comedy of manners we rarely find except in the best novels. His Rupert is a master of using the form of apology as a conversational wedge: "Jerry, I'm sorry. I don't mean to disturb you. I just want to talk to you for a minute." His "I'm sorrys" are frequent and they are always of the preemptive variety, never designed to remedy a wrong done, but to introduce and defuse an offense about to be given. Other instances in this genre are the "I don't mean to bother you but. . . " or his "Really, I don't mind" to Jerry's vexed administrative assistant which skillfully traverses any suggestion that he shouldn't wait around any longer. With the passive aggression of his use of the apology, there is the excessive thank-youing of desperate, but not to be denied, obsequiousness; hands are shaken too often and held too long. First names are used excessively and De Niro gets the style of intrusive familiarity exactly right: he drops Jerry's name to others while in Jerry's presence it becomes a mantra, a magic charm intended to counteract Jerry's desperate efforts at closing their encounter: "Thanks Jerry, thanks. Thanks a lot. It's a pleasure meeting you Jerry. . . . Jerry, Jerry, let me show you a picture of my Pride and Joy. . . . Jerry, seriously, if you ever want lunch, my treat." De Niro gets the accompanying body movements, smiles, tones, and rhythms exactly right in their wrongness.

More than thirty minutes of the film are taken up watching

because others are laughing, for, like embarrassment, laughter is contagious; we also laugh to connect with other laughers, some of whom might be together with us, some of whom are just sharing space with us, but a space defined as one in which laughing is supposed to take place: a comedy club, a movie, a lecture. And we laugh because we have precommitted ourselves to it: we have gone to the video store to rent a comedy because we want to laugh; we have paid for tickets to enter the comedy club; we are invested in laughing. That the comic is supposed to produce laughter makes it easier to laugh. The very label "comedy" cues us to think laughter is expected and thus lowers our critical threshold for what is funny. Comedians have an even better thing going for them than these helpful precommitments and expectations. Much laughter is motivated by social norms that tell us it is inappropriate not to. The comedian, after all, is asking us to laugh and we usually oblige him because it is easier to do that than not to, easier for us to let him maintain his self-respect than embarrass everyone with the truth. The comedian, in short, benefits from our tactfulness, our decency, our capacity for saving someone else's face when that other has jeopardized it by incompetence. That tact is motivated by an uneven mixture of fellow-feeling and the desire to save ourselves the embarrassment of witnessing and participating in another's failures. Sympathy for the poor devil up there partly motivates our concern to save him from himself, save him from the humiliation he will suffer if he could see himself as we see him, because we can only imagine too well what we would feel like if we were being judged at that moment by the likes of us. By saving him we hope to save ourselves.

So the unfunny comedian gets his laughs and the moderately funny one, like Rupert, gets heartier laughs than, strictly speaking, the material deserves because of the added emotional input relief, in its strange dance with embarrassment and amusement, gives to laughter. But if the social rules that make us save another's face, that make us honor his claim to respectful treatment, give the comedian one big assist in gaining laughter without regard to any special merits of the material, that is fair compensation for the impossible situation stand-up comics put themselves in. We usually think that the funniest of things, the things that make us laugh the hardest, are spontaneous, unpredictable, and most often, not contrived, but "real." The bore who prefaces a joke with "I'm going to tell you a joke—it will really make you laugh" has killed the joke before its birth and will only get the laughter that tact, sympathy, and normal politeness can muster. But that is what the comedian does too. The very performance is one big announcement that reproduces the bore's exactly, except with one big difference: the bore bores us without our consent; we have consented to endure the jokes of the comedian and even invested in them. The remarkable thing is that an occasional genius does genuinely make us laugh and the ones who do usually do so by teaching us something about social norms, the same thing I have been trying to do here.

I consider my account too sweet, too filled with empathetic and sympathetic mechanisms or benign ones like embarrassment and relief. We also laugh out of contempt, Hobbes's sudden glory again. This is sticky stuff. Many comedians try to coopt contempt and make themselves the indulgent object of theirs and yours: Woody Allen, Rodney Dangerfield, Rupert Pupkin. Their style is to preempt a kind of cold and malicious contempt, the contempt that borders on disgust and revulsion, the contempt that we would feel for your pretense of thinking you are funny when you are not, with a benign contempt, the contempt that often accompanies amusement at the antics of animals and kids.[18] Some comedians adopt another strategy for dealing with contempt, not being funny on purpose. This is a very self-reflexive style which discovers the comic by thwarting its conventional expectations: the jokes are meant to be bad, the timing is meant to be off, the atmosphere meant to be something less than convivial. The skill here is in signaling conventional competence only to undo the expectations arising from it, the violation of those expectations constituting the basis for humor. This style can also indulge a kind of self-loathing, a contempt for the stock-in-trade of being a comedian in the conventional mode. And this self-contempt has a way of becoming a malign contempt for you. You become the contemptible fool, the butt of his jokes, the sucker. But loathing the audience is not unique to this style. One suspects it also motivates types like Woody Allen. They might pose as sad-sacks, but they let you know that their knowledge and especially their self-knowledge is superior to yours and that that is the respect in which they differ from you.

I know. I know. I can take a hint. My account misses so much of the experience of laughing at Rupert's monologue or any other comedian for that matter. Can it only be a race to see who can hold whom in contempt first? We may indeed have to admit that some gentle contempt figures in our laughing at Rupert's monologue, but then mostly because Rupert gave us permission to have those feelings. We are laughing *with* those who are laughing at Rupert, one of whom is also Rupert. There is a community formed, a community of laughers, and it produces and is produced by amusement and *relief* that he and we survived the threat of our embarrassment at his humiliation. Surely my account is partial: what about the simple fun, the exhilaration, the feeling of freedom and escape that often accompanies the laughter that comedy provokes? And isn't that sense of freedom and escape a liberation from the constraints imposed upon us by the myriad of social norms that keep us civilized if not exactly content, even as those same norms are constraining us, in part, to laugh so as to transcend them?[19]

Let me make one final observation. The discomforts of failed attempts to elicit our laughter seem to be remarkably resistant to variations among visual representational media. Rupert Pupkin can make us just as uncomfortable as any real comedian we see fail on television or live before us in a comedy club. But if we read bad jokes or read cartoons in the newspaper that are not funny we are not embarrassed for their author who remains, for us, a disembodied name. Instead we have contempt for the people who would find such stuff funny. We cannot imagine ourselves as them at all. Thus does our imagination limit the objects of our sympathy. We can sympathize with someone being laughed at, whatever the reason they may be the objects of laughter, but we cannot sympathize with the laughers unless we accept the beliefs and the perceptions which underpin their laughing. It is thus very hard, if not impossible, to sympathize with senses of humor that are not also ours. And nothing elicits our contempt quite so easily as laughter we cannot participate in. Ultimately the whole array of emotional experiences involving the intersection of laughter, the comic, social ineptitude and the emotions it evokes depends on a capacity for imagining ourselves in the other's shoes while we at the same time remain in ours; in effect, we achieve a kind of double consciousness, one part feeling vicariously what we judge the other should feel, the other part feeling as we do when we judge the other. And if we are good enough at that double vision we should never have to say, "I can take a hint."

ACKNOWLEDGEMENT

I wish to thank Larry Kramer, Kathleen Koehler, Carol Clover, and Phoebe Ellsworth for helpful criticism and suggestions.

NOTES

[1]Let me stake out some definitional limits here. I mean to discuss those hints that are subsumed in the category that gives the phrase "I can take a hint" its sense, that is, hints that are distancing and can thus be perceived by the other as somewhat hostile. Although we may give other people hints of encouragement, that is not the type of hint I will be dealing with here. In fact, one could conceive of almost any kind of social indirection as a hint. But little of analytical value would be gained by doing so. Nonetheless, I will have to make some references to a slightly broader class of hints in the discussion that follows than that entertained by the notion of the hostile hint.

[2]The strength of the distancer's right to keep another at bay varies with the moral status and the urgency of the seeker's claim. If the seeker is a child, handicapped, sick, the distancer maintains his distance at the cost of being thought callous, selfish, cruel.

[3]See Erving Goffman, "Embarrassment and Social Organization," *Interaction Ritual: Essays on Face-to-Face Behavior* (New York: Pantheon, 1967), 97–112.

[4]See William Ian Miller, *Humiliation* (Cornell University Press, 1993), 159.

[5]"Sudden glory, the passion which maketh those grimaces called laughter and is caused . . . by the apprehension of some deformed thing in another, by comparison whereof they suddenly applaud themselves." *Leviathan* I.vi.

[6]Both philosophical and psychological literatures generally consider amusement an emotion; see Ronald do Sousa, *The Rationality of Emotion* (Cambridge: MIT Press, 1990); Robert Sharpe, "Several Reasons Why Amusement is an Emotion," *The Philosophy of Laughter and Humor*, ed., John Morreall (Albany: SUNY Press, 1987).

[7]The issue of finding discomfort pleasurable or the witnessing of others' discomfort as pleasurable engaged Aristotle and was much discussed by literary theorists of the eighteenth century; see Aristotle, *The Poetics*, and Steele, *Tatler* No. 82 and Addison, *Spectator* No. 39. Why, for instance, is tragedy pleasurable? Some may find the explanation in a kind of commitment to masochism as the chief motivator of human psychic life; others may prefer a more complex account of aesthetic emotions.

[8]The film was also a box office failure. It exceeded its $14 million production budget by almost $5 million. Its American box office take was less than one-sixth that amount. See Les Keyser, *Martin Scorsese* (New York: Twayne, 1992).

[9]The coding of Rupert's ethnicity is complex and I relegate some brief observations to this note. De Niro's Rupert is not so clearly Jewish as his surname, his nagging mother, and his pushy nerdiness would indicate. His Jewishness fades into a kind of lower-middle class east-coast ethnic, an amalgam of vulgar Jewish, Italian, and Irish styles that itself is the ethnic base of the vulgar showbiz style pilloried in the movie. The Jewish predominates in this mix, as one would expect, but it is not the pure thing. Nor is this style the fashionable way to self-present Jewishly in a film. Brash and pushy confidence, not very self-reflective, as perhaps exemplified in the Marx brothers has given way to the self-involved, obsessively self-doubting, wimpy, intel-

lectualized neuroticism of Woody Allen. Rupert's filmic Jewishness is the old Hollywood; he is manifestly dated.

[10]See Gary Arnold, "Unroyal 'King': Wrong Tone, Wrong Time in Scorsese & De Niro Film," *Washington Post* (April 15, 1983), C1, and Marilyn Beck, "The King of Comedy," *New York Daily News*, Feb. 2, 1983, 37. These writers seem to hint that Scorsese should take special care given that he must bear some responsibility for the production of John Hinckley, Jr., Reagan's failed assassin whose obsession with Jodie Foster dated from her appearance in Scorsese's *Taxi Driver*. See, however, Krin Gabbard and Glen Gabbard, *Psychiatry and the Cinema* (Chicago: University of Chicago Press, 1987), who suggest that the film's closure may be fantasy. But we should never underestimate the American media culture's ability to make such fantasies not quite implausible. Consider the fame of the likes of Oliver North, Amy Fisher, the Bobbitts, etc.

[11]See Keyser, 134–35. Note John Simon's befuddlement (*National Review*, May 13, 1983, 574):

> This is where things become particularly muddled. The monologue strikes me as only slightly less funny than most such monologues, which I don't find very funny either. Are the filmmakers saying that Pupkin's comedy is junk, but that on the Langford Show, introduced by Tony Randall, it enchants an audience of Pavlovian fools? Or are they saying that Pupkin does have that minimal talent needed to make anybody's success in this abysmal business? Is the film about weirdos cannibalizing their betters, or are there no betters, and are large numbers of — if not, indeed, all — Americans a breed of imbeciles? Is the satire specific or all-inclusive?

[12]I owe this distinction to a student, Spencer Gusick.

[13]See Erving Goffman, *Relations in Public* (New York: Basic Books, 1971), 238–47.

[14]Grand social theory tends to ignore the crucial but homely questions that the social theory of Goffman took as central. Some of these are, do bores get bored by bores, boors offended by boors; do nerds have contempt for other nerds? Do we have the self-knowledge to know these things? Can they be answered? Since I have been from time to time both a bore and a boor I draw on my own experience to suggest that evidence warrants answering Yes. About nerds I plead agnosticism, but I suspect yes, for the key to all these character types is not the failure to recognize others for what they are, but to fail to recognize the content of others' recognition of ourselves.

[15]This is not to say it doesn't work well as such a satire. De Niro's genius is given more than an able assist by Paul Zimmerman's psychologically and socially rich script. Another theme the movie deals with is the failure of any characters to connect with any others. All are obsessively self-referential and unwilling to admit the claims of others. Thus it is that Masha can never get a letter delivered to Jerry. When she gets Jerry's unlisted number, he hangs up (and presumably gets a new number). In the end she can only get to him by mummifying him in duct tape and treating him to a one-way conversation. Rupert can never get to Jerry; even Jerry can't get through to his own people when he calls them with the toy gun to his head, for he is indistinguishable from a would-be comedian who does a Langford impression and who also plagues Jerry's office. The opening credits roll against Masha's hands splayed out against Jerry's car window desperately clawing at the glass shield that, like the television screen, separates her TV-idol from her. No one connects. True, Rupert and Masha find each other, but as indicated in the text each is contemptuous of the other; they are only united by the strange convergence of their psychoses.

[16]It is no wonder that he must struggle to find some place to rest his eyes. Places designated as waiting rooms are marked as waiting rooms by having old magazines available to ease the awkwardnesses that attend eye-parking. And, as Rupert has been told, he is waiting in a reception area, not a waiting room. But again, it is not that Rupert is utterly without some inkling of propriety. When he calls Burt Thomas, Jerry's producer, after kidnapping Jerry, he shows some awareness that he might not have a right as yet to first-name Burt: "No, Burt, if I could call you Bu. . . ."

[17]Jon Elster notes astutely that "although we have different feelings when a disaster just misses us, when a probable disaster fails to materialize and when an unpleasant state of affairs ceases to obtain, the single word *relief* covers them all. By contrast, the corresponding emotions defined with respect to positive core emotions are verbally distinguished as regret, disappointment and grief." *Nuts and Bolts for the Social Sciences* (Cambridge: Cambridge University Press, 1989).

[18]This kind of benign contempt has a dark side to it also. It goes hand in hand with some pretty unsavory manifestations of power and hierarchy. It is thus also the contempt of the master for the servant, the white for black, the Christian for the Jew. But this kind of contempt also has its own reciprocity. The lower-status person might as well find the higher-status contemner a worthy object of her own contempt. Few of us have either not been the object or the agent of the blistering contempt of the black for the white, the Jew for the Christian, women for men, and teenagers for adults. The contempt of the high for the low differs in some respects from that of the low for the high. The former might involve disgust, but more often is characterized by a kind of indifference, a refusal even to see the other. If, as Hume theorizes, contempt is a mixture of hatred and pride, then the contempt of the high for the low is made more of pride than hatred, whereas in the contempt of the low for the high hatred would surpass pride; see David Hume, *A Treatise of Human Nature* Bk. II, Pt. ii, Sect. x.

[19]It is a commonplace that comics elicit laughter by breaking various norms of appropriate decorum. Thus Rupert tells about his mom and dad puking, makes jokes about his mother's death, and confesses to having kidnapped Jerry to get on the show. The mirth generated by watching someone break such norms is complexly motivated. There is contempt for the lack of decorum of the comedian vs. admiration for his nerve and insight, nervousness at the breach of deeply held rules vs. delight at the feast of misrule aspects of breaking them, relief over not being punished for breaking them vs. anxiety that we still might be, etc.

ROBERT ZALLER

AFTER THE REVOLUTION:
BERTOLUCCI'S *THE LAST EMPEROR*

The theme of this movie is change. Can a man change?
The story of Pu Yi is a story of metamorphosis. From
emperor to citizen . . . from caterpillar to butterfly. The
extraordinary thing is that the film's story coincides completely with China today. China is changing, a big muta-
tion is in progress. . . . The movie is somehow in synch
with that.

Bernardo Bertolucci[1]

It is axiomatic that an artist's own words are the best guide to his
intentions. It is not necessarily the case with his results. In *The Last
Emperor*, Bernardo Bertolucci has succeeded in making a movie not
about change but about immobility — the immobility of personality,
and the immobility of history. In doing so, he has come full circle as
well in a cinematic project that began twenty-five years earlier in
Before the Revolution. The Bertolucci of that precocious masterpiece
was a young man in search of personal and political transcendence, a
way beyond the bourgeois, Freudian ego in which his class and time
had trapped him. Through purgative madness and disgust in the
manner of Artaud (*Partner*), absorption in the false collectivity of
Fascism (*The Conformist*), temporal reversal (*The Spider's Stratagem*), and sexual privatization (*Last Tango in Paris*), Bertolucci had
explored the avenues of rebellion and escape afforded by his culture,
and found that they terminated in stasis, despair, and death.[2]

Yet each such terminus formed the point of departure for another
utopian projection upon history, another quest for a politics of liberation. In *1900*, the film that marked the crisis of his career, Bertolucci seized upon an idealized peasantry, whose comradeship in the

struggle for social justice in twentieth-century Italy represented the closest approach to an achieved vision of communal and sexual harmony available to him, as the image of his own quest for a reconciliation of personal and social identity. But the image, despite its cinematic virtuosity, was knowingly false: false to history, which Bertolucci stopped in freeze-frame at the moment of the illusory triumph of the peasant-partisan forces in 1945, and false to the reality of desire, which, formed under class relations, could not transcend them in the absence of a revolution that is both the precondition and the result of utopian desire. The result of this was an egregious contrast between the "natural" fulfillment of sexual impulse among the peasantry and the degeneracy of desire among the landed elite. This too rang false, not only by virtue of exaggeration but because the depiction of liberated sexuality in the unliberated peasantry reduced itself to a combination of naivete and prudery that was scarcely more (and, often, perilously less) appealing than the perversions of the elite.[3]

The most retrograde element in this film was that it was made at a time (1976) when no one, least of all the urbane Bertolucci, could have taken the idea of a revolutionary peasantry in Italy seriously. Indeed, the disappearance of this peasantry had been a salient theme of *Before the Revolution*, the absence of a revolutionary class had been the political starting-point of his film career, and the tough-minded engagement with Italy's fascist past had been one of the strengths of his early work.[4]

After the débâcle of *Luna* (1979), Bertolucci's most openly Oedipal romance, he made a partial recovery in *The Tragedy of a Ridiculous Man* (1982), a film which returned him to the scene and scenario of *Before the Revolution*. Bertolucci's ridiculous man is Primo (Ugo Tognazzi), a small factory owner who knows that he is inauthentic, trapped between the memory of his peasant roots and the vision of a harmonious social order that he, as much as any, would gladly see lift the burden of historical responsibility from his shoulders. Thus, he takes pride in the fact that his factory, which processes cheese and pork, is connected with the soil, while his fellow industrialists deal in "inanimate" materials. On the other hand, despite the proprietary satisfaction he takes in his plant, he muses that if it were a cooperative and he its manager he would be safe from the class hatred (and self-contempt) to which he is now exposed.

The convoluted plot revolves around the staged abduction of Primo's son, Giovanni, by a revolutionary group to which Giovanni actually belongs. As Primo's suspicions about the abduction grow, his solicitude for his son turns to cynicism, and he accepts the report of Giovanni's death with alacrity, deciding to use the ransom he has raised to recapitalize his business. The story, whose details need not detain us here, quickly reverts to the familiar Bertoluccian themes of generational substitution and Oedipal conflict. Primo is a father who is not really looking for his son (as Athos, Jr. in *The Spider's Stratagem* is a son not really looking for his father); each is willing to betray the other, Primo to turn his son's reported death to profit, and Giovanni to use revolutionary politics as a pretext for stripping Primo of his fortune. The corruption of all relations within the capitalist order, especially those of its proudest product, the bourgeois family, is foreordained, and the truth about the terrorism of the Red Brigades is the same as that about fascism — they are both degenerative aspects of the same order.

Such a reading, however, suggests only half the issue. As Bertolucci's project has been the attempt to reconcile the individual and the social — posed most starkly by the warring visions of Freud and Marx — so, in the best of his work to this point, he had withheld judgment on the ultimate primacy of the personal or the political. Such a suspension had been possible as long as Bertolucci's films themselves remained fables of bourgeois revolt, fixed within the unsurpassable limit of the capitalist order. But this was an impasse for Bertolucci too; like his heroes, he was fated within that order to repetition, and while the tension of an unresolved quest had given vitality to his art, it also threatened its further development. The constriction of the political situation in Europe had led a number of directors, including Louis Malle and Wim Wenders, toward American subjects, and Bertolucci, declaring his interest in Italian society exhausted, attempted to revive a long-standing project to film Dashiell Hammett's *Red Harvest*.

In the event, Bertolucci's next locale was neither Europe nor America, but the People's Republic of China, and his subject neither Hammett's novel nor (his own first preference for a Chinese project) Malraux's *Man's Fate*, but one urged on him by his hosts: the life of the last Manchu emperor, Aisin-Gioro Pu Yi. What the Chinese hoped for in promoting a film treatment of Pu Yi can perhaps best be gauged by the title of his exemplary autobiography, *From Emperor to Citizen*. What Bertolucci found instead was the tragedy of a truly ridiculous man, the epitome of his film heroes, and the clearest — perhaps the definitive — expression of the political irony that has been implicit in his work from the beginning.

The film pivots on its opening scene, which depicts the return of a trainload of Russian-held Chinese collaborators and war criminals, including Pu Yi, to the Communist authorities of the newly-victorious People's Republic. From this moment, it proceeds backwards in a series of extended flashbacks from the presentation of the three-year-old Pu Yi at the Manchu court, and forward from the point of his arrival at the Chinese internment camp — a very different presentation at a very different court — to his rehabilitation as a citizen of the new order. No doubt Bertolucci's Chinese hosts found this opening highly appropriate, as marking the beginning of Pu Yi's rebirth. For the viewer, however, adopting the perspective of the still-unreconstructed Pu Yi, this narrative choice, centering the film in Pu Yi's memory, makes the long flashbacks a kind of remembered dream, the return to his captive present a living nightmare. It is only as the film turns slowly on this axis that the ends of the dream knit together, and are shown to enclose a single image.

That image is given in the film's first moments. The train bringing Pu Yi to the internment camp pulls into the station where a detachment of soldiers waits for it. The image is doubly ironic: it brings Pu Yi "home" to his native soil, but as a prisoner; and it provides him with a "guard" that will recall the imperial guard that prostrates itself before the boy-emperor, but which leads him instead to a cell. Above all, however, the image of the train itself commands: smoke-wreathed, photographed from a variety of elevations, thrusting itself majestically between the motionless ranks of men. Yet this image belies itself more than any other, for the train's motion is ultimately illusory: shuttling back and forth on its track, it paces and repaces its own steps, like a prisoner in his yard: it can "go," ultimately, nowhere.[5]

The film unfolds this image with endlessly fertile variation, but, in essence, never departs from it. The sequence continues as Pu Yi alights from the train, is recognized by four men who prostrate themselves before him and are driven off by the soldiers, and attempts suicide in the dingy station washroom by slitting his wrists. The blood filling the basin has the effect of a Proustian madeleine: it prepares us for the flashbacks that establish Pu Yi's past.

What Bertolucci finds in the story of Pu Yi's childhood and

infancy is the perfect Oedipal paradigm, the bourgeois child's fantasy of omnipotence lived out as historical reality. The child-emperor, crowned at the age of two, lives in the hermetically sealed world of the Forbidden City, in which his every wish is, literally, law. He lives without sibling or rival, for there are no other children in the Forbidden City. The eunuchs who are his servitors and companions are nonthreatening fathers, for it is they and not he who have been castrated, and no other male dare approach or even gaze upon him. As the Son of Heaven, he is, indeed, fatherless from the beginning. When the wizened Dowager Empress announces to the infant Pu Yi, "The Emperor is dead," and designates him his heir, she makes him symbolically an orphaned son. A crisis occurs when Pu Yi is visited by his younger brother, Pu Je. Pu Je is not only a reminder of the real continued existence of his father (and his continued potency as well), but of a world outside the Forbidden City which, after the republican revolution of 1911, no longer recognized the throne. Pu Yi, shocked by this challenge to his childish omnipotence, seeks to reaffirm it by forcing his elderly chamberlain to drink a tray of ink. It is the most horrific moment in the film, and perhaps the most personally charged one as well: Bertolucci began his own career as a writer, and his father is a poet.

But Pu Yi's father, in his own domain beyond the walls of the Forbidden City, possesses something else that mocks Pu Yi's omnipotence: his mother, from whom he has been separated since entering the Forbidden City. Her place is taken by his amah or wet nurse, to whom he has transferred his maternal needs and affections, without, however, forgetting her absence. Pu Yi's compensation for the loss of his mother is the exclusive possession of her surrogate, by whom he is suckled until the age of eight. Since the amah is the only nubile woman in the palace, this sense of exclusivity is strengthened. When, however, the late Emperor's former consorts, who never approach Pu Yi but observe him from a distance, see that his caresses have become exploratory, she, too, is summarily removed. Pu Yi chases after her, yelling helplessly, while she in turn begs to be allowed at least a farewell: "He is my child!"

In contrast to this anguished scene, the subsequent news of his mother's death leaves Pu Yi seemingly indifferent. When his tutor, who alone among the eunuchs exhibits some sympathy toward him, offers condolences, Pu Yi spurns them. But this event is decisive, for it reveals to him that the Forbidden City, with its promise of omnipotence, is a fraud, since it has withheld from him the one object he truly desired. He attempts to escape, only to have the portals of the City closed in his face. Climbing the roof of the palace, he threatens suicide, only to be rescued by a human chain of eunuchs. These are the only genuine acts of revolt in his life. They serve merely to reveal his true situation as a prisoner.

The now-adolescent Pu Yi is placated by another surrogate. The

As he ages during the film, Pu Yi is portrayed by a succession of actors: Richard Vuu (top left), Tijger Tsou (top right), Wu Tao (bottom right), and John Lone (bottom left).

eunuchs engage him to the sexually assured Princess Wan Jung (Joan Chen). According to imperial tradition, he is also provided with a no less attractive Secondary Consort, thus affording him substitutes for both mother and nurse simultaneously. In a surpassingly erotic scene, Pu Yi takes both women to bed, and the three disappear under a rippling silk sheet where identities as well as bodies merge.

This idyl is menaced both by the ongoing revolution outside the walls and the machinations of the eunuchs within. The latter, who have systematically plundered the palace, set it afire to escape discovery. Pu Yi goes in fear of his life, but finds an ally in the Scots Orientalist, Reginald Johnston (Peter O'Toole), who is brought in to tutor him in "Western" subjects.

Pu Yi's relationship with Johnston puts the final impress on his character. The articles Johnston procures for him are symbolic as well as practical: spectacles for his poor eyesight (the eunuchs, it is intimated, would prefer him to go blind), and a bicycle, which gives him access to locomotion for the first time (though it does not enable him to leave the palace compound). But Johnston brings with him something far more precious: knowledge of the outside world, whose mastery is essential if Pu Yi is to achieve what has now become the ruling passion of his life: dominion in the great kingdom of his father. The first two questions he asks of Johnston are revelatory: "Why are you not wearing skirts?" (i.e., kilts); and, "Where are your ancestors buried?" In the presence of the first true male he has been alone with since entering the palace, and the first foreigner he has ever seen, what Pu Yi wants to know is, Why are you not feminized?, and, Where is *your* father? His anxiety about this latter question reveals itself further when he asks Johnston whether his predecessor had been assassinated. The Emperor Kuang-Hsi is his formal ancestor and, like him, a Son of Heaven, i.e., a son whose earthly father remains hidden. Dare he rule without incurring Kuang-Hsi's fate?

Johnston's replies are candid — another winning attribute in a house of lies — but he perpetuates in Pu Yi the most dangerous illusion of all, that he can in fact some day rule China. Pu Yi gives him his unswerving trust in part because he feeds this illusion, and the illusion is confirmed in part because of that trust.

Johnston's own political interest is obscure. When, while bargaining with the eunuchs for Pu Yi's eyeglasses, he is asked what he really wants, he replies, disingenuously, "The glasses." Johnston "sees" through others in a double sense; he exposes the thievery and self-interest of the eunuchs, yet articulates no perspective of his own. In the end, he appears to be simply the medium through which Pu Yi passes to adulthood. These contradictions are reflected in O'Toole's performance, which goes for the butler manner, sacrificing in substance what it achieves in style. Yet Johnston's influence is pivotal. As the first male in the Emperor's mature life, he sets the pattern of his dependence on masculine authority figures. Pu Yi reveals himself in this relationship as a young man desperately in need of guidance, yet fixed upon achieving a single goal. As such, he will be easily manipulated by anyone who sees what he wants.

Pu Yi (played as an adult by John Lone) is finally not liberated but driven from the Forbidden City by the warlord Feng Yuxiang. Johnston urges him to take refuge in the British embassy, but he chooses the Japanese legation instead. While living through the late 1920s in Tianjin as a Westernized playboy — he and the Empress adopt the names of "Henry" and "Elizabeth" — Pu Yi falls increasingly under the sway of the Japanese, who appear to combine Western efficiency and strength with a hieratic vision of society governed by a feudal code. Despite the warnings of the Empress, he finds a new "tutor" in Amakasu (Ryuichi Sakamoto), a dashing Japanese diplomat and adventurer. When Japan occupies Manchuria in 1931, Pu Yi is easily persuaded to become emperor of the puppet state of Manchukuo.

Bertolucci's Asian fascists are in many ways a reprise of his Italian ones. For the bourgeois, he suggests, — and, under the swank, Manchukuo is very much a bourgeois court — the temptation is always fascism. We are once again in the Thirties, the decade before Bertolucci's birth that is the setting of *The Conformist* and *The Spider's Stratagem,* the period that is always before the revolution. Here, too, as in virtually all of Bertolucci's films, the personal commerce of sexual exchange and betrayal takes place on the dance floor. "Henry" and "Elizabeth" dance among jaded couples in silence; after the music stops, the consort, no less apt a pupil of modernity than her master, says, "I want a divorce."

Pu Yi is able to hold neither of his women. His consort decamps, while Wan Jung drifts into opium and a spiteful, self-destructive romance with his female cousin, "Eastern Jewel," who courts her on the dance floor and services her addiction. Eastern Jewel is Amakasu's mistress as well, and, despite her royal status, boasts that she is a "spy" for the Japanese. She offers herself with insulting casualness to Pu Yi, but her real function is to isolate him from any influence but that of his new mentors.

It is not a difficult task. As Pu Yi relapses into his childhood fantasy of omnipotence, he regresses to a prepubertal state as well. He rejects Wan Jung sexually on the pretext that she, like his mother, is an opium addict, thereby negating the most obvious of his imperial functions, the production of an heir. When Wan Jung announces that she has become pregnant for the sake of the throne, he responds with equanimity if not indifference. Shirking paternal responsibility and stigmatizing his marital partner with a taboo image of his mother, he is psychologically if not physically impotent, a eunuch in effect.

The other dimension of Pu Yi's impotence is revealed to him on his return from a state visit to his Japanese counterpart, Hirohito, whom he fancies as a "brother" emperor. This meeting, like the one with his real brother Pu Je in the Forbidden City, results in the discovery that his power is an illusion. In his absence, his personal guard has been disarmed, and his chief minister sacked. Amakasu presents a decree giving the Japanese plenary powers, and demands his signature. This time the tray of ink is Pu Yi's to swallow. Amakasu also informs him that he cannot allow his honor to be stained by the Empress's infidelity. Her lover—Pu Yi's chauffeur—is summarily executed, her baby is given a fatal injection, and Wan Jung herself is spirited off to a "clinic." Pu Yi chases after her limousine, only to have the palace gates closed a second time in his face.

Bertolucci bypasses the war years, pausing only over the final collapse of the Japanese occupation and Pu Yi's capture by the Russians.[6] The film returns to the narrative present of his captivity in China. The former Son of Heaven is forced to clean his slops and to write his name on the floor. At the age of forty-four he must learn to tie his shoelaces, and—he whose feces were once sniffed and sifted like treasure by his eunuchs—to urinate into the communal bucket at night without waking his cellmates.

At first, Pu Yi adamantly maintains that he had been abducted by the Japanese and forced to assume his puppet throne. A propaganda film showing Japanese atrocities appears to shock him for the first time into realizing the nature of his collaboration. He responds, characteristically, by assuming full blame even for events of which, as his exasperated captors point out, he could have had no knowledge. For

Pu Yi, the question of actual responsibility does not exist; there is only absolute innocence or absolute guilt, just as there is no question of actual political power, but only of impotence or omnipotence.

Pu Yi finally accepts a new tutor in the camp's governor (Ying Ruocheng), who assumes personal supervision of his case. In a crucial scene, the governor confronts him with passages from Johnston's memoir, *Twilight in the Forbidden City*, which contradict his account of having been abducted by the Japanese. In reading Johnston's words, the governor symbolically assumes his mantle, patiently leading Pu Yi to the new "truth" he must learn. He adopts the trade of gardener, and habituates himself to his surroundings. After nine years, he is unexpectedly released. The governor calls him forward at a camp assembly, and, like a school principal graduating his prize pupil, gives him his freedom. "You see," he tells Pu Yi, "I will end up living in prison longer than you."

The governor's remark soon gets a grim twist. In the following scene, an elderly Pu Yi, now employed in the botanical gardens that

Captured by the Russians when Japan was defeated in World War II, puppet emperor Pu Yi (John Lone, 1st row c.) is sent to prison in China for re-education as prisoner 981.

were once part of the imperial grounds, is overtaken in the street by a troop of Red Guards brandishing posters of Mao and leading a group of shackled prisoners. Among them, to Pu Yi's horror, is the governor. Prodded by his captors to confess his guilt, he obstinately refuses, upon which he is forced to his knees in a parody of the kowtow. Pu Yi tries to intercede, telling the Guards that they have made a mistake: "This man is a good teacher!" But he is pushed aside, and history goes its way.

For Pu Yi, there is nowhere to go but home. The film's penultimate and climactic scene shows him in front of the ticket window of what could be taken at first for an afternoon movie. It is instead the admission gate to the Forbidden City, now open to all, but, at this moment of China's history, visited by none. Pu Yi wanders alone through the grounds and the palace. Coming upon his former throne, he begins to mount it. He is stopped by a young boy cadet, who seems to materialize from nowhere, and tells him that no one is permitted to climb the throne. Pu Yi explains that this was his chair, and, to prove it, he retrieves from behind the throne a tiny case containing the cricket he had sequestered there six decades before. The cricket crawls out slowly, brown with age but miraculously alive. Pu Yi turns with a smile, and shows it to the boy.

It is a magical moment — reminding us, among other things, of how much Bertolucci owes to Fellini — and one that brings the film to a conclusion that is as artistically gratifying as it seems politically problematic. In *The Last Emperor* Bertolucci at last lives through the revolution, and comes out on the other side to discover that, although everything has been turned upside down, in a fundamental sense nothing has changed. In Pu Yi, the emperor who is also a revolutionary Everyman, the man who lives the most singular childhood of the twentieth century to become the most anonymous of adults, the extraordinary nonentity who passes, with classic Marxist rigor, from feudal monarch to bourgeois dandy to Voltairean caretaker of what, in Mao's dystopic nightmare, is no one's garden, Bertolucci has found a perfect political analogue for the Freudian human comedy of which, for him, the social order is ultimately a projection. In the end, the emperor has no more escaped his cage than the cricket has; and yet, by the same token, he has always been safe in it. In the palaces at Beijing and Manchukuo, in the Villa Chan in Tianjin, in the Russian and Chinese camps, and, finally, in the open-air prison he shares with a billion fellow Chinese, he is

always in confinement: too sacred to be given freedom, too indis-
pensable to be harmed. Whether worshipped by millions as the Son
of Heaven or the relict bearer of an identity all but forgotten even by
himself, he retains the aura of the last man on earth who has ruled
by divine right. It is true of course that this aura is a tinsel absurdity,
a fraud; it is enough that Pu Yi believed in it once, and, in his heart
of hearts, believes it still.

"May the Son of Heaven live ten thousand years!" This toast, with
which Pu Yi is ritually greeted on state occasions, symbolizes the
immortality of the dynasty and the empire of which the emperor is
the mortal representative. By comparison, the face of Mao, bobbing
up and down on a stick in the arms of the Red Guard, seems a
precarious parody. Mao is omnipresent, and his retouched image has
a counterfeit softness, like an icon worn smooth by generations of
worshippers; yet the revolution that has so quickly devoured its
"teachers" seems destined not to last. One recalls the moment when
Pu Yi rises during the indoctrination film that depicts the Japanese
occupation. Hirohito announces Japan's surrender as the camera
pans over its devastated cities, and the commentator notes that this
was the first time his voice had ever been broadcast. Pu Yi's face
seems to register the fact that his brother emperor, too, has been a
man in a cage; and yet, at the same time, the film seems to acknowledge that only the emperor *has* the power of surrender: his voice
alone can command where all other authority has failed.[7]

Such implicit comparisons might seem paradoxical if not perverse, for of course there can be no substantive equation between the
world-historical figure of Mao and the figurehead Hirohito. It is
striking as well that, in a film ostensibly concerned with the greatest
peasant revolution in history, not a single peasant appears; and still
more so when one reflects on the glorification of the revolutionary
peasantry in *1900*. The very essence of fascism in Bertolucci's early
films is bad faith and betrayal; but how are we to take the portrayal
of a socialist revolution whose only sympathetic representative is
degraded for his pains? It is not difficult from this perspective to
understand Bertolucci's sudden respectability in Hollywood; the
reaction of his Chinese hosts and of his colleagues in the PCI (Italian
Communist Party) is likely to be more equivocal.[8]

In the end, the panorama of Chinese history, as of Italian, serves
Bertolucci as a backdrop for his continuing exploration of the Freudian romance. It is not Pu Yi's presence in the history of his time but

his exclusion from it that constitutes the real premise of the film. The very richness of Bertolucci's effects belies the claustral nature of his vision. The camera remains almost entirely within Pu Yi's physical perspective; a few brief scenes excepted, what he sees is what we see. The result is a revolution shown not through its heroes and leaders but its jailers, whose fate is to be jailed in their turn, and who are perceived through the eyes of a man born to perpetual imprisonment.

The nature of Pu Yi's condition necessarily makes him the revolution's most intrinsically hostile witness. Yet, while confining himself within Pu Yi's construction of reality, Bertolucci refuses to ratify it. The result is an all-pervasive irony. What Pu Yi might see, if that irony were relented, is a man destined to confinement under every regime and dispensation, a man in a cage who can see nothing but a change of uniform in his guards. But Pu Yi is vouchsafed nothing of the sort. He is a captive who fantasizes his condition as omnipotence, drawing out the universal infantile fantasy of Everyman into the make-believe supremacy of his imperial fortress, a delusion separated from madness only by the conspiracy of those around him to support it.

This "conspiracy of the elders," Bertolucci suggests, is all that we, as historical subjects, can know of reality; it is the world we are given but are powerless to make. Pu Yi's fantasy of omnipotence is both the measure of his concrete powerlessness and, as for childhood everywhere, its sole consolation. We do not, of course, remain children; we move forward in time to meet our fate, aided by that last illusion, freedom. What we discover, as our fathers pass, is that our history is no more ours to make than it was theirs; we, as they, are condemned to repeat it. Such is the vision *The Last Emperor* offers. When Pu Yi turns to show the cricket to the boy cadet who is both China's future and his own ageless self, the child in the palace untroubled by the passage of years, he affirms his own sovereignty, passing the scepter of a common destiny over the heads of the generations, the mandate of heaven itself.

It is too rich a gesture to be consummated; Pu Yi turns with his smile, and then disappears. The smile remains, like a Buddha's, fixed in historical memory. It leaves the mystery of authority, which so often abides in the most perfectly powerless, and which can never be quite renounced by those whom it has possessed.

The film ends, then, where it began, with the ancient imperial throne of the Middle Kingdom; and it ends, too, for all practical purposes, with the last emperor beckoning a child to climb it. It is a gesture of renewal, but also one of repetition; a new reign is about to begin, with or without an acknowledged emperor, for what the figure of the monarch symbolizes is the identification of the cycle of history — the collective destiny of all — with the life of one. The absence of monarchy, the overthrow of the old regime, is not, as modern revolutionaries have sometimes naively assumed, the overcoming of the cycle, but only the displacement of its image. The vacant throne, shown in the film's final scene to a tourist group, reminds us silently of the ineluctability of myth.

But Bertolucci does far more than to evoke the commonplace association between the ruler's life span and the historical cycle. By reflecting modern China's history through the man who was its most isolated and yet symbolically implicated figure, and by emphasizing the Oedipal drama as the central theme in that man's life, he offers a strikingly Freudian representation of historical process. Pu Yi signifies the collapse of history into Oedipal fantasy, a fantasy which, since it is shared by all, is retrojected onto the stage of our common life, and symbolized by the figure of the emperor, the immortal child-father of his people.

This representation is all the more effective because it avoids the reductiveness of psychohistory; it offers analogy and metaphor, not explanation. Pu Yi is no Hitler, writing his delusions large on history; his personal life had perhaps less effect on events at the level of agency than that of the humblest soldier in Mao's army. It is, indeed, his very isolation from the historical contest that offers Bertolucci the freedom of analogy. The private and the public realms both retain their autonomy, and no determining reality is accorded either.

In this sense, Bertolucci does not make a "choice" of Marx or Freud in The Last Emperor, but continues to search for ways of evoking the transcendent reality that embraces the vision of each. If what lies hidden in what Arthur Miller calls the "comradely promise" of Marxism is parricide, then the alienation of the Marxist subject of history and the anxiety of the Freudian subject of culture may have a common root too. What is rejected is the millennial aspect of revolutionary Marxism as the final and perfect resolution of history. If it is cynicism to accept the mere historical given, it is folly, Bertolucci now suggests, to attempt the transcendence of history as such. The permanent revolution can only be a revolt against mankind itself.

To maintain one's footing among such issues is no small accomplishment, and to depict a Pu Yi without slipping into bathos or condescension, to render both the crippled human being and the indefeasible symbol, is artistry of a special order. *The Last Emperor* is perhaps not a great film, but it is an important one. It signifies a new maturity in Bertolucci, and suggests, in its ability to reconcile the tragic and the ridiculous, what may finally be the making of a major comic artist.

NOTES

[1]Quoted in Tony Rayns, "Bertolucci in Beijing," *Sight and Sound*, 56, 1 (Winter 1986/87), p. 38.

[2]For more extended comments on Bertolucci's early work, see my "Bernardo Bertolucci, or Nostalgia for the Present," *Massachusetts Review*, 15, 4 (Fall 1975), 807–28.

[3]Cf. Robert Burgoyne, "The Somatization of History in Bertolucci's *1900*," *Film Quarterly*, XL, 1 (Fall 1986), 7–14, for a perceptive discussion of these issues.

[4]*1900* also marked the beginning of a disturbing tendency toward self-piratization in Bertolucci's films. The film opens with a young partisan who has assumed the name and identity of its martyred hero, Olmo, confronting the villainous padron, Alfredo, at the moment of liberation. This scene precisely inverts the plot of *The Spider's Stratagem*, whose hero, Athos, journeys backward in time to discover that his heroic father was a traitor and a fraud. The partisan is permitted to keep his illusion in *1900*; thus, what was emplotted as satire in *The Spider's Stratagem* returns, unmediated, as romance. Similarly, as Pauline Kael has pointed out *(The New Yorker*, November 30, 1987), the brutal squashing of the cat in *1900* is replicated in Pu Yi's squashing of his pet mouse in *The Last Emperor*. Bertolucci's work abounds in self-reference and self-quotation—inevitably, perhaps, in a project such as his—but the manipulation of symmetrically transposed images, symbols, and situations for radically different ends raises serious questions of control and integrity.

[5]Cf. the association of trains and terminals with circularity, immobilization, and temporal regression in *The Spider's Stratagem*. Trains figure prominently in *The Conformist* and *Last Tango in Paris* as well.

[6]Pu Yi's abortive attempt to escape by plane in this scene (the Russians, who descend by parachute, swarm aboard and capture it) underscores the symbolic significance of the train which brings him into captivity—chronologically the next scene in his life, although not in the film's narrative order.

[7]A similar point is made earlier when Amakasu presents Pu Yi with the decree that strips him of his power. Pu Yi has no choice but to sign it, of course, but Amakasu himself wears a pinned sleeve: he has lost an arm. On one level, the scene foreshadows the ultimate collapse of the Japanese empire, but in another, it underlines the ironic dependence of even the most brutal power on even the most spurious legitimacy: Amakasu directs Pu Yi's pen, but it is the emperor's hand alone that can effect the "transfer" of even a power he never possessed.

[8]The Chinese had rejected Bertolucci's first project, *Man's Fate*, on the grounds that it portrayed the revolutionary struggle too negatively.

In *Menace II Society*, Caine, O'Dog, and A-Wax (Tyrin Turner, Larenz Tate, and rapper MC Eiht) meet at a picnic (Top); Mr. Butler (Charles S. Dutton), a caring high school teacher, offers advice to the homiez (Bottom).

GRANT FARRED

MENACE II SOCIETY:
NO WAY OUT FOR THE BOYS IN THE HOOD

In an interview conducted barely a week after the outbreak of the 1992 up-
rising in Los Angeles, Mike Davis was asked what kind of politics he
thought the area's (inner) city youth would produce in the wake of the up-
heaval. Davis, who traced with unrelenting verve and panache the southern California city's political lineage in *City of Quartz*, answered Cindi
Katz and Neil Smith's question in a manner that reveals as much about the
conditions of political struggle in Los Angeles as about what constitutes
politics in that city today. "Part of the problem now," Davis explained, "is
that existing communal structures are being eroded just by the growth in
crime and gangs and so on. Gangs are the major compensatory social
structure that's been generated in the face of structural unemployment,
deindustrialization, etc. I mean the real genius of the city is that it has produced gangs as surrogate families."[1] Within this segregated urban space,
gangs have become the fulcrum of social activity in communities such as
Compton, Echo Park, Watts, and MacArthur Park. The gang is the institution that organizes political and economic life in the Los Angeles hood.
By recognizing how the "surrogate family" structure of L.A. has reconfigured the city's landscape, a gang such as the Crips has been able to locate
itself within the "leading circuit of international trade. Through 'crack'
they have discovered a vocation for the ghetto in L.A.'s new 'world city'
economy."[2] Although the "ghetto" and the "'world city'" overlap to form
complementary axes of the international economy, the populations of
southcentral and downtown L.A. live at a considerable remove from each
other. Young African-Americans, Latinos, Chicanos, and Asian-Americans
experience their daily lives, to say nothing of the means by which they develop political strategies of resistance and survival, in decidedly ambivalent
ways. For African-Americans or Latinos partial economic enfranchisement
coexists problematically with a larger political and social alienation.[3]

The embattled urban communities Davis describes in *City of Quartz*'s later chapters—"Homegrown Revolution," "Fortress L.A.," and "The Hammer and the Rock"—bear a distinct resemblance to the landscape inhabited by the youthful African-American protagonists in movies such as *Boyz N the Hood* and *Menace II Society*. *Menace II Society*'s main characters, the teenage Caine and O'Dog, demonstrate many of the abilities developed by L.A.'s inner city youth—familiarity with the ghetto and an understanding of how the youth service international commerce; the facility to move, high-tech beepers in hand and guns at the ready, adroitly between the realm of formal education and the informal crack-based economic sector. So skilled in the ways of the L.A. economy are the recent high school graduate Caine and his friends O'Dog, Stacey and Sharief, that they appear far more adept and better versed in the gang world than they do in an under-resourced inner city classroom. *Menace II Society* is a youthful world attuned to the demands of global (crack) capital, a world in which the very structure of gangs, and by extension community life, has adapted itself to the realities of inner city deindustrialization. As joblessness came to be the dominant mode of life in the hood, so the "o.g.s"—original gangstas who traditionally occupy senior positions within the gang—found a new niche for themselves as the link between international cartels and the L.A. streets. *Menace II Society*'s o.g., A-Wax, but more commonly known as G, a home-boy in his mid-twenties, performs the functions of middle-management in this corner of Compton. The rather unimaginatively named G's position calls primarily for the supervision of his employees Caine and O'Dog in activities such as gun-running, drug dealing, and car theft. It is telling, however, that in the social sphere—house parties, cookouts, watching television, gambling, in relationships with women, and so on—the o.g. is treated as the equal of his homiez. Outside of his special—crack-derived—economic status the o.g. has no particular authority in the hood. G's limited seniority emanates from beyond Compton, contingent upon the circuit of international drug exchange which he services but over which he has very little control.

One of the consequences of not examining the discrepancies between the o.g.'s status in the spheres of commerce and leisure is that the economic is investigated only vicariously, and therefore insufficiently, via the social. Instead of a critique of the external origins or the internationalism of the drug industry, we have *Menace II Society*'s preoccupation with the local economic and social dimension of the trade. The camera is trained incessantly on Compton, never straying far beyond its confines. The advantage of this particular cinematic strategy is that we get a full portrayal of the social undergirdings of southcentral Los Angeles and the means by which this urban community retains its battered shape. *Menace II Society* focuses on the informal mechanisms of ghetto education—a syllabus grounded in the practice of urban survival—and the process by which the inner city produces intricate webs of social interaction which render the residents dependent upon one another. We see in immense detail how African-American youth rely upon one another not only to survive, but to create a culture that can sustain them all, however temporarily.

Ghetto interdependence forges a distinct culture, one achieved through repertoires of aesthetic representation (dress codes, speech patterns, vocabularies, and modes of transportation), particular forms of socializing (summer picnics or house parties which often hinge on violent, and potentially fatal exchanges of machismo), and the maintenance of the informal industries they manage (drugs, car theft, petty crime). So assiduously is attention paid to Compton that the most removed from the hood we get is Caine and O'Dog's interrogation, by a black cop no less, at the LAPD's downtown headquarters; for residents of Southcentral that short geographical distance amounts to a considerable ideological journey. Because of *Menace II Society*'s insistent attention to the local, the tensions precipitated among the homiez as they move back and forth between the social and economic spaces, and the different relationships and hierarchies which apply there, are left unexplored. *Menace II Society* is provocative in its representation of G as a malcontent among his Compton peers, but the movie fails to explain how the o.g. negotiates the disjuncture between his transient economic authority and his more permanent social parity. Is this discrepancy a rationale for his brooding or his anger? More importantly, however, G is presented as a post-industrial o.g., an original gangsta forced to spend more time engaged in leisure-making than profit-making activities because his share of the economic pie has shrunk so considerably. A Malthusian figure of sorts, G is nevertheless in possession of an incomplete, residual understanding of the links between Downtown and Compton. (Unlike G, Caine's generation has never had to develop even a partial comprehension of the world beyond Compton. For them, there is no possibility of non-coercive interaction with downtown L.A. And, for routine exchanges with the LAPD, Caine and O'Dog were adequately schooled.) The irony is that in reactivating these dormant connections, G fails to anticipate that he is endangering himself as well as those homiez/employees with whom he is disenchanted.

The discontinuity between the o.g.'s economic and social status is symptomatic of the bifurcation between the African-American inner city community's partial economic enfranchisement and its entrenched political disenfranchisement. Cynically implicated in the nexus of the city's economic processes, the hood has no purchase on either the political structures dominated by whites or on the sanctioned practices of that structure. Even as the hood's residents contribute to L.A.'s economic and political growth as an international center, none of that capital is used for the upkeep or improvement of Compton. Political alienation, however, in both the narrow electoral sense and the more complex sense, is investigated only incidentally in the reading of the film. This essay is primarily concerned with the internal tensions and stresses — emotional, personal, sexual, and psychic—that characterize life in this *menaced society*. As a community forced to subsist on the urban peripheries of the body politic, Compton will be explored in terms of its ghettoized space, its limited resources and its severely restricted lifestyle choices.

Compton, in which Caine and his homiez live, is positioned on the outskirts of Los Angeles's political arrangement. To borrow a description from Andrew Ross, Compton is a "south-central Los Angeles neighborhood which is booby-trapped everywhere by the corporate police state for the 'self-destruction' of its inhabitants—gun shops and liquor stores on every street corner, the omnipresence of searchlights from LAPD helicopters circling overhead."[4] Ross's bleak description of southcentral life is consistent with the cinematic representation by the directors of *Menace II Society*, the twin filmmakers Allen and Albert Hughes who were 21 years old when they made the movie in 1993. *Menace II Society* is the world of community-wide unemployment and a dispirited education system (as embodied by Charles Dutton's Mr. Butler, a politically astute, occasionally cynical teacher) whose pupils are looking outside its structure for their economic future. That the life chances of the residents of Compton are few is not incidental. Rather, Compton's general social decay is the result of downtown Los Angeles's policy to accommodate (and accelerate) the "self-destruction" of these communities. Compton's parlous state, Mike Davis points out, has its origins in the city's plan to deliberately underfund non-Anglo areas: "While city resources (to the tune of $2 billion) have been absorbed in financing the corporate renaissance of downtown, southcentral L.A. has been markedly disadvantaged even in the receipt of anti-poverty assistance, 'coming in far behind West Los Angeles and the Valley in access to vital human services and job-training funds'" (*City of Quartz*, 304). The absence of all-purpose shopping malls and the prevalence of "gun shops and liquor stores" represent as much a destructive political strategy as they do the only viable economic activities in the hood. The grocery stores, the drugstores and other vital businesses have long since fled the dangers and unprofitability of the inner city for the lucrative safety of the heavily guarded downtown malls.

The Los Angeles Police Department, in its turn, takes as its Compton brief the surveillance of the hood not only for the protection of the inhabitants or the eradication of the drug trade, but for the confinement of both the hood's inhabitants and drugs to the inner city.[5] If the "LAPD helicopters maintain an average nineteen-hour-per-day vigil over 'high crime areas', tactically coordinated to patrol car forces, and exceeding even the British army's aerial surveillance of Belfast," then why is it not possible to combat the drug trafficking more effectively (*City of Quartz*, 252)? The "booby traps" are cynically, and inextricably, woven into the texture of Southcentral life. The most pernicious features of these traps are as much their ubiquity as the ways in which they prohibit exit from the besieged black enclaves. Ringed by the LAPD from above and on the ground, Caine and O'Dog can only turn inward, back into their depleted community. In this moment of acute economic depression, Compton dwellers have conferred upon the only products which they can acquire the status of vital resources: guns, B'mers (BMWs), black Nissan Maximas, gold jewelry, and, most disconcertingly, women. Within the inner city these resources are the only means by which the young men (the hood is clearly gendered) can secure if not a future, then at least a hiply-dressed and jewelry-adorned today. Compton is a hood in which rival gangs of African-American youth are in competition for an enclosed piece of turf, fighting to stay alive and to keep possession of the only jobs they are likely to have.

The fatally-tagged Caine, whose name resonates with suggestions of the Biblically damned as well as the narcotic (in one of the movie's most sardonic moments, G mockingly calls him "Co-caine"), and O'Dog (whom the voiceover considers "America's nightmare: young, black, and he didn't give a fuck") represent but one band of homiez located within the larger L.A. world-city economic structure. The capacity for conflict between gangs is invariably heightened by the constricted area available to them. Compton represents the impossibility of transgressing the artificially-imposed boundaries of the "carceral inner cit[y]" (*City of Quartz*, 223). Caine and O'Dog's generation has been imprisoned within their hood with an efficaciousness that approximates brutality. The only impact these youth are likely to make on the world beyond Compton, besides their servicing of the drug trade, is by becoming an official statistic of the African-American or Latino male variety. According to a protagonist in the movie *Mi Vida Loca*, these young men's futures are overdetermined. Their life trajectories are such that they will end up in only one of three places: in "prison, disabled or dead by the time they're 21." In a movie of just over ninety minutes, *Menace II Society*'s young men experience these fates with an alarming frequency.

Overdetermination, then, is the dominant trope of this movie. The ghetto is the universe for African-Americans and there is no way out of the ghetto. Arthur Jaffa, director of photography for Spike Lee's *Crooklyn*, endorses the Hughes brothers' representation of African-American life for its unflinching accuracy. "What makes *Menace II Society* devastatingly on target," in Jaffa's view, "is the relentless way in which it assays the cyclic nature of black-on-black violence and the pathological strategies employed by those for whom there is no escape."[6] With the ghetto cordoned off and "no escape" possible, the most "devastating" pathology that can follow is that its residents are destined to be its only victims. Within the tradition of "New Jack Cinema," it is *Menace II Society*'s fierce inexorability, the complete lack of any alternative to the community's seemingly inexhaustible capacity for self-destruction, that distinguishes the Hughes brothers' project from its predecessors in this genre.

"New Jack Cinema" is a genre of African-American filmmaking in Hollywood that takes its name from the Mario Van Peebles movie *New Jack City*, a brand of film which focuses mostly on the experiences of young black men in the post-Reagan inner city. Other movies in the genre include *Hangin With The Home Boys, Juice, Straight Out of Brooklyn* and *Boyz N the Hood*.[7] These late 1980s and early 1990s protagonists, mostly gangsta-type figures who make their living through drugs and informal activities, are portrayed within an inner city context that counterposes crumbling community structures with the home-boy's ostentatious and luxurious lifestyle. The movie's plot is usually premised on a violent conflict between the New Jack character and another African-American male figure who offers the possibility for some form of individual and community regeneration. The intra-community conflict between the young men who manage the drug-based economy and those who propose long-term political and economic restructuring involves the hood in its entirety. New Jack cinema is adept at demonstrating how women (with the ever-attendant problematic of misogyny, patriarchy, and stereotypical representation), older people, young children, the employed, the unemployed/unemployable, and systems of belief—Christianity and Islam—are all implicated in, affected by, and often victims of these internecine conflicts. The violence in these movies about the hood requires the loss of several young lives via shootouts in order to resolve the social antagonisms.[8] This resolution serves to wreak further havoc with the social fabric of the inner city. Termination of the violence is only a temporary phenomenon because while the New Jack man or the destructive forces he represents is defeated, the specter of African-American urban decay remains palpable.

Because New Jack Cinema is a genre in its formative stage, there has been a tendency to make comparisons chronologically—the most recent film is discussed in terms of its relation to its immediate predecessor. Nowhere has this critical predilection been more evident than in the case of John Singleton and the Hughes brothers' movies. *Menace II Society* has been read as an intensification of the violence that characterized *Boyz N the Hood*. "*Menace II Society*," in Harry Allen's opinion, "is like *Boyz N the Hood* on nitro."[9] The reasons for the comparison are self-evident. Both movies take as their principal characters teenage men locked into the declining economy of the ghetto. Singleton and the Hughes twins both set their films in southcentral L.A., an environment where joblessness is the order of the day, with only sports scholarships and drug-dealing offering ways out of the economic malaise. Both movies deal with female protagonists in a very problematic way. However, unlike the "redemptive" *Boyz N the Hood*, *Menace II Society* holds out little optimism for the future of African-American life in the inner city. Within the "pathological" world that is Compton, the Hughes twins see no possibility of urban renewal, no chance of reconstructing life for black inner city communities, and no real life chances for African-Americans. While Singleton's *Boyz N the Hood* is set in a similarly depressed neighborhood dealing with the same kind of street violence, *Menace II Society*'s predecessor is as much a depiction of inner city devastation as it is a critical engagement with the socio-political forces that produce these conditions.

Boyz N the Hood created in Furious Styles, Larry Fishburne's African-American father, a lower-middle-class businessman who performs for his son (and his son's friends), the role of community ideologue and mentor.[10] These young men, who represent a generation of black youth in need of an education about the struggles facing their community, are confronted with precisely such a father. Styles traces the roots of urban decay, addresses the politics of that process (with no small amount of pontificating), and critiques gentrification and the deracinating effects thereof for the young inner city residents. It should be said, however, that much of the currency and political credibility that accrue to Styles's redeemed African-American father—the parental figure organically connected to the hood—derives from an opposition to the inadequate, bourgeois, corporate mother who has raised the son into his teens. Unlike the aptly-named Furious, the mother is represented as a parent who does not understand how the ghetto functions; she certainly does not know how to prepare her son for the challenges young black men have to face daily. It is his father's task, she says as she leaves her son in his care, to teach the youth to be a "man." The ex-Mrs. Styles is a woman unsuited for the responsibility of shepherding the next generation of African-American men to physical and psychological maturity. That function can be performed only by men, preferably those familiar with the mine-filled landscape that is the hood.

With the problematic representation of African-American women left critically unattended, the gender tensions unremarked upon and barely interrogated, Furious is freed to become a mouthpiece for Singleton's several socio-political attacks. The lack of inner city housing, the parlous state of education, the exploitative tendencies of college sport and its expedient recruitment techniques, the artificially abbreviated lives of black males, generational disputes, and even parenting itself fall within the domain of *Boyz N the Hood*'s African-American father. It is the African-American father's critiques, a commentary inscribed with a singular determination to imagine ways out of the devastation and violence of the drug culture, a will to renovate the ghetto without uprooting its inhabitants, that set *Boyz N the Hood* apart from *Menace II Society*.

If we were to provide a parental analogy for *Menace II Society*'s pessimism about the prospects for African-American life against the willed optimism of *Boyz N the Hood*, we would identify Charles Dutton's father as the emaciated analogy for Fishburne. Dutton's father, like Fishburne's, is a street smart man; unlike Styles, however, the local high school teacher Mr. Butler is a desperate man, one so devoid of a strategy for survival in the hood that he is willing to entertain any possibility that will keep his son Sharief alive. Clutching at every socio-political possibility the hood offers, Mr. Butler is prepared to accept the boy's conversion to the Nation of Islam. Mr. Butler is not in full agreement with the Nation of Islam, but he sees the movement as the last resort which can save his son from the menace of the Compton streets. "If Allah can make him a better man than Jesus," Mr. Butler intones in a voice riddled with anxiety, "then I'm all for it." As Mr. Butler echoes the same concern about the production of masculinity as the ex-Mrs. Styles, the ideological differences between the two films are chillingly distilled. Mr. Butler may be politically astute enough to warn Caine and Sharief that the "hunt is on and you're the prey," a lesson delivered in his (empty) classroom, but he cannot save his son when the inevitable shootout occurs. In their own ways, both the fatal shootout (the movie's culminating scene) and the classroom vacated of young, live black bodies, can stand as the central metaphors for the gutted community of Compton. The empty classroom reminds us that even when a resource is made available to this community, there is no one to take advantage of it: the youth are either dead or securing a future which they have come to learn formal education cannot provide.

It is thus brutally ironic, but all too predictable, that Sharief, Stacey, and Caine die in a shootout just as all three of them are about to leave the hood. Sharief and Stacey are about to leave for Kansas where the latter will take up a football scholarship (reminiscent of a scene in *Boyz N the Hood*), while Caine is off to Atlanta to start a new life with his girlfriend Ronnie and her son Anthony. Against the backdrop of the containment of the black ghetto and the superficially restricted movement of its inhabitants, we are compelled to ask: is Atlanta devoid of black ghettoes? Are the Atlanta ghettoes not subject to some form of surveillance? And, most importantly, is escape for the African-American male merely a car trip away? The answer to all these questions is of course a rhetorical "No." The final bloody scene in *Menace II Society* makes plain that Caine and his homiez are so locked into a mode of internecine strife that it evacuates locations such as "Kansas" and "Atlanta" of their geographical specificity, reducing those cities to metaphors and imaginary extra-territorial locations that can have no relevance for those who inhabit the hood. Compton, we are made to see again and again, cannot be escaped. It retains a stranglehold on those who live there and, because of the conditions that prevail there, it is infinitely capable of setting in motion forces that make an easy exit impossible. The film's overdetermination, then, may be unremittingly claustrophobic (for both the Compton residents and the viewers) but it is also key to what sets the movie apart from others in the genre.

Within the configuration of forces designated "external" in Compton, we should list not only the LAPD and international drug cartels, but also black women, that inner city constituency positioned within the hood but outside the homiez's inner circle. Situated within a community that is materially under-resourced and ideologically isolated, the Compton women possess an extremely limited social mobility. They can only move on, and occasionally beyond, the fringes of home-boy culture. As a group that is so marginalized within Compton's dominant culture, the women play a disproportionately large role in the lives of the community's men. The shootout in which Sharief, Stacey and Caine are killed occurs because *Menace II Society*'s chief protagonist has gotten a young woman, Ilena, pregnant and refuses to take responsibility for fatherhood. When Ilena calls Caine with the news, he tells her that it can't be his because, as he says, "The jimmy was real tight." When Ilena's cousin (an unnamed protagonist) approaches Caine and tries to get him to acknowledge paternity, Caine and O'Dog beat him up. The aggrieved male cousin then organizes his homiez "to do" the reluctant father and his friends in *Menace II Society*'s bloody final scene. Ann Powers argues, with a hard-edged irony, that it is Ilena who "destroys Caine."[11] *Menace II Society* is a world in which, Powers claims, it is "girls like [Ilena] (so fertile that even an extra-tight jimmy fails to keep her men free)" who "set the ultimate trap, whether they mean to or not." Is Caine, so clearly marked for disaster by both social context and the lineage of his name, finally undone by neither phenomenon but by a woman, an excessively "fertile" daughter of Eve? In a cinematic discourse that draws upon the trope of the lapsarian moment, the movie converts the social collapse of Compton, which originates in internal and external patriarchal institutions and practices which disempower women, into a political burden for which its female protagonists bear an inordinate amount of responsibility. *Menace II Society*'s representation of women is problematic throughout, but nowhere more so than in the disjuncture between the film's underdevelopment of the female protagonists (the women are afforded very little on-screen time) and their disproportionate implication in the scenes of greatest violence and destruction.

Of the women, Ronnie is most central to the storyline only because she is closely related to two of the movie's principal men, namely Caine and G. Ronnie occupies a focal position within Caine's group of homiez because she represents the main site of sexual tension: not only do Caine and G come to blows about her, but Stacey and Sharief tease Caine about not sleeping with her. Ronnie is also pivotal to the plot because of her relationship with Purnell, the father of her son Anthony, who is serving a life sentence. Purnell acted as Caine's surrogate father by initiating him into the workings of the street. Caine is portrayed in at least two

ways as his mentor's doppelganger: it is he who takes on the role of surrogate father to Anthony by teaching the boy street-talk and introducing
him to guns at the age of five; and, it is Caine who succeeds Purnell as
Ronnie's lover. Even as Ronnie is represented as an independent and
moral working-class woman who refuses money derived from illegal
sources (offered by Caine), a woman dedicated to leaving the hood by
acquiring her high school diploma while raising her son and holding
down a job, much of her character is defined by the men who surround
her. Often Ronnie is simply the vehicle for relating the history of the
Menace II Society's men—she sketches Caine's biography, she situates
him along Purnell's trajectory, and she provides the background to the
Purnell-G relationship.

Ronnie's deep implication in the lives of Menace II Society's homiez
and her fiercely working-class status also serve the cinematic function of
staging her as a counterpoint to the ostensibly bourgeois Ilena—the
privileged teenager who drives around in her flashy sports car. As two
teenage mothers (since abortion is ostensibly not an option for a middle-
class black woman like Ilena) and women located within the constraints
of a patriarchal structure, Ronnie and Ilena are more alike than different. The movie, however, foregrounds their dissimilarities so as to displace the source of violence from the men and the larger social disenfranchisement to the women. In order to establish them as antagonists,
Ronnie is depicted as self-reliant while Ilena is shown to be dependent
upon the men around her. (It is striking that while Ronnie and Ilena are
both at some stage, never simultaneously, involved with Caine, they
never exchange words, let alone hostilities. The articulation and acting
out of antagonism is a strictly male preserve.)

The class distinctions that separate Ronnie from Ilena stand not only
as a marker of the discrepant privileges available to them, but also as a
measure of their very different levels of agency—the home-girl acts on
her own and her son's behalf while the pregnant bourgeois girl has action taken on her behalf. The paradox is that finally Ronnie's agency
means as little as Ilena's lack of voice because they are both reduced to
spectators as the men settle the debate about them. The most poignant
irony is that their affections and their ultimate fates are tied up in the
same home-boy; the black woman's narrative is inextricably bound up in
the lives of black men. When the men act on their behalf, whether it is
Ilena's cousin against Caine or Stacey telling Ronnie to "stay down"
when the shootout starts, the inequities in the two women's social standing are of secondary importance to their shared disempowerment. Class

distinctions have no bearing on how the men of Compton act because for them the hood is a social structure in which class inequities do not apply. The bourgeois Ilena's cousin is then, not surprisingly, as much a home-boy as Caine or O'Dog. Home-boys, their inter-group antagonisms apart, share the same material and ideological relationship to the world of Compton and downtown L.A. However, while women can be uniformly named "bitches" or "hoes" or "pussy," descriptions which litter the script, that does not mean that those terms are devoid of class identification. Bourgeois Ilena is not working-class Ronnie. Or, not to put too fine a point on it, Ronnie is not a "bitch" in the same way that Ilena is a "ho."

While Allen and Albert Hughes's portrayal of women relies upon misogynistic language and shows itself to be unreflexively rooted in a patriarchal discourse, the movie's gender problematic operates in another way which is more insidious. *Menace II Society* is remarkable for its ability to write into its linguistic designations of its female protagonists the depictions of women as catalysts for catastrophe. The movie dramatizes the female body as the site of male desire which rapidly transforms itself into a lightning rod for male disaster. Compton's men can only conduct their lives in relative safety when women are absent. The terms "bitch" and "ho," which depend on popular understandings of women as sexually available, insatiable and promiscuous, rely less on their derogatory connotations than on a reinscription of women as inner city *femmes fatales*—the bearers of male destruction. The *femme fatale* quality—or the Eve factor—results from the entanglement of the men's sexual desire for these women and the social forces which that desire sets in (fatal) motion. The fatality of male attraction to women can be demonstrated by a brief comparison of *Menace II Society*'s two most violent scenes. It is striking that the only scene of group violence which does not originate with women is infinitely more bloody—Caine is carried bleeding profusely into a hospital—but claims fewer lives. The scene to which I am referring revolves unambiguously around Compton inter-group hostilities and deeply personal bonds. Harold, Caine's cousin, is shot by a rival group in a carjacking. Soon after, Caine, O'Dog, and G exact revenge. In terms of the plotline this episode is vital because Caine kills someone for the first time, a rite of passage that marks this home-boy's coming of age in the hood. Set against the larger narrative, however, the "Harold scenes" merely signify a stage in Caine's development—the acquisition of a certain hood maturity, overseen by G.

Although the violent culmination of *Menace II Society* strongly suggests that it is the internal dynamics of Compton that ultimately bury Caine and Sharief in the hood, such a rendering tells only part of the story. The narrative can only be completed if we bring into focus the movie's opening scene. Our introduction to *Menace II Society* is the spectacle of O'Dog shooting a Korean store owner and his wife because the teenager thinks, or pretends to think, that they "dissed" his mother. Caine is a reluctant accessory to this crime. O'Dog, who is streetwise beyond his years, keeps his head enough to take the video of the murder from the store's surveillance camera. Believing that he is safe within the hood because Compton's internal workings are immune from the scrutiny of the LAPD detective squad, O'Dog plays the video for all of Southcentral to see. In fact, he takes a great deal of pleasure in repeatedly going over the shooting with his friends. While O'Dog's actions are in and of themselves brazen, especially when he remarks that he might start selling copies of the videotape for "$59.95," it is his repeated playing of the crime that precipitates, unknowingly, the inevitability of Caine's demise. The video of the Korean store owners' murder becomes, in a swift *dénouement*, the link between internal stresses and violence within Compton and the surveillance system of the LAPD.

Since the Hughes brothers' construction of ghetto devastation inevitably revolves around a woman, Ronnie is the vehicle for the *dénouement*. Ronnie is the *femme fatale* who sparks the tension between men with the crucial exception that in this case, unlike Ilena's, conflict erupts between men within the same group of homiez. What is particularly revealing about the violent intra-group exchange is that it involves two homiez, Caine and G, between whom there has up to now been apparently little animus. Within embattled inner city communities, the bonds of male loyalty can be particularly brittle when confronted with the promises of the female body. While the ties that hold these men together against the outside world are strong on the surface, theirs is in reality a camaraderie especially susceptible to internal dispute and disunity. The timing of the scene between Caine and G is laden with portent because the violence occurs during the farewell party for the Atlanta-bound trio. More precisely, the encounter takes place just after Caine and Ronnie have made love for the first time. G, unaware of this development (though whether that would have altered his responses we can but speculate), harasses Ronnie.

An angry Caine responds by attacking G and administering a humiliating beating about which the other homiez taunt the o.g. G recognizes that he cannot redeem himself without exacting revenge from Caine and, paradoxically, the only means by which he can secure retribution is by exceeding the geographical and ideological boundaries of Compton. O'Dog's videocassette is tailor-made to achieve this end and G, with a maliciousness that impairs his understanding of how the Los Angeles surveillance system operates, sends the incriminating evidence to the LAPD. G, the middle-management Compton gang member, positions himself as the link between the external and internal forces of surveillance. The deprivations and humiliations of the hood, as experienced by G, enable the LAPD to perform its repressive functions without ever leaving their downtown offices. The investigation, arraignment and sentencing, as it were, is being conducted for them by the conditions of disenfranchisement which transform a gang member into a police officer by proxy. The production of Compton as a "carceral inner city" maximizes internal pressures so that the LAPD does not know, and may never know precisely who that "officer" is, but they do know that they have created and maintained the conditions which will encourage persons such as G to perform the tasks of impromptu community policing and inner city surveillance.

In the face of an omnipotent repressive system, one which functions as much by force as it does by deliberate underdevelopment and neglect, there is truly no way out of Compton for Caine or O'Dog or G. If Caine had survived the shootout with Ilena's cousin, which he might have had he not thrown himself over his surrogate son Anthony, then the long arm of the law would surely have apprehended him, be it in L.A. or Atlanta. Caine's gesture toward the young boy is replete with a double irony: in rejecting Ilena, and his (unborn) biological child, and committing himself to Ronnie and Anthony, Caine repeats the Purnell trajectory of fulfilling the role of surrogate parent while not performing those duties in relation to his own child. However, while Purnell was able to guide Caine through his early teens, Anthony will not be the beneficiary of such support and advice. Within the Compton landscape, Caine's is a violent but heroic death. Caine's self-sacrificing act constitutes a rare moment of pathos in *Menace II Society*, an instance in which loyalty and love culminate in a life-affirming act. O'Dog, lone survivor of the gunfight at the Compton corral, will not escape the LAPD's repressive apparatus despite the fact that G's anger was aimed at Caine and not him. The LAPD has the videocassette and it is only a matter of time before they arrest O'Dog, or he meets his end in a fashion similar to that of his best friend. O'Dog, like Caine and Sharief, is too rooted in the lifestyle of the hood to be granted a reprieve. G, we cannot help but think, will go the same way, sooner rather than later.

The relationship among home-boys is predicated upon loyalty, a highly personal structure of intra-group affiliation which shores them up against the rest of the world. Loyalty, however, is a double-edged sword. The first edge is designed to protect them against the external elements, such as other gangs and the LAPD; the second edge, on the other hand, represents a jagged blade that is turned inward, serving no apparent purpose except to be used by the homiez against themselves. The home-boys have constructed out of their besieged ghetto a socially incestuous milieu, one that is most vulnerable to internal dissent. As a dramatic venture, *Menace II Society* thrives upon the malignant quality of the homiez's loyalty to one another. Intra-group bonds, abnormally reenforced from without, are parlayed into an intense commitment to each other, a system of personal connections that seldom fails. If it fails, a homie dies, as in Harold's case. When the bonds of loyalty fray, however, it is not so much a result of the pressures from outside as from the pressures of individual desires. It is when desires conflict and individual needs supersede communal ones that homiez come into confrontation, as happened with Caine and G. In an environment where their individual agency is so contingent, negotiated within such narrow boundaries, within pressure cooker confines, it is inevitable that moments will arise when each home-boy will want to give full expression to his sense of himself. In that moment, a homie will almost certainly find himself in confrontation with his "bros."

Menace II Society, finally, is an account of the production of African-American urban culture. The Hughes brothers provide an estimation of the resources it requires to sustain an inner city community, the key item being whether or not that community is creatively and materially solvent. In conducting this appraisal, the movie finds a culture whose chief assets, its modes of representation (such as its innovative dress codes, its code of inner city fealty, its musical creativity, its richly textured speech patterns), are being liquidated by a combination of the external demands and the costs attendant to those modes. Among those costs are a vicious homophobia (O'Dog shoots a homeless man who offers to "suck his dick" for the $2 it will take the man to buy some crack; this after the homeless man had tried to sell O'Dog a burger for $2), an unreflective misogyny, and a sometimes ambivalent machismo. In its starkest moments, *Menace II Society* is a cold presentation of the costs involved in sustaining inner city African-American culture. Measured against the devastation that marks the ghetto, the dynamism and creativity of the culture is rendered almost negligible, insufficient protection against the "nihilism" (to invoke Cornel West's term) that is wreaking havoc with the social construction that is African-American inner city life. However contentious a description nihilism is, it has a resonance and validity in *Menace II Society* because of the ways in which Compton functions—a community in which there is no way out, except death. The Hughes brothers leave us with an image of the inner city that is hardened by inexorability: the hood is ideologically landlocked, imaginatively and politically bereft of responses to the combined forces of internal/external destruction, a resourceless and futureless ghetto. Its potential implosion may serve as its final resource, however, the only way in which inner city inhabitants can register a protest against downtown. In this instance, the Southcentral implosion could very well be read as an explosion: the reconfiguration of the Los Angeles map by challenging the borders of surveillance and disenfranchisement.

ACKNOWLEDGEMENT

I am grateful to Gitanjali Maharaj for her reading of this paper, particularly her suggestions for the version delivered at the University of Pennsylvania's "Seeking Ground: Figuring a Black Cultural Imaginary" in November 1993. My thanks also to Cynthia Young for her critique of the essay in its later stages.

NOTES

[1]"L.A. Intifada: Interview with Mike Davis," Cindi Katz and Neil Smith, *Social Text* 33, 27.

[2]Mike Davis, *City of Quartz: Excavating the Future in Los Angeles* (New York: Vintage Books, 1992), 309.

[3]See George Lipsitz's "Cruising Around the Historical Bloc: Postmodernism and Popular Music in East Los Angeles" in *Time Passages: Collective Memory and American Popular Culture* (Minneapolis: University of Minnesota Press, 1990) for a critique of the experience of Mexican-Americans, Chicanos, and Latinos in Los Angeles. Lipsitz's chapter on these communities brings together the issues of, inter alia, postmodernity, immigration, deracination, ethnicity, cultural appropriation and exclusion. One of the most effective aspects of his critique is his description of how economic disenfranchisement undergirds all the other facets of minority life in Los Angeles: "For ethnic minorities, failure to assimilate into dominant cultures can bring exclusion from vital economic and political resources" (133). Of course, the prevailing experience of ethnic minorities is deliberate "exclusion" from the realms of politics and the formal economic sector.

ARTHUR MILLER

SNIPS ABOUT MOVIES

I confess to a certain amount of cynicism when it comes to movies, but the form invites trickery and that may even account for the scarcity of films we think of as sincere. After you've said everything it is the cinematographer whose stuff you see and it is up to him to lead the eye toward the story or away from it, toward the mood of a shot or against it. I speak from very little experience but some striking incidents.

John Huston used Russel Metty a number of times, *The Misfits* included, the reason being Metty's scorn for "art." He worked with an electrician and a grip and that was it. He'd set up an interior shot in ten minutes maximum and with a very few lights. When I complained at one point that we were not getting enough background into the film, the noble and permanent Nevada mountains against which the wanderings of men were so unimportant and fleeting, he replied, "They don't buy tickets to see scenery. It's tits and ass all the way." Between shots, when his two assistants were moving the camera around he would disappear to a phone to call Texas to see if an oil well he had invested in had begun to squirt, and that is what *really* interested him. He was not the only cinematographer of that generation who proudly affected an anti-art attitude. It was partly based on their absolute indispensability. You could drop an actor, a scene, easily replace a director or a writer, but the thing had to be shot and if the cinematographer was not the engineer of the train — that was the director — he certainly was the chief mechanic who actually made it all happen on the screen.

They thought of movies as a sort of primitive drum that beat out the simplest, basic emotions — greed, lust, fear, bravado, sobriety, drunkenness, and so on. It was an unalienated art designed for the masses. And that I believe is what it is. Alienated film — Fellini, Bergman, Kurosawa, those visionaries, simply does not penetrate any nation. Fellini, excepting for *8 1/2* never made any money here or in Italy; the masses didn't come. Jerry Lewis made money, no doubt. Fellini continued to get financing from people who never expected to get their money back but were honored to have helped pay for his films. The great postwar neo-realists, DeSica and Rossellini, were all but unknown to their own countrymen who stood in line for Betty Grable, William Powell, Westerns and anything that did not resemble the shambles that Italy was as it emerged from the war. What they wanted was not reality but hope, which is what Hollywood always had by the shovelful.

My European friends who make movies, or try to, are close to despair about ever competing for audiences — and financing — against the American Imperialist film industry. Walk down Champs Élysée and try to find a marquee that is not touting an American movie. In this century the American artist-businessman, sans theory or anything more complicated than happy greed and the navel-level acumen that goes with it, invented the pop culture which is swamping the world. Why we have been so rapturously successful abroad is a good question. I wonder whether it is because this is the first truly multi-national, multi-ethnic culture since probably the Rome of the Empire. Our pictures are not particularly made for export, unless you count Minneapolis and New Orleans as foreign cities. But the variety of cultures in America is such that a movie artist here has a built-in-the-bone sense of what different sorts of people can understand and take to heart. In short, he is an unconscious universalist and if not he dies on the vine.

As I mentioned in *Timebends*, my autobiography, the first movie I ever saw was projected on a white sheet on the roof of our apartment house up in Harlem in the early Twenties. I know nothing about how this arrangement came about but there it was, a sheet in the dark night with a couple of dozen folding chairs facing it. When the show was finished I ran around the sheet to see the people whose pictures I had just seen on it. There was nobody there, only the stars floating over Harlem. Where had they gone? And so quickly!

As for writers and film, who ever heard of somebody buying a ticket to a movie because so-and-so wrote it? And this disregard has its root in the relative importance to the finished product that the writer has, a very contradictory thing at best; he provides the scenario, the warp and woof of the tapestry which are vital for holding it together, but unseen. To the end of time we shall be reduced to congratulating one another for our great works of screenwriting, nobody else will have noticed.

About movie acting, Clark Gable's definition is still the best. After a short scene, the final one in *The Misfits*, I hadn't detected that, as the script required, he had evidenced joy, and I had watched from ten feet away. Later, watching it with him on the screen I saw that indeed he had shown joy. He drew a rectangle around his eyes, "It's all in there," he said, "it's all movie acting is about." The eyes. Since that conversation I've noticed that all movie stars, especially males, have very wide-apart eyes.

One of my early minor shocks was a glimpse on newsreel film of Eisenhower being made up for a televised speech. Sponge, powder-puff, talc, eye marker, the works. He hadn't been made up before launching the invasion of Europe, only to get to be President of the United States. The whole civilization is about performances rather than the real thing. The fog we live in is made of talc.

JIM SHEPARD

FILM-MAKING IN POLYNESIA

"Film-making in Polynesia" is from a novel in progress involving the life and work of F. W. Murnau, who directed films in Germany from 1919-1925 and in America from 1926 until his death in 1931.

Murnau has become somewhat canonical in film studies; at this point he's one of the big three from the silent period, Griffith and Eisenstein being the other two. Murnau is generally considered to be the first to have systematically considered the shot as a space open to every sort of intrusion and transformation; the first to understand the potential of camera movement, to invest his images with a kind of evolving evocativeness that helped revolutionize the medium.

He remains an intriguing and mysterious figure, as filled with contradiction as Weimar Germany itself: a full-blown German Romantic, and a cosmopolitan spokesman for the new art of film; austere, and saddened by his own isolation; intimately linked to his conservative family, and homosexual; extraordinarily well-known, and, in countless ways, utterly private.

My novel takes the form of his working and daily journal, and focuses on four episodes of his life: the making of Nosferatu, *early in his career; of* Faust, *at perhaps the height of his career; his time in Tahiti, working on the film* Tabu *with the renowned documentarian Robert Flaherty; and finally his experiences in the First World War, including the loss of his lover, before his life in film began. "Film-making in Polynesia" is an excerpt—somewhat compressed, and generally fiddled with—from part three.*

July 9, 1929. The first full day in Tahiti, and the production is at a standstill. Flaherty announced almost as I stepped off the boat that no money had been forwarded to meet him. He and his assistant have apparently lived on credit for the last two months. The contract with Colorart by all indications meaningless. The wages of doing business with a 'New Company, on the Rise.' I sent seven cables before an answering cable, unsigned, confirmed the bankruptcy. I imagined a melancholy functionary, the last one at his desk, taking pity on me. The crisis averted only when I offered to finance the film myself, with what remains after the purchase of the *Bali*, and the paying off of its crew. Have no idea if this is even possible. It was agreed: the only person on salary for the time being is Floyd Crosby, our cameraman. All assistants to be recruited locally.

Second meeting with Flaherty not much better. He still wants to make a documentary after the style of his *Nanook of the North*. I asked him if he was hoping now to produce *Saoheri of the South*. This is now not Colorart's money with which we're playing. Everyone was short-tempered. We're here to make a feature film, and he knows it. Crosby put his head on the table and said aloud, "It was at that point that their difficulties really began."

I left bitter dispute behind in Los Angeles so that I might find it here, in the most beautiful place on earth. Still painful to think about *4 Devils*, and the endless battles with Fox. One memo after another, on his wife's faux-Continental stationery, demanding a happy epilogue in the manner of *Der Letzte Mann*: for the doomed hero and heroine! Questionnaires distributed at the premiere, that we were forced to study, as if the Word of the Masters. Three afternoons spent in his office slogging conscientiously through three canvas bags of horrifying suggestions. William Fox, Fox's head of production, and F. W. Murnau all laboring to decipher oceans of childish scrawl. Filmmaking by democracy.

As he reminded me: since *Sunrise* had not recouped its cost, I had little choice. I had become a genius in all but questions of public taste.

It was decided the hero should throw himself at the heroine's feet and beg forgiveness. This was done. The result was execrable. The devastating critical response pleased Fox, encouraging him to believe the film to be now more suited to the general public.

Then *Our Daily Bread*, mutilated and humiliated. The film was too long; the peasants were not American; once more, the gag-men were set to work. I terminated my contract. For the letter I used a stationery even more hideous than his wife's. The film was taken over by an honest man with no imagination, and re-issued under a different title. I wrote him, once the picture was taken away from me, with seven pages of modifications that I thought might please him and save the film. I never received a reply.

And yet such work is what enabled me to fulfill this childhood dream of an expedition to the South Seas.

Stunned upon arrival. Sat nearly senseless while the pilot guided us into the harbor. The peaks and slopes of the volcanic islands of Oceania are so steep and dark and wicked-looking that the coastlines seem gentle by contrast, with pale lagoons that look soothing and sweet. There is always a scrap of mist around the peaks, and the unsettling, below-the-horizon boom of surf on the invisible reefs. The population lives entirely on the fringes of steep and inaccessible slopes, so the villages seem small and crowded.

Moorea's mountains to the west loom dark and spiky, as if always backlit. Local myths claim them to be the dorsal fins of a giant fish. To me they look more sinister, and more alluring. I imagine myself up there, spread across those waterless peaks.

Beneath the green volcanoes, the water is a numinous, shimmering blue, not sea-colored at all, with stunning depths, and shallow coral shelves knobbed and ribbed like bones, rippling with fish. The water is everywhere so bright, like those candy-colored liqueurs and cordials in glass bottles at a bar, lit from below. . . .

I make my notes in English now. But I find I always revert to German in the case of anything critically important.

Everywhere the smell of the *noanoa*—the flowers—especially the *tiare*, a tiny white gardenia the girls and boys wear in the hair and touch to their lips, and then their pelvis, before handing to you. And the trade winds, the trade winds, all night and all morning. The wind never ceases to blow in Tahiti.

Friedrich Wilhelm Plumpe, of Bielefeld, in Tahiti. And yet possible disaster, the end of everything, pursues me from the moment my foot hits the pier.

The Residency supposedly has all the comforts of a club: in this case a bulletin board, a modest liquor cabinet, a map of the world on Mercator's projection, and one of the most spectacular views available on any veranda in the tropics. My fellow guests mostly French officials, German and Scottish merchant clerks. They speak quietly with one another about the young filmmaker, whose plans have apparently come to such grief. The house is commodious. All day, wide, louvered doors stand open and the trades blow over the bare floors.

On weekdays the garden is filled with convicts who set aside spade and barrow and touch hats to visitors like old attached family servants. On weekends the convicts are gone. Dogs of all sizes and ages take their places, sprawled wherever there is shade like the aftermath of a battle.

Behind a ruined wall, the European cemetery, overhung with acacia. Flaherty gives me a tour. English and Scottish and Scandinavians and French. And Germans: one, tipped backward at a vertiginous angle, reads *Veidt*, as if the actor had died here instead of preceding me to America. Grim jokes about finding a headstone for our project.

That first night, a dinner of parrotfish, turtle soup, turtle steak, pork cutlets, salad, and rice pudding. For the others, rum and beer from San Francisco. Slept abominably. Only a few yards away was the pier, where all night the natives rolled one of Crosby's camera dolly-carts up and down its tracks, like a small tram line. One would make a witty remark and the others would roar with delight. Then the great joke became to derail the dolly. This was irresistibly funny. Then it had to go back onto the makeshift rails. Twice I went out to put a stop to it, and became a part of the hilarity. Crosby not in his room.

Eleven-thirty the next morning the welcoming exercises commenced. I sat on the veranda in a sour mood, drinking coconut milk. A good-sized crowd watched. Small boys and girls were continually urged not to approach. Half a dozen strapping natives circulated, impressing everyone with the need for quiet by making a racket themselves. There seems to be no settled style of dress among the males; they wear anything they can get. Then the chief and his delegation arrived, and conferred with Crosby and Flaherty. The chief looked like one of Reinhardt's stage managers on opening night back in the *Deutsches Theatre*. Music began. A half-hidden clutch of young girls sang a beautiful and long-winded song. An oppressive silence followed. I was invited to leave the porch. I did so. A flag-bearer took up a position over my head with the German flag. Another group sang something like a church anthem, repetitious in character. Its words meant, I was told, *Welcome, German*. A group banging tin plates was asked to moderate their zeal. Two dancers seemed to have a roaming commission.

Finally I was led to a group of pigs and chickens herded close together on an island mat. The pigs looked bored. One chicken looked dead. I was told by Flaherty to raise my hand. I complied. This, Flaherty told me, signalled that I accepted the chickens but deferred the pigs for a later feast. Apparently this was precisely the right thing to do.

Crosby had hoped to film all of this. His cameras malfunctioned. The whole thing seemed so fitting that one almost had to smile. While he struggled with them and the assembled multitude worked its way through another welcoming song—they apparently believe I'm much wealthier than I am—I occupied myself by watching a young boy, nearly as tall as I, with beautiful teeth and the tattoo of a coconut palm on his spine. Right below the small of his back, two indentations, like the press of thumbs. He was somewhere between 17 and 21. He devoted the entire welcoming ceremony to the study of Crosby's cameras. He did not move away until he seemed to feel that he had divined the principles involved. At which point he put himself into the line forming to offer individual greetings, the main ceremony now over. When he reached me, he took my hand and laid it against his neck. Then he raised his lips to mine, close, before relaxing back to his previous posture. This clearly meant something to the others in line. I was completely flustered. Flaherty eased over and intervened, indicating the line needed to keep moving. He smiled. "Whatever the virtues of the Tahitian," he said, as if talking to himself, "chasteness is not one of them."

An entire day of no work. Sitting in a sort of a sling arrangement in the shade of a palm, squinting into the intense glare of a cloudless oceanic afternoon. Flaherty and Crosby came by once or twice to check with me, ask how we should begin. Too despairing to answer. They went away worried. Thought I could pick out wreckage perilously near the reef. Near the reef, but off in the area of deep blue that signals the deepest water. Oddest place for wreckage to be. Fragment of a mast and sail?

Tahiti as the New Cytherea, the abode of Venus. When Venus rose from the sea she stepped ashore (according to the poet Hesiod) at Cytherea. Captain de Bougainville was right: this is the world before the Fall, where the golden age still holds. As a boy I committed parts of his Journals to memory. All the creatures associated with the mythology of Venus, he said, were to be found in Tahiti: the dolphin, the tortoise, the gentlest birds, sacred to her memory. He was right. Here there are frigate birds so tame they have red streamers trailing from their legs to keep them safe from hunters.

A camera case has been dropped off the dock. Cleaning the camera has so far been unsuccessful; Crosby tells me the more intimate portions of the mechanism have been coated with salt. Flaherty tells me he is worried about me.

The boy from the welcoming reception comes by every morning. He spearfishes a few hundred yards down the beach, rarely coming closer. At that distance he has the appearance of a Diomedes. His dress is traditional but his spear is metal, and probably from San Francisco. I don't think it's possible any longer to get much of an idea of the old Tahitian customs by observation; it's like staring at a Norwegian hoping to learn about the Vikings.

I asked one of the natives who works at the Residency about him. He described him as a *mahu*, which means an effeminate person.

The Polynesians are subject to a disease of the will instead of the body. I'm told the Tahitians have a word for it: *erimatua*. I cannot find it in my dictionary. Those who contract it are known to succumb, literally dying of discouragement. This is accepted as unavoidable by the victim's family.

My fourth night in Tahiti, after the third day of the boy's show of spearfishing, a tap at the shutter of my bedroom. The boy, standing there in the moonlight, looking up at me. The languages of Polynesia are easy to smatter, hard to speak with elegance. Interpreters abound.

He has a sweet and gentle nature and an acumen for business that is startling. He is an inveterate flirt. He is married. When you say, what about your wife, on Fagatau?, he says, "*Aita pea-pea*": it doesn't matter.

The next morning, just after sunrise, he watched from the veranda, amused, and refused to participate while I flung myself into the smooth warm water of the lagoon. I anchored on my rump a few yards offshore in the soft sand, my face to the bright morning sun, low across the water beyond the Residency. While I flopped about he took his leave. Afterwards, a shower bath and a seat on the veranda, naked under my linen robe, drinking good rich coffee and eating two warm rolls with honey. Flaherty emerged from his room and remarked on the day, watching me. He fetched his own coffee from the kitchen and returned. He hefted his ankles to the veranda rail alongside mine as though we were two Bavarians on the Spree. He looked at me with the cool, poker-playing expression of someone who's experienced a catastrophic setback and fancies it doesn't show on his face.

That morning we walk the beach with Crosby, discussing options. Both of them keenly interested in the idea that I will finance the film myself. They urge the confirmation of the feasibility of this through a series of cables to my bank. Crosby mentions the uncertain weather not so far off. There is some haggling over just how much capital I will have to secure immediately. At one point I slip into German. To their frustration, I sit in the wave's wrack at the edge of a tidal pool: as the rush withdraws, marvels of color and design stream past my feet and through my fingers, with only the occasional conch or miracle spiral caught as proof of what I missed with each wave's retreat.

Lunch. Light lunch. The orange of Tahiti is delicious: small and sweet with a thin, dry rind. The boy visible from the veranda, on the road to the village. His palm tree tattoo accentuates the play of muscles in his back. A sad, minor surprise: he has spent some of the money I gave him, on a straw boater's hat.

The afternoon spent in a kind of stupor. The miracles of the previous night never far from my thoughts. Images of the boy's hands around me while Crosby breaks down the sea-damaged camera for my benefit, demonstrating which parts have been lost to the salt.

Long walks, Flaherty gesticulating beside me. The edge of the reef always fascinating. In many places one is walking on the roof of immense subterranean caverns, into which the sea rushes with uncanny noise, geysering mist and spray through small cracks and holes. The effect makes me feel never more than fifteen years old.

In paths through the interior: streaming sweat, Crosby outlining the difficulties that lie ahead. He carries a day-book to keep accurate count of the impossibilities before us. We dream-walk, amid the vegetation, in a covered house of heat. The air is breathless, and yet overhead the river of tradewinds streams without pause.

A nap. No dinner. Sounds of cutlery and socializing. When I awake again, it's night. Like a child I want time elided to the next moment, the tap at my shutter.

I open my window to him and he climbs through like an immense insect.

I awoke around three, to find the air temperate and scented. I was on my back and could see supernaturally well in the gloom. The boy's three fingers lay around my chin. I rose, naked. All else was surf and silence. The moon was full upon the lagoon. The surf broke and shone around the shore. A black crane fished in the swirling water, stepping brokenly about.

The next morning, some work with Flaherty and Crosby planning casting calls: how the villages will be notified, how the various candidates will be subdivided. Then another nap, this on the beach. Dangerously silly to lie nearly naked under this blistering Oceanic sun; not a single Polynesian will dare it. Also, blatant immodesty. Near the reef, I see natives pointing at me: my red hair, my wrinkles, my sea-air skin. In the looking glass, every morning, my age: my freckles, my weathered coarseness.

I feel awkward dressing in front of him; stepping into clothes while he watches calls forth the old context of shame for me. Lost nights near the Tiergarten. But he doesn't mind, and in fact seems to work out reasons not to leave. "*Kare-peka*," he says: It's all right.

A letter from my mother in the morning mail-packet. Apparently she has just seen *Tartüff* at her local theater. She writes, 'The silver and china are always so exquisite in your films.'

Noon. My shadow cowers around my legs. Some preliminary location-scouting with Flaherty. Flaherty gives me a long, pointed lesson in the local folklore. There is throughout Tahitian culture, he says, an element of dread. The fear of demons and of the dark is very deeply written in the mind of the Polynesian. Certain presences, called *vehinehae*, frequent and make terrible the nocturnal roadside, particularly the crossroads; he's been told they're like so much mist, shaped like men and having the eyes of cats. They represent the dead. When a native says he is a man, he means a man and not a demon, instead of a man and not a beast. Only very recently, Flaherty went on, one demon is said to have taken the youngest of two boys, after twilight, to the edge of the jungle. The demon is said to have whispered, "You are so-and-so, son of so-and-so?" and then caressed and beguiled the boy deeper into the undergrowth while the older boy watched, petrified.

We stand in the shade of the harbormaster's board. It is pasted over with handbills in Tahitian. Beneath the supporting pillars, a small pile of refuse, entertaining bright green flies. Flaherty adds, as a remark, that the natives believe white blood to be a talisman against the powers of hell. It's the only way, he says, that they can explain the unpunished recklessness of the Europeans.

Another boy has taken to following me around. He is thirteen years old and tells me through an interpreter than he wishes to see my ship.

At dinner, the topic is the increase of disease among the Polynesians. One Frenchman, silent up to that point, finally blurted out, "They're dying, poor devils! The main thing is to let them die in peace."

That night, a tap at the shutter, but no entry: the boy makes wave-like motions with his hands when I come to the window. He is not wearing his new hat. He gestures to the jungle. He wishes to show me something.

For a while we keep to the road, an unpaved surface of broken coral. We pass villages spotted with yellow light: those who have recently lost relations keep kerosene lamps burning all night to turn the spirits away. Now and then bicycle riders pass, indistinct ghosts with tinkling bells.

It is so dark that we are without opinions. What to make of sounds or breaths of air, where to put our feet. Soon we're on a path; soon we seem to leave even that. I am completely in his hands. Unknown things brush and sweep against me. The canopy overhead prevents starlight from illuminating our way.

The whole island is so mountainous that the only way to penetrate into the interior is to follow up the valleys. They begin to narrow, the sides growing lofty and more precipitous. We climb for hours. The width of the ravine is now that of the bed of a stream. On each side the walls are vertical, with vegetation in every handhold. Who knows what animals scurry away from our touch?

The ravine finally connects to a narrow track spanning a ridge. We have left the tree canopy well behind. The sky is beginning to pale. We find ourselves above a precipice five or six hundred feet deep, the abyss emerging out of the gloom, partially concealed by the overhanging ferns and lilies. I think: the Alps have a grander scale, but for abruptness of the fall, nothing compares with this.

All this way up, from a little cave the size of a mail-box, he extracts his gift for me, hoarded here: folded up, in a small parcel of leaves, pieces of beef, fish, and an unripe banana. It is some sort of lovers' picnic.

He makes me comfortable, matted grasses at my back, my feet dangling out over the abyss. From here we can see the Residency and the village far below, the coming light rising obliquely over Moorea, the sculpture of its mountain range lifting into relief, the huge gorges emerging from shadow. Attenuated clouds flee overhead.

I am in tears. Who knows what I've left untouched and what I've polluted? Who knows what I have yet to ruin? He takes my hand and places it to his breast. He sees my tears as happiness. Perhaps, but not for him, not enough for him. With this boy beside me, and his smell on my lips, I recite aloud, from de Bougainville's journals, on the discovery of Polynesia, aware that even as I'm inscribed upon, I inscribe these islands: *"We found companies of men and women sitting under the shade of their fruit trees: they all greeted us with signs of friendship: those who met us upon the road stood aside to let us pass by; and everywhere we found hospitality, ease, innocent joy, and every appearance of happiness amongst them."*

MICHAEL ANDEREGG

CAMEOS, GUEST STARS, AND REAL PEOPLE, WITH A SPECIAL APPEARANCE BY ORSON WELLES

Among the several notable features of the recent hit film *Forrest Gump* (1994), one would have to single out the brief "guest" appearances by such famous historical and cultural icons as Richard Nixon, John Lennon, and John Kennedy, among others, all of whom contribute resonant "bits" to Gump's variegated and peripatetic life—conversing with him, shaking his hand, and in other ways interacting with this decidedly fictional character. What makes the presence of these "actors" in *Forrest Gump* of particular interest, of course, is in part the unlikelihood that so many well-known, mainly political figures—three presidents among them—would appear in a Hollywood movie at all, together with the undeniable fact that all of them are dead. As in Woody Allen's earlier film, *Zelig* (1983), but more elaborately, fiction and non-fiction are here deliberately confused not merely on the story plane but in the manipulation of the filmic material itself. Computer-enhanced photography, clever editing, and (not-so-clever) dubbing make it possible for actor Tom Hanks to be inserted into already existing documentary footage and simultaneously create the impression that real historical persons have been brought into the fictional universe of Forrest Gump.

Apart from the necromancy involved in the making of *Forrest Gump*, however, the appearance of real people, even famous real people, in a fiction film is not all that unusual. The melding of the real and the unreal, and the ambiguity that thereby results, has always constituted an essential element of the movies: as one film historian has recently noted, "The fictional film existed long before the notion that people acted in films."[1] With performers, in particular, the line dividing "real" and "not real" is necessarily an invisible one: Forrest Gump may be unreal, but Tom Hanks is certainly real, as real, that is, as Lyndon Johnson or John

Kennedy. Apart from the violation of chronology, there is no reason why Hanks and John Lennon should not appear as guests together on the Dick Cavett Show, as they give the impression of doing in *Forrest Gump*. Both John Lennon and Tom Hanks are, necessarily, playing: the only significant difference is that Lennon is playing John Lennon while Hanks is playing Forrest Gump, an entirely fictional construct.

I

Real people playing "themselves," or some version of themselves, constitutes one aspect of a broad category of film performance that I like to think of as "bracketed" to one degree or another: performances that have been constructed to call special attention to themselves, that are detached—or at least easily detachable—from the flow of the narrative in which they appear, that deviate from various norms that can be demonstrated to govern their contexts. Adopting the useful categories developed by James Naremore for how people in a film can be regarded—"as actors playing theatrical personages, as public figures playing theatrical versions of themselves, and as documentary evidence"[2]—the performances I am particularly interested in would be permutations and combinations of all three, but with a special emphasis on the second and third. These are performances that directly reflect on the nature of performance, that are self-reflexive, that violate, to a greater or lesser extent, the contract that we have with fictionality, either by making excessive demands on our willing suspension of disbelief or, alternately, by attempting to solidify our belief by an injection of hyper-reality, a striving to intensify and even to transcend mere verisimilitude.

Although the kinds of performances I am describing can be found in each decade of film history, they have become more and more prevalent in recent years. Indeed, any fairly sophisticated moviegoer spending time at the multiplex in the summer and fall of 1994 might have thought that virtually every movie—not only *Forrest Gump*—was infected with some kind of self-reflexive, "guest" casting: directors Martin Scorsese and Barry Levinson appear in Robert Redford's *Quiz Show* (with Levinson, a virtually unrecognizable director, playing one-time well-known television personality Dave Garroway), various fashion luminaries play themselves in Robert Altman's *Ready to Wear*, and Quentin Tarantino plays a character in his own *Pulp Fiction*. In *Wes Craven's New Nightmare*, perhaps the most playfully postmodern of all these films, not only does Wes Craven appear as himself but so do, among others, Robert Englund ("Freddie" of the *Nightmare* films), John Saxon, and, inevitably (as the closing credits inform us), the purely fictional character "Freddie"; furthermore, Heather Langenkamp, the young female lead of *Nightmare on Elm Street* (1984) and *Nightmare 3* (1987), plays an actress named Heather Langenkamp, who is asked by the executives (all playing themselves) at New Line Cinema, the company that made the Nightmare films, to reprise her role as "Nancy" in yet another Nightmare sequel, a film that turns out to be, of course, the film that we are watching.

As even this brief catalog suggests, different kinds of "guest appearances," of bracketed performances in film, can be identified: the film "star," or former star, appearing in a relatively small role or cameo (virtually everyone in *Around the World in Eighty Days* [1956]); the famous person who may or may not be a star playing him or her "self" in a historical or biographical film (Babe Ruth in the Lou Gehrig biography *Pride of the Yankees* [1942]; Audie Murphy in *To Hell and Back* [1955]), or a fiction film (Babe Ruth in Harold Lloyd's *Speedy* [1928]); a "nonactor," notable for reasons unrelated to theatre or film, playing a fictional character in a fiction film (lawyer Joseph Welch in *Anatomy of a Murder* [1959]); a film director making a cameo appearance in his or her own film (Hitchcock, most obviously, but many others including Martin Scorsese in *Taxi Driver* [1976], Francis Coppola in *Apocalypse Now* [1979], and George Roy Hill in *The World According to Garp* [1982]) or in someone else's film (Fritz Lang in Jean-Luc Godard's *Le Mépris* [1963]; Sam Fuller and Nicholas Ray in Wim Wenders' *American Friend* [1977]); and a variety of ordinary "real people" and non-actors who either play themselves or who are cast simply because their appearance or manner are thought to contribute verisimilitude to the narrative, are perhaps only the most commonly noted categories.[3] Martin Scorsese's *King of Comedy* (1983), as James Naremore has shown,[4] exhibits virtually all of these performance options.

When real people—not only film directors, a special category in itself, but people who ordinarily have nothing to do with show business—play "themselves" in a film, the effect of that performance depends to a significant extent on context. In his discussion of *Star Acting*, Richard Dyer comments on the appearance of Ava Gardner as "herself" in *Band Wagon* (1953), where she has a brief scene with the fictional character "Tony Hunter" (Fred Astaire): "Gardner . . . by playing herself," Dyer writes, "contributes to the illusion of the other character's existence."[5]

But isn't the effect in fact the opposite of this? Are not all such moments actually a bit embarrassing to the viewer, as if the filmmakers had been caught in an indiscretion, had broken a taboo? The recognizable actor, playing him or herself, I would argue, actually detracts from the illusion created by the fiction and nearly always intensifies the artifice: such performances become instances of *Verfremdungeffekt* whereby the "real" person both appears "unreal," because he or she has been placed in a clearly fictional universe, while at the same time his or her ostensible "realness" intensifies the fictionality of the inhabited space. This is partly what happens when, for example, Woody Allen, in *Annie Hall* (1977), brings Marshall McLuhan, media scholar and guru, from off-screen to contradict a fictional character who is expounding McLuhan's theories. Allen does the same thing, more extensively, in *Zelig*, which features (in a parodic imitation of *Reds* [1981]) on-camera interviews with the likes of Saul Bellow and Susan Sontag, who are then made to comment on the activities of the fictional Zelig. The effect, in both instances, is not to affirm the reality of Allen's fictive world, but to bring that reality ironically into question.

We can see the consequences of real people playing themselves by briefly considering a film which is very precisely about reality, illusion, and the movies. When producer-director Cecil B. De Mille appears as "himself" in *Sunset Boulevard* (1950), he injects into the fiction a self-conscious and slightly awkward realism. His performance, his very presence, calls into question the verisimilitude of the situation in which he is presented and the characters with whom he interacts. The whole narrative becomes, oddly, less believable as a consequence of his presence, and "Norma Desmond" becomes correspondingly more unreal. (Actually, the situation is a good bit more complex than I am presenting it, given that Gloria Swanson, in her performance as Norma Desmond, is also, in part, playing "herself," as are Erich von Stroheim and Buster Keaton and H. B. Warner; as a young star, furthermore, Swanson had been directed by both De Mille and von Stroheim.) De Mille's presence in *Sunset Boulevard* points up a specific and presumably unintended effect of "real people" playing themselves. Because De Mille appearing as "De Mille" would not, one supposes, have agreed to play a character constructed in any way as unpleasant or ruthless, the almost worshipful way he is presented in the film reinforces our impatience with Norma Desmond. De Mille, seldom in real life mistaken for a particularly "nice" man, seems downright benign as well as nearly godlike in this fictional incarnation. His scenes with "Norma" thus generate little tension, provide no real give and take, and certainly no sense of the cynicism, ruthlessness, and lack of sentimentality about Hollywood and its mores that informs other moments in the film.

Much the same effect, though in a virtually opposite form, is created by Babe Ruth's performance as himself in *Pride of the Yankees*. His function in the film, aside from adding "authenticity," is as a foil to Gehrig: Ruth is the flamboyant showboater, media creature, and star athlete; Gehrig (Gary Cooper) the quiet, modest, sincere hero. But the film pushes this contrast further than one might expect. In one sequence, in part reconstructed from newsreel footage, Ruth, in the presence of the press, signs baseballs for kids in the St. Louis Children's Hospital and promises to hit a home run in that afternoon's game for a particularly sick boy. After Ruth and the press leave, Gehrig privately encourages the boy to get well and is maneuvered by him into promising to hit two home runs in the same game. The contrast appears to be all to Gehrig's benefit. Now if Babe Ruth were portrayed by, say, William Bendix, the scene would be unambiguous; the convention, after all, is a familiar one—if your biopic is about the boxer *Gentleman Jim* Corbett (1942), John L. Sullivan is (literally) the fall guy; but if you want to make a movie about *The Great John L.* (1945), then Corbett takes the fall. But the view here presented of Babe Ruth is so harsh and dismissive that it seems impossible he would have agreed to participate in its construction. His actual, physical presence—in other words, our awareness that he is playing himself, that we are seeing the "real" Babe Ruth—produces something like cognitive dissonance: we are left to wonder whether or not we really understand what it is the filmmakers are telling us.[6]

Real people playing themselves, even when not, like Babe Ruth, famous or in some way recognizable to the audience, frequently call attention to themselves by exhibiting "off-centeredness" of one kind or another. In addition to revealing various kinds of discomfort in front of the camera, non-actors often allow the lines of dialogue they are given to more or less "speak for themselves" and fail to provide nuance, shading, irony, or anything like the stylized naturalism we expect from professional actors. Amateur performers either fail to synchronize other elements of performance with the spoken words or they work too hard at convincing us that synchronization is taking place. No matter how well coached by a director, the real person may simply be unable to integrate the various aspects of performance into a coherent whole, and it is that lack of coherence that, as much as anything, signals the amateurishness of the performer.

In other instances, off-centeredness may be the effect of some knowledge brought in from outside the film. Since Hollywood directors, for instance, are seldom immediately recognizable by their physical appearance, their presence in a particular film may have little or no resonance for the average viewer: how many people, without the help of publicity, would have recognized Martin Scorsese in *Taxi Driver* or Sidney Pollack in *Tootsie* (1982)? If you don't know that Otto Preminger is a film director with the reputation of being something of a martinet on the set, the pleasure of seeing him as a Nazi commandant of a POW camp in Billy Wilder's *Stalag 17* (1953) will be, to some degree, lost to you. Preminger's performance smoothly fits its context, and only calls attention to itself, and thereby becomes "bracketed," to a filmgoer "in the know." Director John Huston, on the other hand, is nearly always intrinsically off-center in his "guest" performances; he gives off an aura of pretense, of joking, of slumming, that communicates itself even to a viewer who does not recognize him as his "real" self.[7]

Insofar as all people are, of course, "real" people, all performers, professional and amateur, play themselves to some degree or other. One might want to argue, then, that all performances call attention to themselves as performance and are thus "bracketed" in the sense in which I have been using the term. Although I would prefer to limit my discussion to performances that stand out in a very specific way from the other performances that surround them and in which they are embedded, it is nonetheless true that even, perhaps especially, performers who are also stars can stand out in a particular manner, nowhere more clearly than in films where all available resources have been marshalled to foreground one actor's performance—the so-called star vehicle. Although any film which features a powerful star presence will have a tendency to turn into a vehicle, in practice certain films reinforce the effect by centering on a character who, either through personal eccentricity, marked anti-social tendencies, or physical/mental impairment, already acts as a magnet, drawing to itself all that comes within its force-field. A vehicle of this kind encourages the star to "over-act" and thereby demonstrate his or her "acting" skills.[8] Here, one might simply note the number of "Oscars" awarded to actors who, like Tom Hanks for both *Philadelphia* (1983) and *Forrest Gump*, embody physical or social excess of one kind or another—madness (Vivien Leigh), alcoholism (Ray Milland), mental retardation (Cliff Robertson), mental aberration (Joanne Woodward, Dustin Hoffman), physical impairment (Jane Wyman, Daniel Day-Lewis, Marlee Matlin), and psychopathology (Anthony Hopkins), among others.

When such a character is embodied by a recognizable star performer, the combination almost inevitably results in a showcase film. In these instances, the "bracket" becomes the film-text itself, with all of its formal and expressive devices.[9]

II

I have deliberately held off until now the entrance of my "guest star," Orson Welles, in order to intensify the effect of his appearance, a strategy with which Welles was himself quite familiar, as we know from an anecdote he tells Peter Bogdanovich during a discussion of his performance as Harry Lime in *The Third Man* (1949):

> In theatre, you know, the old star actors never liked to come on until the end of the first act. *Mister Wu* is a classic example—I've played it once myself. All the other actors boil around the stage for about an hour shrieking, 'What will happen when Mister Wu arrives?,' 'What is he like, this Mister Wu?,' and so on. Finally a great gong is beaten, and slowly over a Chinese bridge comes Mister Wu himself in full mandarin robes. Peach Blossom (or whatever her name is) falls on her face and a lot of coolies yell, 'Mister *Wu*!!!' The curtain comes down, the audience goes wild, and everybody says, 'Isn't that guy playing Mr. Wu a great actor!' *That's* a star part for you! What matters in that kind of role is not how many lines you have, but how few.[10]

Although there are other reasons for the effectiveness of his performance as Harry Lime, the Mr. Wu factor, as Welles was quite aware, contributes significantly to the kinds of performances he was frequently called upon to give: Rochester in *Jane Eyre* (1944) and Sigsbee Manderson in *Trent's Last Case* (1952) are notable examples. It was an effect he manipulated even in the films he directed himself, most obviously in *Touch of Evil* and *The Trial*.

Welles, at various times and in a variety of media, has—uniquely, I believe—played variations on all of the "bracketed" performances I have been discussing. He has been a genuine Hollywood star, if only for a brief period, both in his own films and in films directed by others; he has frequently "guest starred" and played cameo roles; he has played versions of himself—played characters, that is, who, though fictional constructs, nevertheless reflect aspects of the Orson Welles persona as it has been constructed over the years; he has played "famous people" in a

Orson Welles lends his compelling screen persona to *Trent's Last Case* (1953), here with Margaret Lockwood, and *Tomorrow is Forever* (1946), with George Brent, Claudette Colbert, and child star Natalie Wood.

manner or context that serves to emphasize a parallel between his own fame, his instant recognizability, and the fame of the characters he plays; and he has played "himself" in documentary films, in semi-fictional films, in the "essay-films"[11] (*F for Fake* [1973], *Filming Othello* [1978]) he directed himself, and in his various guest appearances on television talk shows, variety programs, and commercials of all sorts. Welles, of all film performers, was always both himself—that is, a recognizable "real" person, someone pre- or extra-filmically famous—and a theatrical construct; he was always someone who, even when, perhaps especially when, being "himself," was a performer, and who, even when most disguised in a role, most "performing," was most himself, most clearly "Orson Welles."

Precocious in so many things, Welles was even precocious as a guest star. For his first professional acting job, at the age of sixteen, he tried to pass himself off to the managers of Dublin's Gate Theatre as an experienced actor from New York's famous Theatre Guild; whether anyone actually believed this bluff or not, Welles clearly was seen by the Irish press as an American "guest" at the Gate. Welles *acted* famous before he *was* famous. And he continues to be a guest star of sorts after his death: witness his "cameo" in Tim Burton's *Ed Wood* (1994) or his haunting presence in Peter Jackson's *Heavenly Creatures* (1994). He even appears as a "guest star," a colorful cameo, in other people's memoirs and reminiscences, often establishing his "role" in a single gesture or bold stroke. In Michael Powell's autobiography, *Million Dollar Movie*, for example, we meet Welles over breakfast:

> Orson was down before me in the morning, and eating an enormous breakfast, one course of which was eight boiled eggs, shelled and beaten up with ground black pepper, sea salt and butter in a bowl. We discussed *The Odyssey*. At first enthusiastic, I felt his interest cool when he realised that I didn't want to film the whole *Odyssey*, but only one episode, as one of my *Tales*.

End of cameo, and one aspect of Welles's persona is established: a man of enormous appetite, not only for boiled eggs but for Homer as well: he wants all of the *Odyssey* or none of it.

Although the phrase "guest star" seems to put as much emphasis on "star" as on "guest," Welles was not really a conventional star, if by that we mean primarily a romantic leading man, except for a brief period in the early to mid 1940s, roughly from *Citizen Kane* (1941) to *Tomorrow is Forever* (1945); he was always more of what is popularly known as a

character actor. The distinction between star and character actor, a vocabulary that is part of the Hollywood discourse but may not be entirely
meaningful outside of it, is not clear cut. A "star" is, presumably, not an
"actor" at all, but centrally a performer who again and again plays him
or her self, who is, in a sense, expected to play him or her self. As Edgar
Morin has written, "The star is more than an actor incarnating characters, he incarnates *himself in them*, and they become incarnate in
him."[12] A character actor, on the other hand, is first and foremost an
actor: the "character" part of the phrase suggests a specific construction,
or an infinite sequence of constructions—a character actor, by implication, plays something other than him or herself, plays a "character," by
which is meant not only a precisely delineated individual, but also a role
provided to the actor from the outside.

In practice, of course, this distinction is illusory, if not actually perverse. Some stars are character actors—Paul Muni, Dustin Hoffman—
and many, if not most, character actors come to function very like stars,
become adept at playing slight variations of a single persona, whether
that persona be James Gleason or William Gargan or Brian Dennehy or
J.T. Walsh. Welles, I would suggest, is a star as character actor, or a character actor as star. He constantly played "himself," quite literally when
enacting some version of "Orson Welles," something he began to do
quite early in his career, appearing as "guest star" on the Jack Benny or
Fred Allen radio shows. He was a performer who brought to his roles a
nexus of associations that went beyond, and had little to do with, the in-
tertextual references stars ordinarily bring from the other roles they
have played at other times. The relationship between the role Welles
played in one film and the roles he had played in other films was not
nearly as significant as the way his personality outside of the movies (or
theatre or radio) could be fed back into a specific performance. Starring
as "Orson Welles" always gave Welles his best-known, most recognizable
"role."

In one period of his career as a movie actor, Welles would sometimes
be given star billing for what was essentially a guest performance. In
Prince of Foxes (1949), for example, his billing is virtually equal to Tyrone Power's, even though he occupies far less screen time. But Welles
gives the impression of being more central in part because he has a
grand entrance at the beginning of the film and an equally impressive
exit near the end. In his other moments on screen, he imbues the role
of Cesare Borgia with extra-textual irony and with a flair and sweep that
makes this evil character quite attractive. Welles characteristically works

against the grain of the script; he seems far too self-aware and to hold too ironic a view of life to be the cruel and vindictive despot the film wants him to be. Even the presence in the film of Everett Sloane, a long-time Mercury Theatre associate and cast member of *Citizen Kane, Journey into Fear* (1942), and *Lady from Shanghai* (1948), provides an extra *frisson*; it is to Sloane that Welles delivers his final line in the film: "Then your future's assured—depending on which one of us is hanged first." Here, for a brief but significant moment, something of the "real" Orson Welles world seems to have insinuated itself into the text.

The somewhat paradoxical nature of his billing versus his actual participation in *Prince of Foxes* reinforces the suggestion that Welles became a "guest star" because he was only marginally a "real" star, or, to put it another way, because his real stardom was essentially himself, his public persona. He was a guest because he had no "home" of his own, no stable place in which to locate himself; he was a guest because he had been a guest before, because his identity was that he was a guest, a "guest star," a specialty act. That Welles's performances are nearly always bracketed in the manner I have been discussing both allows us to make sense of an otherwise seemingly incoherent series of roles and appearances in what are often forgettable, and forgotten, films and at the same time goes a long way to explaining the decidedly mixed reception his career as a performer has inspired. Welles, even though he is a professional actor, often seems "off" in a manner parallel to the examples I have given of Cecil B. De Mille and Babe Ruth. Very much like a non-actor or amateur performer, Welles, even when playing himself—that is, when playing a character identified as "Orson Welles"—at times exhibits signs of self-consciousness and discomfort: he doesn't seem to know quite how to be himself, or to remember or reconstruct exactly what being himself might mean. Given the multiplicity of roles Welles has taken up, or been required to take up, in the course of his career, this is not entirely surprising. In *F for Fake* or *Filming Othello*, the effect can be disarming: what may, at some level, be merely unease projects itself as modesty, tentativeness, and self-deprecating humor.

Like the "witnesses" in *Zelig*, Welles has also enacted more or less fraudulent versions of himself, as he notably does in the appropriately titled *F for Fake*. Unlike the various celebrity "real people" of Woody Allen's film, however, Welles's performance does not call forth the discomfort and even irritation we frequently experience when celebrities discuss fictional persons and events as if the latter were part of the same reality as the speakers. Welles's persona, his authority to speak, is always implicated in a good deal of fraudulence, of fakery, of sleight of hand. When Welles speaks authoritatively, that authority necessarily has an ironic component, an irony that has in part been constructed through his always ambiguous relationship to commodification and commercialization. Hence, his early authority as host (as well as producer, writer, star) of the radio program "First Person Singular," produced by CBS without a sponsor for its first season, was very quickly co-opted and compromised when Campbell's soups took over sponsorship at the beginning of the second season. Insofar, in other words, as he was a spokesman for Campbell's soup—or, later, Lady Esther beauty products, American Airlines, Paul Masson wines, etc.—his opinions and his ideas, together with his image and voice, were to a certain extent bought and paid for.

In virtually all of his performances, Welles's "real" identity as "Orson Welles" tends to overwhelm whatever identity he has as an actor. In particular, when Welles appears in his own films, especially in the later ones, we are just as aware of his function as the film's director as we are of his function as a specific character. We are familiar, of course, with the effect of a recognizable director like Alfred Hitchcock making an appearance in his own film; whatever the motive underlying that appearance, it breaks, if only for a moment, the fictional matrix and at the same time introduces material evidence of authorship. But even when the director is also an actor, as with Welles in most of his films, or with, say, Jerry Lewis or Woody Allen or Spike Lee, our knowledge that the performer and the director are one colors the scenes in which he appears. We are conscious of a peculiar "doubling" effect with characters like Hank Quinlan in *Touch of Evil* or Mookie in *Do the Right Thing* (1989); what such characters say and do almost always takes on an authority that seems to speak simultaneously from inside and from somewhere outside the film.

Welles's frequent appearances as "narrator," a role that defines as well as anything can his uniqueness as a performer, also involve a play between inside and outside. His easily recognizable, highly authorative manner of speaking has allowed him to be featured in films and television, as well as the more obvious media of radio and sound recordings, as a voice only[13] to such an extent that "Narrated by Orson Welles" became, depending on the context and occasion, a promise of a variety of specific moods or tones: importance, significance, seriousness; mystery, weirdness, the strange; false seriousness, comic portentousness, camp. In nearly all such vocal performances, Welles is not simply the narrator; he is very much a "guest star," and when the film or video is a documentary, his may be the name that appears first in the publicity material, the name used to sell the project. At its most "serious," the voice of Welles is the voice of God (literally, when he reads paraphrases from the gospels as voice-over for Nicholas Ray's *King of Kings* [1961]); at the other end of the scale, presumably, we have Welles as narrator of *Bugs Bunny Superstar* (1975). But whether employed "straight" or for purposes of parody, each instance of narration depends for its effect on the *authority* of Welles's voice, its ability to transcend the mere materiality of the spoken word, to invest words with an excess of meaning, with, quite precisely, *resonance* in both its acoustic and its metaphoric sense.

III

Though it is perhaps invitable to speak of Orson Welles as always playing himself, he has, of course, simultaneously played a whole gallery of "characters." He made a virtual career of appearing in a particular, and peculiar, genre, what we might call the International Co-produced Historical Spectacle, a genre which presents a number of featured actors from different countries, speaking in a variety of accents or dubbed into a language other than their own, playing historical or pseudo-historical personages in a few brief scenes or single, self-contained segments. A characteristic example would be Abel Gance's *Austerlitz* (1959), a French/Italian/Yugoslav/Lichtenstein co-production which features, in addition to Welles, Jack Palance, Claudia Cardinale, Michel Simon, and Rossano Brazzi. The presence of more or less well-known performers in these films lends "color" and texture and a certain verisimilitude to the narrative, while the limited and often self-contained nature of their contributions conveniently keeps to a minimum their actual time on the payroll. In this genre, the recognizability of the performer becomes a guarantee for the historicity of the character. Our ability as viewers to recognize "Orson Welles" contributes to the aura surrounding "Benjamin Franklin" (*Si Versailles m'était conté* [1954] and *Lafayette* [1960]) or "Cardinal Wolsey" (*A Man For All Seasons* [1966]) or "Louis XVIII" (*Waterloo* [1971]), and entirely constructs the historical reality of lesser-known figures Welles enacted, like "Hudson Lowe" (*Napoleon* [1954]) or "Robert Fulton" (*Austerlitz*).

Welles's Mr. Wu anecdote not only illustrates the effect of a well-timed, delayed entrance; it also shows how a relatively small role can be given a weight and significance far in excess of the amount of time and space it actually occupies. If we think of "character" in film as a complex intertwining of a variety of discourses and signs including audience fore-knowledge, appearance, speech (both of the character him or herself, and what others say about the character), gesture, action, structure, and mise-en-scène,[14] the guest star in a brief or cameo appearance must necessarily rely more on some signs than on others. Audience fore-knowledge—what the spectators already know about either the per-former (star image, for example, but also, in the case of non-actors, fame in general) or the character (historical figures or types), or both, to-gether with such pointers as what others say about the character, will be among the most useful ingredients in the construction of a cameo, whereas matters of structure, action, and mise-en-scène will, of neces-sity, be relatively less important.

As a cameo or guest performer, Welles was thus very likely to play al-ready constructed characters: there is little opportunity, in a cameo, to develop the character through narrative action or even to suggest the possibility of change. Such characters are, in a sense, pre-fabricated, characters who need to be met, to some degree or other, on their own terms; there is nothing to discover about them: he or she is simply there. Their words and actions are pre-ordained because already known, al-ways already known. What else can Louis XVIII do but leave Paris at the news of Napoleon's approach (*Waterloo*)? He has always left Paris. Welles, in his two brief scenes (one of which he plays with the Marshall Ney of Dan O'Herlihy, his 1948 Macduff), lends an element of pathos and comic irony to the king's departure; beyond this, however, there is little he can or needs to give to the role—he simply, for a brief moment, *is* Louis XVIII, though at the same time the king simply *is* Orson Welles.

Even when playing historical characters, however, Welles does not merely inhabit them—his performances almost always provide us with something in excess of or apart from the character he plays, and that something might be described precisely as that which defines Welles as a star, that part of Welles that resists assimilation into the character he is playing. Welles's performance style in film might be said to provide us with a denial of the so-called Kuleshov effect. That famous experiment, as related by V. I. Pudovkin, was meant to demonstrate that the mean-ing we read into a performer's expression is almost entirely a matter of the context created by montage, by editing. Juxtapose a shot of an actor's face with a funeral, and his expression is interpreted as sad, but instead show a laughing baby, and that very same expression will be read as happy. Welles's acting style, however, is a mise-en-scène style, not a montage style. It is nearly impossible to read anything *into* Welles's physical image, impossible for the filmmaker to manipulate the meaning of that image: Welles give us more than the film's editing strategies can possibly reveal. It is not the context provided by other shots that supplies the significance of his performance; rather, it is what is intrinsic to the performance that provides meaning to the surrounding shots.

Welles has, notoriously, been ridiculed precisely for what is frequently perceived as excess in his film performances.[15] Most film critics, of course, and many viewers, understand performance according to a fairly narrow standard. Richard Dyer has summarized the general view of what constitutes "good acting" in film as "the elaboration of character within a loose narrative structure and upon naturalistic devices such as interrupted speech, hesitation, mumbling, tics and other techniques that give an air of improvisation to the performance."[16] By these standards, of course, Welles's performance style in film could seldom be mistaken for "good acting." Though actors are sometimes rewarded for what might otherwise be thought of as excessive performances—John Wayne, an otherwise low-key performer, was awarded his "Oscar" when, late in his career, he gave a highly mannered, self-parodying, *excessive* performance of an eccentric character in *True Grit* (1969)—such performances generally take place within a context where excess is part of the film's essential visual and thematic strategies. The highly flamboyant performance Lee J. Cobb gives in *On the Waterfront* (1954) can be accepted in part because of the contextual support of the method actors who surround him and of Elia Kazan's expressive mise-en-scène and dramaturgy.

Welles's particular excess stems in part from the theatrical mode he nearly always brought to his films, by which I mean that his approach to a role, his method of attack, was closely tied to specific theatrical devices. As Virginia Wright Wexman notes:

> On stage actors are prone to use wigs, makeup, and costume to project a variety of images. On screen they are more likely to employ less obvious strategies such as hair coloring, plastic surgery, and weight control to project a single image that operates intertextually.[17]

Welles, notoriously, nearly always depended on wigs, make-up (he seldom wore the same nose twice), and costume to construct something like a Brechtian effect, to *look* as well as *be* theatrical. His acting repertoire was more or less consciously drawn from a wide range of performance styles, from the "histrionic" at one end to the "verisimilar" at the other, to adopt terminology employed by Roberta Pearson in her discussion of acting in Griffith's Biograph films,[18] just as his roles ranged widely over a historical spectrum.

Even considered in the context of a hit and miss acting career—he appears at times not so much to have chosen his roles as to have been chosen by them—Welles managed to act in films that draw on a variety of theatrical modes, including Greek tragedy (Tiresias in *Oedipus The King* [1968]), Renaissance plays (various Shakespearean roles), American thirties style social realism (as reborn in *Compulsion* [1958]), 1950s family melodrama (*The Long, Hot Summer* [1958]), Theatre of the Absurd (his own *The Trial*), and free-form improvisation (the films he made with Henry Jaglom, especially *Someone to Love* [1988]). In *Citizen Kane*, and uniquely in that film, the distinct acting styles Welles adopts in his portrayal of Charles Foster Kane contribute richly to the meaning of the film by serving to characterize each stage in Kane's physical and moral development.[19] Never again in Welles's career, however, will actor, role, and mise-en-scène mesh so definitively: his control over his own performance has only infrequently been as absolute, even in his own films.

If Welles's film performances call attention to themselves, it is in part because that is one effect of the guest-star phenomenon and in part because Welles, as we have seen, deliberately sets himself against the dominant tonality of the film in which he appears by adopting a style that provides something in excess of, or at least different from, what the project or the role demand. Just as Babe Ruth, in *Pride of the Yankees*, both by his very presence as a well-known "real person" and by the nature of his performance, which consists of delivering every line pointedly, with little modulation, so that everything he says becomes a speech, called attention to himself in a manner at odds with our expectations, so Welles, in his own way, interferes with or works at cross-purposes to, the norm of his context. This is not simply a matter of inflated ego, as if Welles saw himself as essentially superior to the material and hence wanted to draw all attention to his own performance; it is more of a conspiracy with the audience, a conspiracy that seems to say, "you and I, together, can make this work, can salvage pleasure and even significance from what at first sight appears to be unpromising material indeed."

In the thoroughly mediocre *Black Rose* (1950), for example, Welles's performance (as Bayan, a Mongol warrior!) is oddly inflected through the adoption of peculiar speech patterns and, more significantly, by his projection of the impression that the character he is playing possesses secrets not only unknown to the other characters but forever unknown to us as well; here, the peculiarity of Welles's performance is reinforced by the generally lackluster proceedings in which he finds himself. His eccentricities can be interpreted in part as the defensive maneuver of someone with energy and ideas but with no real control over the film-making process. By the same token, Welles can, in a more interesting film like *Compulsion* (Richard Fleischer, 1959), produce something like the opposite effect. Given an overheated, slightly hysterical film style, he withdraws, closes in, and consequently calls attention to himself through restraint rather than histrionics.

On other occasions, Welles gives the appearance of having con-structed a film's mise-en-scène around himself, even to have taken con-trol of a film's narrative strategies. It is difficult to determine how much input Welles may or may not have had on a particular project (he usu-ally tends to be coy and inconsistent on this issue in interviews), so we can only speculate about specific instances. In, for example, *The Long Hot Summer*, directed by Martin Ritt, Welles's presence and persona nearly take over the film, or at the very least the structure of the se-quences in which he appears, even though he has a subsidiary role. Al-though the writers have conceived Will Varner in wildly inconsistent terms—he begins as an overbearing, Tennessee Williams near-sadist, a cross between Big Daddy and Boss Finley, and ends the film as a "sen-timental old fool"—Welles, all greasy make-up, sloppy appearance, and lines delivered in a calculated manner and inflected with a dubiously southern accent, gives the role a larger than life theatricality that bal-ances out the hysterical method "hot" of Anthony Franciosa as well as the self-conscious method "cool" of Paul Newman. Indeed, Welles so dominates the concluding section of *The Long Hot Summer* that the narrative appears to have been about him all along. In five successive scenes, bridged by shots of Will Varner tearing along the Mississippi countryside in his jeep, and each conceived quite differently in mood and tone, Welles interacts with each of the film's major characters, thereby becoming the crucial narrative link among them all while giv-ing the appearance of resolving all the strands of the film's loose narra-tive construction.

Over a period of half a century and more which saw dramatic shifts in modes of narrative and the rapid development of new media, Orson Welles always found a way to be himself—to insist, that is, on his uniqueness as a public persona—while at the same time he parleyed the various aspects of his public persona and public activities into performance, into a wide variety of roles that provided him with the material means to work on his own projects. In playing his many roles, Welles drew on a wide range of performing occasions as well as on performance traditions, occasions and traditions that, for the most part, have little to do with the aesthetics of acting and where questions of realism and verisimilitude have often been of secondary concern. Non-actor, "bad" actor, overactor, underactor: all of these, this performance history suggests, can and do generate pleasure, meaning, and significance. As star, guest star, narrator, host, cameo, or specialty act, among other incarnations, Welles was quite literally a *marginal* performer for most of his post-*Citizen Kane* career, a figure almost always in brackets of one kind or another—part joke, part savant, part fraud, part highbrow, part sideshow freak, part carny huckster, and—an aspect of Welles perhaps too seldom on view—part a witty, commonsensical, insightful commentator on virtually any topic under the sun. All of these roles are themselves commentaries on the complex ways performance has come to be defined, elaborated, and transformed in a movement from live theater to the technologies of radio, sound recordings, film, television, and video, a transformation that parallels the movement, in Welles's own lifetime, from the pre-industrial to the modern to what we now refer to as the post-modern world.

NOTES

[1]Richard deCordova, *Picture Personalities: The Emergence of the Star System in America* (Urbana, Il: University of Illinois Press, 1990), 35.

[2]James Naremore, *Acting in the Cinema* (Berkeley and Los Angeles: University of California Press, 1988), 15.

[3]A separate category here might be the star actor who becomes identified with a certain role, usually a historical figure, and then reprises that role as a cameo, so that both the star and the character simultaneously make a "guest" appearance, as when James Cagney plays George M. Cohan in *The Seven Little Foys* (1955).

[4]*Acting in the Cinema*, 262–85.

[5]Richard Dyer, *Stars* (London: British Film Institute, 1979), 100.

[6]As George Custen has noted, "[*Pride of the Yankees*] attempts to redefine the very terms of heroism and entertainment in sports" (*Bio/Pics: How Hollywood Constructed Public History* [New Brunswick, NJ: Rutgers University Press, 1992], 163). Under the circumstances, Ruth is inevitably downgraded.

[7]By the time he plays an important role in Roman Polanski's *Chinatown* (1974), however, Huston is no longer a director slumming (as is Polanski in the same film); he is a recognizable performer, equally comfortable at meetings of the Screen Actors or the Screen Directors Guilds.

[8]John Ellis notes that because "stars are permitted to underact, compared to the supporting cast," stars sometimes will seek "to reverse this tendency toward underacting in order to produce an effect of 'performance'." (*Visible Fictions* [London: Routledge, 1982]), 104–05.

[9]It is interesting to note, with reference to *Forrest Gump*, how director Robert Zemeckis and company tried to avoid this particular effect by casting Gary Sinise, a highly expressive (some would say, overly expressive), mannered actor as Lieutenant Dan, a physically impaired foil to Tom Hanks's mentally impaired starring role. So volatile are Sinise's various appearances throughout the film that Hanks' centrality, if never entirely negated, is to a certain extent modified.

[10]Orson Welles and Peter Bogdanovich, *This is Orson Welles*, ed. Jonathan Rosenbaum (New York: HarperCollins, 1992).

[11]The term is borrowed from Jonathan Rosenbaum, "Orson Welles' Essay Films and Documentary Fictions: A Two-Part Speculation," *Cinematograph* 4 (1991), 169–79.

[12]Edgar Morin, *The Stars*, tr. Richard Howard (New York: Grove Press, 1961).

[13]As an actor, Welles's first Hollywood film was not *Citizen Kane* (1941), but *Swiss Family Robinson* (1940), for which he speaks the opening narration, albeit uncredited.

[14]These categories are drawn from Dyer, 121–32.

[15]As early as 1946, the *Harvard Lampoon* awarded Welles its "Worst Single Performance—Male" award for *The Stranger* (Cobbett Steinberg, *Reel Facts: The Movie Book of Records*, Updated Edition [New York: Vintage Books, 1982], 333).

[16]Richard Dyer, *Stars*, 89.

[17]Virginia Wright Wexman, *Creating the Couple: Love, Marriage, and Hollywood Performance* (Princeton: Princeton University Press, 1993), 17–18.

[18]Roberta Pearson, *Eloquent Gestures: The Transformation of Performance Style in the Griffith Biograph Films* (Berkeley: University of California Press, 1992), 38–51 and passim.

[19]I discuss Welles's performance in *Citizen Kane* in "Orson Welles as Performer," *Persistence of Vision*, No. 7 (1989), 73–82.

BILLY WILDER

BURT PRELUTSKY

AN INTERVIEW WITH BILLY WILDER

Billy Wilder turned ninety years old on June 22 of 1996. The writer and director of such classics as Double Indemnity, The Lost Weekend, Sunset Boulevard, Stalag 17, Sabrina, The Seven Year Itch, Witness for the Prosecution, Some Like it Hot, *and* The Apartment *still works out of his office in Beverly Hills, where this interview was conducted.*

BP: What sort of home did you grow up in?

BW: I was born in a small town in the old Austrian-Hungarian empire, and we moved to Vienna when I was four. All I ever wanted to be was a writer, although my middle-class parents wanted me to be a lawyer or a doctor. My father was a businessman and, in his own way, a kind of dreamer. But business did not appeal to me. My family were not theatergoers, and there were very few books or classical records in the house.

BP: Did you set out to be a screenwriter?

BW: No, I wanted to work for a newspaper. I had no connections, so I just made the rounds. In those days, in Vienna, there were many papers. One Saturday afternoon I got very lucky. I went up to the third floor of the city's number one tabloid, opened a door and there was the theater critic fucking his secretary. She ran out of the room while he fiddled with his buttons. This was before zippers became popular. He asked me what I wanted, and I told him I was looking for a job. And he said, "You're lucky I was working overtime today."

Newspaper work moved me in the right direction. I went to Berlin to write a piece on Paul Whiteman, who was touring Europe with his band, and I never went back to Vienna. It was in Germany that I began writing scripts. They were silent movies in those days, but I enjoyed writing them even though it was just action.

BP: I have heard rumors that, during your years in Berlin, you occasionally moonlighted as a gigolo.

BW: You could say that. I called myself a dancer. Of course, if I ran into people I knew, I would always say I was doing research for a newspaper story. I wasn't the best dancer, but I had the best dialogue.

The German ladies were usually old and pretty fat, and just wanted someone who'd dance with them at teatime or after dinner.

BP: And did they give you money?

BW: Sometimes. Or I'd be dancing with, say, Mrs. Landau, and I'd say, "Mrs. Landau, I think this might be our last dance. My shoes are wearing out." And the next day, I'd receive dozens of her husband's worn shoes.

I was very popular because I had an American girlfriend and she taught me the Charleston. At the time, there were not many of us in Germany who could do it.

BP: When did you leave Germany?

BW: The day after the Reichstag fire, I left for Paris. From there, I went to Hollywood. Even without the Nazis, I think I would have wound up in Hollywood. But not so quickly.

BP: As a reporter in Berlin, did you ever have occasion to interview Hitler?

BW: No. In fact, I only saw him once. It was at a movie premiere. I looked over and there he was, seated in the loge of honor. I always say I would have shot him, except for two small details—no revolver and no guts.

BP: Did you come to America fluent in English?

BW: No. In school, I had to study Latin, but I had the choice between French and English and, like a fool, I took French.

I arrived in Hollywood when I was 28. It took me about two years before I found myself thinking in English. The accent, of course, I was stuck with. If you come after the age of 12, you don't lose it. In the beginning, I wrote my scripts in German, and somebody would translate them.

BP: How did you come to collaborate with Charles Brackett?

BW: In 1938, I was under contract at Paramount, earning $150 a week. There were about 140 of us writers delivering 10 or 11 pages every Thursday to a studio executive named Manny Wolf. One day, Wolf called me into his office. It seemed they needed someone to write *Bluebeard's Eighth Wife* for Ernst Lubitsch. For some reason, Wolf decided to team me up with Brackett.

I thought it was a fine idea. I already had great respect for Brackett. He was much older than me and had written several novels and many fine pieces for the *Saturday Evening Post*.

BP: You wrote with Brackett for a quarter of a century and then another twenty with I.A.L. Diamond. Did you feel you lacked something in your writing or were there other reasons that you always chose to write in tandem?

BW: I had no confidence when I was first starting out because I only knew English from going to the movies. After Brackett and I split up, I found it too lonely to write by myself.

BP: How did you work with your partners? Would you each write a different scene?

BW: No, we always wrote together in the same room. I'd write on a big legal pad and the other one would sit at the typewriter.

BP: I realize I'm jumping ahead more than a dozen years but why did you and Brackett dissolve what had turned into the most critically-acclaimed, commercially-successful partnership Hollywood had ever seen?

BW: It was like with a match and matchbook. Something had worn out and the spark was missing. Besides, it was becoming like a bad marriage by then. We had begun squabbling over every little thing.

BP: There is an old joke about a starlet who was so stupid that she slept with the screenwriter. Did the truth inherent in that joke in any way make you decide to become a director in 1942?

BW: I didn't become a director to get prettier girls. I have always thought of myself primarily as a writer. The problem was that the directors weren't shooting what Charley and I wrote. Mitchell Leisen, who directed three of ours, would skip lines, even leave out half scenes, and not be the least bit concerned. I'd go on the set and watch Leisen with horror. Then when I'd complain, he'd have me removed bodily from the sound stage. I remember once looking for Leisen to discuss a scene we had written, and I found him in the wardrobe room counting pleats on a dress with Edith Head. You know you're in big trouble when your director would rather count pleats than discuss characters.

In the theater, when you're a playwright, you sit in the second row at rehearsals and the actors ask your permission to change "usually" to "frequently." But in Hollywood, when you're a writer, you're just a pisher.

When people ask me if it's important that a director can write, I say its not so important. What's essential is that he can read.

BP: How did you convince Paramount to take a chance on a fellow who could do both?

BW: Preston Sturges had just made the transition, so I was able to persuade them to give me a shot. You have to remember, movies weren't such a big deal then. I mean, Paramount would produce 50 a year and, because they owned their own theaters, they could pretty much guarantee that none of them would do too badly. Besides, I was of value to the studio as a writer. So Paramount figured, they'd keep me happy, I'd do something artsy-fartsy and fall on my face. Then I'd go back to my typewriter, keep my mouth shut and that would be that!

BP: Instead you turned out one of the biggest hits of the year, the comedy smash *The Major and the Minor*.

BW: Yes, I was very lucky with the casting on that one. Ginger Rogers had just won her Oscar for *Kitty Foyle*. How often does a director get last year's Academy Award winner for his first movie?

An interesting thing about the movie that most people don't seem to pick up on is that, 20 years before *Lolita* came along, this was the story of a man who gets a hard on every time he looks at this woman he *thinks* is a 12-year-old.

BP: You wrote *Double Indemnity* with Raymond Chandler, instead of Brackett. Why was that?

BW: That was entirely Brackett's decision. He wasn't comfortable with the subject matter. He wasn't the only one. I had a hell of a time getting a male lead. I confess I even sunk so low as to offer the part to George Raft. After I told him the story, he was confused. He said, "I don't get it. Where's the lapel scene?" Then it was my turn to be confused. "What's a lapel scene?" "You know," he said, "that's where I turn over my lapel and there's a badge, and I arrest the dame for knocking off her husband."

When I explained there couldn't be a lapel scene because that character had helped the woman kill her husband, Raft turned around and walked away.

I went over the Paramount contract list and saw Fred MacMurray's name. After he read the script, he also turned me down. He said he couldn't do it because he'd actually have to act. For years, he'd only done very light comedies. But I told him not to worry. I told him he'd play the role just like the saxophone player he used to be. And he did, and he was perfect.

BP: Didn't you have to work around the censorship codes in *Double Indemnity*? I assume, for example, that when Stanwyck visits MacMurray at his apartment the first time, they have sex.

BW: Of course, and very good sex, or how could she persuade such a man to kill her husband? I learned from Lubitsch that the scene between the two lovers the next morning tells you much more about their sexual behavior than actually showing them having sex, and pushes the story forward. Now when you see a sex scene, it's usually so hard to figure out what's happening. Is that her elbow? Is that his shoulder?

BP: The following year you and Brackett swept the major Oscars with *The Lost Weekend*. Were you surprised that such a grim story would do so well?

BW: I think we did so well partly because they didn't give me any Oscars for *Double Indemnity* in 1944. So, in '45, they made up for it.

It's very gratifying when you win because for maybe three days your agent can get you more money. It's also a validation of the work. Not as good as box office success, but still very nice.

All in all an Oscar is a very good thing. It helps in the business and it also helps in the community.

BP: How so?

BW: The dentist looks down. "That's an Oscar-winner in the chair," he says to himself. Maybe he's a little more careful with the drill.

BP: You mentioned money. Do you feel you were well-paid for your efforts?

BW: I am very well off but not from the movies. I only made really big money by selling off my art collection and by betting against the Rams.

BP: All through your career, you've fluctuated between drama and comedy. Obviously you were skilled at both. How did you determine what sort of story to tackle next?

BW: People see a comedy, and they assume you were in a good mood when you made it. Wrong. With me, when I'm in a good mood, I write a drama. In a depression, in order to feel better, I do farce.

BP: There were two of your movies which I feel were hurt by inappropriate casting. They were *Love in the Afternoon* with Gary Cooper and *Sabrina* with Humphrey Bogart. Am I wrong in thinking that, good as they usually were, Cooper and Bogart were not ideal casting choices?

BW: We agree. In both cases, I very much wanted Cary Grant. Although he and I were friends, he never wanted to work with me. I don't know why. Maybe it was my accent.

Unfortunately, Bogart knew he was my second choice. All through the shooting of *Sabrina*, he would bring up Cary Grant. He was very mean to me, and I was very annoyed with him. For that role, after all, who wouldn't have wanted Cary Grant? But, when Bogart was dying, I went to visit him at his home. He was very brave and, in the end, I forgave him everything and held him in the highest esteem.

BP: Have there been other occasions when you had to settle for your second choice? Other times when you had to consider writing in a lapel scene in order to nab George Raft?

BW: Fortunately, things never got quite that bad. But there were times when we didn't get who we wanted. For instance, we had Montgomery Clift lined up for *Sunset Boulevard* but at the last second, his agent reneged on the deal and we had to sign William Holden, then a young actor under contract to Paramount. I still don't know why Clift backed out that way.

BP: Wasn't it because of his longtime relationship with the blues singer, Libby Holman, who was twice Clift's age? As I understood it, she had pressured him to turn down the role because she was afraid people would assume that Norma Desmond and Joe Gillis were based on her and Clift.

BW: Fascinating. I'd never heard that. For *Sunset Boulevard* I thought of Mae West, but I dismissed the notion. The age discrepancy was right, but it would have made it a comedy and we would have lost the tragic overtones. And then I realized that it would be best to have an actress who had never appeared in sound pictures. I thought of Pola Negri, and then of Gloria Swanson.

Now, for *The Apartment* I had signed Paul Douglas to play the head of the insurance company. But, three days before the shooting began, he had a heart attack. So I called Fred MacMurray. He absolutely refused. He said he made movies for Disney and he had his wholesome family image to consider, and he would be ruined if he played this terrible adulterer. But I talked him into it, and it didn't ruin anything.

The next time I had to replace an actor, it was Peter Sellers, who died just before we started *Kiss Me, Stupid*. We got Ray Walston, who is a fine actor, but is no Peter Sellers. The movie was a dog. With Sellers it would have been five percent better. So it would only have been 95% of a bomb.

BP: After *Sunset Boulevard* Charles Brackett went off to write and produce on his own. You teamed up with I.A.L. Diamond. After all those years with one man, what were you looking for in a new collaborator?

BW: The point of collaboration is that the two guys have to respect each other, but not think alike. If they agree on everything, it's pointless. You have to be conciliatory and respectful, and I had to remember not to throw my weight around just because I was producing and directing. When it came to the writing, there was no fighting. If we didn't agree on a scene or a line, we just went on to find something we were both nuts about.

Of Diamond, my wife Audrey said, "He's the best collaborator there ever was with the possible exception of Quisling."

BP: Which of your movies do you like the most?

BW: The big hits mostly, although I'm not too ashamed of *Ace in the Hole*, which didn't do very well. I'd say *The Apartment* was the picture with the least mistakes.

I constantly rewrite my movies in my mind. But with *The Apartment*, not so much as with some of the others.

I also liked *Double Indemnity*, *Some Like It Hot*, *Sabrina*, and *Sunset Boulevard*.

BP: Financially, your greatest success was *Irma la Douce*, but you neglected to mention it.

BW: Yes, it was a huge hit. But I'm not sure why. It was a very hard movie to do and it didn't come out quite the way I wanted. It's nothing to be ashamed of, but it's not a movie I think about too much.

BP: *Irma* was originally a French and Broadway musical but you removed the songs. That's interesting because, on four occasions, you have written movies which were later turned into Broadway musicals.

BW: Four? I can only think of three. There was *Sunset Boulevard*, of course, and *The Apartment*, which became *Promises, Promises*, and *Some Like It Hot*, which they turned into *Sugar*. What else?

BP: *Ninotchka* was the basis for *Silk Stockings*.

BW: Oh, yes. That one I never saw.

BP: You're not a fan of Cole Porter's?

BW: I'm his biggest fan, but *Ninotchka* was made for Greta Garbo. And there's no way Hildegard Neff could be Garbo.

BP: You did see *Sunset Boulevard*, though . . . .

BW: Yes. I don't make any money off it, but Mr. Lloyd Webber, who's a very gracious man, invited me to the openings in London and New York. I think it's a very good show, and would make a hell of a movie.

BP: One of my favorite movie trivia questions involves you. Six people who have, themselves, directed movies, have appeared in movies you've written.

BW: Let me think. There's De Mille and von Stroheim in *Sunset Boulevard*. And Mitchell Leisen in *Hold Back the Dawn*. Did you say there are three others?

BP: Otto Preminger in *Stalag 17*, Jack Lemmon, who directed *Kotch*, and Charles Laughton, who directed *Night of the Hunter*.

BW: Very good, I forgot about the two actors. They were very smart. They tried it once and it was enough.

BP: Do you have any unproduced scripts lying around in your files?

BW: No, I'm too practical. I only wrote scripts when people were paying me. What I do have are a lot of ideas jotted down. Once, such a note came in very handy. I had just finished making *Some Like It Hot* and couldn't wait to make another movie with Jack Lemmon. He is wonderful to work with and very talented. So, even before *Hot* was released, I started to figure out what we could do next. I went to my drawer of ideas and on a little piece of paper was written "David Lean's *Brief Encounter*—What about the guy who owned the flat where the lovers met?" Remember? Trevor Howard had a friend who let him use his flat. So, that little note to myself got me thinking. And that's how Izzy Diamond and I came to write *The Apartment*.

BP: After 1963, with the possible exception of *The Fortune Cookie*, none of your movies enjoyed either acclaim or box office success. They were *Kiss Me, Stupid*, *The Private Life of Sherlock Holmes*, *Avanti!*, *The Front Page*, *Fedora* and *Buddy, Buddy*. What happened?

BW: Maybe I lost the spark. I, myself, liked *Sherlock Holmes* very much. I thought it was a beautiful film, but it was not well received. I think part of the reason is that I had to go to Paris, and while I was away the studio cut out twenty minutes.

I should not have made *The Front Page*, though. That was a big mistake. Never do a remake. People remember the original and, with the passing of time, they remember it as much better than it was. The only movie that was ever improved was *An American Tragedy*, which George Stevens remade brilliantly as *A Place in the Sun*. *That* was a very fine film.

BP: Another exception was *The Maltese Falcon*. They made lousy versions a couple of times before John Huston got it right. Who were your role models?

BW: I learned from early Chaplin, from Renoir, from Fellini, from Pietro Germi, from von Stroheim, and, of course, from Lubitsch,

BP: Who are the younger directors you admire?

BW: Among the best things ever shot were Coppola's first two *Godfather* movies and the first half of Kubrick's *Full Metal Jacket*. Scorsese is marvelous and Jonathan Demme is wonderful.

BP: You made two movies with Marilyn Monroe. Are you as astonished as I am that, three decades after her death, there remains this unquenchable fascination with the woman?

BW: It boggles the mind. When I was in Vienna, in the '20s, every week in the Sunday supplements there was a new story about what really happened at Mayerling with Prince Rudolf of Hapsburg and his mistress,

Marie Vetsera. Did they commit suicide in 1888 or didn't they? And did she really go off with him knowing what was in store, because it's always better to go to a hunting lodge and die with a prince than go to the Riviera with some schmuck? If so, she was the "ultimate social climber."

In any case, it was a lot more interesting than Marilyn Monroe, and even that became too much. I swear, if I see one more theory about her death, I'll scream.

You know all the stories about Marilyn Monroe. How she would keep cast and crew and 300 extras waiting all day and then show up at 3 p.m. or 5 p.m. And yet I would gladly have made another movie with her. The camera loved her, the people loved her. She had It.

BP: I think that the biggest laugh of *Some Like It Hot* was the last line.

BW: We were set to film that last scene on a Monday, and weren't satisfied how to close it. What could Jack Lemmon say to Joe E. Brown after he gets a proposal, and what on earth would Brown say back to him? When Lemmon finally announces he's not a girl, Brown says . . . "Nobody's perfect." That was Diamond's suggestion, and I said, that's good but maybe we can do better, let's think about it over the weekend. On Monday we didn't have a better line. Who knew it would become so famous?

BP: Do you do any writing now that I.A.L. Diamond is gone?

BW: A few things, but I don't finish them. I find I miss having a collaborator, a soundingboard, someone whose taste and ideas I respect. Also, having a collaborator makes you come in on time. Now, when I hit an obstacle, I just go on to something else.

I'd still like to make one or two more pictures. It would be a glorious way to go. Actually, making a movie is not so difficult; what's hard is making a deal. How can I go in and pitch an idea to an ex-William Morris mailboy?

BP: Which are the movies you wish you'd made?

BW: Top of the list, *The Battleship Potemkin*, then *The Bicycle Thief, Seduced and Abandoned*, Lubitsch's *The Shop Around the Corner*, Fellini's *La Dolce Vita*, and a couple of Ingmar Bergman's films. But I could not have done what they did. Those directors all had their own handwriting. Particularly Lubitsch.

BP: Did you and Lubitsch emigrate together?

BW: No, we were friends, but he came in the '20s which is when the really talented people came over from Europe. I didn't come until '34. My group just wanted to escape the ovens.

But I lived with Lubitsch for a while. He was not only very talented and unique, he was an outstanding man. He had this very sophisticated French humor, but he, himself, was the son of a Russian tailor.

BP: Has money been important?

BW: Not very much. I have always lived modestly. I never had a house in Palm Springs or a boat on the Riviera. No excess. What money I spent went into art.

BP: Most of which you auctioned off in 1989. What made you part with a collection that was regarded as one of the finest in Hollywood?

BW: It just seemed the right time. I donated some of it to the museum in Jerusalem, and I let Christie's auction off most of the rest. Partly, I was calling their bluff. People kept telling me that prices had never before been so high, and I was a little curious.

BP: How much did it sell for?

BW: About $34,000,000.

BP: Who are the people you wish you'd met?

BW: I would have liked to have met Proust and Mozart. I have known a lot of people, of course . . . Steinbeck, Stravinsky, Thomas Mann, even Freud, who kicked me out of his apartment. If you have a good constitution and a good doctor, you will eventually get to meet a lot of people.

BP: What did you say to irritate Freud?

BW: It wasn't anything personal. He just hated journalists. In 1926, in Vienna, very few people had been analyzed, and the newspapers were always making fun of Freud. So when I went to his apartment to interview him, he tossed me out on general principle. I did get to see the couch, though. It was very small.

BP: Would you advise a loved one to follow in your footsteps?

BW: No. I'd tell him to go do something else—maybe be a landscape architect. With the movies, you not only have to be talented, you have to be very, very lucky.

SAMUEL MARX

THE BOMB MOVIE

Editors' Note: Samuel Marx published three books about Hollywood, concentrating on the first ten of his more than sixty years in the movie business. He was working on his autobiography, which was to cover his youthful experiences as a Broadway journalist in the 1920s and the rest of his career at M-G-M and other studios, when, in March of 1992, he died a few weeks after his ninetieth birthday. The manuscript was far from complete. Marx left draft material, in manuscript and on tape, in various stages of completion, and he had kept extensive files of his fugitive journalism. His wife, Sara Greene Marx, and Robert Murray Davis, professor of English at the University of Oklahoma, have used this material to compile the manuscript of "Mythical Kingdoms," from which this essay is taken.

In 1985 H. S. Nusbaum sent me a photocopy of an article by Nathan Reingold, "Metro-Goldwyn-Mayer Meets the Atom Bomb." Nusbaum said it had not appeared in any U.S. publication and that he had told Reingold to call me. He never did so. But after I read the article, I called him. He hung up on me, so I never got to tell him about my involvement with the movie *The Beginning or the End*.

One November morning in 1945 I got an excited call from my good friend Tony Owen. He wanted me to come at once to the Beverly Wilshire Hotel for breakfast because he had something absolutely fantastic to talk about.

I drove over. Tony showed me a long letter to his wife, the starlet Donna Reed, from a Professor Edward Tompkins, who had been her science teacher in Iowa. Tompkins had quite a crush on that little girl, obviously, but had disappeared during the war.

The letter was fascinating. She hadn't heard from him in seven years, he wrote, because he had been recruited into the scientific group of Professor Enrico Fermi engaged in the development of the atomic pile at

the old stadium at the University of Chicago. He had then been transferred to Oak Ridge, Tennessee, where he worked on the production of
the atomic bombs. He was writing to Donna, his only contact in the film
world, with the idea for a picture about the way the bomb was developed, and how life was at Oak Ridge. He and other scientists would be
delighted to welcome anyone she might send and tell them the fantastic
story now that they were no longer sworn to secrecy.

I agreed with Tony that this was a marvelous idea for a film, and after
breakfast we got into our cars and raced over to M-G-M. I took him in
to Louis B. Mayer. We told him about the letter, and he said that we
should call Carter Barron, M-G-M's liaison in Washington, to find out
whether the government would object to a film being made. The next
day Barron reported that he foresaw no objections. He urged me to stop
at Oak Ridge on my way to Washington to get information, and in any
case, President Truman and Prime Minister Attlee were about to hold
meetings about the bomb and I should be in Washington as soon as possible after they ended. I reported this to Mayer, and he said, "Take the
Starwind [the M-G-M plane] and meet this man in Tennessee and come
back and tell me what you find."

And so Tony and I took off in the DC-3, and we stepped out into a
cold, dreary day in Knoxville to be greeted by Dr. Tompkins, a fairly
young man, and three associates.

It could hardly be more dramatic, under those gray skies, than to have
a man step up to you and say, "Mr. Marx, we are happy to have you here
and tell you what we know, because frankly, we are scared to death."
That was my introduction to the world of the nuclear scientists who had
been involved with the making of the atomic bomb.

Tony and I stayed in Oak Ridge nearly a week. Colonel Parsons, the
temporary commander, saw that we were given passes to various places
inside the huge complex and told that, while we couldn't go inside the
buildings, we could take photographs of the exteriors. In fact, we were
permitted to go into several areas where scientists or workers themselves were unable to go, because they were restricted to the area covered by the color of their special badge. We had several colors on our
badges and far more latitude.

The scientists couldn't go everywhere we could go, but they were now
free to talk. I listened, sometimes to groups considered illegal by the
military. They told us dozens of stories. All were eager to show the world
what they had done, individually. They hated the Army for cooping them
up for the duration of the war, forbidding them to speak of their work

even to their families. After the bomb was dropped, they were warned not to speak out or be charged with violating the Anti-Sedition Act. They were all outraged by the fact that the United States seemed only interested in atomic energy for war. They were really a rather noble group in that respect, but they were certainly chaotic. I couldn't take some of their arrogance, some of their feeling of super-importance, hating the army, hating the military, hating the engineer corps, hating General Groves. They were positive that they'd all been double-crossed, and they wanted only their story shown.

I enlisted Professor Tompkins to be our guide, and I promised to bring him to Hollywood to work as a technical advisor. I kept my promise and regretted making it because throughout the time he was at the studio, he was a spy for the scientists.

The scientists had all formed little societies. The Los Alamos group called themselves the Association of Los Alamos Scientists, ALAS. They were sure that the world was set on blowing itself up. They were also sure that we were going to make a purely commercial film, which to an extent M-G-M was trying to do, and they wanted a picture that would show their side and would have nothing to do with the bomb—which, of course, was the most dramatic part.

A couple of the men I met had actually written letters to Groves and Oppenheimer offering to ride the first bomb down until it exploded as a protest against what was being done. Many of them claimed they never understood that they were only involved with an atomic bomb. They had thought they were involved purely with atomic energy. As a result, they were hostile in all directions.

I learned enough at Oak Ridge to realize that we could make a tremendous film. I telephoned Mr. Mayer and told him so, and he said that I should go to Washington and consult Carter Barron, M-G-M's representative in Washington. Mayer said he would tell Barron to see that I got every help possible. And of course M-G-M and Louis B. Mayer were so powerful that even though he was a staunch Republican and Franklin D. Roosevelt was an equally staunch Democrat, Carter Barron and Louis B. Mayer and M-G-M seemed to have access to anything they wanted.

So Tony and I took Professor Tompkins and James Stangby to Washington. We met with Colonel Swarthout, the Army's liaison to the motion picture industry, and General Groves, and they agreed that, at least as far as making a film went, there was no substantial difference of opinion between the scientists and the Army. General Groves even said that

Samuel Marx (Producer), General Leslie Groves of the Manhattan Project, and
Norman Taurog (Director), discuss the filming of *The Beginning or the End*.

he would allow his name to be used for one of the characters. His wife
said that if Clark Gable played the part, she insisted on playing herself.

We also met with Colonel William Consodine, who was head of
Counter-Intelligence, and General Groves's secretary, Jean O'Leary,
who knew everything from the beginning and was awarded a Congres-
sional Medal of Honor for not telling anything. Colonel Farrell, who had
travelled to Tinian with the bombs and supervised their use, gave us material that we used in the story. Colonel Dupuy was more cautious: he
wanted permission at least from the Secretary of War and preferably
from President Truman.

I also met with Archbishop Francis Spellman. He had been asked to
intervene when a Catholic priest had come to Oak Ridge trying to collect money to build a church. The government didn't want to explain
why they couldn't allow him to do so, and they asked Spellman to call
him off. Spellman himself had said mass on Tinian after the bombing of
Hiroshima and before the bombing of Nagasaki. He regarded the bomb

as equal in importance to the discovery of fire. He deplored the killing of civilians, but he believed that any weapon which could end the war, even one like this that changed the face of the earth, should be used. However, he was doubtful about the future, or whether there would be a future. "This bomb fulfills the third prophecy of the Old Testament," he said. "Man will destroy himself by fire. I hope your motion picture can work to avert such suicide. You had better hurry."

Senator Brien McMahon, head of the Atomic Energy Committee, was more knowledgeable and even more emphatic: "I believe it is the most important happening on the face of the earth since the birth of Christ!"

I listened to Prime Minister Attlee address a joint session of Congress, and then Tony Owen and I were given an audience with Harry Truman. He impressed me as much as any man I ever met and possibly ever will. He was the most controlled person in the most incredibly important job. He had been a haberdasher, he had been a typical politician in the Kansas City political jungle. He was like a great tennis player who suddenly gets a chance at Wimbledon's number one court and plays far over his head. Truman, without doubt, was a great man. He had risen to the opportunity when Franklin D. Roosevelt died. I might say that I have worked for many film people, and I have been impressed by some, not too much impressed by others, but I've rarely been in the office of a film mogul that the phone hasn't rung or he hasn't picked up his mail or he hasn't stopped for any number of interruptions.

Tony and I were supposed to be with Truman for fifteen minutes, but we were there nearly an hour. He was charming and intelligent; he concentrated entirely on the topic; he stressed the importance of doing an important film on the atomic bomb; he knew the perils ahead; he was light-hearted at times.

He told me that when he was head of a Senate committee overseeing government expenditures, he heard about this enormous government enterprise at Oak Ridge, and off he went, only to be stopped at the gate and told he couldn't come in. Now, this was a pretty extraordinary situation, and Truman, in a high dudgeon, as one could expect from him, headed straight for a telephone and put in a call to President Franklin D. Roosevelt and demanded entrance. And Roosevelt, in those dulcet, friendly tones, said "Harry, this is a very special place. I'm going to ask you not to go inside, to put aside your feelings that we've been spending money you should know about, and when you come back to Washington, come and see me and I'll give you some information about this particular place. But please do not go into it now."

When Truman got back to Washington, he was tapped to be vice-president for Roosevelt's fourth term, and then he either forgot to ask, or he didn't want to ask, or perhaps he got so busy that it was impossible to ask. In any case, when Roosevelt died, in July of 1944, and Truman became president, he still didn't know what had been going on at Oak Ridge.

A few days after he became president, he told me, he received a call from the Secretary of War, saying "Mr. President, I would like to bring a couple of men in to see you—Mr. Vannevar Bush, who is in charge of the United States government scientific efforts, and he will probably bring with him another chap, one of the great army engineers, General Groves, and we want to have a talk with you." He also said, "We don't want to come into the White House through the front gate. Please arrange for us to come through the back."

When they arrived, Truman heard for the first time that the United States was attempting to build an atomic bomb. Truman said, "Is it going to work?" And Vannevar Bush said, "The man in charge of our scientific operation, J. Robert Oppenheimer, told us there are four different ways that he believes can result in a bomb. We are going to test the bomb next August, in New Mexico, at the White Sands proving ground, and we also have a laboratory for constructing the final bomb at Los Alamos, in New Mexico nearby. We are confident it will work."

General Groves, who had been the engineer in charge of building Oak Ridge and all the other laboratories, said he was quite certain the atomic bomb would work. And so, Truman said, that was how he not only discovered what was going on at Oak Ridge but also that the United States was in what they considered then to be a race with Germany to develop the atomic bomb.

Then Truman asked me about my home life. I said I had two boys, seven and eight. He said, "That reminds me of an old joke I heard when I was in Missouri." It was about the doctor who gave out prescriptions by number, and he treated some patient and he wanted to give him prescription number fifteen, but he didn't have the right things with him, so he said, "I guess I'll just give you seven and eight." And this was Truman's idea of a funny joke.

On the more serious side, he said that American politics suffered from the fact that it could not bring top people into it. He said, "Everybody that goes into American politics goes in with an idea of graft, of bribery, of only what's in it for him." Coming from Harry Truman, I guess that's pretty ironic. I believe that he had no interest in what was in it for him, except that he wanted to do good things for the country.

As we were going out the door, he asked, "What are you going to call this picture?" I said we really didn't know because we had just come from Oak Ridge and had hardly begun. He said, "I'd like to suggest a title. Call it *The Beginning or the End*, because when you think about it, that is what the world is now up to. How they handle the atomic bomb in the future is going to show them which way the world will go. We are either at the beginning, or believe me, we're at the end."

From Washington, Tony and I went up to New York. I reported to Mr. Mayer that I already had enough material that I was convinced I could get a great picture out of it. So he said, "Well, follow through a bit in New York and then come back and report, and we'll give you a go-ahead at that time. Until then, do what you want to do, but don't make it decisive until you get an answer from me."

In New York I met Bob Considine, whom I was terribly taken with. He was a charming, wonderful man who was himself so involved with humanity that he was anxious to work on this script, and I was sure he'd be the right one.

I met J. Robert Oppenheimer, whom I had known as a boy, and he agreed that if the picture went ahead I could show someone called Oppenheimer on screen. But I would have to come up to northern California to see him—he was then, I believe, a professor at Berkeley, but he lived in San Francisco—and I agreed. I asked him what he might want if we put an actor in his role, and he said, "My wife has been having a hell of a time getting nylons. When you come up to San Francisco, bring her six pair of nylons, and that's all you have to do."

He must have saved M-G-M a million dollars, because every scientist that we impersonated, and ultimately we impersonated a hundred and five living people, the scientists always asked about money, as the Army men did, and I could reply, "Would you like to get what Einstein wants, or J. Robert Oppenheimer?" And of course they would, and then they discovered that Einstein didn't want anything and Oppenheimer wanted six pair of nylons. I wish we had paid them. Some of them admitted that if they had been paid, we could have had total cooperation. Instead, we had nothing but trouble.

Only Professor Tompkins, to my recollection, actually received money. I think we paid him $10,000 for his letter to Donna Reed. Tony took $20,000 for having brought it to me, and when the picture was in production he went to Louis B. Mayer and complained he didn't get enough and he walked away with another $20,000. Next to some of the actors and the high-priced director, all of whom were more or less under contract to M-G-M and certainly far outdistancing my salary, Tony probably got the most out of it.

All the Army men impersonated in the picture got paid, $5,000 to about twenty or twenty-five thousand to General Groves and Colonel Tibbets and General Farrell.

But this was later, of course. While we were still in planning stages in New York, the only man in town and perhaps anywhere who wasn't interested in the bomb was George Jean Nathan, the Broadway critic, who berated me one night in the Stork Club because some people I was with wanted to know about the bomb, and he didn't want anything said about it. He just considered it a bloody bore, and wondered why should anybody be interested. But except for him, everyone was.

I was at a party one night with Earl Tibbets, the pilot of the *Enola Gay*, and a couple of other Air Force men. It was a pleasant party, there was liquor and music, a lot of us were sitting around the floor. I don't remember where it was; it may even have been in my hotel room because I was enjoying the luxury of M-G-M's enormous apartment in the Waldorf Towers. Some girl said, "Is it true that the bomb that was dropped on Hiroshima was dropped with a parachute?"

There was a lengthy silence. Finally I spoke up. "No. The reason that impression seems to have got around is that a lot of instruments were dropped by a plane that flew over those cities first and threw out all kinds of radio material that would broadcast back to the plane when the bomb went off. It would broadcast the heat emanated by the bomb— until the instruments burned up, of course—and the sound, whatever could be caught by a sensitive instrument, up to the moment of its destruction. They were dropped by parachute. Then the observation plane dashed away from there and the plane with the bomb came in and dropped the bomb without a parachute, and when it exploded, it destroyed all those instruments still dangling in the air."

When I finished, one of the boys sitting on the floor thumped his fist down and said, "I'll be damned. I dropped those instruments. I'm not allowed to tell anybody. But here comes a man from Hollywood who knows about it, and nobody's going to stop him from talking."

When I was in New York, I got word that Hal Wallis at Warner Brothers was planning to do a picture on the atomic bomb called "Top Secret." This meant that we were going to be in a race, and so just before Thanksgiving I went back to Culver City and dictated a lengthy memorandum on what I had learned as explanation of why I thought the film must be made and had it mimeographed and distributed to all the executives. It created quite a furor. To say so myself, it was a marvelous reporting job, an awful lot of information that nobody had ever heard and had never been in the newspapers.

On Thanksgiving day, Louis B. Mayer told me that Nicholas Schenk, president of M-G-M, wanted to know more about it and that I must go straight back to New York and have a meeting with him. I don't think I even stayed for dinner with Marie and the boys, I just headed straight back and had this meeting with Nick Schenk and some of his New York people. Everybody was excited about it. I was told I would get every access to every star in the studio. It was going to be M-G-M's big movie.

I returned to the studio very elated, and we now made plans to see Fermi and Szilard in Chicago and Oppenheimer in San Francisco. I was now in touch with everybody involved with the making of the atomic bomb.

The night that Tony and I embarked for Oak Ridge on the DC-3 to bump around the skies they were selling in the airport, at the news stand, a new publication called the Smythe Report on atomic energy for peacetime purposes. This was right after I'd read Tompkins' letter, so I bought a copy and settled down in the plane to read it. It was great reading if you were a nuclear physicist. It was absolute Greek to me. I tried, and I gave up. When I finished the movie a year later, I picked up my copy of the Smythe report, and I could read it like it was a Raymond Chandler mystery story. I had met so many scientists and had been told so much that I had become a kind of nuclear physicist myself.

The picture was caught in a terrible political involvement. For one thing, the scientists and the engineers and the military men engaged in a tug of war. And the scientists knew as little about making a film as we knew about nuclear physics. For example, Szilard contended that he had performed the identical experiment creating fissionable material that Fermi got credit for. He insisted that we show a duplication of almost identical scenes. Movies are supposed to be constructed of scenes that forward the action. This one would have stopped it cold.

There was also a tug of war inside the studio, and I was the one in the middle, serving as the rope. First of all, the picture was assigned by L. B. to James K. McGuinness. Now McGuinness was an intelligent man. He bulled this picture through, and there were many obstacles. But he did it with such partiality to his own pet people that I wound up using people I didn't want and couldn't reject. It hurt the film in the end.

Much worse was to happen, but at least with McGuinness it began to take shape as a project. He agreed to wrap it up. He agreed to Robert Oppenheimer; he agreed to Robert Considine. But he insisted that his friend Frank Wead, who had become a screenwriter after being crippled as a Navy flyer, be the chief writer and that Considine was simply along for the ride. And I could not in any way control the writing of Frank Wead, who had no compassion that I could find.

If you dig back far enough in history, you'll find that the United States Navy flew four seaplanes around the world, practically the first time the world had been circumnavigated, I guess, by aircraft, certainly by seaplanes. Frank Wead was one of the heroes of that expedition. When I met him, he needed two sticks to walk. And the reason for his being crippled had nothing to do with his Navy life or his flying. He stepped off a curb and broke his spine. And he was never able to stand and walk erect again. He was possibly the most embittered man I know. It was literally impossible for anyone to get Frank Wead to write a soft scene for a film, and it immeasurably hurt *The Beginning or the End*.

Bob Considine, who was quite the opposite, couldn't break through. Bob had heart-rending times. And Jim McGuinness was not only under the influence of Frank Wead, but he was also completely influenced by people from his political group, which he even got me into for a little while. It was the antithesis of the anti-Nazi League. It was the Alliance for the Preservation of American Ideals, and it included some pretty important M-G-M people, including Bob Taylor, Victor Fleming, and Cedric Gibbons, whom I loved, and a lot of other boys who were sure, as Jim was, that the United States was about to be taken over by the Communists. Howard Emmett Rogers, Jim's right-hand associate in all this, was as rabid an anti-communist as you could find.

As I said, I even got into this organization for a little while, partly because I was asked by Cedric Gibbons. Also fellows like Eddie Bizzell and Norman Taurog who, like myself, were Jewish, had been persuaded to join to keep watch on what was happening. Jim put it very clearly, and so did Cedric Gibbons. He said, "The first minute you see any anti-Semitism in this outfit, you tell me and I'll quit with you." Well, we never really did, but I considered it about as inept an organization as I've ever seen. They suspected Russian Communists had already invaded and were behind every lamp post in Hollywood.

Norman Taurog was selected to direct *The Beginning or the End*. Norman had directed *Skippy* and many charming, soft little movies. He was as unsuitable to do a hard picture on the bombing of Japan as anybody in Hollywood. But he got the job. I will say for Norman, he was intrigued and ultimately dedicated. It simply wasn't in his nature to make that kind of movie. There were probably ten different directors at M-G-M—Jack Conway, Vic Fleming, Mervyn Leroy, who did *Thirty Seconds over Tokyo*—I could have gone down the list and found a marvelous director who might have given us a great picture. Norman Taurog was utterly unable to do it.

However, the picture was now caught up in the political tides. Dore Schary and a group opposed the film. Somewhere along the line, influence was put to work. Certainly the script by Wead didn't come off as it should. M-G-M was still excited enough by the movie that they bought off Hal Wallis. I don't remember what they paid him, perhaps $100,000. I wish they hadn't done it.

The picture took a year of my life. I was dedicated to it too, but I became a pawn. Instead of Clark Gable playing Tibbets, or Spencer Tracy playing Groves, or an intellectual actor playing J. Robert Oppenheimer, we wound up with a secondary cast, and although they all did their best and many of them too were dedicated when they found out what the subject was, the picture never really came off.

It did have marvelous special effects. Buddy Gillespie and his staff in Special Effects did the entire bombing of Hiroshima. It startled General Groves, and he could never figure out how it was done.

It also startled J. Robert Oppenheimer. Various scientists came to my office during the making of the film, and I took Oppenheimer down to a projection room to see the scene, which we were then making, of the first testing of the bomb at White Sands. Hume Cronyn was playing Oppenheimer, and Oppenheimer sat through the rushes intrigued and quiet, until suddenly in some shots of the bomb being taken to the top of the tower for the test, he leaped out of his seat and shouted, "Not so fast! Not so fast!"

I pushed a button and we stopped the projection machine and the lights came on. I had called Norman Taurog in from the stage to see the rushes with us, and Oppenheimer looked at us and said, "Gentlemen, gentlemen. You're taking that up as if it could get up there in ten minutes. It took me three *weeks* to get it to the top of the tower."

And Norman said, "Dr. Oppenheimer, if it takes me three weeks, I'll be working at Republic tomorrow." Oppenheimer couldn't understand the mechanisms of the motion picture.

Nor could he understand the making of a good salad dressing. I took him to Romanov's for dinner, and he insisted on making his own martini, which was complete gin and explosive enough to blow the top of your head off, and then he wanted to make the salad dressing, and he got all kinds of stuff and he mixed and he mixed and it was easily the worst salad dressing I've ever tasted in my life.

While we were there, Mike Romanov came along. I introduced him. He was tremendously impressed. He sat down and talked knowledgeably about the bomb. He was very taken with Dr. Oppenheimer.

Also there that night was a newspaper columnist, whom you might expect would be rather knowledgeable, and I was proud of my guest, and I introduced Dr. Oppenheimer. The columnist gave him a very perfunctory handshake and said "Glad to know you" and walked away. Later I said to him, "Do you know who that was?" He said, "Oh, is he the guy that writes all those books in England?" He was thinking of E. Phillips Oppenheim, the novelist. So much for Hollywood recognition of great men.

Later Oppenheimer was investigated as a security risk, partly because there was evidence that he dallied amorously with a female communist. Students of espionage know the ploy of assigning a slinky charmer willing to give her all for the cause. Members of the Security Board were horrified when Oppy cheerfully admitted the affair and in fact seemed almost proud of it. They revoked his security clearance.

I can't imagine any temptress, locked in a lusty embrace with a famous scientist, coyly whispering, "Darling, tell me how to make an atomic bomb." It seems plain silly. It seems even sillier to think that he would tell her. However, it's possible that he might have given her the formula of his terrible salad dressing. He was real proud of it.

More than thirty years after the film appeared, there was a scare over a letter about how to make a hydrogen bomb. I remained calm, remembering a documentary-style film called *The House on 92nd Street* which purported to show a foreign spy stealing a briefcase full of directions for making an atomic bomb. General Groves was amused. "Anytime the Pentagon orders me to fill up some spy's briefcase with papers on how to make a bomb, I'll obey," he said. "It's only when they back up a truck that I'll start to worry!"

WILLIAM HARRISON

BIG NAMES, HUGE STORYLINES, GIGANTIC TRUTHS: SHORT TAKES ON THE WRITER IN HOLLYWOOD

The Writer heads over to the studio for a meeting with Tom Cruise's people, his producers and their assistants.

They're all dressed in jeans and $400 shirts. Sipping Diet Pepsi, they repeat the Writer's name in a litany of friendliness.

"We'd like to tell you a story and get your input," one of the assistants begins. "It's a boxing movie. Here's our storyline so far. First, there's Morgan Freeman. He's the fight manager, see, and his boxer is this black kid, a welterweight. The owner is this older white guy and he's crooked. You like boxing movies?"

"Sure, like *Rocky*," the Writer ventures. Unamazed that this imaginary film already has a tentative cast — Morgan Freeman, okay, good, he's a presence — the Writer goes into his usual nods.

"So the white owner and the fighter conspire to throw a fight," the assistant goes on. "When they get caught they blame it on Morgan Freeman, who didn't know anything about it. He's the innocent manager, see, but he takes the rap and loses his license. For a period of one year he loses his license to manage. So during that time he goes out looking for another fighter and he finds this white kid in prison.

"Tom Cruise," the Writer guesses.

"Right, and Tom is a Southern boy, dumb, and he hates blacks. He likes to knock out the black kids in the prison ring. He can hit like a mule. Anyway, Morgan Freeman helps get him out of prison. Like, you know, he's put into Morgan's care. So Tom agrees to let this black guy manage him, but it's just so he can get out of jail. All this is Act One. You follow?"

The Writer smiles and turns his can of Diet Pepsi in his fingers.

188

"Act Two, they go into training. See, Morgan Freeman is a good teacher. And they become friends. Tom learns to box and gets to be a contender."

One of the producers interrupts. He's a ferret of a man who tugs at his $400 shirt and gazes out the window into the parking lot. "Maybe you can tell us what happens in Act Three," he suggests, giving the Writer a little quiz on dramatic structure.

There's a meaningful pause, then the producer levels his gaze at the Writer. All meetings, remember, are auditions. Does anyone have a good idea here? Say something, please, that excites us.

"Oh, at the end of the story Tom Cruise gets a shot at the championship," the Writer says. "And the champion now, naturally, is that black kid who threw the fight with the crooked owner and pinned the rap on Morgan Freeman."

"You got it," the assistant gushes, happy that the obvious has been recognized.

"So they fight for the championship and Tom Cruise gets the hell beat out of him," the Writer says playfully.

Mouths open in consternation at such a sacrilege.

"Just kidding," the Writer says with a grin. "Tom wins. Morgan Freeman gets his vengeance. The end."

The producers and assistants laugh a little too loudly. Good, that's right, very good, we can take a little joke.

"So you already have the storyline," the Writer continues. "What do you need me for?"

"Ah, characterization, you're good at that, aren't you?" asks the other producer, the paunchy one.

"It's Act Two, see, we need to think about that," adds the little ferret. "Morgan Freeman and Tom Cruise become friends. All that. The characterization stuff."

Another pause. The Writer now calculates. How much money are we talking about here? This story is interracial friendship and Tom Cruise-wins. By studio standards, this is a lock: big names, a tip of the hat to major social themes, a Hollywood ending. The Writer's Guild warns its members never to share anything with anybody free, to get a signed contract before even thinking about a storyline or characterization, but in practice this is never how things work. One is auditioning. So the Writer adds to the meeting his affection for a literate advice columnist.

"Morgan Freeman reads Miss Manners," he says. "In fact, he

believes in courtesy the way some people believe in the Bible. So he carries around this big book of etiquette by Miss Manners and constantly reads passages from it to Tom Cruise. While he's teaching Tom to box, he also teaches him table etiquette and how to talk to women. And Tom discovers that courtesy works. This is their bond. In restaurants and out in the streets, it works. With women and blacks and everybody. Tom even quotes Miss Manners himself — in a reverse bit where Morgan Freeman loses his cool."

The producers laugh and slap each other on the backs. Wonderful stuff. Miss Manners, great. It softens the movie with humor, the paunchy one remarks. Wonderful. How'd you think of that? Soon everybody rises and the last handshakes begin.

The Writer drives the freeways going home. He feels clever and successful, thinking he'll certainly be hired for this project after such an impressive meeting. It's a day clear of smog in Los Angeles and some distant Filipino volcano provides a vivid sunset, as if God has used the right filter.

A week later the Writer's agent phones. The producers have decided to go with another writer, a former black boxer who is trying his first script. It's the racial thing, the agent says. Minorities get favored on projects like this.

The Writer remains philosophical, even bemused, but he figures out the truth of that meeting: he was called to the studio so they could take ideas from him, anything that might help a novice screenwriter, anything to enhance the project. They probably had a dozen or so writers stop around, established writers looking for work in the business, picking their brains in a flurry of first names and Diet Pepsi. It's the way of the world here.

He knows, too, that if they ever make that movie about the boxer and his black manager with Tom Cruise, Morgan Freeman, or the next incarnations of movie stars, wherever such a movie goes into production, at whatever studio in this decade or the next, Miss Manners will be there.

He takes an odd satisfaction in this, like a man who has been robbed of his Rolex and says, hey, they got something first class from me, a nice little piece, golden, something that works and sparkles.

*　　*　　*

Where is Robert Mitchum?

Go to Santa Barbara, turn away from the ocean and into the hills, follow a lane, go through a gate, and knock on his door.

The three of us stand there — Producer, Writer, and Assistant — waiting for his presence. Will he say something in Drunkenese? Clutch us to his left pectoral? Throw down a cigarette butt and sneer?

It's a Sunday afternoon, bright with expectation. The television producer has worked through several versions of a script meant to serve Mitchum and his son Chris, a story about father, son, and grandson, but none of the scripts has worked. The Writer hopes to do better, but revision is harder than creation — as though God didn't inherit the void and had to start out renovation with a chaos of bad gasses and sucking black holes. The Assistant is present in order to tell everybody, later, what might have occurred.

Bob opens the door himself, swinging it wide.

He grunts hello, come inside, welcome. The bass voice is profoundly familiar and there he is — broad shouldered, large in the gut, as if he has just taken a big breath and holds it for us. Those eyes we know so well: slits with bags underneath. We love him and we're on his set.

We face a long hallway, maybe forty feet down to the far end. At each side of the doorway are alcoves and in the one on the left sits a baby grand piano.

Courtesies are recited, but from the far end of the hallway a large black dog comes at us. Its paws make little whistling sounds on the tile floor as it gets its legs working, then, this accomplished, it rushes for us. We look for a place to run, but Mitchum, heroic as ever, steps between us and our attacker. He whips out a pocketsized foghorn and extends it, palm upward, so the dog can see it. The dog braces its front legs, scrambles to stop, skidding, its eyes wide, then turns and runs in the opposite direction. Mitchum grunts with satisfaction. The little noisemaker, he explains, hurts the dog's ears, so he only has to see it to turn tail. We nod and smile in relief. But somehow Mitchum is embarrassed by all this, so strides toward the piano where he slides onto the bench, gazes off for an instant while thinking of a tune, and begins to play. He plays well. It's a show tune, maybe Rodgers and Hart. By this time his wife hurries to greet us, ushering us toward a nearby patio where the cold cuts and beer are served.

Mitchum finishes the selection, gets up, and says something in

French with a perfect accent. He tries a smile, but as always when he smiles his face seems somehow broken.

The modest ranch house has been the Mitchum home for years. Nothing fancy, so that everybody is soon laughing, drinking beer and eating. Mitchum tells stories and does voices. A boxing anecdote. He was a prize fighter once, he points out, and he does a Jewish manager, Yiddish mixed in, then he's doing a stiff British drawl with lots of hars and harumphs.

Everybody relaxes, even the Assistant who is paid to be alert. After an hour or so the matter of the script is brought up. Earlier scripts favored the son or grandson. "Clearly," the producer says, "there's just one main part in this project."

Mitchum turns to the Writer to see if he agrees.

"You need some good lines and scenes," the Writer offers.

Mitchum grunts, winks, points a finger at the Writer as if to say, yes, you'll do, then grunts again. This concludes the day's actual business discussion.

More beer arrives. The black dog wanders among us, its tail lashing around, begging scraps. Mitchum says all directors are failed actors. Maybe failed writers. He falls into an Irish brogue, talking about David Lean and the filming of *Ryan's Daughter*, a movie that everyone agrees was far better than the critics allowed.

"Ah, that damn hat blowin' along the strand, do ye remember it?" he asks in his perfect Irish lilt. He goes into how they suffered with that hat, how it wouldn't behave, how they brought down giant wind machines from the cliffs, how the whole production waited for a woman's brimmed hat to tumble perfectly along the beach, how time, ye know, it stands perfectly still, ye wait for nature to cooperate, ye have to get the bloody shot, it's all an act, sure, but ye do take after take, lad, then ye just stuff in it the camera, ye've got it, that's the whole trick of it.

*   *   *

Freddie writes everything and well.

He has translated the poetry of Catullus, written biographies of Somerset Maugham and Lord Byron, scripted radio plays for the BBC, done reviews for the TLS and elsewhere, written novels plain and experimental, and composed volumes of short stories. His movie scripts include *Darling*, for which he won an Academy Award, *Far From the Madding Crowd*, and the brilliant *Two for the Road*.

In all Frederic Raphael may be too brilliant.

His cleverness often flies over the heads of the BBC audiences in England where he lives and works.

He's both naturally and intentionally funny, a comic writer with a flair for zinger dialogue.

His recent scripts, though, aren't getting made into movies. Producers know about him, ask about him, actually commission scripts, read them and think, wait, can Diane Keaton say that? Or, that's a great line, but only Tom Conti is that droll and audiences don't pay to see Tom Conti, for that matter they don't even understand droll.

It's the curse of the screenwriter's art: he must be properly vulgar, understand mass taste or the lack of it, and display storytelling skills far less than sophisticated.

Dinner on Third Street near the Beverly Center at a little Chinese place with Freddie and his wife Beetle. We talk about university creative writing classes and Freddie wonders aloud, "Must we teach the little geniuses to crave the facility of hacks?" We talk about the craft. Movies we've seen. And about another Hollywood writer who Freddie liked so much that after an evening at his house Freddie regretted that he was leaving town and suggested that their friendship seemed worth prolonging with correspondence.

"He told me," Freddie says, laughing, "that, no, he didn't think so, he never writes on spec."

Beneath Freddie's facile surface is a deeply caring, richly educated man with a keen eye both for Hollywood's easy targets and the complicated terrors of contemporary life.

Like most writers of quality, he has been often tempted and seduced by movie money, but there is a purist somewhere who calls out to Freddie — and perhaps to all like him — go away, write novels, swim in deeper waters where we can admire your best strokes, this isn't your place, this isn't your Age, wit just isn't funny anymore.

*   *   *

Gene Lyons phones from Little Rock, Arkansas, to ask the Writer about this Hollywood producer who phoned.

"He wants me to write a script. Make up a story. Anything I want to do," Gene says. "All I want to know from you is how much money are we talking about?"

Gene reviews books for *Newsweek* at this point in his career.

He's a fluid, perceptive writer who sees to the heart of things, but now he's confused about the possibility of being—for once—overpaid for his services.

"They know more about money than we do," the Writer tells him. "So you have to think of a sum of money that you *wouldn't* write a script for. A sum of money so low that it would be an insult and you wouldn't waste your time doing it. The producer will offer you about $500 above that price."

"As low as that?" Gene asks. "You're kidding me."

"The producer probably knew your price before he ever phoned you. That's what I'm telling you. You're only a writer. You don't know money. That's his business."

Ultimately in the dark night of his most mercenary soul Gene decided that he couldn't and wouldn't write a script for $1000. The producer phoned back and after the usual pleasantries offered him $1500.

*   *   *

Pinewood Studios outside London.

The head carpenter comes up to the Writer and pumps his hand. He's a large ruddy man with white hair and the Writer's fingers seem small in his grip.

"Thank you for writing this movie," he says. "You've put forty of us to work here, you know, and we're grateful."

It remains the greatest and most sincere compliment the Writer ever received. Forty men put to work for months. Movie budgets pay real people. A comforting thought in the chaos.

*   *   *

Breakfast with Ridley Scott in Beverly Hills.

Quickly, the deal: there's this Amazon tribesman, a man of the riverine forest, and he grows up, gets educated, and fights the developers who want to rape Amazonia. It's a true story about the noble savage, environmental, big screen, the jungle, what do you think about it?

The more talented of the famous British directing brothers, the director of *Blade Runner* and the magnificent *Duellists*, pushes his fingers through his blond hair and talks to both the Writer and his assistant, Mimi Polk. One suspects that she's the brainy friend, the one who often reads books for fun, who advises, who catches nuances. Assistants are like that here: sitting over at the side while the posing goes on, alert, watching people's eyes during the pitch.

It's a breakfast of sudden intuitions this morning at the Four Seasons. Scott, the Writer decides, doesn't want to be here. The project is fashionably environmental, but like so many Hollywood concepts it's half baked: the real-life character threatens to be a stereotype, there's a point of view problem, and a non-existent climax in an ongoing storyline. Single elements often ignite the imaginations of famous directors or powerful producers and they tend to say things like, "I see a blue canopy of trees, the stars shining through them, a soft night feeling like when you were a kid lying outside in the summer grass, you know, except this is in the jungle, see, this is the Amazon, but with that feeling." From such as this $40 million movies are made.

Anyway, intuitions flare up quickly before the first cups of coffee are cool. The director has just finished filming *Thelma and Louise* and he's tired. He orders eggs, but doesn't eat them. It's early morning and the Amazon is far away and this tribesman, so fascinating once, is becoming a vapor, a mere possibility that the director somehow wants to lift away from the newspaper accounts to a character in a compelling script.

All over the world people are reading newspapers or hearing stories and saying to themselves, hey, that would make a movie. In the film business, though, inhabited by successful millionaire executives, producers, agents, and directors, this common reaction to a good story or an interesting person in the news frequently becomes the impulse to commission scripts. Early on, enthusiasms run high. For one thing, powerful players are surrounded by others who say yes, great idea, brilliant, let's get a script on that. Then reality begins: scripts are difficult and great scripts are rare. Between that first inspiration about what would make a good film and the long, difficult execution of a first-rate script, spirits begin to sink. Sometimes in talking over the project sudden realizations occur, often as little lightning bolts of intuition.

This morning at breakfast the Writer is less than enthusiastic, tries to hide it, but fails. Mimi Polk detects it. And a curious chain reaction seems to occur: she's suddenly doubtful about the project herself, perhaps for the first time, and her silence somehow communicates this to Ridley Scott. In a flash all three of them know: this won't happen, the breakfast meeting is over.

As they stroll toward the lobby, later, the director talks about his children. The Writer replies to a question, saying yes, I'm working on a novel, and, no, I'm not sure it could ever make a film. Mimi Polk, bright and savvy, talks about a recent novel she has read, one that definitely wouldn't make a good script because too much of the inner lives of the characters could never be transposed to images. Smiles all around. Goodbyes.

Intelligent, hopeful people.

Outdoors, the morning smog burns away and bright sunlight illumines workers who are planting a row of palm trees.

*   *   *

Sunday afternoon at Billy's.

The children are out at the pool celebrating little Jack's birthday. Watching over them is a battalion of nannies. Several of the kids are show biz children, Frank Zappa's among others. And each time a little tyke tosses a ball or splashes in the water he gets a round of applause.

"Good boy, Timmy!" a nannie squeals, watching her charge as he bobs up and down. It's Quality Time, Hollywood Style: buy me a nannie, please, who loves me and cheers my every bellyflop.

Out back on half of the tennis court where the hoop is set up, there's a pickup basketball game in progress. Director William Friedkin is short, wiry, and has a good jump shot. His players are all middle-aged jocks, but there's a young TV writer with enough muscle to take the ball to the basket.

Friedkin's compound on Woodrow Wilson Drive looks down on Universal Studios and the congested flatland of the valley. There are two houses on the property, both with red-tiled roofs: a house for the director and another for his new wife, the television newslady. One resists speculation.

Later on during the barbecue the talk turns to the Project, an adventure series for CBS. The director clearly thinks he's slumming, doing TV pilots, although he has been paid $1 million for the effort by a network that hopes some of his old skills as the director of *The Exorcist* and *The French Connection* can be converted to upscale visuals and better than average ratings.

So Billy's eating a hot dog as the kids are ushered indoors to watch a video movie.

"Give me a take on this," he says softly. "Show me how you think." He has a gentle, serpentine manner at this point.

The Writer knows that if he can put a good spin on the project he'll probably be hired to write a script, so he begins.

There is a halo of sunlight overhead.

The two houses stare down ominously.

"Good," the director keeps saying. "Ah, yeah, good." They both continue to add to a possible storyline.

After fifteen minutes they come to agreement. Then Billy says, "We'll work together on this script, but understand that I'll make all the final decisions."

"That's always understood," the Writer replies evenly, smiling. "But I wish you hadn't said it."

Billy's eyes narrow into slits at this arrogance.

But the afternoon soon winds down. The Writer, approved and hired, is dismissed until he meets the director again at the office. Is it a mistake what the Writer seems to detect? Has Billy's face changed? What's happened? Was it that exchange about who is going to be in charge? Later on, the Writer will know: within minutes that afternoon up on the hill, Billy has changed. Power overtakes him like a strange elixir.

Many directors don't work much in the industry. They wait for the studios or networks to phone or hope that a compelling script falls into their hands. For some of them, resentment builds up. They are great talents, they convince themselves, and nobody will give them millions of dollars to put on a play. When they finally get a project they're often strung-out egos, empowered by new employment, petulant, so that they sometimes practice outrageous abuse, scolding assistants, belittling their colleagues who are still out of work, lecturing writers on how to write, and finally terrorizing the actual production. These directors frequently suck up to major executives and movie stars while playing the role of cockbird dictator to those beneath them in the pay scale. Their temperaments often show up in the budgets of films, too. Just as often their mean-spirited whimsy will ruin a scene, fail to nurture a performance, or overrule a good idea.

Later at the office Billy's transformation is complete. He screams at a secretary who has been faithful to him for nine years, sending her off to the women's room to cry. He tells a young assistant to shape up, that he's only a chauffeur, at best, and can be replaced. He demands a new storyline from the Writer, one with lawyers in it, never mind the original action concept.

"I see this as a courtroom drama," Billy says.

A week passes. The Writer looks down at the world from his typewriter high in the Universal Sheraton. Word's out that Billy's new marriage isn't going so well. At the office in Studio City, Billy throws another tantrum. Yet another storyline. He wants one with, maybe, say, nerve gas.

Another week. In the evenings the Writer goes out with pals to El Coyote, the Broadway Grill, Tuttobene.

At the office, again, Billy screams that the Writer isn't working hard for the picture. He wants another storyline, one with trains, those European trains with compartments.

The Writer goes back to the hotel, but Billy has trouble on the home front and doesn't phone. Four days pass, then the Writer leaves a message on a machine and leaves the state.

"You don't quit me, I fire you!" Billy yells over the phone later. Still later, the network pays the Writer after threats from lawyers on all sides, maybe after nerve gas — for work already done on the project.

Actors often act like spoiled children, too, but they're usually powerless and their tantrums are just for display. Directors, on the other hand, inherit power over others when they get work. And often everyone from art directors to script girls, from writers to grips pay the price. There are directors who given the opportunity turn into production tyrants — all in the name of artistic temperament — and exercise their cruelties whenever possible. Such directors usually find work harder and harder to come by until they're eventually out of the business altogether, alone in their high, empty houses, lost in the tantrums of memory.

*   *   *

Margot Kidder walks naked on the beach.

The novelist who lives next door—this is way out in Malibu beyond Zuma and Trancas—also takes his daily strolls along the beach and more than once she has sauntered by him, he admits, and he doesn't know whether to look the other way or just stop and fully admire her every swaying part.

The novelist's wife one day decides they should make a call next door to the actress's rented bungalow. After all, she explains, they are long-time residents, a friendly call is in order, and maybe a personal visit can convince the curvy newcomer that the neighborhood husbands don't need this much excitement.

Miss Kidder's doors are flung wide on the verandah, so the novelist and his wife call out their hellos, then move inside. They call again, entering the living room and listening. Above them in the loft the sounds grow loud and unmistakable: the pounding rhythms of an erotic surf, a real sexual riptide, whitecaps of passion. Without calling out again, they slowly back out of the house.

As time passes the novelist and his wife tell the story on themselves, laughing: their foolishness for dropping by unannounced, their old-fashioned prudishness, the eccentric actress next door, another Malibu story. Eventually the actress gives up the rented house and moves away, but until she does she walks naked on the beach.

Years later a Writer, a friend of the novelist and his wife, meets Margot Kidder in Canada and thinks about telling her this story about her neighbors, but doesn't—although she might have enjoyed it and laughed at it.

"Call me Margie," she says up in Canada. "With a hard g. I want to produce or direct now. Actually, I really want to write."

They are at a conference in Toronto where students in various film disciplines attend seminars. She's one of the older participants. She has a smile full of irony and intelligence and the others want her on their projects. As time goes on, the Writer and Margie find they have friends in common, go out to dinner with others, and try to talk without the usual cynicism for the industry.

The movie business is a place for specialists, each one doing his or her part in the mosaic of a production. One seldom acquires a second specialty. Gaffers do not become directors. Producers might work for kicks as extras, but they don't become movie stars. Few actresses evolve into writers.

Margie's specialty has been an innocent face and a spectacular body, photogenic beauty. Screen beauty of mysterious presence is a gift like a fine tenor voice and one exploits it until it's all used up. Like many clever good-looking women, Margie knows that as the physique fades, somehow, the life of the intellect beckons. So she knows and hates the mean-spirited code of industry typecasting: stay where you are, do your specialty, don't try and get anybody else's job.

She wants to be a writer. Yet so do many major producers, the majority of directors, hundreds of actors and extras, and thousands of crew members. Everybody in town has an idea for a script, if not an actual manuscript. It is an industry that nourishes such hope, but it also wants Margie — with a hard g — to walk forever naked on the beach, carefree and supple, unadorned with thoughts or aspirations, because, after all, it's the movie business and why be anything else when you can be an image?

*   *   *

One Friday afternoon on the set in Munich, John Houseman makes an appearance wearing stiff leather liederhosen, his bony knees and white legs as thin as sticks.

"I've got a driver and a limo for the weekend," he announces. It is the voice of Professor Kingsfield, for which he will become famous in *The Paper Chase* and dozens of television commercials: a stern voice, aristocratic and mischievous. "Let's go down to Mad Ludwig's castle. How about it? Bavarian beer. Schnitzel. How long will it take you?"

On the trip through the black forest he talks about the crude toilets at the castle, the promiscuities of Wagner and all the other visitors. At dinner he talks about actors. He recalls how Anthony Quinn wanted to discuss his role as Gauguin in *Lust for Life*, a movie that Houseman produced.

"When actors want to discuss their roles," Houseman drawls, "they really just want to talk about themselves."

As an actor himself, Houseman has presence, but can never remember his lines. In the Writer's movie Houseman's dialogue is wildtracked, so that he can sit before a microphone in a sound studio and lip-synch the words. These, in turn, are matched to his lips onscreen.

He wasn't much of an actor, but by that spring of 1975 he had worked as a successful grain salesman, had become the business manager of the famed Mercury Theater with Orson Welles, had worked on the script of *Citizen Kane*, had directed the U.S. Armed Forces radio propaganda network in World War II, had produced films and stage plays, and had become the head of the Julliard School of Drama. His life had been long and productive before this stint in his twilight years as an actor, but even now, late at night in a small Bavarian hotel, he has his regrets.

He was nineteen years old, he says. A young European gentleman named Jacques Haussman. And he had written a novel.

"I took it to Leonard and Virginia Woolf in Bloomsbury," he recalls. "They read it and said, yes, they'd publish it. I went around to their flat filled with excitement. And they told me they needed five hundred quid to subvent the publication of the book. I didn't have the money, but I told them I'd think it over. Shortly after that I gave up my literary ambitions and went to America as a salesman for my father's grain company. I look back on it and it makes me sad. Such a curious life. I could've been a novelist. Think of it. A real writer."

*   *   *

Walking along Sunset Boulevard with Bob Rafelson.

He does all the talking. It is difficult directing movies. He was a philosophy major in college. He is Jack Nicholson's very best friend. He was almost beheaded by South American natives, but escaped. He loves adventure. Women over age eighteen have too much mileage and bad karma. He really wrote *Five Easy Pieces* himself, all the good parts anyway.

Above us the Chateau Marmont rises up like a crumbling castle into the smog. Neons along the way announce English pub food, fake fingernails, video rentals, legal advice, and live music.

He once turned a desk over on top of a studio executive who made him mad. He is Dan Melnick's best friend. He hates pretension. He has an eye for talented actors, like Arnold Schwarzenegger. He has a lot of enemies in this town. He sleeps only four hours a night. Energy is genius.

*   *   *

Dinner at The Palm with Oliver Stone.

The thick steaks are good and the stringbeans are great. At the moment he's working with director Brian de Palma on what will turn out to be one of the worst movies ever made, but the money flows, the buzz is momentarily favorable, and life, baby, it just doesn't suck at all.

These are the days after Stone has won an Academy Award for his gritty *Midnight Express* and his fees for screenwriting are growing, even by industry standards, enormous. He flies from his home in Sagaponack, New York, renting villas in the sun, taking meetings, and doing time with de Palma, a questionable talent who at the moment is unquestioned.

The Writer sits at Stone's table in the noisy restaurant because Stone has optioned his novel. Everything will happen, Stone says with confidence. I want to direct. My ambition is, well, big.

The crowd at The Palm gorges itself, chattering and screaming, adding a frenzy of hope. As the French painter Edgar Degas once observed, there is a kind of success that is indistinguishable from panic. He must have been in Hollywood when he dropped that line.

Stone has dark hair, heavy brows, and eyes that take on a penetrating look, yet the gaze is somehow melodramatic and wrong, as if he practices ferocity before bathroom mirrors. He means to convey intelligence, intimidation, and authority, but there's a comic uncertainty about him.

The Writer eats his steak, not wanting to acknowledge this. He wants Stone to turn his recent novel into a money hole. He wants Stone to be stable and clever, what everybody wants of everybody else in the industry.

The conversation drifts toward books. Stone admits that he doesn't actually read books anymore. He used to read Hemingway. The conversation moves to universities and education. The Writer teaches at a relatively obscure boondock university, but this seems to make Stone anxious, as though his eastern education isn't enough and as if the Writer has credentials and he doesn't. He points out that Vietnam interrupted his studies. He was an intellectual who became a grunt, he explains, and, okay, war teaches a man damn good lessons, it makes good material.

As Stone and the Writer trade anecdotes and look around at the pop murals on the walls of The Palm, everything does begin to seem possible. The city is built on this debris of hope, although just below the streets are the tar pits, the fault lines, and the bones, of writers who believed that glitter wasn't necessarily glitter, but something finally more meaningful.

The Writer wakes up the next morning at the Beverly Wilshire. He reads the *LA Times* and dines on croissants and honey.

Then Oliver Stone phones, raging.

An item in the *Hollywood Reporter* has sent him into orbit. It states that the Writer's new book has been optioned and goes on to report that, quote, "Oliver Stone — remember him? — hopes to direct it." This cruel aside on the part of the columnist has made Stone frenzied and paranoid.

"Your people put that item in the trades!" Stone accuses the Writer.

"My people? Are you kidding? You think I've got a press agent?"

"You bastard! What kind of line is that? Remember him? I'm no goddamned has-been! I'm going to bust this town wide open, but you or your people have screwed up our deal!"

"Hold it, I teach out in the boondocks, remember? I don't even know anybody who talks to the trades!"

"Our deal's off!" Stone screams. "I don't have to take this shit!"

The money hole hangs up.

The Writer is left to study the walls of his suite: brocade wallpaper, aqua colored, pastel.

Stone goes on to become a man who ascends to Hollywood power, one of the few writers ever to do so. He directs big films, thriving on controversy, celebrating violence while disapproving of it, sticking the American public with the knife of guilt and twisting it, blaming everybody with abandoning the boys in Vietnam and murdering JFK in a giant conspiracy.

When writers become powerful in the industry they usually do it by moving into the director's chair, often managing to finance and produce their own work. Woody Allen might be considered such an auteur and entrepreneur. Some regard him as our little Ingmar Bergman on the east coast while Stone is our Barnum and Bailey of oversized hysterics in the west. Certainly, Allen concentrates on characterizations and wit while Stone hammers at the big themes, stereotypes, and announces the cultural importance of his every project.

Even so, that columnist in the *Hollywood Reporter* gave him a snide shot.

The option on the book was dropped, by the way, but picked up by another director who managed after years of hardship to make it into a bad movie.

Irony, it is a common fruit out west. Like the avocado.

*   *   *

Independent producers and amateurs.

A Peruvian restaurateur flies the Writer out to LA and puts him up at the Westwood Marquis. Rolls of money appear, actual rolls bound with rubber bands, allegedly cash from cocaine. The penthouse. Club sandwiches. A guy with a gold chain who was recently a busboy at Aspen who might direct the movie. Hey, everything is rolling. The woman who played Emmanuelle signs on, a race car is built out of balsa wood as an exact replica of Al Unser's famous formula model, rock music is commissioned, and, oh, wait, better get a script before we all head for Monaco! Get me a writer, queek! The little Peruvian appears, saying, "Lee-sin, ever'body, I am een to power!" Hardy laughter rings out around the penthouse, then abruptly stops. The guy is serious. And the Writer pays his own ticket home.

Another time there is a high school football coach who makes movies, he says, with rented cameras. His uncle owns a single oil well in El Dorado, Arkansas, and their project is the story of Titanic Thompson, a 1930s golf hustler and proposition man who was a favorite of Damon Runyon's. Rights to Titanic's story are owned by the gambler's son — a card mechanic of some repute himself — and these rights have been sold, most recently, to a dentist in Dallas who teamed up with an advertising executive from Fort Worth. It's complicated, the football coach explains. Like all movie deals. Yet the Writer is paid a modest sum and writes a script that makes everybody laugh. After months, the studios don't respond, so the dentist, very disappointed, sells the whole project to a group of eager businessmen from Oklahoma City.

Finally, there is a doctor from Houston. The Writer gets paid well to do research and write a script about the Vietnamese who came to South Texas after the war to become shrimp fishermen. The Writer travels to Port Aransas and other spots along the Texas coast, gets intrigued with what he sees, thinks about a storyline, then talks to the doctor who says this should be a love story about a veteran who lives in a lighthouse. Maybe the girl lives in the lighthouse, but the

Vietnamese fishermen are secondary players, sort of background color. When the script is delivered the Writer is oddly proud of its characterizations and structure, but the doctor says, no, hold it, there are too many Vietnamese refugees here, never mind what we said, let's take them out and concentrate on this lonely veteran. Maybe he can have a war wound. As the Writer thinks this over, a New York consultant is flown in. He sees this as an action movie — drug dealing and gun running among the shrimp fishermen. The Writer is flown to New York and stays at the consultant's house. In the consultant's family there are dozens of Irish cops and the talk is how these Irish Catholic cops were honest for decades, then how the drug money came and subverted the whole system. The script and the Houston doctor float away in all this.

A writer with screen credits is often offered work by amateurs who want their dreams set forth in movies. Under the right circumstances, writers agree and do their best. Occasionally they become engaged — with the fascinating Vietnamese refugees who became, in time, the best shrimp fishermen in South Texas, say, or with other characters and subjects — and they give the amateurs *some* of their best work.

*   *   *

Jim Harrison visits town and sits with the Writer and others for lunch at The Grill.

On the chalkboard menu is a daily special none of the regulars have seen before: Venison Stew. Everybody gets excited and orders a bowl of it. It's so good that everybody orders more and years later Jim will write in *Esquire* that there's just one place in America that serves an excellent venison stew: that famous grill on Dickson Street. No one ever tells him that he was eating Arkansas road kill that day — and that this wonderful dish never again appeared on the chalkboard menu.

Jim writes poetry, novels, food columns, travel articles and essays while living with his family and dogs up in Michigan and while using Hollywood opportunities without ever seeming to be used himself. He likes to tell the story about how for years he and his pal Tom McGuane wrote scripts at ever increasing prices although none of their work ever appeared on movie screens. McGuane's place in Montana and Jim's in Michigan, one surmises, both came largely from payments for screenplays and both have enjoyed mobility and freedom because of the money.

As Jim tells it over venison stew, a sad thing happened when the McGuane script for *The Missouri Breaks* actually weht into production. Even the formidable presences of Marlon Brando and Jack Nicholson couldn't save that oddball western from critical and box-office disaster. The result was that McGuane's reputation and price as a screenwriter began to sink. (Years later Jim's own status took a blow when his own bomb, *Revenge*, came to movie houses.)

"But around the time Tom was having his troubles, Ray Stark phoned me," Jim says, dipping his cornbread in the stew. "He asked me to go to South America, live in Rio, and write a movie about horse racing in Kentucky."

As Jim tells it, it made a kind of California sense.

Stark, one of the industry's most powerful producers, had gone to the Bluegrass and had become enamored of possibilities. He had come to Jim with a seductive line of money and talk. Jim, he said, was one of America's greatest writers. An author. He could give the public the greatest horse racing movie of all time.

Jim says the money sounded wonderful, but he told Stark that his life was in upper Michigan and that he didn't know anything about Kentucky or horses.

"No problem," Stark insisted. "Take the money and go to my Copacabana penthouse in Rio. Live there for a year. Take your family. You're a great American writer and it'll come to you."

Jim struggled to get this straight. Brazil?

"Go there all expenses paid," Stark insisted. "You're a great American writer. An author."

Jim took his family and went.

Weeks passed. Good food, drink, and the pleasures of Rio. But nothing remotely intelligent occurred to him concerning a horse racing story.

Stark phoned periodically and finally, after months, became concerned over Jim's lack of progress. One day he phoned to say that he'd fly down to Rio for a breakfast meeting.

At the famous breakfast Stark said, "You know, flying down here the whole story came to me. You're a great American writer, that I know, but you need a storyline."

Jim agreed that any help was appreciated.

"Okay, here it is," Stark said dramatically. "Our horse wins."

Not long after the breakfast, Jim says, he packed up and went back to Michigan for the hunting season. He never wrote the Bluegrass movie, although he was highly paid for a while.

The professional scriptwriter except in rare situations must live and work in either New York or Los Angeles, trying to get meetings with directors or producers, making pitches, and taking the brunt of whatever cruelty a harsh commercial world can muster. Even if he finds work he must look ahead to the next assignment and unless he's just had a big commercial success or a highly praised critical success he knows that future work is doubtful. The winter winds of Manhattan are always at gale force for screenwriters. Meetings with producers or directors — perhaps because there are so few — seem impossible. The West Coast is sunny and promising, yet perhaps even more deadly: everybody hears stories, gets glimpses of celebrities, and dies for work. It's a palm tree world, a halter top world, and phrases like Malibu or development deal roll off the tongue, but one lives on a professional fault line where everything is shaky and terrifying.

Oliver Stone refers to authors like Jim Harrison as "the real writers" who do books and take screen work if it's offered. Like many others in Hollywood, Stone has little respect for the other hacks.

Jim remarks that, "Writing fiction is like trying to remember in vivid detail things that have never happened." That struggle lies close to the heart of authentic creative work. The craft is hard and its struggles and victories are largely private, coming out of memory, the wit of the imaginative psyche, reading, travel, and time. There are elitists, of course, who contend there is something noble about the truly literary author that will always keep him from hacking it up along Sunset Boulevard or out on the Warner's lot and that by his very nature he can't be an industry professional.

It's an old argument. Those less pure point out that the line between the original artist and the hack is frequently blurred and that most authors have within themselves the capacity to be practical and blatantly commercial. Shakespeare played to the groundlings and it can be argued, for.instance, that in spite of his genius he was an uneven playwright who was willing to knock off thin comedies and a shallow piece of raw violence like *Titus Andronicus*. Both Dostoyevsky and Dickens serialized their potboilers in the newspapers and would probably write mini-series for TV if they were alive today. Bill Faulkner toiled over 150 scripts in Hollywood and his biggest screen credit was called *Land of the Pharoahs* with Joan Collins as Cleopatra. Both James Joyce and Vladimir Nabokov yearned to write for the movies — and Nabokov was especially flattered to have worked with Stanley Kubrick on the screenplay of *Lolita*.

Serious writers want to be original. The great journalists want their work to have innovative spin and real style. The original voice, compelling structure, the rich characterization that blows away the stereotypes, these are the standards that set the more original storytellers apart from the hacks. And no one can argue with where originality comes from. The real writer must lead a secret life away from the mainstream, out of the offices of literary commerce, and off the freeways of the next big deal. Yet talented writers are often occasionally practical and try to live in a world where patronage and creative possibility exist together — and where if they want to write their own works they must occasionally consider writing somebody else's.

The trick, they'll tell you, is to conspire toward greatness in the screenplay, in the novel, in the short story, and in all the genres, and to hope — in fact, to swear to oneself — never to compromise in any of the essentials. Just remember, buddy, these writers will tell you, Michelangelo was hired by the Pope.

III. Screening Films

VACHEL LINDSAY

A SPECIAL DELIVERY LETTER TO MY PARTICULAR FRIENDS

Vachel Lindsay, one of America's most famous poets in the second and third decade of this century, also published an influential book of film theory, *The Art of the Moving Picture*, in 1915. "If it is the conviction of serious minds that the mass of men shall never again see pictures out of Heaven except through such mediums as the kinetoscope lens," he wrote in that book, "let all the higher forces of our land courageously lay hold upon this thing that saves us from spiritual blindness." But by 1925 he had become disillusioned with the movie industry, and especially with what he considered the immoral stories and erotic imagery of high-budget Hollywood films. The following essay, written between 1925 and 1927 as a newspaper feature but never published till now, casts a cold eye on the movies and recommends censorship of the industry. It is part of the Vachel Lindsay Collection in the Clifton Waller Barrett Library of the University of Virginia. Another manuscript from that collection, Lindsay's analysis of *The Thief of Bagdad*, appeared in the Spring 1992 issue of MQR. The editors are grateful to Michael Plunkett of the Barrett Library for his assistance, and to the poet's son, Nicholas C. Lindsay, for permission to publish this manuscript.

The lull after the great war is over, and every little war is on. Some of these wars are terrible indeed, and heartbreaking, and destroyers of the entire patience of the soul. But one war which waxes hotter is exhilarating, a restorer of one's hope in his mind. It is the war on the bad movie. Thank God censorship bills are being introduced or about to be introduced into every legislature that exists on American soil.

The Movie Corporation magnates seem to be like the Germans. They have learned nothing, and forgotten nothing. Certainly they need the scare of their lives, and I hope every legislature gives it to them, or annihilates their business altogether. Any man who cannot get past any censorship bill on earth is simply lacking in brains. And the unutterable stupidity of the photoplay corporation magnates is their first crime. From the dictionary to the encyclopedia, from the medical school to the biology class, gentlemen will always have the privileges of speaking their minds and rotters are likely to get hurt.

There are a lot of patients that have to be given nourishment through a small rubber tube through the nose. The movie men, poisoned by easy money, have lockjaw of the mind. I, for one, will be delighted if they are tied up one and all, and fed through a tube called Censorship. It will do them good. No, there are no exceptions. When you mention even casually that there are possible exceptions, why Rahab, Jezebel, Ahab, and Nero breathe easier and think they are being forgiven and proved to sentimentalize about themselves. Whoever you are, I mean you.

I have done myself the honor to read all the press-clippings on this book, after the manner of vain authors. How, from first to last, all the practical practitioners deny the relationship to the arts of the present or the future. How I am not interested in poetry criticism. How many poets have been active in this field, and how they will testify that I have remained silent. How I am much more interested in the canons of an art I approach in a purely recreational way, as a citizen.

This book, *The Art of the Moving Picture*, has, so far as I know, never been contradicted or challenged, except for one chapter which I have now thrown out, substituting new material.

It so happens that people interested in my other three books of prose and in my four books of verse, have considered this treatise a thing apart, have read it separately, disconnectedly, though its aesthetic theory has never been challenged in any way, its sociological discussion has never been argued up or down, and its theory of the relation of the photoplay to the American Future has never been in any way disputed by radical conservative, mystic or scientist. No, the book has not been ignored. I have grown unutterably weary of seeing articles in the leg-show movie magazines stolen bodily from this book, sermons written straight from this book by movie magnates with their tongue in the cheek, articles prattling about uplift, written however to advertise stupidity, thickness of mind and smut, smut, smut. Romeo and Juliet are the movie magazines' two tadpoles to leer about. Their greatest act is to teach cheap whores to simper, and the magazines are an index of the business. Then they have the gall to steal my sermons without acknowledgment, and the magazines and magnates give a brothel turn to every device outlined in this book. They do not acknowledge that they found it here before they spoiled it. This book written in 1915 anticipated most of the new devices. They were carried out because they were there prophesied, or they were there suggested. But the principal suggestion was ignored.

Before God I urged upon these men to say their prayers. I meant it with all my soul. I am not the first who have urged it. It was not an original suggestion. But I did urge it, and it is still there in the text. I had a right to urge it.

I am fighting the assumption that a book on the movies must be necessarily outlaw and cheap in intent, a thing apart from all other activities of the human mind and soul and all the other aspirations of the world's holy temples. If everyone assumes the photoplay is a brothel, a definitely segregated district of the human mind, why it remains a brothel. I have just as much a right to fight for a clean redeemed spiritualized beautiful movie, evolved in prayer, based on a love of God and beauty and hope for America, as I have to fight for a clean town, or clean politics, or anything else clean. I have a right to ask that people who take my other books as part of myself, understand that this book was also written in my heart's blood, and not to pass the time of day. It is not a trick book to teach smart office boys to write scenarios, though I know well though the book has sold extensively most copies have been bought by people in the business college state of mind. They are appalled that I ask them to pray.

The photoplay art should be literature, and a sacred book, not a smutty scrawl on an alley fence. It has the possible dignity of Egyptian hieroglyphics and Egyptian temples, and the possible splendor of the painting of Michelangelo and Titian, the possible epic grace of the Russian Dancers. It should have the apocalyptic gleam that will be the glory of the future, the prophetic fire already in our most vicious papers that point toward the future, The Declaration of Independence and Lincoln's Gettysburg Address. And with all these possibilities, we are treated to floods of unutterable stupidity. To go to the films is like trying to read the literature of a great nation with nothing left but the inscriptions scrawled at Pompeii. I go to the four movie palaces at my home town all the week and every day. I began with the first films that came to Springfield from the days before the Biograph and I shall so continue to go to such films as may be had till I die, and my heart is there, and when I die my ghost will come and look. I know when they leave commerce, they will appear in the school. I declare this filmmaking is the beginning of a great literature, though it be as far now from great literature as was the first tadpole from the lordliest mastodon. But I say my heart is in this promise of new life, and nothing shall shame me out of it. Every day here in my home town, the magnificence of the medium and the dignity of the unused hieroglyphic alphabet still dazzle me, and the poorest film and the rottenness has always five minutes of power, power which the movie corporation magnates, try as they may, cannot destroy.

They are all damned rotters, and should be put out of business. The device will remain, and civilized people will take it up and use it. I counsel censorship that practically destroys film-making as a business. A commercial oil-well, the Colleges, Churches, Universities, Highschools, the state, city, and national governments, any or all of these uncommercial agencies can take up the films at once, as soon as censorship wipes these other fellows out.

There is just one hope for the movie men. Let them flee from the wrath to come. Let them say their prayers. Let them send for the Paulist Fathers, or Rabbi Wise, or Gypsy Smith, according to the places where they worshipped in better days. According to the various faith of their cleaner and brainier childhood, let them send for the recognized evangelists of their various peoples. Let the evangelists go to Los Angeles, and drive these movie men to their knees with whips of scorpions.

Whatever the temples of these photoplay men, they have defiled them. Whoever is their mother, they have unutterably shamed her. They have insulted with equal stupidity the most primitive ethics of the oldest writings in the old testament and the most exalted aspirations of the new. And they have been stupider and more unpatriotic than they have been vicious. If America is their land, they have despised and degraded her. Wherever in the films men should pray, they have put in a leer instead. Wherever men naturally and simply hope for tomorrow they have put in idiocy and shame. Whatever is their college or their school or their home town, they have shamed them, they have shamed all pride of the mind, all tradition, and all hope of wisdom. Let them say their prayers, and that speedily. They have no right to defile the total mind of the American youth and get off free. Better men get the third degree every day. They have no right to the world. They are no saner or sweeter than Nero or Heliogabalus, and they have no right to power. Let them show fruits meet for repentance, or be quickly legislated out of existence. The films will go on. Like Nero, the movie magnates are burning Rome, and fiddling while it burns. But Rome will be rebuilt; I say, drag the madmen down. In God's name, what right have they to wear the crown of all the world, to dictate the total future of the newest art? Let us legislate them out of existence.

DIANE KIRKPATRICK

SEE YOU AT THE MOVIES:
THE CINEMA IN ART

The collective experience of going to the movies has been with us one hundred years. Since December 28, 1895, when the first paying audience watched a film projected on a screen in Paris by the Lumière brothers, the cinema has fed our dreams and shaped our notions about reality. Almost from the beginning, artists joined the enthusiastic crowds fascinated by the magic of this illusionary world. Avant-garde artists seized upon the new medium as one appropriate weapon in their joyous shattering of boundaries between high and low subjects, materials, and styles in the shock tactics with which they sought to awaken humans from the torpor which the artists believed had been induced by the stifling artificiality of societal conventions. These adventurous artists rang many changes on cinematic expression. In the first half of the century, Marcel Duchamp and Hans Richter played Dada games with film. The Italian Futurists captured on film a version of their dystopic vision. Fernand Léger created a cinematic ballet with the mass-produced objects that inspired his painting of the modern world. Man Ray and Joseph Cornell, among others, exploited cinema's grand capacity for surrealist hallucinatory fantasy. László Moholy-Nagy made films that transformed the physical world into one seen by "Vision in Motion." Since then many artists, including Robert Breer, Tony Conrad, Michael Snow, and Robert Frank, have invested the film medium with their own vision. Not surprisingly, as movies became an increasingly integral part of the physical and mental landscape of twentieth century society, they also formed part of the subject for visual artists interested in depicting contemporary life. In honor of the moving art's one hundredth birthday, this essay examines fourteen works that provide a cross-section from this rich body of artistic interpretation.

216

THE EXPERIENCE OF MOVIEGOING
a portfolio

Fig. 1. Ed Ruscha, *Trademark 2*, 1962. Ink, pencil, and oil on paper. 8 3/4"
× 14 1/4" (24.8 × 36.2 cm). San Francisco Museum of Modern Art. Purchased through a gift of Dr. and Mrs. Allan Ross.

Fig. 2. George Segal, *Cinema*, 1963. Plaster, illuminated plexiglass, metal.
118" × 96" × 30". Albright-Knox Art Gallery, Buffalo, New York. Gift
of Seymour H. Knox, 1964.

Fig. 3. Reginald Marsh, *Twenty Cent Movie*, 1936. Egg tempera on composition board. 30" × 40" (76.2 × 101.6 cm). Collection of Whitney
Museum of American Art. Purchase. 37.43.

Fig. 4. Edward Hopper, *New York Movie*, 1939. Oil on canvas. 32 1/4" ×
40 1/8" (81.9 × 101.9 cm). The Museum of Modern Art, New York.
Given anonymously. Photography © 1994, The Museum of Modern Art,
New York.

Fig. 5. Eduardo Paolozzi, *Wittgenstein at the Cinema Admires Betty Grable*, no. 12 in *As Is When* (Interpretations of Ludwig Wittgenstein),
1965. Silkscreen. 38" × 25 3/4" (96.5 × 65.4 cm). Published by Editions
Alecto, London. Printed by Kelpra Studio, London, England. Photo:
Diane Kirkpatrick.

Fig. 6. Cindy Sherman, *Untitled Film Still # 56*, 1980. Gelatin silver print.
20.3 × 25.4 cm. The Art Institute of Chicago. Restricted gift of Allen
Turner, 1988.389. Photograph © 1994, The Art Institute of Chicago.

Fig. 7. Cindy Sherman, *Untitled Film Still #6*, 1977. From *Untitled Film
Stills*. Published by Rizzoli International Publications, 1990. © Cindy
Sherman and Schirmer/Mosel, Munich, Germany.

Fig. 8. Salvador Dali, *Mae West*, © 1934. Gouache over photographic
print. 18.3 × 17.8 cm. The Art Institute of Chicago. Gift of Mrs. Gilbert W. Chapman in memory of Charles B. Goodspeed, 1949.517. Photograph © 1994, The Art Institute of Chicago.

Fig. 9. James Rosenquist, *Marilyn Monroe*, 1962. Oil and spray enamel on canvas. 7′ 9″ × 6′ ¼″ (236.2 × 183.3 cm). The Museum of Modern Art, New York. The Sidney and Harriet Janis Collection. Photograph © 1994, The Museum of Modern Art, New York.

Fig. 10. Andy Warhol, *Double Elvis*, 1964. Acrylic on canvas, silkscreen. 82 ¼″ × 59 ⅛″. Purchased with funds from The National Endowment for the Arts, PONCHO, and The Seattle Art Museum Guild. Seattle Art Museum, Seattle, WA. Photo credit: Paul Macapia.

Fig. 11 Andy Warhol, *Six Marilyns (Marilyn Six-Pack)*, 1962. Acrylic and silkscreen ink on canvas. 43″ × 22 ¼″. Collection Emily and Jerry Spiegel. Photo credit: Charles Uht.

Fig. 12. Ron Kitaj, *Amerika (John Ford on his Death Bed*, 1983–84). Oil on canvas. 60″ × 60″ (152.4 × 152.4 cm.). Metropolitan Museum, New York.

Fig. 13. Thomas Hart Benton, *Hollywood*, 1937. Tempera with oil on canvas mounted on panel. 53 ½″ × 81″. The Nelson-Atkins Museum of Art (Bequest of the artist). © 1993, The Nelson Gallery Foundation.

Fig. 14. Man Ray, *Admiration of the Orchestrelle for the Cinematograph*, 1919. Ink and gouache airbrushed on buff paper, with traces of pencil. 26″ × 21 ½″ (66 × 54.6 cm). The Museum of Modern Art, New York. Gift of A. Conger Goodyear. Photography © 1994, The Museum of Modern Art, New York.

1

2

3

4

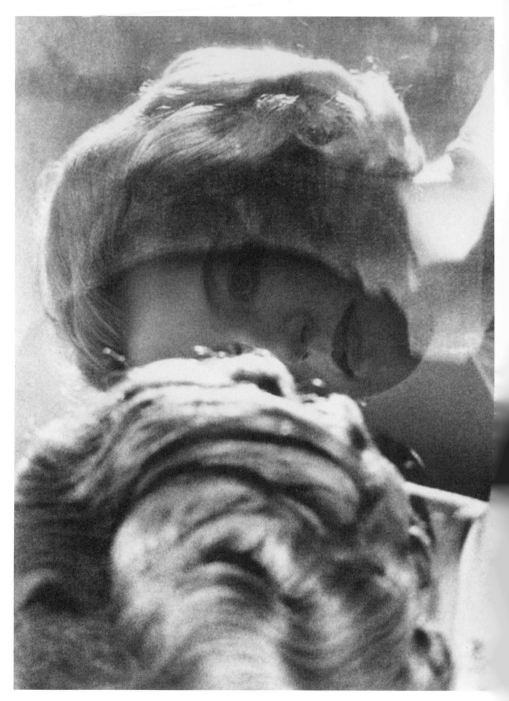

7

8

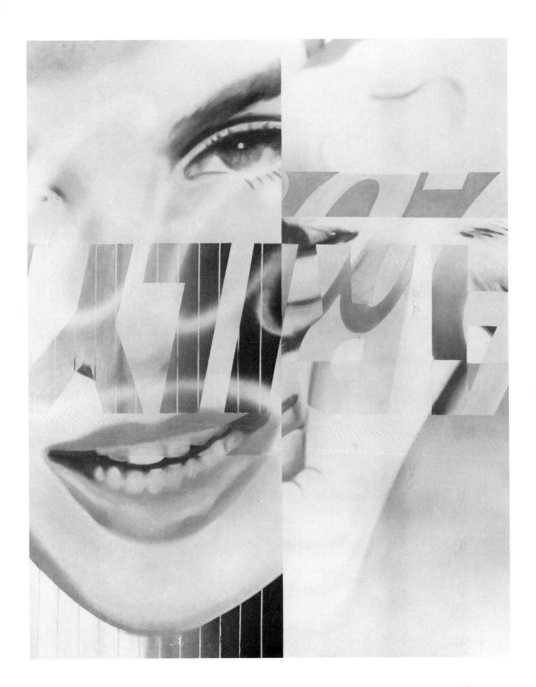

9

10

11

12

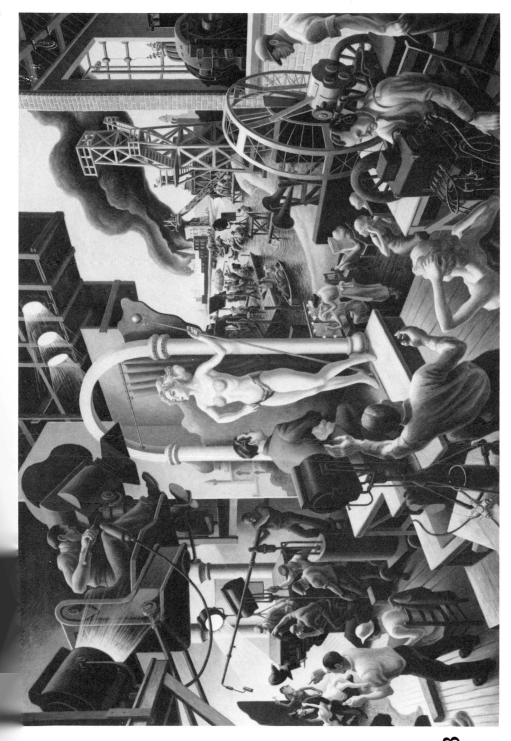

Admiration of the Orchestrelle for the Cinematograph

man ray

14

I

Ed Ruscha's *Trademark 2* (1962, Fig. 1) is a symbolic portrait of a film studio. Raised in Oklahoma, Ruscha fell in love with Los Angeles on a family vacation when he was a kid. He won parental permission to move there in 1956 to study art at the Disney-sponsored Chouinard Institute, and has lived in or near the city ever since. Ruscha loved southern California's zany visual environment of sleek hotrods, movie glitz, and laid-back designer style. He built his early paintings with emblems snatched from that scene and rendered them with the icy illusionism of commercial art against stark monochrome backgrounds.

In *Trademark 2*, the 20th Century Fox logo rises as a vast signboard-cum-building, recalling the giant white letters that sprawl across the Hollywood hills to spell out that community's name. Ruscha thumbed his nose at "good" art composition, by pushing the massive trademark and its backdrop of searchlight beams to the far left. Our eyes are trapped and held there, while the remaining four-fifths of the image stretches in our peripheral vision away to the right. This makes the words rush toward us as if carried within a huge beam of light. It also adds solidity to the elongated mass that carries backward from the letters, suggesting the kind of pre-pop architectural practice that shaped buildings as common objects to create identifiable signs for the products and services inside. The cool, precise style of Ruscha's bold forms is borrowed from a mixed world of advertising hype and architectural rendering. The blend generates a vibrant emblem for Hollywood's big-studio business.

II

George Segal's *Cinema* (1963, Fig. 2) snatches its subject from outside a movie theater. Segal (the sculptor not the actor) glimpsed this pregnant moment between program changes as he drove late one night from Manhattan to his home in New Jersey: "I saw . . . a fellow reaching up to pluck off the last letter from an illuminated sign and it was like seeing an exalted moment." Back in his studio, he translated that vivid memory into *Cinema*.

The artist turned from abstract expressionist painting to figurative sculpture in 1958, to explore "real space." His first figures were ungainly life-size constructions made from wire mesh and plaster. Then a student introduced him to the plaster-impregnated bandages newly developed by Johnson & Johnson for setting broken bones: "Immediately I knew what I wanted to do. . . . I had found my medium."

Segal was especially drawn to the kind of moment that caught his attention for *Cinema* — ordinary individuals involved in everyday actions: "I love to watch people. I'm interested in their gestures and I'm interested in their experiences and mine." He asked friends to take poses that mimicked those in the scenes he wanted to recreate. His white figures are full of life, in part because the heavy plaster wrapping presses down to capture the unmistakable individuality of each clothed body as it acts out the artist's direction. Once the figures were complete, Segal constructed the settings with appropriated items and things he made from scratch to imitate what he had seen. In the case of *Cinema*: "I rebuilt those objects, emphasizing a set of formal qualities . . . composing with bits of real objects from the real world."

Emotive as Segal's figures might be alone, the haunting stopped-time quality of his works springs from his rare ability to choreograph convincing vignettes based on real life. Displaced from life into art, the objects become potent talismans for their counterparts, as the Dada readymade and the Surrealist found object had demonstrated before.[1] In *Cinema*, the man's posture and the eerily suspended panel on which he works combine to recreate the artist's original glimpse of work taking place high overhead. We forget that the figure stands on the same floor as ourselves, and respond to the pose of a person perched on narrow scaffolding who must stretch to the side to pluck the last letter from its place. The formal structure of this work underlies and reinforces its content. The empty spaces of the illuminated plane (spare as those in a Mondrian painting) emphasize the isolation of the lone figure and its absorption in the task of changing the announcement of one program.

III

The films playing at the theater in Reginald Marsh's *Twenty Cent Movie* (1936, Fig. 3) emphasize the lures of human flesh. References to "Bio Feature" (for Biograph Studio pictures) and mainstream star "Frederic March" pale in the welter of lurid phrases. "A love written in blood" "Joys of the Flesh" "Stripped Bare" "Dangerous Curves" "Blood." Said aloud in the mind, the words call out in hucksterish tones more suited to burlesque (which Marsh adored) than to Hollywood fare. How to explain this vision?

Marsh was born in Paris to expatriate American artists who lived a comfortable life financed by rich Chicago grandparents. The young artist had an illustrator's gift for capturing detail and character, and his work soon appeared in a variety of newspapers and magazines. He was especially attracted by people with very different lives than his own: office workers, bums, and street characters. Perhaps these subjects had for him that fascination for the "other" which has been the subject of much recent critical writing. In any case, Marsh became known as a "realistic" chronicler of the less affluent parts of American urban life.

Twenty Cent Movie is constructed like a proscenium theater set. We view the space from a distance, with the detached and elevated perspective of someone seated in theater stalls or on a passing bus. The figures who people this entrance are a curious mixture of "respectable" girls and rough men. Transparent washes of tempera paint make the figures shimmer and shift as if hovering at the edge of our consciousness. Female viewers may not easily find themselves in this scene. Men can identify with the street toughs and enjoy the spectacle of the "Marsh girls," whose suggestively clinging clothing and air of respectable vulnerability had made them favorites since their first appearance in the *Yale Record* during the artist's undergraduate days. The aura of prurient interest is strengthened by the short men in rumpled suits and hats at the back who scrutinize posters and ogle twin nudes, whose scale and elevated position suggest mass-market copies of some Botticelli/Medici Venus. Like the films on show inside, the scene at the front of Marsh's theater is a voyeuristic male dream.

IV

In contrast to Marsh's scene, Edward Hopper's *New York Movie* (1939, Fig. 4) is strangely empty. The artist found his favorite theme of introspection and urban isolation even at the cinema. Only one patron watches the program of repeating shows. A uniformed attendant waits in the lighted side aisle to show any newcomer to a seat. A thick wall separates her from the darkened audience space. Unable to lose herself in the film, the woman sinks instead into her own thoughts. Her figure is almost lost within the cavernous hollows carved by the play of light and shadow around her.

Hopper's talent for picturing the existential loneliness of modern life was grounded in his realist training in New York City with Robert Henri, who taught the young artist to look hard at everyday scenes. Hopper's strong interest in literature and psychology leavened any impulse toward straight documentation. He looked constantly "for something that says something to me." When he found it: "I think about it. Just to paint a representation is not hard, but to express a thought in painting is."

Once the idea was set, a painting could begin to take shape through careful research and studies for the scene. *New York Movie* incorporates details from sketches Hopper made at the Strand Palace, Republic, and Globe theaters, and of his wife posed as the usherette in their apartment hallway. The final stage was the trickiest: "What you put on canvas is concrete, and it tends to direct the thought. The more you put on canvas, the more you lose control of the thought." Everything had to be stripped of superfluous detail to let the idea float free.

Hopper worked powerful magic with his small-scale figures and vast architectural voids. The cavernous spaces of *New York Movie* fill our eyes, pinpointing mercilessly the minute human island in their midst. For Hopper, a movie house is simply another setting for the inescapable isolation of one human being from another.

V

We expect Eduardo Paolozzi's *Wittgenstein at the Cinema Admires Betty Grable* (1965, Fig. 5) to depict someone at the movies. But this jazzy kaleidoscope of overlapping forms and bold striped pattern is clearly not a realist work. It is number 12 in the *As Is When* portfolio, designed by the artist as an abstract homage to the philosopher Ludwig Wittgenstein. The compositions were inspired by the thinker's writings and by a double biographical memoir written by two of his former students.

Why Wittgenstein? Paolozzi saw similarities between the way he assembled his artworks from found fragments and the philosopher's descriptions of the word games possible because language is a picture of reality. As the son of Italian immigrants and classified an "enemy alien" in World War II Britain, Paolozzi also empathized with Wittgenstein's position as an Austrian expatriate teaching at Oxford. And the artist shared the philosopher's fascination for American films and culture.

The title *Wittgenstein at the Cinema Admires Betty Grable* reflects Norman Malcolm's vivid description of the philosopher rushing from his lectures to see American movies and "sitting in the very front row of seats so that the screen could occupy his entire field of vision . . . [and he could] become totally absorbed in the film." Malcolm cites Wittgenstein's special fondness for "the film stars Carmen Miranda and Betty Hutton." There is no mention of Betty Grable. The name switch could have been an error, or an allusion to the artist's personal favorite. In any case, the print is primarily an amalgam of resonant signs for Paolozzi's own cinema admirations, including his ironic appreciation for the lusty nastiness of Disney's early Mickey Mouse.

Paolozzi is a master collagist. In 1952, he mesmerized an Independent Group audience at the ICA in London by projecting mass-media images, in no discernible order, as rapidly as possible with an opaque projector to create a stream of consciousness visual flow. A flood of two- and three-dimensional assemblages followed in his own work. Collaged montage is similar to cinema montage in the way that each bit is seen as itself, and at the same time, each shape engages in a visual dialogue with its neighbors. In this sense, *Wittgenstein at the Cinema Admires Betty Grable* speaks to and through the moviegoer in each of us.

VI

Cindy Sherman's *Untitled Film Still # 56* (1980, Fig. 6) takes us into the world of the cinema bit-player, essential for a moment to the plot, but interchangeable with a host of others in the minds of the viewer. We must stand near this small work to see its details. The head of a young woman fills the space. She looks at herself in a mirror. Her face is barely discernible in shadow from the strong back light that makes a halo of her bouffant hair. There is a strong impression that what we see is a shot from either one of Hollywood's *films noires* or one of the European films inspired by that style. The composition makes sense only within such a context; the paucity of visual information urges us to take this for one instant in a narrative film. Sherman's ability to suggest that we are looking at an actual frame of film is due partly to the way in which she has adopted her experience with still photography to the frames within which she stages her carefully constructed scenes.

For each of the roughly 70 Untitled Film Stills made between 1977 and 1980, the artist immersed herself in a stereotypical role of the sort that filled the stylized black and white films of the '50s and '60s. As a girl growing up in suburban New Jersey and Long Island, the artist enjoyed "dressing up" and watching movies at home on television or with her parents at a movie theater. These interests, together with a strong love of drawing, followed her to art school and then to New York City, where she arrived in 1977. Along the way she amassed a collection of second-hand '50s and '60s clothing and accessories. And she discovered European films, which intrigued her by the way their bottom-of-screen subtitles became captions that suggested a separate narrative for each image.

Having decided on a role for an Untitled Film Still, Sherman became director, producer and designer — establishing the right costume, props, setting, camera position, and lighting. Then as actress she stepped before the lens. Sometimes others tripped the shutter, but mostly she preferred working alone within the controlled environment of her studio.

Sherman's Untitled Film Stills call attention to the gendered nature of our film viewing. The subjects in her Untitled Film Stills are women caught in moments of self-absorption.[3] As a female viewer, I merge with the person in *Untitled Film Still #56*. I imagine what she has done and what she will do next. Even with a less ambiguous image like *Untitled Film Still #6* (1977, Fig. 7), I am forced into an empathetic participatory connection, connecting remembered adolescent fantasies about sexuality with the inward turning gaze, lowered mirror, open robe, and sensual pose of Sherman's scantily clad young woman. Men respond differently. They look at the figures in Sherman's Untitled Film Stills as outside themselves — women available for male scrutiny and assessment. In the words of Peter Schjeldahl, all of these images have a sexual charge: "As a male I . . . find these pictures sentimentally, charmingly, and sometimes pretty fiercely erotic." Sherman's vision is so on-target that these works can trigger powerful emotions on both sides of the gender gap.

VII

Hollywood's leading ladies have played key roles in the fantasies of countless male admirers. The Spanish artist Salvador Dali, never one to be shy about matters of sexual obsession, tackled the subject head-on in *Mae West* (c. 1934, Fig. 8). Like many Surrealists, Dali wanted his art to help liberate humans from social conventions which inhibited the union of psyche, flesh, and conscious and unconscious thought. An avid reader of psychological texts, with special attention to Freud and Krafft-Ebbing, Dali developed his own aesthetic theories. He said: "My whole ambition in painting is to manifest the images of concrete irrationality in terms of authoritative precision . . . images which for the moment can neither be explained nor reduced by logical systems or rational approaches." To this end, he used what he called his "paranoiac-critical activity . . . [a] spontaneous method of irrational knowledge based upon the interpretive-critical association of delirious phenomena." Using this he could combine the seen and unseen worlds, producing works "every one of which includes an entire systematic structure . . . [that] only becomes objective *a posteriori* by critical intervention." In practice, this approach led Dali to invent bizarre double images which flip-flop uneasily between representations of two quite different subjects.

Mae West shows both the well-known sultry features of the actress and the interior of a spare but sensual room. The impression of a face is strongest from a distance; that of the room is most unavoidable at close range. At mid-distance, there is an unnerving double vision which swings wildly back and forth like the uneasy scene shifts in a nightmare. Dali saw twinned images everywhere he looked. In *The Secret Life of Salvador Dali* (published in 1940), he gathered those connected with *Mae West* into a montage page of related images under the title "The Mouth as an Aesthetic Form." Two of these illustrations — natural rock formations near his birthplace in Cadaques and a painting of his own containing "Mysterious Mouth appearing in the back of my nurse" — are clues to the multivalent power of the mouth for the artist.

Dali fills *Mae West* with visual puns suitable to its original title: "The Face of Mae West which might be used as an apartment." Boudoir and siren are one. Female tresses become drapery swags that swing back to admit us to an inner chamber. Soft chins form the entry stairs. Floorboards become luminous skin, yet limn a deep space. A dark plane is simultaneously flat wall and mysterious mask. Framed pictures merge with sexy eyes. Pert nose and saucy clock combine into an erotic fireplace. The doubling of pursed lips and soft couch offers a special welcome. Dali later produced an edition of *Mae West Lips Sofas*, complete with satin fabric specially manufactured to match the actress's favorite pink lipstick. And he turned *Mae West* into an actual room in his museum in Cadaques. But the hallucinatory power of the vision remains strongest in the original painted photograph, which creates so well the sensation of the dreams that movies can inspire.[2]

VIII

James Rosenquist takes a different tack in *Marilyn Monroe I* (1962, Fig. 9). Marilyn was a worthy successor to Mae West. But Rosenquist's out-of-order jigsaw puzzle says less about the actress's individual charms than about the transmission of her image through the impersonal mass media. We work hard to recognize Marilyn's famous sleepy gaze and open-mouth smile in their inverted positions. Scattered letters only gradually slide into focus as blocky "a. . .ily. . .n." The effect is rather as if our memory had collected a stray assortment of details from the visual clutter in a late twentieth century American city.

The artist invented this style out of his experience hand-painting billboards throughout the Midwest and New York City. Working high above the ground, Rosenquist learned to paint his assigned daily picture chunks with the peculiar brushy illusionism that convinces the eye speeding past at a distance but turns cool and mannered when seen close-to. When he began making art for himself, the artist used his billboard experience as a carrier of special meaning: "I decided to make pictures of fragments, images that would spill off the canvas instead of recede into it. . . . I thought each fragment would be identified at a different rate of speed. . . . I wanted the space to be more important than the imagery. I wanted to use images as tools." To viewers in the early '60s, Rosenquist's use of billboard style and mass-media imagery seemed deceptively like that of other artists then appropriating banal popular subjects and commercial graphic techniques in reaction to the heavy emotionalism of Abstract Expressionism. But Rosenquist's compositions had a density that set them apart from much Pop art.

Marilyn Monroe I departs from Rosenquist's usual desire to "choose images common enough to pass without notice, old enough to have been forgotten, but not old enough to trigger nostalgia." Marilyn was a star who could disappear at will into a carefully constructed public persona. She could oscillate with ease between plain Norma Jean and the Marilyn Monroe made famous in the media. In a sense, Rosenquist's composition is a record of the painter's own experience as moviegoer. In this work, he joins other artists who honored Marilyn as a tragic symbol of the destructive nature of fame, where one's being may dissolve in the glare of fiction roles, media hype, and public acclaim.

IX

Andy Warhol's *Double Elvis* (1964, Fig. 10) is a compelling portrait of a male film star. And it is more. Elvis floats directly before us in a bare and undifferentiated space. His figure crouches in the classic gunfighter's stance. He wears jeans, boots, and open-necked shirt. His right hand aims a pistol snatched from the holster that hangs low on his right hip. His eyes gaze steadily in the direction of his gun's barrel. Clearly he is ready to do in a bad guy. This is a studio publicity shot for a Western film designed to showcase Presley's attractions.

Warhol loved films, and he was attracted by the mystery of fame. For his art he appropriated public media images of well-known people whose lives were tinged with tragedy — Marilyn Monroe (Fig. 11), Elizabeth Taylor, Jacqueline Kennedy, Elvis Presley. Such works are poignant reminders about how our knowledge of the world around us in the late twentieth century is shaped more by media picturing than by direct experience. Many of Warhol's "celebrity" canvases, including several of his Marilyn Monroes, repeat the chosen iconic representation across a gridded format that recalls an assembly of magazine covers on a newsstand. Minute differences in color placement and shadow differentiate the individual faces, but simplified shapes and harsh commercial hues create a series of masks that become powerful metaphors for the prison of modern media fame.[4]

The repeated media image in Warhol's Elvis Presley canvases works differently. Elvis was a special kind of movie star. He came to film from the hothouse land of rock music where female and male artists stand in front of crowds and sing in a manner that makes them equally the objects of sexual fantasies in the imaginations of their audiences. Elvis's screen roles incorporated his rock star appeal and turned him into a teen's movie idol, more mature in appearance than many who came after him.

Warhol used this appropriated studio photo as a silkscreen stencil in variant Elvis compositions. For the *Double Elvis* diptych, the artist chose a size just large enough to squeeze one and a half Presley figures into the left half. The right holds hazy traces which may indicate that more Elvises were once there. Warhol carefully subverted his mechanical process so that it could not duplicate images with a machine's accuracy. His careful sloppiness with the silkscreen technique was well known. Sewall Sillman, who produced a print with him at Ives-Sillman in New Haven, talked about how hard it was to achieve just the degree of misalignment and smudging that satisfied Warhol as declaring the unmistakable intervention of the human hand.

The shifts in appearance caused by the artist's screenprinting technique and the odd cut-offs at the edges of this canvas create the quality of action seen within a cinema space. The repeated figure and its cropping by the canvas edge imply a sequence in time. The twin Elvises are not quite alike; the right-hand one is placed a wee bit higher on the canvas. And the marks of squeegee and ink are not identical within the two forms. The figures move before us and invest the media image with life. *Double Elvis* resurrects memories of the star and transports anyone who saw him in action backward in time into the mental space in which we saw him perform.

X

Ron Kitaj's *John Ford on His Death Bed* (1983–84, Fig. 12) is an unusual meditation on this major director and his life. More than any other director, Ford gave flesh to the heroic myth of the Western film, in which self-reliant men and supportive women tame the American frontier while upholding clean moral values and unerring justice. Ford also had a gift for tales of heart-warming comradeship and strength in the lives of ordinary working people. His rich legacy includes *The Informer* (1935), *Stagecoach* (1939), *The Grapes of Wrath* (1940), *How Green Was My Valley* (1941), *They Were Expendable* (1945), *Wagon Master* (1950), *The Searchers* (1956), and *The Man Who Shot Liberty Valence* (1962).

Movies had been important to Kitaj since his youth in Cleveland and Troy, New York. Many details in earlier works were inspired by movies or occasionally a single film frame. In 1971, Kitaj had direct contact with the film world during a visiting professorship at UCLA, where: "We took a house within old Hollywood . . . and I visited some of the great old directors like John Ford and Renoir, Mamoulian, Milestone, and Billy Wilder. I sketched them for a painting I never made about Hollywood." The idea for a work about film directors surfaced years later back in England as part of Kitaj's desire to create paintings that would "register my American self from afar and in exilic fantasy."[5]

The close-packed references in *John Ford on His Deathbed* are typical in Kitaj's work. His paintings reflect his equal attraction to "the compendious nature of certain modern poets and writers . . . who try to get the world in . . . [and] the more intimate confessional ones . . . whose world-view is more in their own mirror." From early in his career, the artist has based details of his work on items from his collections of mass media images. His richly-textured combination of universal and personal references requires such careful attention from the viewer that the artist often adds interpretative texts to help in decoding the images.

In Kitaj's painted theater of the mind, John Ford appears three times, identified by the billed cap he favored late in his life. His figure is based on a photograph the artist took of the director during their Los Angeles meeting. The action is pushed into the four corners of the canvas, with the director occupying three and his work crowding the fourth. At the lower left, one Ford lounges in a director's chair and barks orders through a megaphone. A second Ford leans forward intently at the lower right, his eyes unshielded by the dark glasses he used to protect the weak eyes that plagued him throughout his career. This Ford peers toward a transparent screen at left center, where two figures lock in an energetic fight or dance. Behind him, a script girl consults her manuscript. At the upper right, the third Ford holds court from his bed with a cigar firmly clamped between his teeth. The rosary dangling from his right hand symbolizes both his Irish heritage and his "Irish" films. This Ford scrutinizes the commanding figure of John Wayne at the far left, who wears the uniform that carried him through Ford's cavalry trilogy: *Fort Apache*, *She Wore a Yellow Ribbon*, and *Rio Grande*. Up the middle of the canvas runs a hollow space, topped by a frame suspended in midair. Its legend — "The End" — is a fitting marker for the film director's demise.

XI

Thomas Hart Benton was the Cecil B. De Mille of the brush; he painted American history as a heroic saga of ordinary people. In Hollywood on assignment for *Life* magazine in 1937, Benton spent a month poking his head into every aspect of film production. The resulting 800 or so drawings he made of extras and technical support folks fed into the design for *Hollywood* (1937, Fig. 13).

By the time he made this work, Benton had perfected a means of painting his montages of American life by dividing his canvases into pockets of space that interconnected, yet held to the picture plane in the manner of cubist compositions. To unify his ideas and work out each design, the artist constructed elaborate small-scale relief models in clay. Raphael Soyer, a fellow painter who saw Benton at work in Hollywood, reported that the models were "illuminated so . . . that there were shadows." The painting faithfully followed the effects, with the result that the eye rolls through Benton's *Hollywood* as if watching a film.

Light and shadow, solid forms and interlocking space pull us back and forth between *Hollywood's* three film sets. At the left, we catch a glimpse of action on the set of a drama. In the right distance, a reconstructed city burns during the making of *In Old Chicago*, which was in production during Benton's visit. On the way to the outdoor set, our eye passes through a starlet dressing room. The glamour shoot of a statuesque blonde occupies center stage in the composition. This almost nude beauty is identified by Henry Adams as Benton's tribute to the recently deceased Jean Harlow, who had shared the artist's home town of Kansas City. The technical action that swirls around this central figure spreads along a band that runs from upper left down the center and across to the right. This clever device not only frames the side scenes but also puts female beauty clearly at the center of Hollywood studio production.

Benton wanted *Hollywood* to go in the lobby of a movie theater. Failing to find a patron, he made a panel painting instead. *Life* magazine found the scantily-clad blonde unsuitably risqué and refused to publish the work they had commissioned. In an ending worthy of a Hollywood romance, the painting won its way into the magazine two years later when it made art news by taking the "Popular Prize" at Pittsburgh's Carnegie International exhibition.

XII

For Man Ray and his Dada friends Duchamp and Picabia, machines were intriguing alternate life forms. *Admiration of the Orchestrelle for the Cinematograph* (1919, Fig. 14) is a symbolic diagram of Man Ray's fantasy that the *orchestrelle* sound system (devised to provide musical accompaniment for movies) anthropomorphically serves and adores the vision system that, in the language of the artist, "writes with cinema."[6]

Man Ray was fascinated by the mechanics of motion. He had represented it earlier as a series of overlapping flat colored planes in the painting of a *Rope Dancer Accompanying Herself with Shadows* (1916) and a series of collages called *Revolving Doors* (1917). In these he worked out a vocabulary of silhouette forms and diagram devices to carry the physical and dream realities of his subjects. For *Admiration of the Orchestrelle for the Cinematograph*, the artist combined the language of mechanical drawing and illusionistic shading to articulate a dream space. An ascending strip of numbered boxes at the upper left suggests film running through a projector and disappearing into the dark. In the center, the dainty *orchestrelle* picks up sound from its spinning mechanical-organ platter and amplifies it through a morning glory horn. Lines and shaded edges hint at the *orchestrelle's* position on a platform high above the rectangular movie screen at the lower right. As it plays, the music machine is transformed into an alter ego, which lifts its sound-horn skirts and dances below in twirling admiration before the "cinema-tograph."

The fantasy setting of *Admiration of the Orchestrelle for the Cinematograph* is enhanced by its airbrush technique. The airbrush (which Man Ray had been using for his commercial work) was perfectly suited to his artistic needs. With it he could improvise on the spot in the manner of a good Dadaist, using any shape at hand as a stencil and spraying color through it and around it, or painting free hand, varying at will the density of hue by moving the nozzle closer to or away from the paper. The images appeared as if by magic. As he jubilantly exclaimed: "It was wonderful to be able to paint a picture without touching the canvas."

Admiration of the Orchestrelle for the Cinematograph is a fitting work with which to end this tribute to the interplay of inspiration from movies to the visual arts. Man Ray's gentle poetic vision of a world in which machines themselves are captivated by the big screen symbolizes well the power of the moving image to provoke wondrous dreams.

NOTES

[1] Segal was introduced to Dada ideas by his friend Allan Kaprow, then teaching at Rutgers University and later well-known for his Happenings, some of which had Segal as a participant.

[2] Dali created occasional film dreams too. In Paris, with Luis Buñuel, he made the classic surrealist films *Un chien andalou* and *L'âge d'or*. In Hollywood in 1946, he painted backgrounds for the aborted Disney film *Destiny*, and designed part of the dream sequence in Alfred Hitchcock's *Spellbound*.

[3] Sherman did do a few as '50s/'60s male bit-players, but found it harder to think herself into those male roles.

[4] The Marilyn Monroes by Warhol and Rosenquist speak to very different aspects of the contemporary media experience. Warhol's use of "cool" mass-media techniques with publicity and news images produces a very different expression from Rosenquist's surreal conjunctions of personally resonant fragments inspired by the vast scale and hand-painted quality of advertising billboards.

[5] Initially titled *Amerika (John Ford on His Deathbed)*, this painting was a pendant to *Amerika (Baseball)*. Kitaj borrowed the German spelling for both works from Franz Kafka's novel with its outsider's view of the United States.

[6] Man Ray played on the Greek origins of the word "photograph" in naming various techniques he used for his art. "Rayograph" was his term for cameraless photographs. "Airograph" was the word he coined for airbrush paintings. And cinema became "Cinematograph."

BIBLIOGRAPHICAL NOTE

Biographical facts and artists' statements in this essay were based on the following sources: RUSCHA: Dave Hickey and Peter Plagens, with introduction by Anne Livet and foreword by Henry T. Hopkins, *The Works of Edward Ruscha*, NY: Hudson Hills Press, in Association with the San Francisco Museum of Modern Art, 1982; SEGAL: Martin Friedman and Graham W.J. Beal, with commentaries by George Segal, *George Segal: Sculptures*, Minneapolis: Walker Art Center, 1978; Segal in Henry Geldzahler, "An Interview with George Segal," 1964; Phyllis Tuchman, *Segal*, NY: Abbeville Press, 1983. Modern Masters Series; MARSH: Edward Lanning, *The Sketchbooks of Reginald Marsh*, Greenwich, CT: New York Graphic Society Ltd., 1973; HOPPER: Gail Levin, *Edward Hopper: The Art and The Artist*, NY and London: W. W. Norton & Company, in association with the Whitney Museum of American Art, 1980; Gail Levin, *Edward Hopper As Illustrator*, NY and London: W. W. Norton & Company, in association with the Whitney Museum of American Art, 1979; PAOLOZZI: Norman Malcolm, *Ludwig Wittgenstein: A Memoir*, London: Oxford University Press, 1966, with a "Biographical Sketch" by Georg Henrik Von Wright; DALI: Ercole Arseni, Leone Bosi and Massimo Marconi, *Walt Disney: Magic Moments*, Milan: Arnoldo Mondadori Editions, 1973; Salvador Dali, *The Secret Life of Salvador Dali*, translated by Haakon M. Chevalier, NY: Dial Press, Burton C. Hoffman, 1942; Robert Descharnes and Gilles Neret, *Salvador Dali*, Cologne: Benedikt Taschen Verlag, 1989; ROSENQUIST: Judith Goldman, *James Rosenquist*, NY: Viking Penguin, Inc., for The Denver Art Museum, 1985; SHERMAN: Gerald Marzorati, "Imitation of Life," ARTnews, Sept 1983; Peter Schjeldahl and I. Michael Danoff, *Cindy Sherman*, New York: Pantheon Books, 1984; WARHOL: John Coplans, with contributions by Jonas Mekas and Calvin Tomkins, *Andy Warhol*, NY: New York Graphic Society Ltd., c. 1978; KITAJ: Marco Livingstone, *R.B. Kitaj*, NY: Rizzoli International Publications, Inc., 1985; "John Ford," *Biography*, Arts and Entertainment channel, December 1994; "John Ford," David Quinlan, *The Illustrated Guide to Film Directors*, London: B.T. Batsford Ltd., 1983; BENTON: Henry Adams, *Thomas Hart Benton: An American Original*, NY: Alfred A. Knopf, 1989; MAN RAY: Arturo Schwarz, *Man Ray: The Rigour of Imagination*, NY: Rizzoli, 1977.

GRETA GARBO

H.D.

BEAUTY

In a poem of 1920, Hugh Selwyn Mauberley, *Ezra Pound deplored the vulgar taste of the age for a "prose kinema," an aesthetic of accelerated movement rather than the "sculpture of rhyme." His friend and fellow poet Hilda Doolittle, who used the pen name H.D., took a different view of the cinema. She celebrated it as a modern revelation of the "Beauty" derived from classical literature—the figure of Helen of Troy, for example. "It is the duty of every sincere intellectual to work for the better understanding of the cinema," she writes in this early appreciation of Greta Garbo. H.D. acted in films directed by Kenneth Macpherson in the late 1920s, and contributed regularly to the film journal* Close-Up. *Her articles on film have never been reprinted. This one appeared in the issue of July, 1927.* MQR *is grateful to James Laughlin and New Directions Publishing Corporation for permission to reprint this essay.*

I suppose we might begin rhetorically by asking, what is the cinema, what are the classics? For I don't in my heart believe one out of ten of us high-brow intellectuals, Golders Greenites, Chautauqua lecturers, knows the least little bit about either. Classics. Cinema. The word cinema (or movies) would bring to nine out of ten of us a memory of crowds and crowds and saccharine music and long drawn-out embraces and the artificially enhanced thud-offs of galloping bronchoes. What would be our word-reaction to Classics? What to Cinema? Take Cinema to begin with (cinema = movies), boredom, tedium, suffocation, pink lemonade, sawdust even; old reactions connected with cheap circuses, crowds and crowds and crowds and illiteracy and more crowds and breathless suffocation and (if "we" the editorial "us" is an American) peanut shells and grit and perhaps a sudden collapse of jerry-built scaffoldings. Danger somewhere anyhow. Danger to the physical safety, danger to the moral safety, a shivering away as when "politics" or "graft" is mentioned, a great thing that must be accepted (like the pre-cinema days circus) with abashed guilt, sneaked to at least intellectually. The cinema or the movies is to the vast horde of the fair-to-middling intellectuals, a Juggernaught crushing out mind and perception in one vast orgy of the senses.

So much for the cinema. (Our "classic" word-reaction will come along in due course.) I speak here, when I would appear ironical, of the fair-to-middling intellectual, not of the fortunately vast-increasing, valiant, little army of the advance guard or the franc-tireur of the arts, in whose hands mercifully since the days of the stone-writers, the arts really rested. The little leaven. But the leaven, turning in the lump, sometimes takes it into its microscopic mind to wonder what the lump is about and why can't the lump, for its own good, for its own happiness, for its own (to use the word goodness in its Hellenic sense) *beauty*, be leavened just a little quicker? The leaven, regarding the lump, is sometimes curious as to the lump's point of view, for all the lump itself so grandiloquently ignores it, the microscopic leaven. And so with me or editorially "us" at just this moment. Wedged securely in the lump (we won't class ourselves as sniffingly above it), we want to prod our little microbe way into its understanding. Thereby having the thrill of our lives, getting an immense kick out of trying to see what it is up to, what I am up against, what we all, franc-tireurs, have to deal with.

First as I say, amazing prejudice. The movies, the cinema, the pictures. Prejudice has sprouted, a rank weed, where the growth of wheat is thickest. In other words, films that blossom here in Europe (perhaps a frail, little, appreciated flower) are swiftly cut and grafted in America into a more sturdy, respectable rootstock. Take "Vaudeville", for example, a film that I didn't particularly revel in, yet must appreciate, Zolaesque realism which succeeded admirably in its medium, was stripped by this gigantic Cyclops, the American Censor, of its one bloom. The stem is valuable, is transplanted, but the spirit, the flower so to speak of "Vaudeville", we called it here "Variété", the thing holding its created center, its (as it happens) Zolaesque sincerity—is carefully abstracted. A reel or in some cases an artist or a producer, is carefully gelded before being given free run of the public. This is no fault of the public. The lump heaving under its own lumpishness is perforce content, is perforce ignorant, is perforce so sated with mechanical efficiency, with whir and thud of various hypnotic appliances, that it doesn't know what it is missing. The lump doesn't know that it has been deprived of beauty, of the flower of some production or of the fine flower of some producer's wit and inspiration. The lump is hypnotized by the thud-thud of constant repetition until it begins to believe, like the African tribesman, that the thump-thump of its medicine man's formula is the only formula, that his medicine man is the only medicine man, that his god, his totem is (save for some neighboring flat-faced almost similar effigies) the only totem. America accepts totems, not because the crowd wants totems, but because totems have so long been imposed on him, on it, on the race consciousness that it or him or the race consciousness is becoming hypnotized, is in danger of some race fixation; he or it or the race consciousness is so doped by mechanical efficiency and saccharine dramatic mediocrity that he or it doesn't in the least know, in fact would be incapable (if he did know) of saying what he does want.

He learns that there is a new European importation for instance of a "star"; this importation being thudded into his senses for some months beforehand, his mind is made up for him; she is beautiful. We take that for granted. There I agree, the leaven and the lump are in this at one. The lump really wants beauty or this totem of beauty would not be set up by its astute leaders. Beauty. She is beautiful. This time "she" is a northern girl, a "Nordic", another word they fall for. A Nordic beauty has been acclaimed and we all want to see her. I am grateful (it was my privilege) that I, for one, saw this grave, sweet creature before America claimed her. I saw her, as I see most of my pictures, more or less by accident. At least the divine Chance or classic Fortune that more or less guides all of us, led me one day to worship. I, like the Lump, am drawn by this slogan, "Beauty", though this particular enchantress was not particularly head-lined on the provincial bill-boards. In fact, the whole cast was modestly set forth in small type along with the producer and I thought "well it looks harmless anyhow" and it was raining and so in Montreux, Switzerland, I happened (as it happened) to see my first real revelation of the real art of the cinema.

I am led a little afield in trying to realize in retrospect the vast deflowering that took place in at least one rare artist. I dare say it is a common occurrence but in this particular case particularly devastating. I saw "Joyless Street" ("Die Freudlose Gasse") in Montreux, some two or three years ago when it was first "released" from Germany to take its tottering frail way across Europe toward Paris, where it was half-heartedly received, to London, where it was privately viewed by screen enthusiasts, only last winter, at one of those admirable Sunday afternoon performances of the London Film Society. In the meantime, I had seen Greta Garbo, deflowered, deracinated, devitalized, more than that, actively and acutely distorted by an odd unbelievable parody of life, of beauty, we were efficiently offered (was it at the Capitol about a year ago?) "The Torrent".

Greta Garbo in Montreux, Switzerland, trailing with frail, very young feet through perhaps the most astonishingly consistently lovely film I have ever seen ("Joyless Street") could not be, but by some fluke of evil magic, the same creature I saw, with sewed-in, black lashes, with waist-lined, svelte, obvious contours, with gowns and gowns, all of them al-most (by some anachronism) trailing on the floor, with black-dyed wig, obscuring her own Nordic nimbus, in the later "Torrent". The Censor, this magnificent ogre, had seen fit to devitalize this Nordic flower, to graft upon the stem of a living, wild camellia (if we may be fanciful for a moment) the most blatant of obvious, crepe, tissue-paper orchids. A beauty, it is evident, from the Totem's stand-point, must be a vamp, an evil woman, and an evil woman, in spite of all or any observation to the contrary, must be black-eyed, must be dark even if it is a Nordic ice-flower and Lya de Puttiesque. Beauty is what the Lump and the Leaven alike demand. So "beauty, here it is," says the Ogre. The Ogre knows that the world will not be sustained, will not exist without that classic, ancient Beauty. Beauty and Goodness, I must again reiterate, to the Greek, meant one thing. To Kalon, the beautiful, the good. Kalon, the mob must, in spite of its highbrow detractors, have. The Ogre knows enough to know that. But he paints the lily, offers a Nice-carnival, frilled, tissue-paper rose in place of a wild-briar.

Beauty was made to endure, in men, in flowers, in hearts, in spirits, in minds. That flame, in spite of the highbrow detractors, exists at the very center, the very heart of the multitude. It is the business of the Ogre, the Censor, to offer it a serpent for an egg, a stone for bread. It is the duty of every sincere intellectual to work for the better understanding of the cinema, for the clearing of the ground, for the rescuing of this superb art, from its hide-bound convention. Perseus, in other words, and the chained Virgin. Saint George, in other words, and the Totem dragon. Anyhow it is up to us, as quickly as we can, to rescue this captured In-nocent (for the moment embodied in this Greta Garbo) taking frail and tortuous veils of light and shadow, wandering in photogenetic guise that Leonardo would have marveled at and Tintoretto radiantly acclaimed. Greta Garbo, as I first saw her, gave me a clue, a new angle, and a new sense of elation. This is beauty, and this is a beautiful and young woman not exaggerated in any particular, stepping, frail yet secure across a wasted city. Post-war Vienna really wrung our hearts that time; the cheap, later clap-trap of starving stage Vienna had not yet blighted and blunted our sense of proportion and reality. Before our eyes, the city was unfolded, like some blighted flower, like some modernized epic of Troy town is down, like some mournful and pitiful Babylon is fallen, is fallen. The true note was struck, the first post-war touch of authentic pathos, not over-done, not over-exaggerated, a net of finely spun tragedy, pathos so fine and so intolerable that after all, we can't wonder that the flagrant, Parisian, commercial "buyers" must disdain it. London could not (being governed also by a brother to our American Cyclops) allow this performance to be broadcast. War and war and war. Helen who ruined Troy seems to have taken shape, but this time it is Troy by some fantastic readjustment who is about to ruin Helen. Little Miss Garbo (I think of her as little; I believe from the columns of "gossip" I read dished up in various Hollywood camera news productions that "Greta Garbo is taller than John Gilbert", a thing they seem in some subtle way to have, among many other things, against her) brought into her performance of the professor's elder, little daughter in "Joyless Street" something of the quality that I can't for the life of me label otherwise than classic. As long as beauty is classic, so long beauty on the screen, presented with candor and true acumen, must take its place with the greatest master-pieces of the renaissance and of antiquity.

For there is no getting over this astonishing and indubitable fact. Beauty as it has existed in pre-Periclean Athens, in the islands of the Cyclades, in the temple of Karnak, in the frescoes of Simone Martini and the etchings of Albrecht Dürer still does find expression, still does wander veiled as with dawn, still docs wait for a renaissance to hail her. Miss Garbo is a symbol, was, I should say, a symbol as I saw her in "Joyless Street". She may again become some such glorified embodiment as flung itself in its youth and its strange, statuesque abandonment across the wretched divan of Madame what-ever-was-her-name's evil house. Beauty, the youth and charm, by just a fluke, wasn't tarnished in that atmosphere. The odd thing was that this story of poverty and fervid business speculation and the lady of the world and her lovers and her pearls and the young financier and their meeting in this ill flavored establishment and the secret murder, wasn't commonplace, wasn't trivial, partook of the most etherial overtones of subtlety. Tragedy rang like little bells, fairy bells almost. Tragedy didn't dare, those days, to stalk openly in its ornate purple. Not in Europe, not in London or Paris or Vienna. Murder and pearls and speculation seemed perilously a part of life in those days. Tragedy was a muse whose glory was for the moment over-shadowed with an almost mystical, hardly to be expressed quality that one might possibly define as pathos. Beauty and the warrior were at rest. For the rest of us in London and Paris and Vienna, there was something different, something too subtle to be called disintegration or dissociation, but a state in which the soul and body didn't seem on good terms. Hardly on speaking terms. So it is that this fine little Greta Garbo with her youth, her purity, her straight brows and her unqualified distinction found a role to fit her. She had, it is true, appeared, I am told, creditably in other films; it was my good fortune to meet her first in this "Joyless Street" or, as it was billed in our Lake Geneva small-town, "La Petite Rue Sans Joie". The theater, I need hardly say, was half empty. The performance began with a street (will I ever forget it) and the somber plodding limp of a one-legged, old ruffian. No appeal to pity, to beauty, the distinguished mind that conceived this opening said simply, this is it, this is us, no glory, no pathos, no glamour. Just a long, Freudian, tunnel-like, dark street. Nothing within sight, nothing to dream of or ponder on but . . . the butcher's shop with its attendant, terrible, waiting line of frenzied women.

Life is getting something to eat said the presenter of this "Petite Rue Sans Joie". Getting it somehow, anyhow. Beauty itself must come to me, says La Petite Rue Sans Joie and one after another through sheer boredom with starvation, the "girls" of the neighborhood, the banal, the merely pretty, the sometimes ambitious, and the sheerly slovenly are drawn within the portals of la Petite Rue. For in the little street there is a shop that rivals even the butcher's for gaiety and distraction. It is neatly disguised, yet thinly. Clothes are bought and sold by a certain suave Madame (the performance of this entrepreneuse whose name I have forgotten, was amazing) and the little bigger of the little daughters of the proud, utterly destitute, brilliant, youngish, middle-aged professor strolls from time to time discreetly to its portal. Madame who is so suave, so kind (will I ever forget the subtlety of her make-up, that suggested shadow of a mustache across her sly upper lip) one day offers the little Mademoiselle a fur coat to wear home, she needn't pay for it yet, just wear it and keep warm, things are so hard, Madame is so suave, so genuinely sympathetic. The little lady loses her job through the insidious gift. A fur coat. Everyone knows what that means in post-war Vienna. The Manager of the office is pleased, didn't know this wild-flower was a game one. He summons her, offers a rise in salary, the usual denouement, of course, she being she, can't possibly accept it. La Petite Rue Sans Joie seems perilously near to swallowing our Beauty. Helen walking scatheless among execrating warriors, the plague, distress, and famine is in this child's icy, mermaid-like integrity. Her purity shines like an enchanter's crown. We *know* nothing can happen to her, yet do we? Things happen, we ourselves have known them to happen . . . one by one, our audience (already meager) has risen, has blatantly stamped downstairs. I hear words, whispers, English. "A thing like *this* . . . filthy . . . no one but a *foreigner* would dare present it." La Petite Rue Sans Joie was a real, little street. It was a little war-street, a little, post-war street, therefore our little picture palace in our comparatively broad-minded Lake Geneva town, is empty. People won't, they dare not face reality.

And beauty, among other things, is reality, and beauty once in so many hundred years, raises a wan head, suddenly decides to avenge itself for all the slights that it has negligently accepted, sometimes through weariness, sometimes through sheer omnipotence, sometimes through cynicism or through boredom. Simonetta, the famous Medician Venus (though I don't care for her), one and one and one, all stand as witnesses that once in so often, beauty herself, Helen above Troy, rises triumphant and denounces the world for a season and then retires, spins a little web of illusion and shuffles off to forget men and their stale formulas of existence. Well beauty has been slurred over and laughed at and forgotten. But Helen of Troy didn't always stay at home with Menelaus. Beauty has been recognized and for that reason (as the world will not face reality and the ogre, the Censor, this Polyphemus knows well enough that beauty is a danger), Miss Garbo has been trained, and that with astonishing efficiency, to sway forward and backward in long skirts with pseudo-Lillian Gish affectation, to pose with a distinct, parrot-like flare for the Gloria Swansonesque. Her wigs, her eye-lashes have all but eclipsed our mermaid's straight stare, her odd, magic quality of almost clairvoyant intensity. She simpers. Something has been imposed, a blatant, tinsel and paper-flowers and paste-jewel exterior, yet it doesn't quite dominate this Nordic ice-flower. Beauty brings a curse, a blessing, a responsibility. Is that why your Ogre, the Censor, is so intent on disguising it, on dishing it up a vamp charm, as stale, Nice-carnival beauty-as-we-get-it-in-a-beauty-contest? Greta Garbo remains Greta Garbo. Let us hope she takes it in to her stupid, magic head to rise and rend those who have so defamed her. Anyhow for the present, let us be thankful that she, momentarily at least, touched the screen with her purity and glamour. The screen has been touched by beauty, and the screen, in spite of all the totems, must finally respond, Polyphemus of our latest day, to the mermaid enchantment.

LAURA ANTILLANO

GONE WITH THE WIND

"What does that matter? Your words are valid for your reality, my words are valid for mine. When we mix them, they lack meaning."
                                                    Liv Ullman in Autumn Sonata.

The frames of her glasses are getting old, they're a style typical of the 1940s. She never changed them, she only uses them to watch the projection in the darkness of the theater, probably because there she can feel like someone else without being ashamed.

The benches in the plaza out front are showing wear from the impetuous and irreverent rain and sun. Today doesn't seem like Sunday, but it is Sunday.

With her ticket, which the boy in the cashier's booth has just sold her, she stops in the doorway to look outside. She is waiting for the chance to enter the theater to choose her seat; there is little movement from the public and this delays the start of the film.

Her daughter looks at her, contemplating her distant air, and for a few moments tries to initiate a conversation, without success. It occurs to her daughter, then, that she can offer her mother something from the candy stand (which is run by a woman seated on a stool, intensely engrossed in a tabloid magazine).

The grayness of the street has become a grayness inside; the daughter offers her mother sugared gum, Savoy chocolate, a package of popcorn, and it all remains in her hands with no response, a slight smile traced on the lips of her mother (as if she were trying to thank a stranger who was definitely unfamiliar with her affinity for sweets). A final silence and she continues to look at the trees in the plaza, the children in the plaza, the sky over the plaza. . . .

Clark Gable is eating a raw carrot. He bites into it making noise with his teeth, and he looks (with a look of desire) at the imposing figure of Scarlett O'Hara, alias Vivien Leigh. She is determined to save their love; she needs it. She has lived through so much torture in this war and her "pure-southern-belle-soul," inherited from a "powerful-cotton-growing-slave-owning-family," has undergone the most bizarre transformations.

The lenses of her 1940s eyeglass frames seem totally fogged up; she lifts her hand to her face with absolute serenity and takes them off to one side. She opens her purse and takes out a handkerchief with lace trim to clean her glasses, but her eyes remain glued to the screen, while the girl at her side keeps her eyes glued to her mother. The girl's hand tries to touch her mother's hand in a timid gesture (she wants to remind her that surely Clark Gable also loves Scarlett O'Hara, it's just that he can't express it because his pride won't allow it. Besides, Vivien Leigh, alias Scarlett O'Hara, doesn't inspire confidence in him. Deep down, she profoundly despises him, and this is a new game to trap him now that he has become a "prosperous man"). But her mother removes her hand from the armrest, thinking that that was what her daughter wanted at that moment.

Now the camera pans over the hundreds of bodies strewn about. They are wounded soldiers, their arms and legs intertwined in a makeshift hospital in the passageway at the station. Now she appears among so much destruction, so many faces asking for water, so much complaining, so many raised hands, so many carts hauling dead bodies. She walks majestically among them, wearing her sun hat with its black ribbons framing her face, with her hair carefully curled and shining, she appears with her sleeves bordered by buttons and her well-sculpted waist. And now the soldiers raise their hands pleading as she passes, and she looks at them without seeing them. She looks at them and reviews in her mind those parties in her parents' mansion, before the war when everything was sun and young ladies laughing and the wind lifting beautiful skirts and great elegant feasts, everything in harmony with those good black slaves, capable of working and working and loving their masters and Scarlett alias Vivien is nauseated by everything she now sees, the filth of half-dead soldiers lying on the floor in the passageway of her beloved station. And she stops in front of a soldier who is lying just below the hem of her long and elegant dress, and she looks down on him seriously, with a reflective look; the man's head is wrapped with a piece of old, dirty rag, which surely is an attempt to keep his brains together, which are about to fall out. At that moment the girl

can no longer concentrate as she watches the screen because she has
heard her mother sob, who again takes off her glasses to clean them
with her little lace handkerchief. This time the daughter doesn't try
to touch her, she only looks at her and thinks. She can imagine a
town, a house and a room with a cement floor, very clean, shining
from use, ferns hanging everywhere, forget-me-nots and orange
blossoms (like the song says), velvet chairs, the fragrance of cilantro
and cinnamon, women seated in a circle. There's a radio on the
table and once in a while one of them has to hit it so they can
continue to listen to the announcer, interrupted by some Glenn
Miller melody or Los Panchos. The women's laughter is an ingredi-
ent in the conversation; they all wear wide skirts, and on their laps
rest their sewing baskets, thread, needles, and lace sticking out of
them. The conversation is a monotonous murmur with the radio
playing its musical background. One of the women stands up; she's a
young girl, not pretty but possessing a certain grace of movement.
She says, "Ready! It's all finished."

She puts her basket on the chair, and lifting a pink diaphanous
gown with her hands, she puts it on over the dress she is wearing.
Holding on to it firmly, she spins in front of the other women, who
watch her with great enthusiasm.

> "It's beautiful!"
> "It fits you perfectly!"
> "Do you think so?"
> "Yes, it's identical. . . ."

Identical to the one worn by Vivien Leigh alias Scarlett O'Hara,
when she cries. She sees everything destroyed and she cries, and
there is nothing but fire and disaster, ruin all around her, and she
cries, remembering what she has lost. But no, she won't allow herself to die; she grabs that curtain from the floor, she picks it up, she
embraces it, she holds it against her chest while she cries, and then,
Vivien Leigh alias Scarlett says yes to life and no longer feels impoverished and defenseless. She looks for a needle, thread, and scissors,
and she sits on the floor to make the most marvelous dress that any
young lady has ever worn during the Civil War, the most beautiful
dress ever designed to win back Clark Gable and to tell him, "Here I
am, ready for whatever comes, my love." Everything is pink; the
wide skirt below, the low neckline above, the velvet ribbon at the
waist, and the broad-brimmed straw hat on her head, everything

beautiful and fresh (but no longer so fresh inside, because as every-one knows, the world has changed, life has changed, and Vivien Leigh knows about poverty and disillusionment and desperation).

The daughter can no longer take her eyes off her mother, who now does not even bother to put her glasses back on. She allows the tears to flow, they overflow in a pool, a permanent flood. The lights come on in the theater and everything becomes the noise of chairs returning to their normal position, skirts brushing against legs, candy wrappers rolling around, whispered words, some laughter, a kiss and a sleepy hug good-bye.

The two stand up and the daughter timidly tries to extend her hand to her mother's shoulder, and her mother says softly, "Let's go," and she looks at the floor, as if wanting to say, "It's alright, leave me alone."

Under a gray sky they cross the plaza, with its pale aging benches set among the trees, and both mother and daughter carry their hearts in their hands, without daring to leave them in the first trash can and not daring to put them back in their chests, while a light rain begins to fall peacefully, covering everything.

From: *Cuentos de películas*. Caracas:
Publicaciones Seleven, 1985.

Translated from the Spanish by Kathy S. Leonard

WILLIAM PAUL

SCREENING SPACE: ARCHITECTURE, TECHNOLOGY, AND THE MOTION PICTURE SCREEN

Where do you like to sit when you go to a movie? The conventional view of the movie theater holds that it doesn't really matter. As theater historian Maggie Valentine has written, "Measurements that govern seating arrangements are less crucial [in movie theaters][1] because there are no 'bad' seats, given the size and angle of the screen." But the screen is, in fact, a more difficult object than Valentine recognizes. A twenty to twenty-five foot screen in a large auditorium—roughly what could be expected in most of the movie palaces before the wide screen revolution of the 1950s—creates greater distinctions in what people see in the front rows and the back rows than a similarly sized screen in a small auditorium. This does not mean conversely that all small auditoriums present more favorable viewing conditions than large ones. A narrow and deep hall provides more variable impressions of screen size than a wide and shallow space which provides more variable impressions of image coherence. The long hall presents different members of the audience with both a big and a small screen, while the wide hall shows a big screen to all, but also a distorted image to many.

All this suggests that the placement of the screen in architectural space is a key determinant in how we experience a movie image. 1995 marks the 100th anniversary of the first projection of motion picture film upon a screen, yet what exactly do we know about the motion picture screen itself? Oddly, this most visible piece of filmic illusion is the one thing both film history and theory have most overlooked. In this regard, film scholars seem to be following in the footsteps of exhibitors, for whom the creation of the image was often a secondary concern. The big picture palaces we tend to regard nostalgically today treated the screen as an afterthought, something that had to be fit into pre-existing designs

244

for theaters that featured live stage performances. And theater owners who sought to maximize their audiences were content to have seating arrangement dictate dimensions and placement of screen, rather than the other way around. Situating the projection booth was often regarded as a more important issue, since the space for the screen—the stage—already existed in conventional theater design.

As the key element in our experience of watching a movie, the most distinctive aspect of the screen from the first motion picture performance on is what has also remained most constant about it: the screen leads a double life. It is both the final link in the chain of film technology as well as an element of architecture, defining—and being defined by—the space it inhabits. If the screen has been overlooked in both its roles, this is because critical writing on both architecture and film technology has seen the screen as essentially passive. Consider, for example, Maggie Valentine's encomium of Moderne theaters from the thirties and forties designed by S. Charles Lee: "Together with the light pattern on the ceiling, the walls blended the interior in shape, color, and harmony, translated as great swirling patterns that led the eye to the screen" (106). It's a rather odd notion that patrons sitting in a darkened space would need any help directing their eyes to the one brightly illuminated area, yet it's easy to arrive at this notion if you do not begin with the premise that the screen is the theater building's most prominent architectural element, if you begin, as Valentine does, with the assumption that a film theater is built around the projection booth.

A comparable sense of passivity has affected our view of the screen in its technological role. Most of the writing in film studies on the "technological apparatus" has focused entirely on image creation (the camera, lenses, lighting, film stocks, etc.) and, to a lesser extent, image production (the projector).[2] As a reflecting surface the screen apparently limits itself to giving back unchanged the images presented to it. It is for this reason that the screen has found its place in film studies primarily as metaphor, its very passivity facilitating its transformation into other things.[3] But in point of fact the motion picture screen has always played an active role, both as an element of architecture and an element of technology. And it has done so in a way that reflects back on other aspects of film technology. The activity of the screen is not a static phenomenon, one that transcends its history. Rather, both the architectural screen and the technological screen have changed in their 100 years, and changed in ways that directly affect our perception of the movie image. Once we understand the activity of the screen and its historical role, we can begin to trace an evolution in the *way* we have looked at movies, a history that parallels and complements the history of the movies themselves.

THEATER SPACE AND FILM STYLE

Rather than attempt a complete history, I'd like to establish a critical way of thinking about the screen in its history. My starting assumption is that there are both constant and variable dimensions of the screen in its dual architectural and technological guises. If I can establish the constants, I can then chart a history of the screen by looking at the variables. The variables have generally centered on size in relation to theatrical space, shape, the placement of the screen in the auditorium, and reflectance. In this essay, I will concentrate on screen size and reflectance by looking at two periods that sought the most radical changes in screen history: the failed move to wide-gauge filmmaking 1929-31 and the more successful wide screen revolution of the 1950s. In doing this, I hope to demonstrate how the screen itself might have influenced the development of film style.

Architecturally, the one constant is a seemingly simple one: the screen always occupies a fixed point in architectural space. In this regard, the screen does place definite constraints on theater architecture. To take the most obvious example, in spite of the Lumières' early experiment with a two-sided screen, a conventional film screen will not allow for a theater-in-the-round.[4] It dictates an audience placed in front of it, and it limits the spaces that the audience may inhabit. From this simple condition of fixity, the screen establishes the possibility for fairly radical departures from traditional stage theater design. The screen might reflect a good deal of movement, but the audience's attention is effectively always fixed on one object, the screen itself. With the stage theater, on the other hand, audience attention may be selectively directed by movement along the whole width of the proscenium. For this reason, stage and screen theaters create a different spatial relationship between spectators and spectacle. Ben Schlanger, "the dean of movie architects," formulated this difference as a horizontal orientation in the stage theater versus a vertical orientation in the movie theater.[5] For Schlanger, this difference mandated important design differences that encompassed among other things a startling reworking of floor slopes to emphasize the vertical axis. Schlanger's architectural aesthetic reflected general modernist trends in architecture that made function dictate form; for him, the function of the movie theater had to make the screen dictate the form of the theater.

But this was often not the case, and most especially not during the great period of movie palace construction, from the teens through the early thirties. As a consequence, the positioning of the screen in architectural space might function as a constant, but the construction of the space around it is a variable. The earliest writing I have found that defines the proper relationship between movie theater space and the screen is a 1931 *Journal of the Society of Motion Picture Engineers* article:

> The proper size [of the screen] should be chosen:
> (A) Minimum desirable width is one-sixth the distance of the screen from the farthest seats.
> (B) Maximum desirable width is eight-tenths the distance of the screen from the front seats.
> (C) Intensity of lamps is an important factor limiting the size.[6]

To some degree, this formulation still treats the screen almost as an afterthought, since theatrical space here determines screen size. By 1937 Ben Schlanger reversed this determination and let the screen dictate theatrical space: the first row of seats should be set at a distance equal to 0.87 times the width of the screen; the last row should be no further than six times the width of the screen; and the width of the rows of seats should fall within a 60° angle originating at the screen.[7] This formulation was subsequently repeated with some frequency in the pages of *Motion Picture Herald*, the most important trade journal for movie exhibitors.[8] The point of both these sets of rules was to live up to the democratic promise of the movie theater, to make every seat a good seat indeed and allow the camera eye alone to serve as the viewer's eye.

The recommendations came fairly late in the development of the nation's theatrical plant, they didn't have the force of law, and, finally, they even represented something of a compromise since "studies of viewing conditions have indicated a factor of 3.5W [i.e., a maximum distance of 3.5 times the width of the screen] as a reasonable one for such visual limits as 'long shots' generally."[9] Furthermore, other considerations could end up dictating architectural design. The dual function of the movie palaces, the attempt to combine a live stage theater with a movie theater, obviously ruled out even the ambition of building a theater *around* the screen. And the desire to make every seat a usable seat had economic motivation, of course. Seats could be placed both closer and further away than these rules dictated so long as patrons were willing, if not entirely happy, to sit in them. Until the fifties, *Society of Motion Picture and Television Engineers* surveys found an *average* distance for theaters of 5.2 times the width of the screen.[10] Since this was an average that included a balance between large and small houses, the distances in the movie palaces would have far exceeded the six times width recommendation.[11] Finally, the great width of the palaces also dictated that many seats were placed on angles outside the 60° arc.

For theater chains, and most especially the parent film companies that owned the theater chains, size was a virtue in itself, enabling them to turn their minority percentage of the nation's theaters into the majority percentage of box office receipts. But size also meant a large number of seats that either stood at a great distance to the screen or an extreme angle. In fact, George Schutz, the editor of the "Better Theatres" section of *Motion Picture Herald*, estimated in 1948 that one third of the audience in the large first-run theaters saw a distorted picture.[12] Consider, too, the relationship of screen size to the depth of the auditorium. First of all, the screens are doubly framed, a smallish rectangle of light set in black masking that is then framed by a fairly large proscenium. Over the years, various reasons were offered for the masking: the dark surround made the image appear brighter, which helped with general problems of illumination; it squared off the image to make less apparent the keystoning caused by sharp projection angles of high projection booths; it concealed the vibration of projection equipment. Whatever the justifications, masking had the odd effect of making a small image seem even smaller and, by virtue of the double framing, at a fairly great remove from the audience. Secondly, these very small screens in very large halls necessarily made it difficult to see details in any shot further back than medium distance. And black masking actually exacerbated the situation: a two-year study by the Illuminating Engineering Society of Great Britain reported in 1939 that a dark border around a light picture perversely had the effect of reducing visual acuity, making it more difficult for the eye to resolve detail.[13]

Given the size of the image, the double framing of black masking and proscenium, and problems in visual acuity, I want to suggest that the decoupage of the standard Hollywood film, with its emphasis on telling close-ups to direct audience attention, might in part be a function of the conditions of reception. Through much of his writing on film theater architecture, Ben Schlanger saw precisely this connection:

Cinematographic technique depends to a great extent on the ratio be-tween picture size and viewing distance. If we said, for example, that a picture had to be viewed from a distance equal to ten times the width of the image, we would know that the story would have to be dramatized pretty much by the close-up method. The *scenic* material, which is certainly important to an illusion of reality, would be without detail to many members of the audience.[14]

Schlanger is exaggerating the width-distance ratio here for the point of ar-gument, although some of the largest theaters like the Roxy did in fact ap-proach this configuration. Even in theaters that didn't reach this extreme, however, the small screen in the large space was at a minimum conducive to a style that relied on medium to close shots to make narrative points.

Can we assume that there is a correlation between film style and ar-chitectural space? Barry Salt's statistical analysis of Hollywood films of the twenties does demonstrate a generally closer position for the camera in the twenties than in the teens, and the camera seems to get progres-sively closer as the decade wears on.[15] Since this shift in style follows upon the explosion of movie palace construction for prime first-run the-aters throughout the United States in the teens and twenties, it seems likely that the places of exhibition had some impact on the product that was exhibited. Conversely, when Salt's figures on European films point to much greater camera distances, I'm not inclined to regard this as purely a cultural preference for distance. A survey of international the-aters published in *Exhibitors Herald World* in 1929 suggests that one possible reason for this difference lay in the differences in exhibition:

> With approximately 27,000 theatres in Europe seating 12,000,000 people, *only* 19 have a seating capacity of over 3,000; 23 seat from 2,500 to 3,000; *only* 84 have from 2,000 to 2,500 seats; 267 have a seating capacity from 1,500 to 2,000 and 1,250 from 1,000 to 1,500 seats each. There are more than 18,000 theatres (*a good proportion of which barely qualify as motion picture theatres*) with less than 500 seats each. The average cinema capacity in Europe is less than 480.[16]

As my added emphases indicate, this writer clearly thought there was something very wrong with the small size of these theaters; some of them might not even be theaters! While Europe at this time had more theaters than the United States, the writer's attitude might make sense if you consider that the New York metropolitan region alone probably exceeded all of Europe in the number of theaters with over two thousand seats.[17] These marked differences in theater architecture between the United States and Europe might well explain another odd fact that Salt's analysis of camera distances reveals: the American films of Alfred Hitchcock and Fritz Lang generally have a much higher number of close shots than their English and German counterparts.[18]

If the deep distance of architectural space possibly had an impact on the distance of the camera, let me speculate further by considering the width of the auditorium. I can evoke the problem most clearly if I use Radio City Music Hall, the last of the great picture palaces and one of the largest. Until the wide screen revolution of the early fifties, the Music Hall utilized a screen approximately 33 feet wide, one of the biggest in the country, set in a proscenium 100 feet wide, set in an auditorium approximately 200 feet wide.[19] This means that a fair block of seats at the Music Hall lay outside the 60° arc of the screen with a resultant distortion of the image and often extreme distortion at the ends of the rows. This has one direct consequence for the kinds of image projected on the screen, as noted by theater architect Schlanger in 1932: "Distorted views of form and background on the screen are accented most when the forms and background appear in sharp perspective." In noting this, Schlanger is actually objecting to dominant cinematographic practice of the time, for he adds: "A view taken in sharp perspective in motion picture work is one of the most forceful and effective instruments of the motion picture art. Thus, it is necessary that the means of exhibiting must be allied with the production of the motion picture as well."[20] By pointing to problems of distortion and stating his own preference for sharply defined images, Schlanger effectively offers one explanation for why deep focus, a common feature of cinematography up through the teens, was not a good cinematographic style for large movie theaters.

I don't want to claim a one-to-one causality here, but I think it worth noticing that the advent of shallow focus as a dominant style follows the large theater expansion of the teens and twenties. André Bazin assumed that shallow focus resulted from cutting procedures geared toward focusing audience attention: "Soft focus only appeared with montage. It was not only a technical must consequent upon the use of images in juxtaposition, it was a logical consequence of montage, its plastic equivalent."[21] Bazin posits a very specific causality here, with cutting procedures determining cinematographic practices. But it is just as likely that both cutting and shallow focus style are in part determined by another, external constraint, that of theatrical space.

A TEST CASE: *THE BIG TRAIL* (1930)

These are frankly speculative observations, and perhaps never fully susceptible to proof or disproof. But in claiming that an exploration of film theater architecture points to ways of rethinking important aspects in the history of film style, I have taken my lead from Ben Schlanger because he was a major theater practitioner contemporary with developments I have been describing. From his earliest writings on, Schlanger expressed a strong awareness of the ways in which theatrical design in the teens and twenties had consequences for the cinematography of what we now call the "classical Hollywood style." Schlanger was not a filmmaker, so that his writing, however suggestive, always operates at a remove from actual production circumstances.

There is nonetheless one concrete piece of evidence that might limn the extent to which filmmakers were thinking about the screen in relation to architecture as a stylistic constraint: the early attempts at wide gauge filming in 1930-31. Because there was no way of reducing the wide gauge image onto conventional 35 mm film as CinemaScope would eventually allow, filmmakers had to shoot two different versions, one in the wide gauge and one in 35 mm. The wide gauge versions, intended for exhibition on screens at least double the size of the screens in even the largest deluxe theaters, made possible something that had never existed before: an image that came close to filling the spacious prosceniums, an enlarged image more commensurate with the enlarged dimensions of the movie palace itself.[22] As such, wide gauge film powerfully changed the existing relationship between image and theatrical space in a manner that had consequences for conventional stylistic practices. I propose that differences between 35 mm and wide gauge versions offer a likely test case for determining how the period understood the relationship between the screen and its architectural space.

Consider Raoul Walsh's *The Big Trail*, filmed in "Fox Grandeur," a 70 mm system, restored in a 35 mm anamorphic print by the Museum of Modern Art. The film has also long existed in a standard 35 mm print. At first glance the Grandeur print seems a radically different film because its shooting style departs from other films of the period, with images much denser and the camera much less directional, often to the point that you occasionally have to search through the image in a given scene in order to find the speaker.[23] Still, direct comparison of the two versions reveals that the cutting patterns of the 70 mm version are fairly similar to the 35 mm. The key differences actually come in areas I've been suggesting up to this point, camera distance and depth-of-field. Let me cite three specific moments from the film to demonstrate this.

I) Indian scout Breck Coleman (John Wayne) visits family friend "Mother" Riggs (Marcia Harris). In the Grandeur version, the scene begins with an extraordinary shot of six women by a fence in the front yard washing and combing their hair (Fig. 1). The women are arranged in the image so that five form a diagonal line that moves to the right of the image where Coleman will enter through an opening in the fence. A woman sitting on the far right balances the image, but there is no clear centering of focus since lines converge toward the opening in the fence on the right. As Coleman starts to walk out of the image, there is a cut to a three-quarter shot of "Mother" Riggs at a pump feeding dogs. Coleman walks up to her in the center of the image and greets her. A fence on the left and a cabin on the right frame the image, but the background remains clearly defined and full of action: a wagon drives by as well as a number of horseback riders (Fig. 3). In the 35 mm version, one woman is eliminated from the first shot, while the remaining five form more of a circular grouping with a center point near the center of the image (Fig. 2). The shot is compositionally less complex, and it is held accordingly for a shorter period of time. After Coleman walks in on the far right, there is a cut to a long shot of "Mother" Riggs in the center of the image feeding her dogs, with the pump to the left of her. Here the shot is actually further back than in Grandeur, but the background is closed off by the cabin on the right and a tree and a fence on the left. Furthermore, as soon as Coleman says hello, there is a cut to a loose medium shot and a shift in angle so that the two are standing against the indistinct background of the house, which effectively acts like a shallow focus shot since no distinct lines are visible and all attention is allowed to concentrate on the centered foreground activity (Fig. 4). As they walk toward the house at the end of the sequence, there is a pan to the doorway, as if to suggest the limitations of what the camera can see. Although the doorway is not visible in 70 mm, there is no camera movement in that version.

II) This sequence introduces the heroine, Ruth Cameron (Marguerite Churchill), an impoverished Southern woman who is moving west with her brother Dave and much younger sister, "Honeychild." It also introduces the first of two villains, Mr. Thorpe (Ian Keith), an

Fig. 1: *The Big Trail* in Grandeur (70mm)

Fig. 2: *The Big Trail* in 35 mm

Fig. 3: *The Big Trail* in Grandeur (70 mm)

Fig. 4: *The Big Trail* in 35 mm

Fig. 5: *The Big Trail* in Grandeur (70 mm)

Fig. 6: *The Big Trail* in 35 mm

equally impoverished Southern gentleman who has become a river gambler. Again, the 35 mm has the need for one additional shot, but the general purpose of the cutting in both versions is similar. In 70 mm, it is as follows:

1) A long shot of the upper deck of a boat looking out toward the river; the boat and the people on it fill the left and bottom of the image. Miss Cameron stands in the center of the image, while her sister sits to the right on a railing which her brother, further right, leans against. The Captain of the boat enters from the left and walks up to Miss Cameron (Fig. 5). He speaks: "Well, Miss Cameron, we be—"

2) Approximately a three-quarter shot with the four characters spread out across the image and no real center to the shot (Fig. 7). The Captain and Miss Cameron face each other, occupying the left half of the image. The Captain completes his sentence: "—landing in a few minutes." The Captain tries to talk Miss Cameron out of her plans to go west, but she objects: "Why there's no place to turn back to." Captain: "Why,—"

3) #1. The Captain finishes: "—there isn't a home in all the South that wouldn't welcome the daughter of Colonel Cameron." Mr. Thorpe appears from the crowd to the left of the Captain, walks forward to the right and leans against the railing, obscuring our view of Honeychild and Dave (Fig. 9) as Miss Cameron tells the Captain, "We must keep the family together." As she turns around to her sister, Mr. Thorpe walks to the left and out of the image. On his leaving, Miss Cameron says, "And our brother Dave is almost a man grown."

4) #2. Dave: "Ruth is right, Captain. The Cameron tribe must stick together."

In the 35 mm version the camera is more emphatic, both through cutting and mise-en-scène:

1) A long shot of the upper deck of a boat looking out toward the river, but the shot has been moved closer in than in 70 mm, reducing our view of the river and trees to a fringe at the top of the image (Fig. 6). Here the railing is moved into the center, so that the family grouping of Miss Cameron, sister and brother is now more centered and symmetrical. The Captain enters from the left and moves behind Miss Cameron, beginning to speak, "Well, Miss—"

2) A close medium two-shot symmetrically balanced of the Captain and Miss Cameron (Fig. 8) as he finishes his sentence: "—Cameron, we be landing in a few minutes." There are people behind them looking out at the river and land, but what we can see of river and trees is distinctly

Fig. 7: The Big Trail in Grandeur (70 mm)

Fig. 8: *The Big Trail* in 35 mm

Fig. 9: *The Big Trail* in Grandeur (70 mm)

out of focus. The cut on dialogue is slightly different here, taking place when Miss Cameron says, "Why there's no place to turn back—"

3) Full shot, with the railing now to the right of center as in #1 of the 70 mm version. While there are four characters spread across the image as in #2 of the 70 mm version, here Miss Cameron is definitely in the center as she finishes, "—to." Mr. Thorpe enters and moves forward to the center, partially blocking our view of the Captain and Miss Cameron as the Captain tries to talk Miss Cameron out of her plans, "It's a tough proposi—"

4) #2. Captain: "—tion, girl, this pioneer life in the savage wilderness." . . . Miss Cameron: "We must keep the family togeth—"

5) #3. Mr. Thorpe is now leaning on the railing, fully blocking our view of Miss Cameron (Fig. 10) as she finishes her sentence: "—er." Mr. Thorpe starts to walk off as Miss Cameron turns to her sister, and he walks out of the image as she says, "And our brother Dave is almost a man grown."

III) Coleman has his first exchange with the second and more treacherous of the two villains, Red Flack (Tyrone Power) inside a trading post. The key difference here is substituting cross-cut singles for a two-shot, but there is a significant difference in cinematography as well. In Grandeur, the confrontation takes place as follows:

1) Long shot of the interior of a trading post with the large and bright entryway in the background to the right of center. In the foreground the bottom image is framed on either side by Indians counting furs. Other people and objects are visible in the image. As Coleman, left of center, tells the trading post owner, right of center, he'll scout for the wagon train, and the owner tells him Red Flack is the wagon boss, Flack himself enters from behind the boss to the left and walks to the center (Fig. 11). Boss: "Likely you two've met be—"

2) Medium two-shot of Coleman, left, and Flack, right (Fig. 13). Although focus on the background is somewhat soft, setting, furs, other objects, and two men who enter a door and walk to the right are all definable. The boss (off-screen) finishes: "—fore." Flack (looking Coleman up and down): "Nah. . . ." Coleman (with a steady gaze): "I reckon not." Boss (off-screen) "Coleman's gonna scout for the train. And he understands, Flack, that he's to have final say in all matters dealing with the Indians." Flack: "Yeah, well, who's got the final say about bossing the bull—"

3) #1. Flack: "—train?" As Flack says this, the Indian on the right moves forward toward the center to place a fur in a pile.

Fig. 10: *The Big Trail* in 35 mm

Fig. 11: *The Big Trail* in Grandeur (70 mm)

Fig. 12: *The Big Trail* in 35 mm

Fig. 13: *The Big Trail* in Grandeur (70 mm)

Fig. 14: *The Big Trail* in 35 mm

Fig. 15: *The Big Trail* in 35 mm

The 35 mm again requires one more shot:

1) A three-quarter shot of the interior of the trading post, with Coleman on the left and the boss on the right, part of the doorway visible to the right behind him. The top of an Indian's head may be seen in the foreground right of center; his activity is not clear. The boss starts to move back further to the right at the sound of o.s. steps; Flack enters and moves into the center (Fig. 12). Boss: "Likely you two've met be—"

2) Close medium shot of Flack (Fig. 14). Boss (o.s.): "—fore." The doorway light is behind Flack and a passing shape seems to be a person, but otherwise the background focus is soft to the point of abstraction. Flack (looking Coleman up and down): "Nah. . . ."

3) Close medium shot of Coleman (Fig. 15). As in #2, the background focus is soft to the point of abstraction. Coleman (with a steady gaze): "I reckon not." Boss (o.s.) "Coleman's gonna scout—

4) #1. Boss: "—for the train." The scene continues as above.

Although the patterns and purposes of the cutting are the same in both versions, in all three sequences, the 35 mm camera is clearly more emphatic in directing viewer attention. This is why each sequence contains an extra shot in 35 mm. Even on the rare occasion when the 35 mm version uses a longer camera distance, as it does briefly in the first example, the mise-en-scène moves the viewer's eyes to the foreground center by blocking off the background activity. This scene also presents the most overt attempt at directing attention in that the ensuing conversation plays against the nondescript background of the cabin, while the Grandeur version loads the background with competing activity. This neutralizing background cannot simply be a function of the lesser width, but, rather, a consequence of the overall smallness of the image in relation to the vastness of the auditorium space. On the postage stamp screen of conventional 35 mm installations, the competing activities of Grandeur would have to register more as distraction than enhancement.

In trying to understand the different stylistic choices here, we have to keep in mind that original expectations for the Grandeur screen looked to a greater height as well as width. This suggests that even in longer shots characters might occupy approximately the same space on the screen they would have had on smaller screens in close shots. Arthur Edeson, the cinematographer on the 70 mm version of *The Big Trail*, indicated as much when he wrote, "Grandeur reduces the number of close-ups considerably, as the figures are so much larger that semi-close-ups are usually all that is needed."[24] In general, throughout the film, the camera is simply further back in the 70 mm version, and it never gets closer than what Edeson calls a semi-close-up distance. If the 35 mm cuts to a tight medium shot, the 70 mm is likely to cut to a loose medium or a three-quarter shot, and occasionally it won't cut at all. Because relative size of character was likely similar in the two versions *as projected*, cutting patterns remain similar between the two versions: the cutting always brings a movement in, even if the 70 mm is rarely as close and never as isolating on detail. Further, lines of dialogue are generally overlapped across the cut, but the 70 mm seems more likely to let them play in long shot because it is easier to pick up detail on the big screen.

On the other hand, compositional strategies are frequently different, often seeking to establish different playing areas in 70 mm while the 35 mm tries to establish a definite focal point. Where the brushing and shampooing women in the first example form a tightly encircled grouping with a center point near the center of the image, the comparable shot in 70 mm creates a center point of two intersecting diagonals toward the right of the image. Similarly, in the second example, shot #2 in 70 mm has four people effectively set in two different spaces, with most of our attention focused on the left where the two speakers stand. The comparable shot in 35 mm, #3, also has four characters, but now Miss Cameron, the central speaker, is made central in the image as well. While both versions dramatically contrive to have Mr. Thorpe block our view of a family member just at the moment Miss Cameron asserts that the family must stay together, in the 35 mm he does so from the center of the image so that he blocks our view of Miss Cameron herself. In 70 mm he appears further to the right, blocking our view of the sister and brother, and eliminating the need for a cut-in to Miss Cameron as she starts to deliver this line, which is what happens in the 35 mm version in order to keep both Miss Cameron and Mr. Thorpe a strong presence in their respective images. When we consider the screen in its technological guise, we will see reasons for the more insistent centering of the small 35 mm image that is so apparent here.

Finally, there is the matter of cinematography. Compositional matters aside, the general look of the film is fairly similar in both versions except when the camera moves into medium and closer distances. Then, one of two things happens. Either the mise-en-scène is set up so that background detail is eliminated, as in the first two examples, or the depth-of-field is rendered shallower in the 35 mm version. In general, while backgrounds in the 70 mm might be somewhat soft in closer shots, they never approach the extraordinarily shallow depth of field of closer shots in the 35 mm. Cinematographer Edeson noted at the time, "The chief requirements for lenses for wide-film cinematography are, first and foremost, extremely wide covering power, and secondly (and of quite as great importance) extremely great depth of focus. . . . [E]ven in close-ups, the depth of focus demanded by Grandeur makes the background an important part of the picture." (9, 21)

The difference in handling background is most forceful in the final example. The scene might seem a prescient example of later theorizing over wide screen aesthetics that preferred two-shots to cutting, but I find the backgrounds here even more striking.[25] In 70 mm, the background is soft, but clearly defined, and, as always, very active. The cutting to singles in 35 mm, on the other hand, makes the actors' bodies truly imposing in their detachment from the background. It also ensures, importantly for the period, I think, the absence of lines of perspective that could foreground distortion. At an early demonstration of Grandeur in 1929, an *Exhibitors Herald World* technical writer thought it worth highlighting "No Distortion Anywhere": ". . . I sat in a box which was one flight up, way over to the right side and down front. I of course expected a heavy side angle distortion, but could see none at all. Don't ask me why. I don't know. It just was so far as I could detect, not there."[26] Clearly, motion picture professionals were well aware of the distortion evident in side seats,[27] and a larger image offered one possible way of dealing with the problem, much as it made detail more evident without the necessity of close camera distances.

TRANSFORMING SCREENS

To this point, I have been writing about theater architecture as a condition of our perception of the image and a possible determinant of film style that takes us away from the previously exclusive focus on production to a real concern for reception. Now, turning briefly to screen technology, I feel I have to emphasize that there *is* technology here. It's easy enough to think of the screen as little more than a fancy bed sheet hung on a wall, but movie screens are not simply *built*, they are also *engineered*. In the history of motion pictures, this was made most evident to audiences with the Cinerama screen, which was promoted as an engineering marvel. Justly so, since it did present an ingenious solution to a problem that was central to the Cinerama experience. Cinerama could play on depth perception not just by extending the width of the screen, but moving into areas of peripheral vision, which necessitated a deeply curved screen. The deep curve, however, created a light problem, as light from left and right panels could reflect against each other, thus washing out the left and right portions of the image. To ensure even illumination across the image, Cinerama engineers devised a screen made up of a series of strips, with the angle of each strip adjusted according to its position on the screen.[28] Strips toward the ends of the screen were angled out to the audience, maximizing directional reflexivity of the light and minimizing spill-off onto other portions of the image. Much as Cinerama's three projectors tried to create the illusion of a single image, the Cinerama screen itself presented the illusion of a single, continuous surface that was not in fact there.

The Cinerama screen represents an admittedly extreme example, which is why I have begun with it. Still, since the beginning of sound film at least, the impression of a continuous image we have in watching any movie theater screen is in fact an illusion, as much an illusion as the Cinerama image. With speakers placed in back, the sound screen had to be shot full of tiny holes to allow for sound transmission, generally "42 perforations per square inch, each perforation being 0.005 in. in diameter."[29] This perforated screen remains a standard for theaters to this day. From these two examples of the louvered and perforated screen it should be evident that the screen as an element of technology does not simply receive an image. In fact it would be most accurate to say that no image exists until the screen acts upon it, reflecting light back toward the audience in a way that allows interpretation of a coherent image even if the screen actually fragments that image.

This leads me to point out the one constant we may note of the technological screen: it must always offer sufficient light reflectivity to produce an image that is clearly discernible to the entire audience. No format other than Cinerama demanded such a radical reworking of screen design, but through much of the screen's history its activity as a reflector was the central concern for screen engineers. With the sound screen, for example, could you have perforations sufficiently large to transmit sound yet sufficiently small to remain imperceptible to the audience? If you get close enough to the screen in today's theaters, you can in fact perceive the perforations, so the surface of the screen does have some impact on the seating plan of the theater. And while the holes do not interfere with the illusion of the image for most seats, they do nevertheless always affect reflectance, with the Society of Motion Picture and Television Engineers estimating that the average screen reflects back only 70 percent of the light projected onto it.[30] Further, while the engineering of the Cinerama screen sought to solve an illumination problem caused by the deep curvature, curved screens existed well before Cinerama, all the way back to 1912, in part to solve problems of illumination and focus.

Screen reflectance, then, is no simple matter. Clearly, you do not want a screen made of material that absorbs all light, but how much light do you need to create a coherent image, and what level of coherence are you willing to settle for? Since projected images have been around for about three-and-a-half centuries, it might seem likely that all these issues had been settled by the time motion picture images were introduced. But the screen's central activity as a reflecting surface remained a problem until the fifties. Consider, for example, the result of a Society of Motion Picture And Television Engineers survey of theaters after World War II:

> . . . it was found that approximately 50% of the theatres had illumination intensity and screen brightness *at or below the minimum* recommended value. About two-thirds of the projectors provided side to center illumination ratios as low as 50%.[31]

The extraordinary popularity of drive-ins in the post World War II period and the wide screen revolution of the early fifties eventually led engineers to find solutions for most problems in screen illumination because of the much larger screens necessitated by both phenomena.

But previous to this period the limitations of the technological screen had consequences for film style similar to those created by the constraints of the architectural screen. For one thing, problems in fulfilling the demands of the screen's one technological constant of sufficient reflectance were as conducive to a close-up style with shallow focus as the problems created by architectural space. Objects seen close-up in an insufficiently illuminated image are simply more intelligible than those seen at a distance. Visual acuity increases with screen brightness.[32] As a consequence, insufficient illumination operates as a kind of parallel to the problems created by great distances: it leads to a preference for close-up in order to show detail, since detail would not stand out sharply on its own given the illumination problems in a majority of theaters. Furthermore, at low illumination levels, shallow focus helps an object stand out against background more forcefully than it would in a sharply defined image which gives all objects equal value.

There is some evidence that the production side of the industry was aware of problems in exhibition and might have sought adjustments that would deal with these problems. In a 1930 address to the *Society of Motion Picture Engineers*, Irving Thalberg reported on the formation of a "Producers-Technicians Committee" by the Academy of Motion Picture Arts and Sciences in 1929. Of the six areas the committee was to investigate, five had to do with production and film processing, but the sixth was "screen illumination." Noting "The problem of the quality of the projected picture seems to center on brightness contrast," Thalberg promised, "Minimum standards will be formulated for illumination attainable by the majority of theaters. Because of economic considerations, de luxe houses will exceed these and very small houses will not be able to reach them, but they will be practicable for the great majority of houses. The density of release prints can then be related to this standard."[33]

A long-standing problem of illumination across the surface of the screen possibly impacted on film practice in one other aspect. Illumination of the screen is both a matter of light source—i.e., the projecting apparatus—and the actual composition of the screen material. The choice of screen material, however, was in part a function of space the screen inhabited, which is to say space determined the type of screen used. Essentially two types of screen were available for theater use until the fifties: the "specular" screen, which reflects light back in the same direction it was sent and thus retained more of the illumination directed at it, and the "diffusive" screen, which disperses the light over a larger angle. Until the fifties, the specular screen was considered most appropriate for narrow theaters where patrons could be assured of remaining within a narrow angle of vision. The dispersal screen was necessary for larger houses, but this accentuated a problem in illumination, namely that the sides of the screen reflected only 64.5 percent of the visible light at the center.[34] The centering of the image which has both been made a hallmark of the Hollywood cinema and interpreted in ideological terms could in fact be a consequence of the sharp drop-off of light toward the edges of the image.[35] If nothing else, the example of *The Big Trail* in 70 mm demonstrates that even Classical Hollywood could abandon centering as a stylistic imperative. On the other hand, the small screen and the vast theatrical space coupled with the problem in even illumination likely contributed to making the center of the image dominant.

How exactly do conventions get established? Much academic writing over the past decade or so has made ideology the dominant determinant, but this is as reductive as laying claim to any one factor must be. I doubt if we can ever pin down the precise origins of artistic movements and procedures, but we can at least attempt to cast as wide a net as possible and remain open to modification of our original assumptions. We might best understand specific conventions by attempting to trace a history of how those conventions have been understood, allowing for the possibility that practitioners using the same conventions at different points in film history might understand those conventions differently. Procedures, established for reasons subsequently forgotten, may nevertheless take on a life of their own and remain standard practice as if they were addressing a seemingly essential need.

Consider, for example, a striking difference between the 70 mm version of *The Big Trail* and *The Robe*, the first movie in CinemaScope. When *The Robe* was released in 1953, contemporaries thought it worth noting that close-ups could still be used and used effectively. There was concern about this issue precisely because the close-up had become such an *essential* part of Hollywood storytelling. Compare this attitude with an *American Cinematographer* article on the production of *Happy Days* (1930), the first film made in Grandeur: "Viewed from a practical viewpoint, the *Grandeur* proportions offer many advantages to all concerned. The director can film his spectacular scenes and stage or dancing numbers to their best advantage, with fewer cuts—and no need of close-ups."[36] The key issue in 1930 was not the use of close-ups on a wide screen but making the image large enough to obviate the need for close-ups. *Happy Days* and *The Big Trail* were made at a time when the advent of the procedures we now ascribe to the classical Hollywood cinema were still relatively fresh, but by the time of *The Robe* procedures had taken on the force of doctrine. Hollywood practitioners in 1930 saw the enlarged screen as a solution to a problem; in 1953 they saw it as a problem. By the fifties, the need for a close-up, what early filmmakers had called the "big head," became absolute.[37]

This shift in attitude is all the more astonishing if we consider the difference in proportions between the first Grandeur and CinemaScope screens. Coincidentally, both *The Big Trail* and *The Robe* premiered at the grandiose Roxy Theatre in New York: within a proscenium arch opening more than 70 feet, Grandeur utilized a screen 40 feet wide, while the CinemaScope screen twenty-three years later was 64 feet wide. CinemaScope and most other wide screen processes of the fifties produced big heads that were simply much bigger than early practitioners of the Hollywood classical style would have dreamed possible—or possibly even desirable—on the old 35 mm screen (Fig. 16). Arthur Edeson thought it important to keep his camera in *The Big Trail* generally more distanced than in conventional 35 mm filmmaking; he wanted

Fig. 16: *The Robe*: the biggest head of Victor Mature

Fig. 17: *The Robe*: an insert shot of Pontius Pilate washing his hands

a big head that would be no bigger than that on a conventional screen. While *The Robe* can use long shots as effectively as *The Big Trail*, using the added width to enhance film's inherent propensity for the spectacular, in its dialogue sequences the camera quickly settles into medium shots, generally shooting at closer distances than *The Big Trail*, even though *The Robe* had the benefit of a larger screen. Although insert shots are a form of close-up that is primarily informational, generally lacking the emotional force of the big head, *The Robe* even makes use of insert shots (Fig. 17), while the 70 mm version of *The Big Trail* has none.[38] Although *The Robe* has fewer shots than the average Hollywood film of its period, it also looks far more conventional than *The Big Trail*.

In noting the conventional aspects of *The Robe*, I don't want to minimize the effects of the wide screen revolution; in fact, I would argue that the early fifties transformation of the screen in both its architectural and technological guises represented a radical break with the past comparable to the alterations introduced by the movie palace building in the teens and twenties. While there was certainly a continuity in Hollywood's stylistic practices, there were also changes in style. For example, Alfred Hitchcock has spoken of pressure he received from Paramount Pictures executives while shooting in Paramount's wide screen process, VistaVision, to make the image as sharp as possible throughout its depth of field since the process was being touted as "Motion Picture High Fidelity."[39] But Paramount was selling size as well as shape with VistaVision: they wanted theaters to feature screens as wide as CinemaScope but taller. To make the process distinctive, they had to distinguish it from earlier attempts at simple magnification which resulted in images with very visible grain and poor focus.[40] For this reason, they insisted on deep focus photography in an image that could both fill the proscenium and appear sharper than conventional film because of a larger negative area. This is a distinction whose value was tied to a particular period of time and not a necessary consequence of either new spatial relationships or the technology itself. But it was also a distinction made possible by new spatial relationships and a new technology.

If distinctions were not inevitable and the force of old conventions could operate against change, the new way in which the screen found itself situated in relation to architectural space did at least allow for the possibility of approaches that could not have worked effectively in movie palaces before the early fifties. Barring a systematic study of films in the post wide screen era, I would tentatively suggest these differences occurred chiefly in the realm of camera distance and compositional strategies.

The insistent extreme long shot style in works as different as Stanley Kubrick's *2001* (1968) and Franklin Schaffner's *Patton* (1970) moves them decisively away from Classical Hollywood. And the emphasis on extreme long shot is not simply a consequence of the wider screen, but also the much larger screen, the screen that dominates the space it inhabits and the spectator's field of vision. Similarly, improvements in screen illumination have at least made possible the spreading of detail across the screen beyond the once-brightest spot in the center. The decentering procedures of *Summer of '42* (1971) and *Alien* (1979) are dissimilar—*Summer of '42* features odd zoom shots where the object of the zoom inevitably ends up on the side of the frame, while characters seen in close-up single in *Alien* are as likely to turn up on the extreme left or right of the image as in the center. But both films depend upon an even illumination across the image to inscribe a stylistic tension between center and side.[41]

The relationship between film style and theatrical space is a subject well worth pursuing up to the present moment since there has been a radical rebuilding and redesign of the theatrical plant over the last couple of decades in the United States through the multiplex, a transformation that is starting to spread to Western Europe and beyond. However much theater design might change, viewing a film in a theater will remain in part an experience of architecture. Because the screen is the point at which architecture and image technology converge, changes in theater and screen design must matter. Throughout the screen's history, its double life as an element of architecture and an element of technology has had an impact not only on the way we receive the images from the screen, but also how those images are put together. This is a fact that all future histories of film style must take into account.

ACKNOWLEDGEMENTS

I would like to thank Tanya Falk of the Interlibrary Loan Department, Hatcher Graduate Library, University of Michigan, and Sean Cavazos-Kottke for their tireless efforts in securing much of the material that provided the foundation for this essay. And I am very grateful to Andrew Greenfield for his prodigious computer skills and selfless donation of time in preparing the accompanying stills.

NOTES

[1]Maggie Valentine, *The Show Starts on the Sidewalk: An Architectural History of the Movie Theatre, Starring S. Charles Lee* (New Haven: Yale University Press, 1994).

[2]See, for example, Raymond Fielding, ed., *A Technological History of the Motion Pictures and Television* (Berkeley: University of California Press, 1967; rpt. 1983), an anthology of articles on different technical subjects from *The Journal of the Society of Motion Picture and Television Engineers*. None deals directly with the screen itself although screen brightness was a long-standing concern in the pages of the *Journal*. In film studies, the screen has received most attention from John Belton in his impressively thorough *Widescreen Cinema*, but in spite of his title even Belton focuses most on the technological apparatus embodied by camera and projector. Belton, *Widescreen Cinema* (Cambridge: Harvard University Press, 1992).

[3]The most thoroughgoing example of this approach may be found in Robert Eberwein, *Film and the Dream Screen: A Sleeping and a Forgetting* (Princeton: Princeton University Press, 1984).

[4]For a 1936 *Journal of the Society of Motion Picture Engineers* article, Louis Lumière described an enormous screen (approximately 100 feet wide by 80 feet high) used for the Paris Exposition of 1900: "As a fabric for the screen I had selected a material that reflected, when wet, as much light as it transmitted, so that one could see the projected images from any position in the big hall." Lumière, "The Lumière Cinematograph," rpt. in Fielding, 50.

[5]Ben Schlanger, "Auditorium Floor Slopes for Motion Picture Theatres Today," "Better Theatres" Section, *Motion Picture Herald* , September 20, 1947, 17. The description of Schlanger comes from Larry May in a provocative article that seeks to relate changes in theater architecture of the thirties to an increasing desire to find distinctly American forms that throw off European influences. May, with the assistance of Stephen Lassonde, "Making the American Way: Moderne Theatres, Audiences, and the Film Industry 1929–1945," in Jack Salzman, ed., *Prospects: An Annual of American Cultural Studies* (New York: Cambridge University Press, 1987), Vol. 12, 97–99.

[6]Francis M. Falge, "The Screen—A Projectionist's Problem," *Journal of the Society of Motion Picture Engineers*, July 1932, 910–11.

[7]Ben Schlanger, "Motion Picture Theaters," *The Architectural Record*, February 1937, 19–20. Later, when this formulation had been accepted as a guiding principle, Schlanger would recommend somewhat more stringent guidelines. In one 1946 article, he actually recommended an auditorium distance-screen width ratio of 5.2:1 for the furthest seat and at least 1:1 for the closest seat, about which he added, "It is desirable, indeed, to make this distance one and a quarter times the picture width wherever possible." Schlanger, et al., "Planning the Small Motion Picture Theatre," "Better Theatres" Section, *Motion Picture Herald*, June 1, 1946, 19.

[8]See, for example, Gio Gagliardi, June 3, 1950, "It's High Time to Give the Screen the Attention Due It!," "Better Theatres" Section, *Motion Picture Herald*, June 3, 1950, 27.

[9]Ben Schlanger, "Sizing the Picture for 'Wide-Screen,'" "Better Theatres" Section, *Motion Picture Herald*, October 10, 1953, 18. See also Schlanger, "The Motion Picture Theater Shape and Effective Visual Reception," *Journal of the Society of Motion Picture Engineers*, February 1939, 128–35.

[10]Schlanger, October 10, 1953, 16.

[11]In 1948, Ben Schlanger reported that a 1938 "survey of 500 theatres showed [a] variation [of screen sizes] to range from a width of from one-third to one-eighth of the max-

imum viewing distance in the auditorium." Given the size of the palaces and repeated references in the trade press to "postage stamp screens," they likely account for the high end of this range. Schlanger, "Proposing a Larger Picture for a More Effective Show," "Better Theatres" Section, *Motion Picture Herald*, July 31, 1948, 29.

[12]Schutz, "The Screen Theatre: Bringing Architecture to the Picture House Through a Third of a Century," "Better Theaters" Section, *Motion Picture Herald*, Sept. 25, 1948, 4.

[13]H. C. Weston, E. Stroud, "The Lighting of Cinema Auditoriums for Visibility and Safety," *Transactions of the Illuminating Engineering Society of Great Britain* (London: Illuminating Engineering Society of Great Britain, 1939), cited in R. Gillespie Williams, "Dynamic Luminous Color For Film Presentation," in Helen M. Stote, ed., *The Motion Picture Theater* (New York: Society of Motion Picture Engineers, 1948), 83.

[14]Schlanger, "Now How About Our Auditoriums?" "Better Theatres" Section, *Motion Picture Herald*, January 7, 1950, 18.

[15]Salt, *Film Style and Technology: History and Analysis*, Second Edition (London: Starword, 1992).

[16]Nathan D. Golden, "Sound Motion Pictures in Europe," "Better Theatres" Section, *Exhibitors Herald World*, November 23, 1929, 51. Given the current physical plant for exhibition in the United States, these differences might not seem as striking to us now. But when I lived in Berlin in 1964–65, a period when the palaces still dominated American first-run exhibition, I was generally surprised by how very tiny the theatres were. Even the one downtown theater from before the war that still stood, the "UFA Palast" (where, I believe, *The Blue Angel* premiered), possessed a name that had to suggest something a good deal grander to an American ear than the theater I actually saw.

[17]Because I have not been able to locate a precise theater breakdown from 1929, I am using a theater census from 1948. This should still offer an apt comparison in terms of large theaters since the only significant change in the physical plant of U.S. exhibition in the intervening period was the loss of small, marginal theaters and the building of theaters in the under 2,000 seats category. The census listed 589 theaters operating in New York with an additional 60 in Newark and Jersey City. My claim for the higher number of large theaters is based on the fact that the average number of seats per theater was 1,228 for New York and 1,282 for the New Jersey cities. Since Manhattan and Brooklyn possessed some of the largest first-run theaters in the country, with many "neighborhood" theaters with seating capacities substantially over 2,000, it is evident that large theaters dominated first- and second-run exhibition. The census also revealed 16,880 movie theaters "open more than three days a week and more than three months a year." Although this number is only 62 percent of the number of theaters in Europe in the 1929 survey, there is a far higher proportion of large audience theaters: 92 over 3,000 (which the survey actually breaks down further, with 17 over 3,999), 348 from 2,000 to 2,999; 2,199 from 1,000–1999. Where two-thirds of the theaters in Europe had fewer than five hundred seats, approximately one-third of the theaters in the U.S. had fewer than 401 seats (the cut-off point in the 1948 survey). "16,880 Operating Theatres, 7,442 Buyers, Study Finds," *Motion Picture Herald*, May 1, 1948, 16, 18.

[18]Salt, 219, 221–22.

[19]George Schutz, "The Big Picture," "Better Theatres" Section, *Motion Picture Herald*, May 9, 1953, 76. This was the size given for the 1.33:1 screen at the time the Music Hall began utilizing a 1.66:1 screen fifty feet wide. It is likely that the Music Hall screen in 1932 was actually smaller.

[20]Ben Schlanger, "New Theaters for the Cinema," *The Architectural Forum*, September, 1932, 254–55.

[21]Bazin, "The Evolution of the Language of Cinema," *What Is Cinema?* (Berkeley: University of California Press, 1967), 33.

[22]This would have been true at least for the grandest of the movie palaces. While the proscenium opening in the mid-sized palace was always sufficiently large to give a postage-stamp appearance to the screen, in many instances it may well have been too narrow to accommodate the enlarged screens that were at least feasible with wider gauge film. In any case, individual articles on new theaters that appeared in the *Better Theatres* Section of *Exhibitors Herald World* 1929–30 and its successor *Motion Picture Herald* in 1931 inevitably note that the proscenium was built large enough to accommodate enlarged screens.

[23]While I have seen one reel of this film projected in its wide screen aspect ratio on a screen, I have only seen the Grandeur version in its entirety on a letterboxed television broadcast. I mention this to indicate the possibility that seeing the film projected on a properly proportioned screen might well leave a different impression, with the position of the speaker within the image more apparent.

[24]Edeson, "Wide Film Cinematography: Some Comments on 70 mm. Camerawork from a Practical Cinematographer," *American Cinematographer*, September 1930, 21.

[25]See Charles Barr, "CinemaScope: Before and After," *Film Quarterly*, Summer 1963.

[26]F. H. Richardson, "Wide Film: What It Is—How It Works," *Exhibitors Herald World*, Oct. 19, 1929, 33.

[27]See, for example, Daniel B. Clark, A.S.C., "True Film House Is Yet to Come," *American Cinematographer*, April 1927, 22.

[28]John Belton specifies the original Cinerama screens as having 1,100 strips, but later enlarged to 2,000 strips for larger theaters. Belton, 101, 262.

[29]The quote actually reads "0.050 in. in diameter," but I have corrected what is quite clearly a typo. Perforations 0.050 in. in diameter are impossible since the perforations alone would cover a space larger than a square inch, while the 0.005 inches is congruent with other dimensions in the article. Charles R. Underhill, Jr., "Practical Solution to the Screen Light Distribution Problem," *Journal of the Society of Motion Picture and Television Engineers*, June 1951, 681.

[30]"Review of Society of Motion Picture Engineers Work on Screen Brightness," in Stote, 216.

[31]George Schutz, "Screen Light and Projection Tests," "Better Theatres" Section, *Motion Picture Herald*, March 24, 1951, 46.

[32]See Gagliardi, June 3, 1950, 28.

[33]Thalberg, "Technical Activities of the Academy of Motion Picture Arts and Sciences," *Journal of the Society of Motion Picture Engineers*, July 1930, 14.

[34]Underhill, Jr., 680.

[35]See, for example, David Bordwell, "Space in the Classical Film," in Bordwell, Janet Staiger, and Kristin Thompson, *The Classical Hollywood Cinema: Film Style & Mode of Production to 1960* (New York: Columbia University Press, 1985), 50–1; Stephen Heath, "Narrative Space" in *Questions of Cinema* (Bloomington: Indiana University Press, 1981), 19–75; and Jean-Louis Comolli, "Technique and Ideology: Camera, Perspective, Depth of Field," trans. Diana Matias, in Nick Browne, ed., *Cahiers du Cinéma 1969–72: The Politics of Representation* (Cambridge: Harvard University Press, 1990).

[36]William Stull, A.S.C., "Seventy Millimetres: The First of the New Wide Film Processes Reaches Production," *American Cinematographer*, February 1930, 42.

[37]In the early seventies I had the good fortune of interviewing Raoul Walsh, the director of *The Big Trail*, together with my colleague and dear friend Andrew Sarris. Throughout the interview, Walsh always used the term "big head" when he intended

close-up. I think the term is especially telling in this context where the actual size of the screen is a key issue.

[38]There are no insert shots per se in the 35 mm version if an insert shot necessarily implies a cut. In his later films, however, Walsh often pans to a set-up that works as an insert shot, and the 35 mm version of *The Big Trail* offers one striking instance of this. When Breck Coleman discovers the corpse of Red Flack's partner in crime, the camera pans from a loose medium shot of Coleman (Fig. 18a) to the corpse seemingly frozen in the snow with a single hand rigidly reaching up toward Coleman (Fig. 18b). In the 70 mm version, the action is seen in long shot with no camera movement (Fig. 19).

[39]The occasion of the remark was a meeting with film students at Columbia University in 1972 when he was receiving an honorary doctorate. Hitchcock seemed a bit surprised by the question of how he liked the VistaVision process and dismissed it as an insignificant feature in his films at Paramount.

[40]From the mid-1920s on, deluxe theaters would occasionally make use of "Magnascope," a simple blowing up of the image that was reserved for isolated sequences in films, usually those involving spectacle of some sort, like the storm sequence at the end of *Portrait of Jennie* (1948) and Busby Berkeley's water ballets in *Million Dollar Mermaid* (1952). Technical difficulties kept the use of magnascoping limited: what the image gained in size it lost in quality, with a perceptible increase in grain and decrease in illumination. One of the most curious uses of the Magnascope was the practice at the New York Roxy in the 1930s of showing its newsreel on a screen about 44 feet wide, then reducing it to half that for the feature ("Report of the Projection Screen Brightness Committee," *Journal of the Society of Motion Picture Engineers*, August 1946, 139). Since newsreel film often appeared grainier than that in feature film work, it is likely that the image degradation could be discounted as generic. The increased size also suggests that newsreel material was regarded as purely spectacular.

[41]For the record, I should note that the first two of these films were shot in 65 mm, released in 70 mm (2.2:1), while the other two were in 1.85:1 35 mm and 2.35:1 (Panavision) 35 mm respectively. I have deliberately chosen films in different gauges and aspect ratios to suggest that the wide screen itself is the factor here. Further, I have tried to keep the selection far enough away from the first decade of wide screen since radical departures often occur when innovation motivates filmmakers to foreground the new technology as an attraction in itself. The stylistic departures from Classical Hollywood in these films were facilitated by new technologies, but not a consequence of them.

A note on frame enlargements. Stills reproduced here have been made from videotape versions of *The Big Trail*. The 35 mm frames, seen in the 1.33:1 aspect ratio currently used by commercial television, slightly misrepresent the original film. In the early sound period, the film frame, making way for the encroachment of the sound track, became more square. This means that the 35 mm frames here are missing some height.

Fig. 18a: *The Big Trail* in 35 mm—as John Wayne looks down . . .

Fig. 18b: the camera plans to create an insert showing what he sees

Fig. 19: *The Big Trail* in Grandeur—a stationary and distanced camera

LEO BRAUDY

"NO BODY'S PERFECT":
METHOD ACTING AND 50s CULTURE

In the summer of 1975 I began teaching a course on the 1950s at the University of California, Santa Barbara. As far as most of the students were concerned, the 50s seemed incredibly far away. A good number of them had been born in the late 50s, they knew the 60s as early teenagers, and even that decade was growing dim. So they toured the 50s with me as if it were an exotic and somewhat outlandish country, and only rarely understood its relation to their own lives and tastes and desires.

During the semester, Michael Wilson, who lived nearby, came to class to talk about the period from the perspective of a member of the so-called "Unfriendly Nineteen." Wilson was a blacklisted Hollywood screenwriter, who had written *The Salt of the Earth* (the only feature made by members of the Hollywood Ten), had his screenwriting credit removed from *Friendly Persuasion*, and had anonymously co-written *Bridge On the River Kwai*, for which the non-English-speaking Pierre Boulle received the credit—and the Oscar. The class asked a few questions, but in general they regarded Wilson as if he were someone from outer space. It was clear they felt little connection with that strange world and time when people lost their jobs, families, and even their lives as a result of being accused either of having the wrong opinions (communist), or of having the right opinions at the wrong time (premature antifascist). The fact that Michael Wilson dressed for the occasion in a bright red jumpsuit only added to its fantastic atmosphere.

For several years now, however, students in later versions of that course have been much more attuned to the basic rhythms of the period—and the course itself has evolved into one in film, fiction, and popular culture. In part, this affinity has come about because their own high school teachers have been having them read *Catcher in the Rye* or *Invisible Man* or *The Bell Jar*. But it has also occurred because, with the

275

1980s, there came a more general realization that we were still living in the aftermath of the 50s, still reacting against its terms, still following out its themes, and still appealing to some version of its imagery as a way of understanding our problems.

As the 1980s wore on into the 1990s, 50s music and 50s dress style were constantly revived. Starting with blockbusters of the late 70s like *Star Wars* (1977), 50s B-film plots were blown up into elephantine films—costing many millions to produce rather than the original one or two—that extended the elephantine genre revival into the 80s and beyond. *Raiders of the Lost Ark* (1981), *Body Heat* (1981), and *Blade Runner* (1982) were only a few; we can all name the most recent. Nationally, the 80s were also marked by a 50s fear of Russia, a 50s emphasis on economic success that was virtually indistinguishable from naked greed, a 50s sounding off about who's loyal and who's disloyal, and a tinge of the 50s belief that American citizens were being manipulated by diabolic foreign powers ("comsymp" was *Time*'s old word). This was all carried out under the aegis of Ronald Reagan, a 50s-style President, who in 1946 had become the staunch anti-Communist head of the Screen Actors Guild, having recently shed his previous incarnation as a New Deal Democrat.

Even now, despite or perhaps because of the end of the Cold War, the effort to understand the 50s continues. Whatever view historians take of the period, they seem to agree that it marked a crucial shift in American culture. In the 50s begins the effort of the United States to deal with a world entirely changed by the gigantic scale of World War II—its mobilization of millions of people, millions of tons of equipment, and billions of dollars. During the 50s occurred American society's first effort to face changes that we are still trying to absorb—the affluent society of suburbia, the new medium of television (along with the expansion of advertising, experiments with 3-D, and the dominance of color film), new attitudes toward the discussion of sexuality (marked by the Kinsey reports of 1948 and 1953), and the political effort to include more and more groups in the definition of what it means to be an American. It was a society filled with new passions and exuberance, in which the future, especially as defined by consumer goods, access to education, expansion of universities, and the general sense of what it was possible to achieve in the United States, seemed more endlessly open than ever before.

But if from one perspective the future never looked brighter, from another it was shadowed with anxieties and paranoias, some perhaps justified, but others helping to create what they most feared. In terms of the

national state of mind, the 50s were a very medieval period, characterized by a daily psychic tug of war between personal identity and social
identity, or, in 50s terms, individualism and conformity, alienation and
patriotism. After the solidarity against Nazism in World War II, and the
sense of expansiveness in joining with the Allies, a closed-down defen-
siveness about the rest of the world dominated national politics. Intent
on looking inward, the 50s were the last American period before the in-
ternationalization of culture and commerce that would come firmly into
being by the late 1960s. It was the last stand of a nineteenth-century
America that had been delayed by wars and Depression, and thus provided a laboratory environment for the definition of the America to
come.[1]

Popular journalism has accustomed us to turning the characteristics
of a decade into retro-fashion, and perhaps zeitgeist criticism always has
an aspect of nostalgia. Yet if we are to try to think historically at all, and
pay some respect to the differences and the similarities between our
own time and the past, we need a keener sense of how to define a period, a decade, an era: what has lasted, what is significant, and what
should be culled for revival. Dead-ends might be as instructive as tri-
umphs: why was science fiction so popular in the 50s only to virtually
disappear for 15-20 years, then re-emerge in new force by the late 70s?
Can we chart a cultural baseline through a variety of phenomena—films,
theater, popular fiction, "serious" fiction, advertising, photography—
without sacrificing the sense of difference and contest that makes culture move and change?

Two such baseline interpretations of the 50s have been particularly
powerful. From the left, the period has been seen as a time of repression and paranoia, with McCarthyism rampant and rigid official values
entirely in the saddle. Such an interpretation dates from the period itself and was reinforced academically by historians, political scientists,
and film critics who began writing in the 1970s under the impact of the
1960s. From the right, in a mirror image, the 50s are seen as a period of
booming economic expansion, in which the American Dream became a
possibility for the many rather than for the few. This view is also firmly
rooted in the period, but it became more popular in the 1980s, when
Reaganomics and a neoconservative search for origins gave it the necessary injection of teleological energy.

Both of these views have some truth in them. But I want to try to look
at the 50s from a different angle, in hopes of dissolving at least some of
their artificial polarity. My title invokes the famous last line from *Some*

Like It Hot (1959)—with a little shift in its spelling—because it so beautifully and succinctly signals my central topic: the place of the body, particularly the acting body, in 1950s culture.

By "acting" I mean the body in action as well as the body in performance. In the language of Method acting this is often called the "instrument" or physical/emotional body of the performer. But the Method language and preoccupation with the body extends to other arts as well: the gestural emphasis of so-called "action" painters (like Jackson Pollock or Helen Frankenthaler); the celebration of bodily and emotional memory that animated so much of the fiction of Jack Kerouac, the poetry of Allen Ginsberg, and—in somewhat different ways—the so-called "confessional" poetry of Robert Lowell, Theodore Roethke, and Sylvia Plath. This emphasis on patterning a movie, a play, a painting, a novel, or a poem on the non-textual or extra-textual energy and agency of the performer's, the artist's, the author's, or the subject's physical presence constitutes a linking metaphor by which we might know some crucial elements of the 50s more clearly. Like Michael Wilson in front of my puzzled students in 1975, the performer's body in 50s art gave the lie to easy generalizations, plots, and appeals to authority.

But even though I would like to post roadsigns to the art, literature, and theater of the 50s, I do not have the time here to pay an extended visit. My central subject is the Method and the movies, and how a postwar ambiguity about the actor's authority, rooted in the fragility of male self-definition, affected still other sources of artistic authority—in film direction, plotting, and characterization.

✿   ✿   ✿

In the light of the 50s political preoccupation with the "unamerican" in culture, it is intriguing to note that Stanislavsky's founding of the Moscow Art Theater in the 1890s, along with his development of the "System" for actor training, was part of an effort to re-nationalize theater and performance. With the help of Chekhov's plays, Stanislavsky was trying to create a Russian tradition to replace the dominant European one. Similarly, the goal of the Group Theatre (founded in the 30s) and the Actor's Studio (founded in the late 40s), together with the plays of Clifford Odets, Tennessee Williams, and Arthur Miller that they often featured and drew upon as models, was to extricate American theater from a dependence on European plays as well as upon European styles of acting and being.

The Group Theatre was of course a product of the political and social ferment of the 30s. In the 50s the memory of its seemingly selfless emphasis on the community of the ensemble and on repertory performance was often used to attack the individualist and even star implications of the Actor's Studio and the Method. But as far as the 50s were concerned, the Method's preoccupation with individual authenticity had quite a different enemy, summarized in 1951 by the observations of that noted theater critic Holden Caulfield:

> In the first place, I hate actors. They never act like people. They just think they do. Some of the good ones do, in a slight way, but not in a way that's fun to watch. And if any actor's really good, you can always tell he knows he's good, and that spoils it.[2]

Self-congratulation drives Holden crazy, and he sees it everywhere, especially in American performers in the Anglophile tradition like Alfred Lunt and Lynn Fontanne: "They didn't act like people and they didn't act like actors. It's hard to explain. They acted more like they knew they were celebrities and all. I mean they were good, but they were too good" (126). What Holden instinctively dislikes—and the Method defines itself against—is an acting that apes some buttoned-up, usually English, style of official selfdom, especially when tarted up with noblesse oblige. As he says about Olivier's Hamlet, "He was too much like a goddam general, instead of a sad, screwed-up type guy" (117). Since no body's perfect, it's even worse to pretend to be.

Self-conscious artistry, obvious skill, and a condescending professionalism are the heart of the problem for Holden. Like many of the emotionally tangled characters in 50s films, Holden is not looking for perfect performances but for models of being, especially models of growing up. His disgust with performers and his railings against the movies indicate how much the search for models of social behavior in postwar America focused, as it never had before, on the examples the movies furnished. For all his disdain, Holden is hardly immune from the combination of theatricality and solace the movies bring. As he says after indulging in a particularly vivid revenge fantasy of guns and death, set off by a losing encounter with a sleazy bellhop, "The god-damned movies, they'll drive you crazy" (149).

The star system of the 20s and 30s encouraged more worship than imitation. But the 40s and 50s ushered in a preoccupation with film actors as social symbols, Rorschach tests by which individuals could connect their dreams across the American landscape. This search for emblematic stars, for admiration and for psychic support, became central to postwar culture, and it was hardly confined to the movies. We had won the war and now who were we? *Life* magazine was a particularly sedulous bearer of the spotlight. Already in 1946 it was telling its readers that an otherwise obscure and difficult New York painter named Jackson Pollock might be America's greatest artist. In 1953 it celebrated Hemingway as America's greatest writer by putting him on the cover and all of *The Old Man and the Sea* inside.

Life also told its teenage readers why they shouldn't become beatniks and discussed whether or not going steady was acceptable, even while it clued their parents in on what arcane terms like "square" and "cool" meant. Of course, a prime social function of popular media is to dispense etiquette in the guise of information. But the codes of behavior celebrated in *Life* or *Cosmopolitan* or *Redbook* sold themselves as an etiquette of not just social success but also personal aspiration—a sort of advice whose goals were less controllable than what to wear to the prom. Character could be the armature of subversive change as well as official acceptance. For every reader who shuddered at *Life's* picture of the beatnik pad, how many others found it mysterious and intriguing?

❖   ❖   ❖

What were the characteristics of these new people, these about to be famous names or cultural types that Holden might approve of? In contrast with Anglo-mimics like the Lunts, whose acting style projected a refined and orderly self that was to be contemplated as a product, these newly-celebrated images of character implied that depths of feeling could be found in everyone, not just in the inner life of the sensible classes. More protean in both their class and their sexuality, they helped establish an art based on the armature of the body. It was a text of the anti-text, a return to flesh and feeling, the magnification of a vulnerability that denied traditional forms along with their more detached commitment to order.

Intensifying this emphasis on emotion, the most characteristic plots of 50s drama therefore focused on the character vulnerable to contradictions and irresolution rather than either the stock types of earlier social realism, or the archetypal figures of romance or agitprop. These were often characters with unfinished, unresolved business in their pasts. Dramatic structures thus frequently built toward an explosion of the past into the present, in which some unmentionable event or feeling had to be unveiled, a primal scene—the revelation of parental sin, a homosexual act, a betrayal usually associated with illicit sexuality—that required exposure and confession for absolution, a public revelation of the wounds of private feeling.

That much of the personal experience to be mined was inner, psychological, and tinged with traits conducive to alienation and rejection corresponded to the outsider position of many of the artists who created such works—outside by religion, by sexual orientation, by politics, by birth, by class, by language. For them, an emphasis on the self was not ahistorical and quietist. Instead, it took a definite attitude toward history and authority, usually one of contempt and resistance if not outright rebellion.

In the process of forging that social marginality into a cultural centrality, a layered self was created, whose interleaved areas of conventionality and rebellion have usually been reduced or dismissed, by the insider/outsider models favored in the Freudian contrast between repression and sublimation, as well as by the Marxist contempt for diverting political energy into fruitless emotional self-involvement. Yet there was something more at stake in, say, the plays of Tennessee Williams, the novels of Jack Kerouac, and the poetry of Robert Lowell than a simple bipolar pingpong match between florid personal superstructure and ignored politico-economic base. It was the interplay, the tension between these seeming opposites, that energized their works and gave them a permeability and an inconclusiveness that characterized Method acting as well.

W. T. Lhamon, Jr., calls "ethnographic" what he sees as common impulses in Strasberg and Kerouac to reach beyond the confines of an outmoded bourgeois realism: Strasberg as immigrant Jew and Kerouac as Catholic French-Canadian both bringing disturbing, disparate, and as yet unassimilated voices into the American conversation, "the irrepressibility of the repressed." Borrowing from Clifford Geertz, Lhamon defines both Kerouac's writing method and the Method actor's physical style in terms of their "thick description," the effort to make reality real by accumulating detail and gesture and especially feeling. But he glosses over the significant shift in generations between Strasberg and Kerouac. Like Edward Steichen in *The Family of Man* photography show he created for the Museum of Modern Art in 1955, Strasberg emphasized the basic psychic similarity beneath the ethnic, racial, and gendered differences. Of the great influences on acting in the 50s, it is Elia Kazan, rather than Strasberg, who is attracted by an alternative: "ethnographic" views of social experience marked by a semi-documentary style, the casting of non-professionals, and the anchoring of characters in their physical environments. Strasberg's theories thus incline him more to assimilation and even resolution than Kerouac or even Kazan usually allows.[3]

In line with its fascination with the divided character, the characteristic 50s strategy on the level of story was to face up to and contain its contradictions, instead of reconciling and thereby subduing them in the mirror relation of social order and dramatic closure. The implication, for both actor and character, underlined the choice between social assimilation (and subduing one's personal nature)—or trying to bring some aspect of inner psychology and past with you, and making explicit and unmistakable the cost of what was left behind. The 50s search for the new text and the new character thus proceeded by investigating and invigorating what was difficult if not impossible to assimilate: the individual, the inarticulate, the mad.

The result in actual performance was a kind of Jekyll-and-Hyde conception of character, what some Method teachers formulated as the difference between the part in you, and the you in the part. In this emphasis on the performer's ability to tap into his or her emotions and past, the Method also took a position at least implicitly suspicious of language as a tool of reason and articulation, and more than one critic has remarked on "the suspicion of the text that haunts the Studio." This suspicion had its roots in Stanislavsky's own mystical side, but was particularly strengthened in the 50s by the interest in the anti-theater theories of Artaud, the plays of Alfred Jarry and Eugene Ionesco, and the cultural emphasis on the artist as prophet/guru that enveloped figures otherwise as different as Hemingway, Kerouac, and Salinger. Reflecting its ambiguous attitude toward the written text or even language itself, the Method motto, if it could be said to have one, was "acting between the lines."

In the public imagery of the 50s, the Method actor was repeatedly characterized as a raw nerve mumbling and scratching himself. Yet such characters also clearly appealed to an audience as interested in recalling and renovating their emotional lives as were the actors, and equally attracted to family dramas as the context of self-discovery. Rather than the polished social surface of character and situations, the new style of acting dramatized the extraordinariness of ordinary private nature.

Kazan has remarked that the Method took root in the United States so easily because of the similarity between its emphasis on the great soul of even the most inconspicuous person and the attitudes of American democracy. Certainly the uniting of all groups and classes and genders to fight the enemy was a staple of World War II propaganda. But there was also a particularly hot-housed growth of this connection in the postwar period, as books like Dostoyevsky's *Notes from Underground* raised the banner of existentialism over paperback intellectual culture.[4]

The way the Method drew upon empathy as well as emotional and sensory memory in the creation of a role thus reflected the way the personalities and emotions of performers were beginning to be seen as ways of validating the inner lives of individual members of the audience. But Strasberg's creation of the "Method"—like Stanislavsky's of the "System"—was at base a professional effort to codify what had before in theater history been due to genius, luck, or a mechanical application of a rhetoric of gesture. Even though they found the source of energy, inspiration, and authenticity in personal memory and feelings, their goal was a greater professionalism for the performer. Like the endless etiquettes of the mass market magazines, these more confused and contradictory personalities engaged their audiences through a relation to the American self-help tradition. The raw materials of the old self were to be shaped to make a new one through a process of endless work— much as Strasberg and other acting teachers developed techniques for actors to make their personal experience "useable" by tapping from the unconscious what Strasberg called "affective memory."[5]

Because of this primary stress on craft and control in the elaboration of the Method, we need to be delicate if we are to make any general cultural point of the anti-textual similarities of the Method actors, the Beat writers, and the action painters: Kerouac's automatic writing and his perpetual drawing and re-drawing on his memory of his own life and those of his friends; the broad bodily gestures and even broader brushstrokes of Pollock, Motherwell, Kline, de Kooning, and others. Instead of seeking to organize emotions for later retrieval, Kerouac in particular continually resists the pressure of consciousness and control, and a pre-existing official literary history, to shape his work. His solution, like that of many others, is in the urge to divert consciousness and thereby to tap into non-official and anti-official orders of being.

Only one of the more prominent aspects of this effort was the Beats' romanticized preoccupation with the particularism of racial, ethnic, and dropout subgroups—reflected in Mailer's *The White Negro* and Kerouac's *On the Road*, as well as criticized by James Baldwin in his essay "The Black Boy Looks at the White Boy." Drugs also united both the dropout and marginal with the search for an altered consciousness that would be further propagandized in the 1960s. Jazz and other modes of improvisation forced tradition and melody through the immediacy of personal expression (which might even be recognized in what a Maria

Callas, for example, did with the traditional opera repertory). Like the image of the artist as prophet, the interest in Asian religion generally and Buddhism particularly allowed a turning away from Judeo-Christian organized religion and celebrated non-expository modes of understanding that included meditation, incantation, and repetition. Finally, in the realm of the body, Reichian psychoanalysis emphasized orgasm as the expression of ecstatic health, and sexuality generally as the prime antidote to the totalitarian political consciousness.

In short, practices and people considered marginal by normal society became defined as central by a significant proportion of 50s artists in all fields. In literary terms, for example, Hemingway's sense of the honed (and thereby external) professional craft of the writer was to be replaced by the standard of the internal self. Kerouac particularly sought to revive a literature of feeling, affect, melodrama, and even sentimentality to do battle with the lords of literary discipline. He became very upset when Ginsberg sent him the manuscript of *Howl* because there were words crossed out and emendations made. For Kerouac that was already a compromise. As he noted in a series of aphorisms for writing printed as "Belief and Technique for Modern Prose," "Something that you feel will find its own form." The better way was to write automatically. Like the automatic writing that lay behind Yeats's *A Vision*, Kerouac's also sought to look into the inner workings of personal time: "Like Proust be an old teahead of time." The fabled roll of teletype paper on which he wrote the first draft of *On the Road* is an apt metaphor for the redefinition of both news and novel that he sought. Kerouac's goal was to connect artistic work to real, immediate autobiography and memory, so much so that Ginsberg dubbed him "Memory Babe." Once again, this memory was not ahistorical. But the history sought by Kerouac, Ginsberg, and even Burroughs—along with poets such as Lowell, Plath, and Roethke—was a personal history that would correct and replace the bankrupt history of public events.[6]

Some of the anti-techniques by which the writer could divert the demands of a restrictive and repressive formal order came of course from the history of literature itself. The accumulated details of observed reality (Lhamon's "ethnographic" impulse) resembled the theory of an evolutionary literary realism, ever more mindful of the "real" world, argued most influentially for the 1950s in Erich Auerbach's *Mimesis* (translated in 1953). Significant predecessors could be chosen as well. On the more visionary side, Allen Ginsberg invoked the poetics of Blake and the incantatory line of Whitman as two significant influences.

Still another dip into the literary past revived the picaresque, a form that always seems to reappear in periods impatient of received traditions and looking for new structures based on new people, especially those, in Kerouac's words, attuned to "our one and noble function of the time, *move*."[7] In a polemic that is indelibly tied to the picaresque form, the new academic and popular interest in American literature, dating to the late 1930s and expanding after the war, also helped bring back the nineteenth-century motif of the quest. Bellow's Augie March and Henderson the Rain King, Ellison's Invisible Man, Plath's Esther Greenwood, Salinger's Holden, Mailer's Rojack—all in their different ways satisfy this model. Unlike the archetypal picaresque hero, Ulysses, however, their goals are not the domestic resting place, the refuge of family, but an ever-receding and elusive personal wholeness.

The exuberance of movement in Kerouac's prose, Pollock's splashing paint, and Brando's metamorphic amble therefore barely cover the sense of loss that animates their quest. It is a search for a lost past, a lost identity, and—frequently—a lost masculinity. With the end of World War II—perhaps with the ending of every war until women become an equal part of the military—a master historical narrative defining and even guaranteeing masculinity abruptly vanishes. All the problems, disturbances, and other anomalies of masculinity, previously swept up and plastered over by the single-minded male war role, reemerge in more baroque forms. With the licensed male bonding of wartime gone, homophobia takes on a crucial importance in the definition of masculinity. In the vacuum of masculine certitude after World War II, popular culture from western movies and detective novels to military crewcuts and barbershop-quartet singing supply alternate narratives and motifs for compensation and solace. Immediately after the war, more realistic film stories of returning veterans stress the problem of re-entry into a world (primarily of women) that has gotten along quite well without them. One of the more extreme meditations on male weakness and frailty—*The Best Years of Our Lives*—receives the Academy Award for Best Picture in 1946. In another, more mythic and cartooned aspect of this cultural preoccupation, soldiers without guns in real life read about dicks with guns in detective novels, intent on seeking revenge on an uncaring or hostile world for their murdered friends, their lost values, and their own wounds.

What had been lost was on the epistemological level a sense of unity and on the personal a sense of integrity. Total war and the Bomb that ended it had rendered all over-arching meaning suspect and threatened to level all existence into atomic sameness.[8] Into one version of that gap flowed what William S. Burroughs called "the control addicts," substituting paranoia and repressive order for the lost harmony; in another appeared a more soothing abstraction, like that of Andrew Marvell's "The Garden," a poem celebrated in 50s New Criticism—"Annihilating all that's made/Into a green thought in a green shade."

But the most culturally pervasive response to the postwar vacuum of masculinity was the rise of new male stars, whose images often explicitly challenged older forms of masculinity, even while defining a new kind of masculine beauty and assertiveness. Montgomery Clift, for example, plays in his first film, *The Search* (1948), a soldier who adopts a young German war orphan. In his second, *Red River* (also 1948), he plays cattleman John Wayne's adopted son, who challenges Wayne's aggressive authoritarian ways with his own more humane and sensitive—but still sharpshooting—brand of leadership. Another new young actor, Marlon Brando, scores a tremendous success on Broadway as Stanley Kowalski, the bare-chested "gaudy seed-bearer" of *A Streetcar Named Desire* (1947), who can still break down from his need for his wife Stella. Brando then begins his Hollywood career playing a war-wounded paraplegic in *The Men* (1950), for which he prepared by living with paraplegic veterans while confined to a wheelchair himself.[9]

The fabled rebelliousness of Clift, Brando, and later, Dean—along with that of the characters they played—defined itself against a generation of missing or failed fathers, who were either overpowerful or impotent. In the Oedipal politics that shadowed the period, the object of the personal search for meaning is often a father, literally or figuratively absent, like Old Dean Moriarty in *On the Road*, "the father we never found." It is striking, in fact, how pervasive is the oedipal structure of much narrative drama and fiction of the 1950s. Even for women, the problem is more often with fathers than with mothers (e.g., Judy in *Rebel Without a Cause* and Esther in *The Bell Jar*). In *On the Road*, however, the quest for the lost father is only a pretext for Kerouac's unending mission to capture on paper Neal Cassady, the real person on whom Dean Moriarty is based: "In praise of Character in the Bleak inhuman Loneliness." Through him, Kerouac focuses the desire for a family of choice rather than one dictated by necessity and inheritance. What urges their journey of personal discovery forward is the effort to find the lost father, however disreputable and inadequate, even so that he may be finally rejected.[10]

❖   ❖   ❖

Animated by a cold-war suspicion of unitary intellectual systems, the recourse to gesture, thought, feeling, and memory that characterizes Method acting, action painting, and Kerouac's poetics re-establishes the individual on a ground separate from society and its compulsions. But it is the films of the 1950s that express these conflicts and ambiguities in a way that literature and painting, with their solitary creators, and theater with its social setting, cannot quite accomplish. If there is an argument to be made for the centrality of the metaphor of Method acting practices to other aspects of culture in the 1950s, it must center on the films. I don't want to argue here that the Method works better on film than on stage. But the cinematic tension between physical action and dialogue, between the meaning conveyed by visual image and the meaning conveyed by verbal construct, allows film more fertile and complex play with its contradictions.[11]

It is particularly the actor who reflects and intensifies the struggle between resistance and assimilation in 50s art. Just as we should withstand either a totalizing view of the 50s as dark and paranoid, or a totalizing view of the 50s as progressive and expansionist, we need to contest an interpretation of the Method as either a patriarchal repressive ethos based on outmoded Freudian assumptions, or the Method as an uncomplicated ethos of freedom and self-determination. Its true usefulness as a metaphor is not its actual pedagogy but its practice—the tensions between the individual and the group that it tries, often unsuccessfully, to subdue.

The actor's empathy, emotionality, and physicality—fostered by the Method and Method-like acting techniques—plays against the pressure for the character to conform to text, closure, and stereotype. Even if at the end of the story the character seems to assimilate, the subtext of the vulnerable and emotional body allows the audience to be still aware that this process is also explicitly imposed from the outside. Instead of merely naturalizing the authority that brings about the ending, the narrative keeps the question of personal nature and its allegiances to the social order in flux. Perhaps this also constitutes a demonstration of how much of cultural change proceeds: not by a series of assertions that have the character of a logical syllogism, but by contraries and contradictions.

To underline this irresolute allegiance of 50s art between character and plot, performer and medium, I want to consider three crucial films: *Viva Zapata!* (1953), *On the Waterfront* (1954), and *Rebel Without a Cause* (1956). The endings of all three of these films involve betrayal, on both the thematic and the narrative levels. But instead of glossing over that betrayal, each dramatizes its incompatible elements, and thus has attracted critics who want to choose one univocal interpretation or another and reorganize the entire film in relation to that choice.

But in the actual, more ambivalent practice, the conflict between director/group/mise-en-scène and actor can be focused on most profitably, I think, by raising the question of how these films end, how they often fail to resolve the conflicts they raise dramatically, and thus how they show that the conflict itself is the issue rather than the resolution. By examining the inconclusive endings of the films, we can better see how the tension between the form that wants to end and the character who wants to go remains a fruitful contradiction.

❖   ❖   ❖

Elia Kazan's films are a particularly rich field for exploration of these tensions for several reasons, including his crucial role in the founding of Actor's Studio, his political background in the Group Theatre, and the unresolved conflict between his own social and individual imperatives indicated by his testimony as a "friendly witness" before the House Un-American Activities Committee. Kazan's films have also been generally dismissed by film theorists as part of the social-problem, kitchen-sink realism of the 50s. Yet in fact they often contain a pervasive questioning of realistic visual premises[12]

Kazan's visual patterns in *Viva Zapata!*, for example, are often indebted to Sergei Eisenstein's, not only in the way characters are arranged within the frame and set in the landscape, but also in the way objects function in a foreboding, fatalistic way that reflects the director's absolute knowledge and control. Nevertheless there is a potential for evasion and escapability that the performer embodies. When the theme is the body, the aims of the writer, the actor, and the director grow closer together. Kazan in this way, I would argue, shows an uneasiness with his own authority as a director and, like Kerouac or Pollock, reaches out to the performer as an alternate model of coherence and meaning.

The last sequence of *Zapata* is set up as a ritual death, of which Zapata the character is himself fully aware. As he rides into a fort, to get help from supposedly rebellious troops of the Mexican army, he pauses knowingly in front of several machine-guns on boxes aimed directly at him. In addition to this proleptic fatalism, there are shadowy crosses and mourning peasants to provide an overlay of Christian symbolism—one way in which many of the seemingly realist texts of the 50s made a universalizing claim for the significance of their frequent violence toward the male body. Inside the fort, Zapata is greeted by a Judas kiss from a man named Jésus. The camera meanwhile focuses on Brando's eyes, shifting, thinking, wondering, remembering. Zapata, like Terry Malloy in *On the Waterfront*, is the Brando hero as non-intellectual, mostly inarticulate, and close to nature. He then sees his lost horse, a personal symbol of his own past. He physically connects with the horse, touching it, talking to it. Jésus unnecessarily says "It's your horse." On the sides of the courtyard the old men and women wait silently, knowing what will happen. Then the assassination, like the director's-eye-view, comes from above, in the form of hundreds of soldiers pumping bullets into Zapata's body.

Fernando, who is simultaneously the most abstractly motivated and the most opportunistic character in the film, then rushes forward. As a man of debased language who understands only the ways words force meaning, not how they expand it, Fernando wants Zapata's horse killed as well: it could become a symbol. But the horse has run away and so Fernando opts for the rhetoric of brutal realism: throw the body onto the village square; then they'll know he's dead.

The body lies on the wellhead, the church steeple above it, the water flowing from a pipe below. But despite Fernando's effort to take control of Zapata's myth, the meaning the villagers draw is their own. Through their conversation over the body, their ironic refusal to believe it is Zapata, they take imaginative control, denying the exclusivity of either the realistic or the symbolic reading. The body is not Zapata's, they say, he's fooled his enemies again. But Zapata, they continue, is also not a spirit or a myth. He's a man.

The final shot of the film seems corny—the white horse free in the mountains, unsaddled and unbridled, the wind in its mane—in part because it's irrelevant to the conclusions drawn by the Zapatistas in the village. Its inadequacy as a final image is the inadequacy of the directorial attempt to force closure through the audience's complicitous acceptance of a specific, unambiguous image. In the end of *Viva Zapata!* we see an essentially inconclusive disquisition on a wide variety of ways cinematic meaning is created. The movie must end, but the discussion continues, because the effort to obliterate the individual has in effect failed.[13]

This is far from what has traditionally been called realism either in literature or in film. The realist assumption is that the audience is presented with a familiar and reassuring world, which merely enhances what it already knows. No work is necessary, only congratulations to the artist for presenting such a compelling imitation of nature. But in *Zapata* as in many of Kazan's films, the conflict between realism and its alternatives is the actual message. The terms, and therefore the cultural meaning, of realism and naturalness are themselves turned into problems by an underlying and constant reference to how film specifically and visual representation in general inflects meaning.

❀   ❀   ❀

Although the ending of *On the Waterfront* has been argued about for the last twenty-five years because it seems to involve a hollow social reconciliation, it actually intensifies many of the issues of male performance and self-sacrifice dramatized in *Zapata*. Terry Malloy, the longshoreman played by Brando, is a former boxer whose personal awakening is expressed as a willingness to get back into the ring, physically as well as legally and morally. As we approach the end of the film, Terry has already testified at the Waterfront Crime Commission hearing. (Interestingly enough, we see only the preliminaries, not the testimony itself.) In this courtroom, ill at ease, in a torn suit jacket, Terry looks out of place, unnatural. And so he needs another kind of theater, a non-official theater, a non-institutional theater, in which to justify himself.[14]

But theater it still is, and very self-conscious theater at that. Before the fight, Terry gestures broadly and expansively toward the crowd of longshoremen watching him while he attacks Johnny Friendly verbally. Whereas Zapata is usually upset about such visual prominence, Terry is playing to an audience. He knows it, and he exploits it, When the fight begins, the wild line spoken by one of the watchers—"That boy fights like he used to"—on one level refers to Terry's return to energy and self-confidence; on another it means he's back on stage. Similarly, the impersonal, symbol-preoccupied directorial gaze that had signaled to us Zapata's fate has precipitated into *Waterfront* in the form of two fathers: the evil gangster Johnny Friendly and the good priest Father Barry. Yet, like all authorities, however benevolent, the good father is a manipulator as well, and the film visually underlines his premeditation by focusing on Karl Malden's shifty eyes, as he thinks how to persuade Terry to become a symbol of resistance to the union bosses.

Even more than in *Zapata*, everyone in *Waterfront* but the Brando character has a rhetoric. As Terry, Brando just has a body. Throughout

Waterfront, Terry's body and what to do with it takes center stage in the dialogue. "How did you recognize me?" he asks Edie Doyle in the park. "By the nose?" All the characters are fighting over him as an object, a prize that must be seized. "When you weighed 168 pounds, you were beautiful," says his brother Charlie, trying to soften him up to prevent him from testifying. Earlier, struggling to explain Terry's defections to Johnny Friendly, brother Charlie uses the cargo language of the docks: "The girl and her father have their hooks in him so deep he doesn't know which end is up." And throughout, as a former boxer, Terry has been owned as a body. "Johnny had a piece of me," he explains to Edie." "I think he still does," she responds.

Central to the way the 50s dramatized the problematic relation of individual to community is the self-consciousness of the character as a performer. The actor especially—and the actress as well—is playing someone who appears in performatory situations in which they are defined by the bodies they often precariously inhabit. This definition through the body is often dramatized with a certain hostility from the point of view

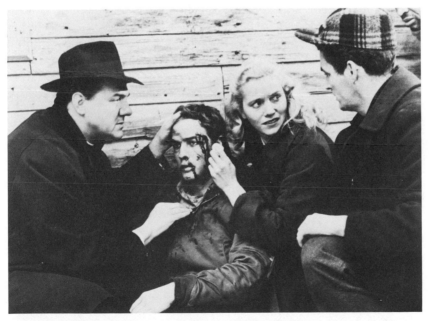

The physical assaults on Marlon Brando in his movies of the 1950s call attention to a vulnerable body (and psyche), as here in *On the Waterfront*.

of plot and direction: the victimization of a Marilyn Monroe can be matched by the number of times Marlon Brando is physically attacked in his films.

Thus the willful, passive theatricalizing of the figure of Terry here (as so often in other roles played by Brando, Clift, and Dean), resembles that of Jackson Pollock and Ernest Hemingway peering out from their pictures in *Life*. All are focused on and thereby manipulated, in a way reminiscent of how the figure of the woman has been theorized in classical cinema. "The male figure cannot bear the burden of sexual objectification," writes Laura Mulvey in her classic essay on the male gaze in films, and Mary Ann Doane says that the reversal situation—in which the man is the object of the gaze—is an aberration. But their arguments ignore the particular demands of this 50s cultural thematic I have been sketching, and the way in which theatricalized masculinity stands at the heart of it, a masculinity that demands an audience just as often inside the film as outside—yet is simultaneously crippled and manipulated by it.[15]

The precedents for such an audience focus on the spectacle of the male body are in plays of the 1930s, like Clifford Odets's *Golden Boy* (1937, with Luther Adler in the lead; film version 1939 with William Holden), in which the drama of "making it" in America is projected in the form of a rising athlete (as in *Waterfront*, a boxer). What constituted a proletarian style of male ambition and physicality in the 30s has by the 50s metamorphosed into the Method. Its lineage might be traced from *Golden Boy* through John Garfield's performance in *Body and Soul* (1947), Biff in *Death of a Salesman*, the great high school football player who fails in everything afterwards, and Brick, the alcoholic and impotent ex-football player in *Cat on a Hot Tin Roof*.

Paul Newman, who plays Brick in the film of *Cat on a Hot Tin Roof*, is one figure who combines the Method training of inwardness with a bare-chested masculinity to create characters who often only seem to be in charge of themselves physically. Newman plays a boxer in *Somebody Up There Likes Me* (1956, the biography of Rocky Graziano) and does a cameo in *Hemingway's Adventures of a Young Man* (1962), in both of which, especially the latter, his handsome face is almost unrecognizable. Biblical and classical epics, in contrast, represented a cinematic space in which the male body could be portrayed as more ideal and sufficient, in a sword-and-sandals exhibitionism that became more and more campy as the decade progressed, until both it and the self-satisfied Christianity it sponsored were definitively parodied in *Life of Brian* (1979). In his first movie, *The Silver Chalice* (1954), Newman embodied this ideal. Although he repudiated the film in a famous *Variety* ad, the iconic importance of his body continued to be one of his trademarks as an actor. In films with a contemporary setting, however, the central image is of the once-sufficient male body that no longer works, either sexually or socially. Not so much the sufficiency of Newman as the frailty of Clift, Dean, and even Brando.

The genre of the boxing film, on which *Waterfront* draws, emphasizes man as performer—and Terry is the boxer who has thrown the bout. He has taken his fall before an audience, and so must regain an audience, first Father Barry, then Edie, then the other longshoremen who mocked him. Terry tells Edie he's going down to the docks "to get my rights." But what he is really after is not so much the moral (and invisible) sense of having done the right thing, but to win the fight in front of other people.[16]

In the climactic fight with Johnny Friendly and the goons, Terry is battered until he's almost unrecognizable. His physical body has taken more than its share of punishment. But then the priest, with calculating eyes, whispers that Terry needs to zip up his jacket, hide his wounds, and display his symbolic body before the longshoreman crowd. *On the Waterfront* thereby seems both to argue in favor of informing, and yet to demonstrate that Terry has been manipulated into doing it. "If Terry walks in, we walk in with him," says an appreciative member of the audience within the film. And so they do, to work for a big ship owner in a fancy coat much like Johnny Friendly's. What Terry doesn't realize, but what the film dramatizes with its own ambivalence, is the combination of moral and erotic spectacle his punishment and redemption have become, as well as the actual lack of thematic resolution this spectacle diverts us from. The insufficiency or at least the ambiguity about Terry's or anyone's ability to make a difference reflects similar structural ways in which *Waterfront* questions its own realist sufficiency. Rather than an ideological polemic, *Waterfront* from this point of view seems more like an anarchist critique of any authority, Marxist or capitalist, generated and sustained by the director's empathy for the actor's self-conscious effort to escape all categories. The closing door at the end speaks of no uplifting reward for Terry's sacrifice of blood. Like a dropping theater curtain, closure has been forced; the play may be done, but the story is not over.[17]

✿   ✿   ✿

Rebel Without a Cause is an even more explicit example of seeming narrative resolution and reconciliation that undermines itself. *Rebel* was

In *Rebel Without a Cause*, James Dean's oedipal rebellion against his father (Jim Backus) is happily resolved through his loving relationship with Judy (Natalie Wood).

directed by Nicholas Ray, who had a long background in the Group Theatre, and its script was heavily influenced by pseudo-documentary research into the actual lives of some of the teenagers who played roles in
the film. Unlike *Zapata* and *Waterfront*, whose central characters are
adults, *Rebel* poses these questions of conformity and rebellion in terms
of the teen-age male (although James Dean was in fact 24 at the time).
Plato (Sal Mineo), the boy who is brought up by his black maid, whose
own parents have nothing to do with him, has joined the "family" of Jim
and Judy, whose fathers are inadequate or self-centered, while their
mothers are shrewish or passive. As the film draws to an end, Plato has
taken a gun to protect himself from the gang, and run away, first to an
empty mansion where he plays the child to Jim and Judy's "parents," and
then to the Griffith Planetarium. Jim has tried to talk Plato into giving
up the gun. When Plato refuses, Jim essentially tricks him into letting
Jim take a look at the gun, whereupon he removes the bullets. It is an
act supposedly done to protect Plato, but, as the climax unfolds, it serves
only to make him more vulnerable.

What transpires is another of the double endings so characteristic in
works of the 50s, in which assimilation and acceptance is bought at the
price of an explicit betrayal. A one-sided reading of the end would assert
that Jim Stark buys his parents's acceptance of him and his relationship
with Judy at the expense of Plato's death, and furthermore that the film
agrees, and proceeds to ignore Plato to focus on the story of Jim and
Judy. But my point is that this betrayal is exactly what the ending explicitly dramatizes for us: first, Jim seemingly takes control by showing
himself theatrically in front of the searchlights of the police cars. Plato,
on the other hand, the more hidden, weaker male, is upset at the focus
of the lights and goes out of control, ultimately to his death, which Jim
has unwittingly helped engineer. Behind the credits at the beginning of
the film, in a scene improvised by James Dean, we see Jim lying on the
ground in a fetal position, playing with a child's toy monkey. By the end
of the film, for Jim to become a man, it seems that he must help kill off
Plato—the ethnic, gay, intelligent, misfit self. Acceptance by the family
("Dad, this is Judy. She's my friend.") is the closure/acceptance you seek.
But you also have to know what you sacrificed to get it.

When Jim and Plato first meet, it is in the Planetarium after a lecture
on the destruction of the world that the speaker ends with some bland
"scientific" remarks on the emptiness of interstellar space. Plato
emerges from behind the seats to ask Jim, "what does he know of man

alone?" It is like an echo of similar remarks about the legacy of the war and the Bomb. Faced with apocalypse, everyone is a teenager.

As Father Barry zips up Terry's jacket in *Waterfront* to keep the blood inside and make the symbolic gesture more powerful, Jim lends his bright red jacket, the emblem of his body and physical presence, to the cold and dying Plato. Whatever was rebellious about Jim is somehow distilled into that jacket and purged, along with the Plato side of himself. And the camera underlines what is lost and left behind, bringing us back to the maid grieving over Plato, even as Jim's parents, and then Jim and Judy, have walked away. In an important way, both text and subtext, expression and repression, have been dramatized. The death of Plato is the price of returning to the approval of a patriarchal world in which there are fathers one can approve of in their turn.

❖   ❖   ❖

In 50s films, as in 50s popular culture generally, there was more pressure than ever before on stars to act out the audience's fantasy life, especially interwoven fantasies of impotence and rebellion. The endings of these three films indicate how often the 50s effort to establish a standard of individual nature against which to battle abstractions and institutions produces works that may nominally end, but still remain vitally unresolved. None of them comes down on one side or another of the basic questions they raise. Like much of the poetry, fiction, and visual art of the 1950s, they affirm only that making a connection between emotion, physicality, and personal time was worthy artistic work to do. The implicit questions were: Is masculinity exclusively identifiable with individualism? What is growing up? What is gained and what lost in the connection to adult society and traditional forms? In the 1950s the teenager in Hollywood films became a special vehicle of ideological subversion. But the questions raised were relevant not just for teenagers but for others as well. At the core of this exploration was an emphasis on the performer—not as a vehicle for words so much as an artist of the self, who used his or her own life and feelings to reinvigorate outmoded forms.

Despite many theories to the contrary, I think we can never quite be sure what is conformist and what is subversive in the artifacts of popular culture, of high culture, or of any cultural level. Because of the central importance to the culture of the 50s of the conflicts I have been describing, there are quite different messages available in *Viva Zapata*, *On the Waterfront*, and *Rebel Without a Cause*, both official messages of assimilation and subversive messages of resistance and even rebellion.

Our lasting preoccupation with the struggles of the 1950s implies that the conflicts describable by the metaphor of Method acting, with its emphasis on the physical, feeling body, may be as unresolved now as they were then. But what was hammered out in 50s culture were some lasting strategies to approach issues of ambition, realism, and the never-ending conflict of individual and communal desires essential to American culture. "No body's perfect" because each is different, escaping generalization, never completely a subject, but also not merely an object either.

ACKNOWLEDGEMENTS

I would like to thank Joe Boone, Seymour Chatman, Carol Clover, Rip Lhamon, Laura Rosenthal, and Rob Silberman for their contributions to the final form of this essay.

NOTES

[1]What constitutes "Americanness" has, of course, always been an evolving and constantly debated issue throughout our history, long before the House UnAmerican Activities Committee came on the scene in the late 1930s. The issue seems especially polarized after wars: the sense of disillusionment and loss of revolutionary fervor after the War of 1812, which helped bring about the cult of the Revolution and Lafayette; the financial expansion complete with industrial greed and monopoly of the Gilded Age after the Civil War; the isolationism, Jazz Age hedonism, and alien exclusionism after World War I.

[2]J. D. Salinger, *The Catcher in the Rye* (New York: Little, Brown, 1951), 119.

[3]W. T. Lhamon, Jr., *Deliberate Speed: The Origins of a Cultural Style in the American 1950s* (Washington, D.C.: Smithsonian Institution Press, 1990). Lhamon takes the almost oxymoronic phrase "deliberate speed" from the *Brown v. Board of Education* decision of the Supreme Court. In his book it refers to "the new form of the era—momentous spasms of energy frequently linked together amorphously" (25). On the issue of ethnicity, Steve Vineberg observes that in the 1930s the Group Theatre was enthusiastic about producing Clifford Odets's *I Got the Blues* (an early version of *Awake and Sing!*), due to their personal connection to the accents and stories of its Jewish characters, although Strasberg was, "oddly enough," strongly opposed to it. But the universalism of Strasberg's theories of acting and his anti-"ethnographic" impulses make his opposition quite logical. See Vineberg, *Method Actors: Three Generations of an American Acting Style* (New York: Macmillan, 1991), 42. Vineberg also comments on Kazan's relation to Italian neo-realism, which carried forward the early Soviet film's experimentation with non-professional actors (95). A counterexample—and one more in accord with Strasberg's views—would be the very non-ethnic performance of Lee J. Cobb in the original production of *Death of a Salesman*. The speech rhythms of Willy Loman are clearly New York Jewish, yet Kazan, Cobb, and Miller collaborate on a universalized story set in Jo Mielziner's dreamlike stage space. One mark of the difference between the emblematic uses of ethnicity in the immediate postwar period and the present is how Dustin Hoffman's 1984 performance (film, 1985) emphasized the Jewishness of the character.

[4]Michel Ciment, *Kazan on Kazan* (New York: Viking Press, 1974), 39. The precedent of nineteenth-century Russian literature for the holy fools of the 50s is intriguing. When Allen Ginsberg meets Carl Solomon (to whom he later dedicates *Howl*) at Columbia Psychiatric in 1949, he introduces himself as Prince Myshkin. In response, Solomon says that he is Kirilov. Ann Charters, *Kerouac* (New York: Warner, 1974), 139.

[5]Just as the Group Theatre descended into the Actors Theatre, perhaps 30s American social consciousness theater, with its odd combination of 20s expressionist fatalism and revolutionary aspirations, may also have a parallel evolution into the individualist rebels of the 50s. The athlete as archetypal proletarian hero, and the preoccupation of writers of the 30s and 40s with boxers above all, is an intriguing sidecurrent in this argument. The central cultural importance of Joe Louis (especially as an anti-Nazi symbol) is significant here. But the line stretches from Ernest Hemingway, A. J. Liebling, Norman Mailer, and Budd Schulberg—to name just a few—down to its latter-day version in Joyce Carol Oates. Now, of course, when a writer chooses to memorialize sport with that kind of attention, it is usually the elegiac and bucolic world of baseball rather than the urban struggle of boxing.

[6]For Kerouac's response, see Barry Miles, ed., *The Annotated Howl* (New York: Harper & Row, 1986), 149. The two aphorisms/maxims are from "Belief and Technique for Modern Prose," *Evergreen Review*, 2, 8 (1959), 159–160.

[7]*On the Road* [1957] (New York: Penguin, 1976), 133. Later, Sal Paradise asks "Where we going, man?" and Dean Moriarty answers "I don't know but we gotta go." See also John Clellon Holmes's novel, *Go* (1952).

[8]An intriguing formulation of the disintegrating pressure of the Bomb and the concentration camps on the sense of personal identity appears in the first paragraphs of Norman Mailer's *The White Negro* (1956).

[9]*The Search*, which, like *The Men*, was directed by Fred Zinnemann, deals centrally with the fact of the concentration camps, whose emotional reality Clift had to include in his performance. Of late this anxiety about (or nostalgia for) a missing core of meaning in masculine experience has been called male hysteria, although hysteria seems too reductively diagnostic a word for such gloom and melancholy. Kaja Silverman discusses the "'dominant fiction" (about masculinity) that is breached in a film like *Best Years* in "Historical Trauma and Male Subjectivity," *Male Subjectivity at the Margins* (New York: Routledge, 1992), 52–124. Her Lacanian view can be usefully compared with Dana Polan's more sociological and historical discussion of the general narrative collapse of assumed modes of coherence and closure in *Power and Paranoia* (New York: Columbia University Press, 1986).

[10]Dana Polan in *Power and Paranoia* associates the oedipality of much of 50s culture with the death of Roosevelt, and the frequently-noted connection between Method exercises and Freudian therapy and the Studio taste for family drama is also relevant here. Compare the frequently missing mothers in Robert Heinlein's teenage-boy oriented science fiction novels, together with his vision of the father as pal/partner (*Farmer in the Sky*, 1950) or nemesis to be won over by his heroic son (*Puppet Masters*, 1950).

[11]The conflict represented by the Method appears more fertilely in film than it does, say, in art, where the tug between abstraction and representation constitutes a fight with art history as much as an assertion of self. The first generation of abstract expressionists, such as Jackson Pollock and Robert Motherwell, implicitly carried on this fight while the younger generation of Robert Rauschenberg or Richard Diebenkorn, not so actively hostile to representational forms, could thematize it within the individual work. Not to say that the process can be so neatly distinguished by generation. Ad Reinhart, for example, although also an abstract artist, worked in a comparatively non-autobiographical and non-psychological mode. The painted surface was smooth, the evidence of the brush and the

artist's gesture in making the brushstroke was virtually erased. Yet even this erasure implied the intense labor necessary to achieve the effect (especially in the context of Pollock's drip-paintings). Reinhart's paintings, like those of other abstractionists, still demand that the viewer do a good share of the work. They engage the eye instead of reassuring it.

[12]Kazan's work in theater is similarly divided between the social orientation of Arthur Miller and the lyric individualism of Tennessee Williams. In his characteristic mises-en-scène from the 50s, realism and anti-realism play against each other, as do realist characters (Biff in *Death of a Salesman*, Stanley Kowalski in *Streetcar Named Desire*) and fantasist characters (Willy Loman in *Salesman*, Blanche Dubois in *Streetcar*).

[13]See Foster Hirsch, *A Method to Their Madness* (New York: Norton, 1984) for some interesting comments on Kazan's way with symbols and objects. *Viva Zapata!* is also a notorious example of how different audiences can take a film and use it for their own purposes. What to many critics in the 50s and later constituted a politically quietist attitude toward power became in the early 60s an inspiration to the activist founders of Students for a Democratic Society. For the negative reading, see Peter Biskind, *Seeing is Believing: How Hollywood Taught us How to Stop Worrying and Love the Fifties*, (New York: Pantheon, 1983).

[14]There is a touch of the cowboy confrontation on main street here, as Terry Malloy goes down to confront Johnny Friendly. Leonard Bernstein's score underlines the parallel musically by quoting Aaron Copland's *Billy the Kid*.

[15]Laura Mulvey, "Visual Pleasure and Narrative Cinema," *Screen*, 16 (Autumn 1975), 6–18; Mary Ann Doane, *The Desire to Desire: The Woman's Film of the 1940s* (Bloomington: Indiana University Press, 1987). Compare James Naremore in *Acting in the Cinema* (Berkeley: University of California, 1988) on the femininity of the male image in Brando. Peter Manso in his biography of Brando (*Brando*, New York: Hyperion, 1994) recounts, for example, Eric Bentley's review of *Streetcar Named Desire* in *Theater Arts* magazine, which implied Brando was homosexual with the caption: "It's his eyes that give him the lie" (281).

[16]Dana Polan, in *Power and Paranoia*, discusses how 1940s films such as *Pride of the Marines* dramatize the way male injury turns a previously selfish and narcissistic man into a more human member of a larger community (87–90). *Waterfront* follows this pattern intriguingly, elaborating the distinction between Johnny Friendly's corrupt union gang and the downtrodden rank and file. When Edie asks Terry what side he's on, he replies "On my side, Terry." Later, Father Barry mocks Terry's loyalty to his brother Charlie: "Let me tell you, you got some other brothers too."

[17]In an odd but significant moment, as Terry stumbles down the gauntlet of longshoremen toward the door of the pier, Edie clutches Father Barry's arm. He looks down as if in surprise. Perhaps her years with the nuns at Tarrytown have made symbolism a turn-on for her as well. In any case, it is an ambiguous gesture whose reach outside the narrow needs of the dramatic moment emphasizes the Method effort to develop a character not totally defined by what the script says.

JANSET BERKOK SHAMI

I OFFER MY LOVE TO YOU

When I was twelve, three important changes took place in my life. My elder brother left Istanbul and went to study in Ankara. My mother hired a lizard-like young woman as a new maid. A new girl who had transferred from another school appeared in our class.

But before I continue about how these changes affected me, I would like to go back to one of my earliest memories, the first movie I ever saw.

I was six years old when my mother took me to the cinema to see *Les Miserables*. I don't know what prompted her. She didn't enjoy movies herself. Whatever her reasons, she must have regretted her idea as she saw me weep throughout the last half of the film. When Madame Fantine began to call her daughter's name with her dying breath, "Cosette, Cosette," my sobs became very loud.

"Don't cry, little girl," said the gentle voice of the man sitting next to me. "Tomorrow Cosette's mother will be well and alive."

I stopped crying for a while and considered what he said. I tried to believe him. But how could I? If I was taken to the cinema the next day, Cosette's mother who would be alive at the beginning of the film, would die again toward the end. If I went to the film a hundred times, the poor woman would die a hundred times. There was no escape. Did the man think I was stupid? Let my teachers think so, let the whole world think so, I wasn't stupid. I understood much more than that man who sat next to me might think.

I remember my mother confirming what the man said. "The kind gentleman is absolutely right, Yasemin. Cosette's mother will be alive tomorrow."

After I tell you about the three changes in my life, you'll see that my mother was not very bright. When I tell you about my further involvement with the cinema in the following three years, and my mother's ignorance of that involvement, you'll see what I mean.

I do not hesitate to categorize my mother among the "not very bright" in spite of her intellectual friends who often come to visit. I think that my mother calls them "intellectuals" because they are good bridge players and because they speak differently from the mothers of my friends. They pronounce their own language in such a way that one might mistake them for foreigners. The words roll sideways and backwards on their tongues before they come out, and often lead to the ordinary subject of fashions. But they somehow make it sound different. Thank God that the fashions of the nineteen-forties are dying out, thank God we'll get rid of our burdensome Napoleon overcoats, they say, but they keep on wearing them. They will stop wearing hats and gloves, they say, but I saw one of them coming to our school with a pillbox hat on her head. Perhaps the hat was to impress her daughter's class teacher.

It is time to come to the three changes in my life.

Both my elder brother and I had a good ear for music. We were very fond of musicals. My mother allowed me to go to the movies with my brother. She was sure that he would not take me to see violent films.

Our favorite films starred Nelson Eddy and Jeanette MacDonald. If we were going to watch one of their movies, my brother would carry a notebook and a pencil to the cinema and write down the words of the songs. The lyrics of "Indian Love Call" looked like this in his notebook: "*Ven ay colon you, vial you anger tu? Det mins ay ofer may lav tu you, to bi yor ovn.*" My brother studied English at his high school. I am sure he could have done better than that. I think he wrote the words the way they would be spelled in Turkish so that I could read them. After all, my English didn't go any further than "yes" and "no."

We added these mutilated lyrics to the melody and sang the song on our way home. We sang it softly so as not to be heard by people on the street. The song sounded quite all right in spite of the Turkish spelling.

At home we polished our singing with the help of our ancient, out-of-tune piano. My brother's skilful fingers jumped over the uncooperative keys so nimbly that the accompaniment to our halting song sounded quite successful.

My brother didn't have the rich baritone voice of Nelson Eddy, but somehow he brought more feeling into the songs. My voice? It was still a child's voice, lacking all expression.

When my brother moved out, I was more or less left in the permanent company of that lizard-like, mud-colored nanny-maid. At the beginning I was so hostile toward her that I couldn't say her name. "Will you bring me a glass of milk?" "Will you tell my mother that I need a new school bag?" I said without even looking at her face. Each time she patiently chided me saying, "My name is Nuran. Nu-ran." Did she think that her name was so difficult to pronounce? Didn't she understand that I didn't want to have anything to do with her?

I took my separation from my brother so hard that I thought my life was coming to an end before it had properly started. "Time heals everything, time heals everything," I said to myself, clinging to that grown-up myth in order to preserve my courage. I looked forward eagerly to his visit during the half-year break.

In the meantime I discovered something which surprised me pleasantly. Nuran was as fond of movies as I was. She was so fond of movies that she had found herself a projectionist boyfriend.

Although the looks of the boyfriend were even less appealing than Nuran's, I could not but be grateful that she took me to the cinema every weekend. We watched the films from the small opening through which the projector transmitted the pictures onto the screen.

At the beginning I found it hard to adjust to this uncomfortable viewpoint. I couldn't see the films properly. Only after several times did my eyes finally adjust themselves. After that I felt that I was seeing the films even more closely than before.

Nuran's boyfriend was proud of his speed in changing the reels of the films. "I don't give a chance to the teenagers down in the hall to stamp their feet and to whistle," he said. He was fast, I had to admit that, and yet once or twice I heard some stamping of feet reaching up to us in the projection room.

My mother did not know about our constant visits to the cinema. She thought we spent the time at the nearby Municipality Park.

She didn't know about Nuran's boyfriend either. I heard my mother speak to one of her intellectual friends about me and Nuran. "Nuran has become so attached to Yasemin that she spends even her leisure time with her."

I had not suspected at the time that while we were keeping my mother in the dark regarding our trips to the world of the white screen, Nuran was turning me into a collaborator in order to blackmail me and use me for her protection if the necessity arose.

Nuran was pregnant. Not from the projectionist boyfriend, from someone else. She was already pregnant when she came to work for us but it didn't show at the time. Her hope for solving her problem lay in luring the projectionist boyfriend into marriage. She used every opportunity to mention to him the amount of money she had saved.

If she succeeded in leading him to the civil marriage registrar's office, that would be fine. If, on the other hand, she failed in her efforts to get married before the baby was born, she was going to bring me into the picture. I was to plead with my mother to keep her, and thus save her from losing her job.

What would happen if I didn't? She would tell my mother all about the movies she had taken me to see. She would tell her how much I enjoyed Myrna Loy's flirtation with Tyrone Power in *The Rains Came*. She would tell her how I had memorized the last scene of the movie. ("What is it?" the Maharanee, Tyrone Power's mother, asks the young Maharajah, "What do you hear?" Tyrone Power answers, "Nothing, your Highness, only a song." He keeps on listening to the love song with a thoughtful expression on his face, the song Myrna Loy and he had heard when they were so much in love.)

She would tell her that I had already seen the Barbara Stanwyck films *Banjo on My Knee*, *Double Indemnity*, *The Lady Eve*, and her film with Robert Taylor, *This is My Affair*. She would tell her that I had already seen the Bette Davis film *The Private Lives of Elizabeth and Essex*, in addition to many films with Joan Crawford.

Nuran called Joan Crawford trough-mouth, *yalak ağızlı*; she called Bette Davis pop-eyed, *patlak gözlü*. She had to give a nickname to each actor and actress. It wasn't easy for her to pronounce these foreign people's strange-sounding names.

The films I watched occupied my mind only for a day or two. It would have taken a long time to get used to living without my brother's companionship if I and Berrin, the new girl in our class, had not become good friends.

Now at the age of fifteen I look back to this friendship wondering about the turns and twists of life. Our friendship would not have developed so fast, it would not have become so strong, if the teacher had not seated her next to me. When I think of Berrin, I feel that someone is trying to steal something from me. Is it her that the mysterious being is trying to steal? Or is it me, myself, who is going to be stolen? I wrap my arms around myself, to protect my most valuable belonging.

Berrin was a very studious and quiet girl. Although she knew the answers to most of the questions the teacher asked the class, she rarely raised her hand. Most of the time she whispered the answers to me. She wanted me to impress the teacher, she wanted me to raise my hand.

I did it a few times just to please her. I was an average student, I didn't want to shine bright in the skies of the classroom all of a sudden. I couldn't keep it up in the written exams. I was also an honest girl.

Berrin was not only studious, she also had artistic talents. She kept herself busy drawing during the history lessons. The teacher approached our desk one day and asked her what she had just said. She looked determined to punish her if Berrin couldn't answer. My clever friend began to repeat all that the teacher had said about the occupation of Istanbul by Fatih Sultan Mehmet not forgetting to add the date, 1453. The expression on the teacher's face was of obvious amazement. She couldn't stop Berrin's long recitation although she was already convinced.

After that the teacher didn't interfere with Berrin's Picasso-like drawings of one nose here, one staring eye over there.

Berrin's art was not always for my private viewing. Sometimes the class would return from our recess before the bell rang just to watch her draw on the blackboard. She would clean it thoroughly before pulling out the box of colored chalks from the pocket of her uniform.

Her drawings were of the logos of various film companies like Paramount, 20th Century-Fox and Metro-Goldwyn-Mayer. We would sit in a respectful silence while the exact replicas of what we saw at the cinema were reborn on the blackboard. When the recess was over, every move of Berrin's hand removing the logos from the blackboard would be followed by our sad looks. It wasn't easy to watch a piece of art disappear.

Sometime after Berrin became my best friend, I discovered that our houses were not far from each other. That's when I began to talk about her to my mother. I told her how clever my friend was, how beautiful she looked, how perfectly clean and well-ironed were the white collars she attached to her uniform. I hoped that if my mother heard my praises long enough, she would eventually allow me to go and visit Berrin. She would let Nuran take me to her house.

My mother is full of surprises. She has always been that way. She excused herself from a bridge game one afternoon and took me to visit Berrin herself. On the way home, she told me that Berrin must be a good girl since she had a pleasant mother who kept her small house so tidy and clean.

I studied Berrin's mother during my following visits and agreed that she was pleasant in addition to being a hard worker. It was lucky that my friend had taken after her mother and not her father. Her father was not pleasant at all. He was a monster, an absolute monster.

He was terribly unfair to Berrin and her little brother. The short, square man squeezed the spirit out of his children. He wrung them like washing to be hung. His reasons? His reasons for acting the way he did were so stupid that one would laugh, if the suffering of Berrin and her brother were not so real, so intense.

He punished Berrin because she collected postcards of movie stars. He punished the little boy because he allowed his hair to be put into curlers by his sister.

Nuran's brother looked like Shirley Temple. Nuran knew that Shirley Temple was already a teenager, much older than her brother, older than us. We knew that most of the movies we saw were five or six years old by the time they reached our country. That didn't matter to us in the least. We wanted the ages and the looks of the actors and actresses to freeze on the screen. As far as we were concerned, Shirley Temple was not a day older than six years. It was for that reason that Berrin wanted her brother to look like that six-year-old movie star by putting his hair in curlers.

Naturally she stopped curling her brother's hair when their father began to beat the little boy. She wouldn't allow her brother to suffer at the hands of their father because of her. She would rather suffer the beatings herself.

Berrin was not beaten by her father. All he did was to forbid her from occupying her time with anything except going to school, studying, eating, sleeping and saying "yes sir, yes sir," to him. He insisted that she add *efendim*, my sir, to the end of every answer she gave him. He also didn't want her to own anything. Berrin had realized this when she arranged snapshots of her friends in an album she had bought. Her father had thrown away the album with all the pictures in it. "Isn't it enough that we have a family album?" he had said as an answer to the frozen tears in her eyes.

Lately he had made a habit of tearing up the movie star postcards she collected. As soon as he returned home and put on his slippers, he rushed to her room with high expectations of finding what he was looking for. It was like a competition between father and daughter. She bought them; her father tore them up. She bought more; he tore them up as well.

The official excuse for this destructive activity, which broke his daughter's heart, was that collecting these cards and looking at them for long periods of time had an unfavorable effect on Berrin's studies.

He must have known that this was a lame excuse. Berrin was the best student our school had had for many many years. This is what our class teacher had told her mother when she had visited the school. This is what her mother had related to me, trying not to sound too boastful. She had blushed when she repeated the teacher's words.

I thought that he objected to her collecting those postcards because he was a religious man, and he disapproved of the scantily-clothed actresses. This wasn't the case. He couldn't have been a religious man. I learned that he was the manager of a factory producing that milky alcoholic *Raki* which makes people very drunk.

What did he have against his daughter then? Why wouldn't he allow her to collect these postcards and enjoy looking at them? What was wrong with it?

Berrin told me that it was her mother who gave her the money to buy those cards. She told me that her mother made some money by hand-hemming about a dozen chiffon scarves daily. The poor woman spent all her free time at home doing that tedious work. But then perhaps she kept herself busy to escape her husband's company, not to be obliged to go out with the monster.

One day Berrin proudly told me that she had discovered a good hiding place for her cards. She said that she arranged them in a large flat box and put them under a loose plank in her room. She was certain that her father would never find them.

After that, several of her father's searches were fruitless. When he asked her where the cards were, she told him that she had stopped buying them. He changed the timing of his raids. He hoped to catch her red-handed, looking at the photos. His attempts failed. Berrin never looked at them while her father was at home.

But one day when he barged into her room without knocking, as was his habit, one of the wooden planks creaked under his feet. He immediately ordered his daughter to turn down the carpet. When he saw her hesitate, he was certain that he had made a discovery. He raised his voice. "I said, turn down the carpet!"

The naked floor showed that the plank under which the box of cards was hidden was not at the same level as the rest.

Berrin told me between sobs that after he made her take out the box and place it on the desk, he settled down on her chair, and began to tear up the cards one by one.

I didn't have enough money to replace her collection, but I immediately offered her all my savings. Her refusal left me with no other solution. All I could do, then, was to cry with her. I shared her pain, I shared her hate for her father.

I find it extremely hard to continue. But since I started, I must go on.

A few days after our bitter tears, Berrin who was so regular in her attendance at school, was absent. I told Nuran and she got my mother's permission to take me to Berrin's house the very same afternoon.

When we approached, we saw a commotion near the building where she lived. We heard a man's voice reading Suras from the Koran. We saw people descending from the second floor where Berrin's apartment was. We saw a coffin being carried out. Nuran immediately clasped my hand.

"What's going on?" she asked the two women who stood at the narrow door of the building.

One of the women was crying. The other one answered. "The girl, the daughter of Zeki bey, she shot herself. She is dead."

I thought I screamed, but there was no sound. Nuran tightened her grip on my hand and made me walk to our house with fast steps. She came to my room later on and I saw teardrops slip down Nuran's muddy-colored cheeks. Now that I think about it, this was the only time I saw Nuran cry. Even when she gave away her baby three months after that tragic event, I did not see her shed a tear.

It is strange that I remember Nuran's reaction to Berrin's tragic end more clearly than my own. That afternoon I felt that I had disappeared together with my friend. Even when my mother searched my face with her eyes before I went to bed, I felt that she couldn't see me, I felt that I wasn't there. I began to feel the throbbing, biting, tearing sorrow the next day.

I was excused from going to school. My mother might have been afraid that I would neglect to dry the constant flow of tears and would disgrace myself by sitting in the classroom with a wet face and a runny nose.

My mother asked Nuran to make me a glass of lemonade every hour or so. She said that if I did not drink enough, my body fluids might dry up, I might become dehydrated.

I wished my body would lose all the fluids it contained. I wished I would die.

According to people, including my mother's intellectual friends, Berrin had found her father's loaded gun in the drawer where he kept his underwear, had carried it to her room, put the muzzle in her mouth and pressed the trigger.

Every time I heard this unlikely story, flames leapt up and down my body. The sharp fingers of those flames pointed at Berrin's father. "Don't tell me that my twelve year old friend committed suicide! Don't tell me that!" I wanted to scream. But to whom? The police said that there were only her fingerprints on the revolver. I was the only one not convinced by the evidence.

What if her father wore gloves, pushed the gun in her hand and made her place it in her mouth?

I could not contain myself longer than a day or two. I thought of telling Nuran. Then I changed my mind and opened my heart to my mother. She became very angry. "Don't be crazy. Don't repeat it to any-one. Do you understand?" she said, raising her voice and forgetting to roll her words sideways on her tongue. When she calmed down, and said "Where did you learn such things?" I felt that she was becoming suspi-cious about my outings with Nuran.

I obeyed my mother's orders. I didn't repeat my ideas to anyone else, not even to Nuran. If I had told her my theory Nuran might have taken me to the police station. The station was only two blocks from our house. Could I have stopped the tragedy that followed if I had been courageous enough to talk to the police officers? I suppose I'll be asking these silent questions all my life.

I was too young. Too young to do anything about what happened.

Within a month, Berrin's brother was also shot dead. This time in the heart. The police were convinced that he had learned where his father hid the gun during the investigation following his sister's death, and he had taken it out to play.

What a stupid assumption! Would the boy want to play with the gun after he had seen how dangerous it was, how it had ended his sister's life?

I think the monster killed him too. Perhaps he killed him simply be-cause he looked like Shirley Temple. Perhaps one day, after his sister's death, the little boy tried the curlers on his hair just to remember his sis-ter. Perhaps his father caught him in the act and killed him.

What proves my theory is that almost as soon as the little son was buried, the mother of the two dead children left her husband. She sim-ply disappeared.

She must be doing some hand-hemming somewhere. She must be having difficulty keeping the chiffon scarves from getting wet with her tears.

When it became obvious that Nuran was pregnant, my mother gave her a lecture. "I should send you away. I would too, but my hands are tied. I would be hurting Yasemin's feelings. I know that she is very fond of you. I'll keep you if you manage to get rid of your baby."

I don't think my mother meant her to get rid of the baby in the way that Nuran did. She must have imagined that Nuran had some relatives to look after her baby boy.

But the mud-colored nanny-maid had no relatives. No mother, no father, nobody. So she took the forty-day-old baby to the Government Child Clinic and found a seat between the other mothers who had brought their babies to be examined. After sitting for a while as though she was waiting for her turn, she asked the woman sitting next to her to help her for a few minutes with her baby, She told her that she needed to go to the ladies' room. The woman smiled and took the baby. Nuran escaped through the other door.

Last month, on the seventh of May, my mother arranged a birthday party for me. She filled our large house to capacity by adding her friends and their children to the list of girls I wanted to invite. My chiffon full-length dress was light blue and I had a crown of flowers of the same color in my hair. I thought I looked so childish.

My mother's intellectual friends apparently did not share my view. They gave me one look as I greeted them and began to flood my mother with compliments.

They compared me with their "immature" children and told her that she should be proud of me. They told her that I was very beautiful, very graceful, and well-adjusted. They told her that I was on my way to becoming a mature young lady.

My mother must have been pleased with what she was told. Probably she accepted the compliments without questioning them. I was the one who did the questioning. The ladies are entitled to their opinions regarding my grace and beauty. But my being well-adjusted? How would they know just by looking at me? And as for maturity, I have a long way to go.

While the coming years will bring me maturity, I'll carry the songs of Nelson Eddy and Jeanette MacDonald in my heart. The good and the bad I have seen on the white screen will accompany me. I must remember Jeanette MacDonald's response to Nelson Eddy when he sang, "When I'm calling you, will you answer? That means I offer my love to you, to be your own. If you refuse me what shall I do?" Jeanette MacDonald didn't reject Nelson Eddy's gift of love.

I believe that Berrin and I would have been life-long friends if she had lived. I believe that my brother will always love me as much as he loves me now. I believe that Nuran will find her son in an orphanage one day, and they'll be together again. They'll live happily ever after. I be-lieve that if my father had not died when I was still a baby, he would have never behaved like Berrin's father. I'll forget the unhappy movies. I'll bear in mind that my mother has no faults other than spending too much time with her intellectual friends. If somehow we became separated, and if, God forbid, my mother fell ill, during her delirium she would re-peat my name. "Yasemin. Yasemin," she would say.

IV. The Poetry of Film

DIANN BLAKELY SHOAF

REUNION BANQUET, CLASS OF '79

"What happened to Charlotte Rampling?" — the vamp
and villainess of freshman year's remake,
Farewell, My Lovely. I can't recall the plot,
nor which boyfriend I went to see it with,

none villains. Freshman year, girls learn to drink;
we spent weekends bombed in years that followed,
often with those old boyfriends, some seated
in nearby chairs as we discuss *Three Women, Klute*

("poor Sutherland — what was the bomb that followed?"
"Fellini's *Casanova*"; Jane Fonda
changing women from fat dateless klutzes
to lean wives, marrying "that Turner guy,

a fellow Casanova before Jane.")
Chinatown, Looking for Mr. Goodbar,
Diane Keaton ferrying from guy to guy
then killed. *Helter Skelter*, a TV movie

looked at with Chinese food and tepid beer,
that crammed dorm room (soph year? junior?), our knees
jellied. Hell, what's better than the movies
for filling gaps, for steering talk away

from this crammed corner's melodramas, its queens
of bad luck? Emma's three miscarriages —
"children fill a gap"; talk tries to veer away
but she tells us about her absent husband,

313

who blames their bad luck on her mom's DES,
how she spends Saturday nights now, fevered
by secrets she doesn't tell her husband:
chlymidia and one nostril scarred from coke,

for instance. *Saturday Night Fever*!
someone yelps, and Nan's atop the table—
clam sauce spotting her skirt, a Diet Coke
spilled in the famous John Travolta pose;

someone yelps as Nan tips from the table,
as Layne prescribes a single mom's sanity:
sitcom repeats, like the John Travolta show
about the teacher, while she plugs into

tapes that prescribe ways to keep your sanity
while raising a small boy alone. Virginia
weeps—loudly—about the teacher who plugged her
senior year, and the men at the next table

rise to leave. "So long, boys," and then "virgins,"
sneers Laura, meaning none have been divorced,
not since senior year, when one at their table
tied the knot and wanted out weeks later.

The Deer Hunter. Most seated here are divorced,
and childless too. *Lipstick. Who'll Stop the Rain*?
I untie my knotted napkin, wanting out. It's late.
Woman under the Influence. Badlands.

"What happened to our apple charlottes?" Vanished,
like our lipsticked smiles, the bottles of wine.
We're women fluent with address pads and pens:
farewell, my lovelies. "I'll call, or write."

CHARLES H. WEBB

FANTASY GIRL

"You're the fantasy girl, aren't you?"
—Bruce Willis to Jane March in *Color of Night*

Indian & Spanish? French & Chinese? Black & White?—
what collision of genes made this perfection that's just rear-ended you,
wearing a yellow scoop-necked blouse, eyes flashing diamonds,
voice a whisper, "I've got no insurance. Please don't bust my chops."

You can't help talking to yourself when she appears: "Here she comes,
wearing a backpack like a little girl, and falls into his arms."
It could be corny, but it's not because she's young and beautiful,
and nothing's corny about beauty and youth. Instinctively you know

it doesn't matter if someone leaves a diamondback in your mailbox,
if a red Ferrari tries to run you down, if you find a hose
flooding your living room, and stand on the veranda clutching
a butcher knife as tympani roar in your ears, and the house alarm

goes off like a scream. Later, as you clean up, harps will play
her theme and she'll appear. "Hi. Remember me," a breathy intake
after "hi" and "me," as if she's run a marathon. "There she is:
an angel dancing on the head of a pin," you'll say, transfixed

by her flowered dress through which a pubic halo gleams,
by lips and teeth so perfect they could be superimposed. Kissing,
she breathes "Oh, oh," as porno music surges—strings and electric
fuzz guitar. You make love, slow-motion, in the swimming pool.

When the scene cuts to hang-gliders, it's not corny; and when she leaves
you strapped by one hand to the bed, you laugh—it's just enough
depravity. It doesn't matter if she fucks half L.A., including women—
if she stabs her therapist thirty times, hangs an S & M freak by his
    heels,

carves "Rich Bitch" into his hide, and slits his throat—if she used
the same body moves, same whispers, same smile she's using on you.
It doesn't matter if she's cooked for them too—*ahi* with steamed
greens and rigatoni perfectly arranged on white bone china

with a brown checked border—wearing the same ruffled French
maid apron, nipples glowing through, slim derrière
(ass is too crude; butt is too blunt) with her rose tattoo bared
as she bends to pull perfect sourdough biscuits from the oven—

yours; she's broken into your house to cook for you.
(Chimes in her theme now: sex and danger sautéed.)
It doesn't matter if she's a psychopath or has multiple personalities:
one a murderous boy, one a slut who wears a gash of red lipstick,

glittering hoop earrings, mascara thick as mud. You know,
because she's young and beautiful, that your suspicions can't be true.
You know you'd enter hell to save her, lightning flashing
as you sneak past a gigantic welded Jesus, then cages and machines,

griffins and krakens, racks and screws. Satanic choirs can't mask
sobs gliding down like wounded birds around you as you push
through spiderwebs and blood-splatters, upstairs. She's sitting
in a shredded shirt, stripes lashed into her back, hands nailed

to her chair, driven psychotic by her brother, crazed himself
by child abuse, the one sin even the '90's can't forgive.
You know you'll face him with his crucifying nails—that just
as you saved her, she'll save you with a spike between his eyes

as he's about to sand off, inch by inch, your skin. You know
his death will purge her madness, but that someone so young
and beautiful can't live with fratricide, so she will climb—
in thundering rain, as lighting flickers like a faulty bulb—

an iron ladder that beanstalks up. You follow, begging her
"Come back." Souls in pigeon form explode heavenward
as, her wet shirt a sacrament, she stands on a roof patterned
like a waffle iron. She wants to jump, like someone else—

someone you loved but couldn't save. This is your chance
to be redeemed, and so you plead, "Come back to me. Come back . . ."
She reaches for you like Eurydice. But death's wind
hurls her down, so you jump too, catching a chain

and then her arm as she swoops by, both of you penduluming
over the abyss where tiny car-lights cross and twitch.
You're not afraid; you know you'll swing her to safety,
then clutch each other in the rain. Her theme will rise,

all strings this time, as lightning blinks off—on—off—on.
Your own madness broken too, you watch the credits
to see what name goes with such beauty and youth.
Jane March? Absurdly plain. You hit rewind, pop out the tape,

place it by your doorway for morning return, then plod to bed
and let your wife—with no gaffer to back-light a transparent gown
or bounce diamond-glitter off her eyes, with no director
to coax out each breathy line, with no shadowy, hellish past,

only the usual dark and tortured human history
to heat her kiss, only her arms that would have pulled out
of their sockets if she dangled like Jane—draw you back
into her body, back into this flawed and precious life.

MARGARET ATWOOD

AVA GARDNER REINCARNATED
AS A MAGNOLIA

Somehow I never succeeded
in being taken seriously. They made me
wear things that were ruffled: off-the-
shoulder blouses, the tiered skirts
of flouncing Spanish dancers, though I never
quite got the hauteur — I was always tempted
to wink, show instead of a tragic
outstretched neck, a slice of flank. Now look
at me: a vaginal hot pink,
vibrant as a laxative bottle —
not, given the company, a respectable
color. Let's face it: when I was in
the flesh, to be beautiful and to be
a woman was a kind
of joke. The men wanted to nail
me in the trophy room, on the pool
table if possible, the women simply to poke
my eyes out. Me, I would have preferred
to enjoy myself — a little careless
love, some laughs, a few drinks —
but that was not an option.

What would have given
me weight? Substance? For them.
Long canines? Vengeance?
A stiletto hidden in my skirt,
a greyish rainbow of fate
like an aureole of rancid lard —

or better: dress up in armor,
ride across the steppes, leading a horde
of armed murderers. That gets you a statue,
copper or stone, with a solemn frown,
—jaw clenched as if chewing—
like those erected by the sober
citizens, years later,
for all the sad destroyers.

Well, to hell with them. I'd rather
be a flower, even this one, so much like
a toilet-paper decoration
at a high-school dance.
Even that, to be trampled
underfoot next day by the janitor
sweeping up, even the damp flirtation,
the crumpled tulle, even the botched smooch
in the parking lot, the boy with the fat neck
and the hip flask, even the awkward fumbling
with the wired bodice, cheap perfume between
the freckled breasts, would have been better
than all their history, the smudged
flags, dry parchments, layers of dead bone
they find so solemn, the slaughters
they like to memorize, and tell
their children also to pray to

here, where they hate bouquets, the pleasures
of thoughtless botany, a glass
of wine or two on the terrace,
bare leg against white trouser
under the table, that ancient ploy
and vital puzzle, water-
of-life cliché that keeps things going,
tawdry and priceless, the breeze
that riffles through what now
may be my leaves, my green closed
eyes, my negligible
vulgar fragile incandescent petals,
these many mouths, lipsticked and showy

and humid as kisses opening
in a hothouse, oh I'd give anything
to have it back again, in
the flesh, the flesh,
which was all the time
I ever had for anything. The joy.

IRA SADOFF

AT THE MOVIES

An October drive through the leaf parade:
blood reds, pumpkin yellows with a cast of green.
Whatever's knocking around inside has opened the shutters

and gone for a walk. Common stuff suddenly blazes
in particular: you know how you put off
the optometrist, trying to deny your diminished vision,

but the new glasses brought clarity to your whole life,
meaning definition and composition, shape
and structure? That's how I feel about the movies.

Maybe there's an afterlife already composed of
our favorite scenes, a harp concerto by Handel, a plate full
of granted wishes. Maybe our spirits just loom

eternally, with a doctrine full of footnotes untangling
natural disasters, stillborn children and history's
handful of malice. Still, I'll take my chances with my eyes

open wide in this very dark place, consuming images
in the pews of someone else's choosing. Of course my taste
is cheap, corrupted by greed, TV, a compulsiveness

and fear of desolation just vast enough to be conceived.
But you can't convince me Heaven satisfies
more than *That Obscure Object of Desire*, where everyone

waits forever to be served. Secondly, suffering's
formless, unjustifiable, saturated with shame
and an art based on resignation and hate. Whereas

On Golden Pond, filmed a few short miles from here,
phony as a sermon on the virtues of the family,
transformed an inconsolable death into miracle,

and gave me a place to grieve and rest my feet.

MORDECHAI GELDMANN

PORNO

Under different circumstances I could fall in love with her—

The beauty of a French woman was mixed in her
with the beauty of unidentified Orientals;
the beauty of her body, her face, the beauty of her walk,
have made all the women I've seen until now seem ugly.
Her beauty remade the body's loveliness
into a cruel question—for a moment the cruelest of questions.

To desire her together with all the others—
those acting with her in the film, making it with her before my eyes,
and those watching her with me, creaking in their seats—
old men holding onto their final lusts,
queers cruising along the rows,
blacks who migrated to Tel Aviv to whiten their fortunes,
their frightened strangeness visible even in the gloom,
Arab workers homeless and filthy
jerking off in the corner in hopeless desire,
hoping for the cancellation of the Bride Price
and the expulsion of the oppressor,
quiet bashful Vietnamese who work in restaurants
and others—anonymous in the heavy darkness
pierced by a ray of light
bringing her delicate beauty to the screen,
the lighty echo of her supposed being.

Is to desire her among all these
like finding Euryidice in the underworld
passing through, white and smooth

with strawberry lips
in the consuming mists of the land of death?
This is a banal simile flattering
the poet who sees himself as Orpheus:
to desire her among all these is to find
on a deserted beach
      among volcanic pebbles and tin cans
      among seaweed and goat droppings—
                  a polished pearl

Translated from the Hebrew by Karen Alkalay-Gut

JANET SYLVESTER

NO BOY WOULD TELL HIS MOTHER HE WASN'T HUNGRY

I have watched them watching one another.
That's what we call the gaze with hands,
its fingertips so small he cannot trace
their soft meander across the broadcloth
edifice of a suit to its taper
where his waist might be. She cannot raise
to a stain the fingerprint that causes silk
at her breast to press slightly forward
as when the breath's indrawn. The Renaissance
drew little arrows discharged from taut bows
to figure how the skin, as if grazed
by fingernails, quickens beneath the eye.
No one, I think, has ever sketched the arrows
in collision in mid-air, their meeting
swift as a synapse firing before
they spin away. Sophisticated
as middle America, he holds the beat
a second or two too long before he
breaks, an athlete's internal torque
greasing with velocity his escape.
Model, she asks the empty place he's left
what he might mean. It's 1943,
and *Andy Hardy's Double Life* causes
the wringing of the bowels that torsion is
in the pause of an underwater kiss.
In the studio still, black and white,
Mickey and Esther fused at the mouth,
exchange fluid oxygen, their bodies

the bright platinum of satin sheets
in the California sun, sifting down, his hair
silver in her hand, her legs drifting
like diamond wings behind his right shoulder
in the foreground. We cannot see his face.
She's the angel Louis Mayer invented
for men brought up in the abundance
of yellow-curtained kitchens with hooked rugs
and jumpy with lovesickness their wives ignore,
or will, later on. Lips against his lips,
she whispers this. Who knows what he's thinking?
In studio portraits, sex would never be
happy. Even a male ingenue,
red-haired, open-faced, aspired to glitter
with resolute disdain, the hint of fake
that's glamour and slides the plate away
to prove, though desire's ghostly, it won't starve.
In one important scene, the lovelorn Andy
refused to eat. *You lied to me!* screamed Mayer,
the factory boss, whose product had just walked off-line,
You've let Andy insult his mother!
No boy would tell his mother he wasn't hungry!
In dailies, then, the young star ate and ate
and ate monotony, spit-flavored air.
Cash flowed through the limbic system
of America into the studio,
into sixteen films that millions
of handsome girls and pretty boys, all eyes
those futureless Saturday afternoons,
the theater lights brought down,
would turn from, bored, to one another.
Taking all this in, the shadow figure
behind the scrim still is Mr. Mayer,
whispering, *My little ones,* his audience
of children, mouth to mouth, and craving more
of wherever he procured that sameness.

DAVID WOJAHN

BEGINNING IN LAS VEGAS, 1985

". . . in his hotel room watching Ambersons *late one evening. The door was ajar, and as she neared the room she could hear the voices and see the reflection of the film in the window. She was about to enter, but stopped. . . .*

—Citizen Welles

He is weeping on the bed. He is weeping hugely
on the bed. She was about to enter but stopped.
Dark room and the memorizing, chastening light upon

the ice house scene, refrigerated sound stage 4
at RKO. He is weeping on the bed as cornflakes
method act a freezing rain, then snow. *It worried me*

because you didn't see people's breath.
She was about to enter, but closed the door
and left. *The Man Who Broke the Bank*

at Monte Carlo's sung, image cloning image—
snow filling screen, and the window's
image of the screen, and the window's image

of the weeping him. And she closes the door,
goes out. . . . In the City of Nets
he is lost. And how to speak of him?

Dropped globe of snow, the shocked entangled hands
constricting Desdemona's throat.
And how to speak of him? . . . The tape I've rented's

colorized, and version three. *I was trying*
to hold on to something, but they. . . .
The minutes shaved. One thirty-three

to one one seven, and then the keyboard symmetry
of eighty-eight, inflammable celluloid
like barber-shop hair, whisk broomed in long shot

on *RKO* linoleum. *Lucy and George for example in*
the one-horse open sleigh. And did I tell you how we. . . .?
The cadaver sewn back up and weeping

hugely. Forensics and the entrails read. Hair, fiber,
semen, blood, but the hair recombed, some rouge
for the cheeks. And how to speak?

Whisk-broomed like barber shop hair,
like the man and his son inching up
a February beach in Provincetown,

their fishtailing truck in the new
wet snow. To beat the Institute for Coastal Studies
team, the Museum of Comparative

Biology. Moonlit low tide, and now
they can reach her, forty feet and tons,
faintly her lavender flanks aglow, already scored

with knife-cuts, graffiti. The truck
in the water, up to its doors, and in rubber boots
they wade out to touch her, peel off their gloves

in the headlights' yellow wands of mist,
before the son pulls the chainsaw cord—
recoil and the smell of gas, the father

pointing to the jawline where the son
now aims, sputtering toward the first
of twenty hand-sized teeth. Leviathan

aglow. Leviathan's ivory molars
ensilvered and pulsing in the father's hands,
the tide and the sea's white foam:

the Chinese and the scrimshaw carvers eat them up.

PIER PAOLO PASOLINI

MARILYN

Of the ancient world and the future world,
there remained only beauty, and you,
poor little sister,
the one that runs after her big brothers
and laughs and cries with them, to be like them,
and puts on their scarves
and secretly touches their books, their pen-knives,

you, little sister,
you wore that beauty humbly,
and your soul, the soul of a daughter of humble people,
never knew you had it,
because otherwise it wouldn't have been beauty.
It vanished, like a shower of gold dust.

The world pointed it out to you.
And thus your beauty became its own.

Of the stupid ancient world
and the savage future world,
there remained a beauty which wasn't ashamed
to point to your little sister's breasts,
and your little belly so readily uncovered.
And this made it beauty, the beauty
sweet black beggarwomen have,
and gypsy women, and the shopkeepers' daughters
who win the pageants in Miami or in Rome.
It vanished, like a golden dove.

The world pointed it out to you,
and thus your beauty was no longer beauty.

But you kept on being a child,
silly like antiquity, cruel like the future,
and all the stupidity and cruelty of the present
got in between you and your beauty,
which had been taken by power.
You still carried it with you, like a smile among tears,
but you had become unclean through passivity,
indecent through obedience.
Obedience requires many swallowed tears.
Giving yourself to others,
the too cheerful smiles which beg for their pity . . .
It vanished, like a white shadow of gold.

Your beauty, which had survived from the ancient world
and was needed by the future world, was taken
by the present world and thus became an evil.

Now finally your big brothers turn around,
leave off for a moment their cursed games,
come out of their unbreakable distraction
and ask themselves, "Is it possible that Marilyn,
little Marilyn has shown us the way?"
Now you are the first, you, little sister,
the one who doesn't count, the poor little one, with her smile,
you are the first outside the gates of the world
abandoned to its destiny of death.

Translated from the Italian by Andrew Lear

LAURENCE GOLDSTEIN

VERTIGO, A SEQUEL

When Alfred Hitchcock traveled underground
And settled his famous bulk in Charon's boat
("A star vehicle at last!"), and heard the sound
Of oars, and felt the deathship float,

He turned for one last framing glance
At the cool blondes, the shapely auburn-haired,
Whose shades whirled about him in a bawdy dance,
Lifting their crimson dresses, bosoms bared.

His fingers trembled toward Grace
Who modeled once more the postures of sin.
He read the brazen line on her painted face:
"I don't like cold things touching my skin."

He would kill her, again, for saying that.
Strangle or stab, in living room and shower. . .
Hell swung into view like a Hollywood matte;
Kim and Tippi spun beyond his power.

At the helm, some likeness of their leading men
Directed his freight toward the *paysage triste*,
But their king-sized genius, scissors in hand,
Gazed backward till their movement ceased.

DAVID LEHMAN

TOWARD A DEFINITION OF LOVE

I.

Another time they were making love. "It's even better
When you help," she said. That was the second thing
He liked about her: she had memorized hours
Of movie dialogue, as if their life together
In the close apartment, with the street noise,
The crank calls, and the sinister next door neighbor,
Consisted of roles to be played with panache,
If possible, and with a song in her heart. Was she lying
When she told him she loved him? Or was she
The nude in his bed, with her back turned to him
As if he were a painter in Paris in 1870
And she were a model in Brooklyn in 1992,
And what separated them was a painted ocean
Representing the unbridgeable distance between them,
As between age and youth, Europe and America?
A condition of their romance was its impossibility —
She would have panicked if he had proposed,
Because love was passion consuming itself
Like a flickering cigarette, an ember in an ashtray.

2.

When she went back to sleep, he thought about her
Some more, and what they had done the night before:
Something holy, but with awful consequences,
Like a revolution about to enter its reign of terror.
In the movie, he was the jilted soldier ("don't you still

Love me?") or the Scandinavian philosopher ("he wondered
Why he had to give her up"). But their lines so truly parallel
Though infinite could never meet, and there was no use
Arguing against the despair that had wakened his longing
For her, now that she was gone. There was no way
To make it last, to prolong a moment of such pleasure,
Sweet and intense, that Faust would have bargained away
His soul for it. In public they acted married. One day
She left. She phoned from the road. A morning of tears
In honor of the first morning he had woken up beside her
With the shades rattling in the window, and the rays
Of light seeping weakly into the room, and the noise
Of the kids playing with a ball in the gutter.

CONTRIBUTORS

MICHAEL ANDEREGG has published books on William Wyler and David Lean, as well as many essays on subjects ranging from Shakespeare and Thomas More to the films of the 1940s and 1950s. He is currently writing a study of Orson Welles as a performer. He teaches at the University of North Dakota.

LAURA ANTILLANO, born in 1950, grew up in Venezuela, where she currently teaches at the University of Carabobo. Her book of stories, *Cuentos de pelicula* (1985), is entirely about movies, especially classic Hollywoood cinema. She has published eleven other books, and has just completed an historical novel, *1700*. Her translator, KATHY S. LEONARD, is Assistant Professor of Spanish at Iowa State University. She is currently finishing work on an anthology of translated fiction titled *Broken Blossoms: Short Stories by Latin American Women*.

MARGARET ATWOOD is the author of more than twenty-five books of poetry, fiction, and non-fiction. Her most recent novel is *The Robber Bride*; her newest book of poetry is *Morning in the Burned House* (Houghton Mifflin). She lives in Toronto.

LEO BRAUDY is the Leo S. Bing Professor of English at the University of Southern California. He has written books on Edward Gibbon, Jean Renoir, film theory, and most recently, *The Frenzy of Renown: Fame and Its History* (Oxford University Press, 1986). He is currently completing a study of the culture of the 1950s and a book on war and masculinity.

ADRIENNE DONALD teaches in the English Department at Princeton University. She is currently working on a book on Wordsworth and Enlightenment discourses.

H.D. (née Hilda Doolittle) is a major American poet of the Modernist period. Her *Collected Poems 1912-1944* has been published by New Directions. Further information about her is contained in the headnote to her essay.

335

GRANT FARRED is the editor of *Rethinking C. L. R. James* (Blackwell, 1996), and the author of essays in *Social Text* and *Research in African Literature*. He is completing a manuscript, *Midfielders' Moment*, on contemporary South African literature and politics. He teaches English and comparative literature at the University of Michigan.

BONNIE FRIEDMAN's book of essays, *Writing Past Dark*, was published by HarperCollins in 1993. Other essays have appeared in *The New York Times Book Review* and the *Times'* travel section. "My Gertrude Stein," an essay about her sister, was anthologized in *The Sister Plot* (Doubleday, 1995). She has taught at Dartmouth College and the University of Iowa.

MORDECHAI GELDMANN, born in 1946 in Munich, now resides in Israel, where he works as a psychotherapist. He has published six books of poetry. His translator, KAREN ALKALAY-GUT, is the author of several books of poetry and translation, as well as a biography of the American poet Adelaide Crapsey.

LAURENCE GOLDSTEIN, Professor of English at the University of Michigan and editor of *Michigan Quarterly Review*, has published most recently *The American Poet at the Movies: A Critical History* (University of Michigan Press, 1994) and a volume of verse, *Cold Reading* (Copper Beech Press, 1995).

WILLLIAM HARRISON is the author of eight novels and a volume of short stories. His screenplays include *Rollerball* and *Mountains of the Moon*. His most recent work of fiction, *Upriver*, was bought in manuscript by Steven Spielberg and is forthcoming as a novel and movie.

DIANE KIRKPATRICK is Professor of the History of Art, and Chair of the Department, at the University of Michigan. She has published a book on the work of Eduardo Paolozzi, and is currently writing a study of Sonia Landy Sheridan, a Chicago area computer artist, as well as a book to be called *Art as Information*.

IRA KONIGSBERG is Professor of English and of Film/Video Studies at the University of Michigan. The author of books on Samuel Richardson and narrative theory, he has also published *The Complete Film Dictionary* (New American Library, 10th printing, 1995).

DAVID LEHMAN's third book of poems, *Valentine Place*, was published by Scribner in 1996. He teaches at Columbia and in the core faculty of the Bennington MFA program.

VACHEL LINDSAY (1879-1931) wrote the first book of film theory in America, *The Art of the Moving Picture* (1915), as well as some of the earliest poems about movie stars. See the headnote to his work for more information about him.

SAMUEL MARX began his career in film as a story editor at M-G-M under Irving Thalberg. He produced *Lassie, Come Home*, among other classics, authored *Mayer and Thalberg: The Make-Believe Saints* (1975), and served as consultant for the series about M-G-M, "When the Lion Roars."

ARTHUR MILLER's play *The Crucible* in its film version will star Daniel Day Lewis, Emma Thompson, Paul Scofield, and Winona Ryder, under the directorship of Nicholas Hytner. His novella *Homely Girl* has recently been published.

WILLIAM IAN MILLER is Professor of Law at the University of Michigan. He is a student of the Icelandic sagas and has a special interest in honor, vengeance, and the emotions that maintain us as responsible social actors. These themes figure centrally in his book, *Humiliation* (Cornell University Press, 1993).

PIER PAOLO PASOLINI, the distinguished film director, is best known for movies such as *Accatone, The Gospel According to Saint Matthew, Medea*, and *Edipo Re*. His collected *Poems* appeared in 1996 from Noonday. His translator, ANDREW LEAR, has also published translations of Homer and Sappho, and has edited Laura Argiri's novel, *The God in Flight*, for Random House.

WILLIAM PAUL is Associate Professor of English and of Film/Video at the University of Michigan. He has published a book on Ernst Lubitsch, and, most recently, *Laughing Screaming: Modern Hollywood Horror & Comedy* (Columbia University Press, 1994). His current project is a study of the diversity of screens in film history.

BURT PRELUTSKY is an award-winning writer for *MASH, Mary Tyler Moore*, and *Dr. Quinn*, and the author of TV movies such as *Aunt Mary, Hobson's Choice*, and *A Winner Never Quits*.

IRA SADOFF's new and selected poems, *Delirious*, will appear from Godine in 1997. *The Ira Sadoff Reader* was published as part of the Bread Loaf Contemporary Series in 1992. He teaches at Colby College and the Warren Wilson MFA program.

JANSET BERKOK SHAMI was born in Turkey and currently lives in Jordan. Her stories have appeared in *The Malahat Review, Confrontation*, and *The Nebraska Review*, among other journals, and her first novel, *Cages on Opposite Shores*, appeared in 1995 from Interlink.

JIM SHEPARD's most recent novel is *Kiss of the Wolf*. His collection of stories, *Batting Against Castro*, appeared in 1996 from Alfred A. Knopf. He teaches at Williams College.

DIANN BLAKELY SHOAF's first book of poems, *Hurricane Walk*, appeared in 1992 from BOA. Recent publications include *Agni, Boulevard, The Nation, Ploughshares, The Southern Review*, and *Pushcart Anthology XIX*. She teaches at a girls' preparatory school in Nashville.

JANET SYLVESTER is the author of *That Mulberry Wine* (Wesleyan, 1985), and the manuscript of a new collection of poems which includes a poem featured in *Best American Poetry, 1994*.

CHARLES H. WEBB has coedited *Grand Passion*, an anthology of poetry by Los Angeles poets. His poem "The Shape of History" appeared in *The Best American Poetry, 1995*.

DAVID WOJAHN's most recent collection of poetry, *Late Empire*, appeared in 1994 from the University of Pittsburgh Press. He teaches at Indiana University and in the MFA program at Vermont College.

ROBERT ZALLER, Professor of History at Drexel University, has written essays on Bertolucci (*Massachusetts Review*) and Philip Guston (*Critical Inquiry*), as well as several books including *The Parliament of 1621* and *The Cliffs of Solitude: A Reading of Robinson Jeffers*.